Thomas Hall Pearne

Sixty-one years of intinerant Christian life in church and state

Thomas Hall Pearne

Sixty-one years of intinerant Christian life in church and state

ISBN/EAN: 9783337263287

Printed in Europe, USA, Canada, Australia, Japan

Cover: Foto ©Lupo / pixelio.de

More available books at **www.hansebooks.com**

REV. THOMAS H. PEARNE.
(At the age of 30 years.)

SIXTY-ONE YEARS OF ITINERANT CHRISTIAN LIFE IN CHURCH AND STATE

BY

THOMAS HALL PEARNE, D.D.

AUTHOR OF

"THE WORLD HARVEST," "THE TWO CHURCHES," "THE TWENTIETH CENTURY," "CINCINNATI SUNDAY SALOON," "RAILROADS AND CIVILIZATION."

Printed for the Author

CINCINNATI: CURTS & JENNINGS

NEW YORK: EATON & MAINS

1898

DEDICATION.

To my dear daughter,

VIRGINIA WYOMING PEARNE,

This Volume

Is affectionately dedicated.

THOMAS HALL PEARNE.

PREFACE.

THIS volume is due to the partiality of my brethren of the Cincinnati Conference, who, by a resolution passed at their session in 1896, requested that it be prepared. It was thought by them that a record of my experiences and observations, extending through a ministry of over sixty years, would be of interest and value to the Church, and contain suggestions that might lead its readers to a more active and better spiritual life. In accordance with this resolution the work was undertaken, and the present book is the result.

The author has not written these pages in the form of a diary, nor has he given a detailed narrative of his life. He has attempted rather to present the more striking events with which he has been connected, and to depict some of the great incidents of our ecclesiastical and civil history which came under his notice, together with occasional sketches of the prominent actors with whom he has been more or less associated from his younger years. He has endeavored to be a faithful chronicler, and to describe persons and scenes as they were, or, at least, as they appeared to him. Most of what is given has been written from recollection. The events of my earlier life still seem fresh and vivid. If I have lost somewhat of the buoyant spirit of childhood, I trust that the high hopes then conceived have in a measure been fulfilled through my ministry, and that I have not labored in vain in the Lord.

For whatever success I may have had in preaching the Word and in cultivating the field given me by the great Head of the Church, to him be the glory. **T. H. P.**

Hillsboro, August, 1898.

INTRODUCTION.

THE influence of Methodism upon the marvelous growth of what was once called the Great West, upon its educational and its religious life, will never, probably, be accurately measured nor fully acknowledged. A distinguished jurist, judge of the Supreme Court in one of the Western States—a professed Deist—is reported to have said, on one occasion: "But for the Methodist Church and the Methodist ministry, this country would have sunk into barbarism." This may be an extravagant statement; but the early Methodist itinerants were, undoubtedly, a remarkable class of men. It is said occasionally, in a half apologetic tone, that these hardy and adventurous pioneer preachers were men for *their* times; and so indeed they were, and nobly did they fulfill their mission. Some of these sturdy heroes were the vanguard of our early frontiersmen, who, advancing westward from the Atlantic seaboard, over the Alleghanies and across the Mississippi Valley, swept onward over the Rockies to the Pacific Ocean, thus spanning the continent with a splendid type of Christian civilization.

It is certainly within bounds to say that Methodism has been second to no other human agency in promoting the remarkable growth of the West; and it so, the publication of the many biographies of the pioneers of this pioneer Church, which have been issued in recent years, is amply vindicated; for these books are an important part of the history of the country.

Many notable and most valuable contributions have been made already to this biographical literature of the Church, including sketches of such recognized leaders as Francis Asbury, Jesse Lee, William Watters, Henry Smith, Elijah Hedding, James B. Finley, David and Jacob Young, James Quinn, Peter Cartwright, Thomas A. Morris, Granville Moody, William I. Fee, and many others. The writer of this autobiography ranks easily with these and other distinguished men of the denomination, and it is eminently proper that a life of such varied and protracted usefulness should find a permanent place in the history of the Church. It may be said truthfully, I believe, that no man in the ministry of American Methodism has sustained an effective relation in the itinerant ranks for so many years, consecutively, as are embraced in this volume, and it will be the earnest prayer, I am sure, of all who read these thrilling pages, that the author may long be spared to the Church he has so nobly served.

The sixty-one years of active and conspicuous service which Dr. Pearne has given to the Church already, covers a most interesting period in the history of the world—the most remarkable period, perhaps, in the nineteen centuries of the Christian era; for in that time, and on this continent, and in this Republic, humanity has reached its high-water mark of material, intellectual, and political thrift. The fact that this splendid Western civilization is the highest now existing, is due largely to the labors of the pioneer preachers in the formative and history-making epoch in which they lived. Certainly these born leaders of men are worthy to be held in affectionate remembrance by those of us who have entered into their labors.

And yet, worthy as is this volume of a place in every Methodist library, it is not probable that its preparation would have been undertaken but for the action of the Cincinnati Conference, in 1896, as follows:

"WHEREAS, Dr. Thomas H. Pearne, an honored and able minister of this Conference, having had large experience in public and journalistic service, has in many ways accomplished great good in both Church and State; therefore, be it

"*Resolved*, That we express to him our high regard, with the hope that he will be able to place his Reminiscences in printed form. If it be feasible, we suggest and request that he prepare such a volume, which we believe will be of great interest and value.

"C. W. BARNES,   J. A. STORY,   C. L. CONGER,
"D. LEE AULTMAN,   M. M. KUGLER,   JOHN PEARSON,
"F. G. MITCHELL,   G. W. DUBOIS,   WM. RUNYAN."

The reader of this volume will note the division of the author's life into five periods, each marked by distinctive conditions and duties. The first fourteen years of his ministry—from 1837 to 1851—were spent in Central New York and Northern Pennsylvania. Here all the characteristics of the Church and of society were marked by more or less culture and maturity, even at that early time, rather than by the rudeness and hardships of pioneer life; and yet it was, after all, the transitional period between the old and the new—the evolution from the earlier and simpler forms of life to the higher civilization of the present times. The common-school system was then in its infancy; the Sunday-schools were crude and comparatively inefficient; railways were unknown; steamboats were in their earlier stage, limited to river transportation; there were then no ocean steamers; the daily newspaper was a luxury, only to be enjoyed in the largest cities; and telegraphic news from all parts of the world, printed daily, was not even dreamed of as a possibility. Methodism, then, was of the primitive type. The class-meetings, band-meetings, love-feasts, were given great prominence, and strangers were admitted to them cautiously, and not more than twice or thrice. Instrumental music was very generally excluded from the services of the Church. Its introduction was stoutly opposed as an innovation, forbidden alike by precedent, prejudice, and the claims of spiritual worship. It would be a great mistake, therefore, to suppose that the life of an itinerant Methodist preacher, even in that favored region, would be destitute of hardship, romance, and such thrilling incidents as constitute the web of all human history. Of Dr. Pearne's marked success as a preacher and pastor in this initial period there is abundant evidence, apart from that furnished, incidentally, by his autobiography.

The second period—1851 to 1865—was that spent in Oregon. No part of Dr. Pearne's ministry, it is safe to say, has been more influential in molding opinions and shaping results than the fourteen years passed in Oregon. He was selected for that work by one of the wisest men on the Episcopal Bench, and the outcome fully vindicated the wisdom of the choice. The country was new, and the foundations of civil, educational, and religious institutions were being laid. A man of force, courage, and ability was needed to take leadership in the plastic stage of our Church life in that important and strategic field. Of Dr. Pearne's work in Oregon, as a presiding elder and an editor, this is not the place to speak at length. The following pages will reveal how great was his opportunity, and how fully he met the demands of the situation. That country was receiving, at that time, large accessions to its population from all parts of the Republic; these accessions were swelled, no doubt, by the contiguity of the recently-opened gold-mines of California. Dr. Pearne's position naturally brought him into close relations with the pioneer leaders of that section, in religious, civil, and military life, and so impressed were these leaders in civil affairs with the Doctor's statesmanlike qualities that he was once importuned to stand for an election to the United States Senate. Dr. Pearne did not encourage this movement, because, as he felt, he could not relinquish the work committed to his hands by the Church.

The third term included five years spent in the South, in the "Reconstruction Days" following the Civil War. His work was in East Tennessee, and in connection with the first Conference of the Methodist Episcopal Church organized in Tennessee after the overthrow of slavery, and the rehabilitation of that State with sovereignty. The war, indeed, was over, and armed rebellion was subdued; but the fierce passions aroused by the long and bloody struggle, and the bitter prejudices excited by that unhappy, fraternal strife, still existed. Dr. Pearne's position here was a most delicate, difficult, and even dangerous one, as will be noted by the reader in the thrilling narrative of that period.

From this important work Dr. Pearne was called by the Administration at Washington to serve his country as United States consul in the British West Indies. Of course, the duties of this position were secular rather than sacred; and yet amid the engrossing duties of his official position in Jamaica, the Doctor found time to respond to the frequent calls made upon him to occupy the various pulpits of the city, and also of the island of Jamaica, in all of which he preached frequently, except in those of the Roman Catholic Church and the Church of England.

The last of the five periods into which the Doctor has divided his life—from 1874 to the present time—has been spent in the regular work of the itinerancy in Ohio, as a member of the Cincinnati Conference. Entering this body at an age when ministers are generally supposed to have crossed the "dead line," Dr. Pearne took at once the position in the forefront which he holds now, and is likely to hold until his voluntary retirement from the effective ranks. Whether as pastor or presiding elder, his rare ability as a preacher, his genial personality, his fidelity to every trust, and his faithful discharge of every duty, have made him one of the most acceptable and useful ministers of his day.

The Church will be grateful to Dr. Pearne for this valuable contribution to its pioneer literature, and it will be read, I have no doubt, with increasing interest as the years go by, and greater distance lends still greater enchantment to the heroic days of American Methodism.

JOHN F. MARLAY.

SPRINGFIELD, OHIO, August, 1898.

CONTENTS.

First Period—Beginning Itinerant Life.

CHAPTER I.

Ancestry—Birth—Conversion of Parents—Early Childhood—Removal to New York Mills, Oneida County—Happy Home-life—Father a Local Preacher, then an Itinerant—Old-time Veterans—Conversion, and Call to Preach—School-life—Serious mistake, ... Page 21

CHAPTER II.

Begin preaching as a Supply—Truxton Circuit—First Appointment—First Sunday—Changed to Madison Station—Marriage—Amusing Incident—Appointed to Marcellus—Funeral—James Jay, an Old Wesleyan Preacher—Skaneateles—Visit there in 1864—Auburn—Returned to Madison—Revivals and Church Improvements, ... 31

CHAPTER III.

General Conference of 1844—Personal Recollections, . . . 41

CHAPTER IV.

Binghamton—Eel-pot Church—Wyoming—Great Revival—Elisha Harris my Helper—Conversion of Payne Pettebone—Letter from Rev. R. W. Van Schoick, ... 53

CHAPTER V.

Francis Asbury, Personal Reminiscences—Wilkesbarre—Bishops Soule and Waugh, who Ordained me—Bishop Roberts, ... 63

CHAPTER VI.

Associations and Experiences—Fathers of the Oneida Conference — Marmaduke Pearce — John Dempster — Joseph Castle—George Harmon—The Paddock Brothers—David A. Shepard—The African Missionary—W. W. Ninde—Elias Bowen, ... Page 77

CHAPTER VII.

Jesse T. Peck—George Peck—George Gary, ... 91

Second Period Life in Oregon.

CHAPTER VIII.

Transfer to Oregon— Conditions inducing—Voyage—Steamer Associates—Delay in Aspinwall—Passage up the Chagres River—Incidents—San Francisco Delay—Port Oxford—Indians—Portland—J. H. Wilbur—Oregon City—Salem—Ministers, ... 109

CHAPTER IX.

The Name Oregon—Description—Columbia River and Valley Willamette River—Umpqua and Rogue Rivers—Washington—Climate—Camp-meeting Lunatic — Rook Creek Camp-meeting — "Two-seed" Baptist — Santiam Camp-meeting—Doctrinal Preaching, ... 123

CHAPTER X.

Toils and Hardships—Muleback Riding—Trip to Washington in December, 1852 — An Inhospitable Priest — Lost—A Bitter Cold Night—Narrow Escape from Freezing—Christmas Walk in Deep Snow Twenty-six Miles — Floods out, ... 134

CHAPTER XI.

Sloughs—Weddings and Funerals—Incidents, ... 124

CHAPTER XII.

Jargon—Wolves—Trip with Bishop Simpson—Bishop Ames in Oregon in 1853—Organization of Oregon Conference—Educational Plants—F. S. Hoyt—Other Preachers—Conference of 1854—Bishop Simpson's Sermon—Reminiscences of his Visit to Oregon—Incident, ... Page 148

CHAPTER XIII.

With Bishop Simpson on the Columbia River—Bishop Baker at Oregon Conference, 1855—Delegate to General Conference—*Pacific Christian Advocate* Founded—General Conference Incidents—Elected Editor—Fortieth Anniversary of the *Advocate*, ... 166

CHAPTER XIV.

Bishop Simpson's Last Visit to Oregon, 1862—Buggy-ride with him to Yreka—Appeal Case tried before Bishop Janes—National Republican Convention in Baltimore, 1864—Oregon a Free State—Contrasts, ... 180

CHAPTER XV.

A Stage Trip from Oregon across the Plains, in 1864, . . 194

CHAPTER XVI.

Adventures with Indians and Wild Beasts, ... 215

CHAPTER XVII.

Oregon and Slavery—Secession—Editorials in Advocate, . 224

CHAPTER XVIII.

Thanksgiving Sermon, 1862—Christian Patriotism—The Rebellion, ... 238

CHAPTER XIX.

Oregon and the Northwest Boundary—General Scott—Our First Mission House in Oregon, ... 258

Third Period—Reconstruction.

CHAPTER XX.

A Year's Absence from the Conference for Rest and for Work in the Army—Christian Work in the Army—City Point—Care of Hospital Ward—Work During a Bloody Engagement at Hatcher's Run, ... Page 271

CHAPTER XXI.

Bishop Clark's Visit and Work in East Tennessee in 1865—Organizes the Holston Conference of the Methodist Episcopal Church—History of the Proceedings, ... 281

CHAPTER XXII.

History of the Reorganization continued—Letter Concerning Bishop Clark's Work in the South, ... 300

CHAPTER XXIII.

Letter from Nashville Concerning Reconstruction—Editorial in *Western Christian Advocate*—Work on Knoxville District—Visit to Asheville—Perils—Misunderstandings, . 310

Fourth Period—As United States Consul.

CHAPTER XXIV.

United States Consul to Kingston, Jamaica—Reasons superinducing—Duties of the Office—Cuban Excitements—Steamer *Edgar Stuart*—Steamer *Virginius*—Captain Fry's Farewell to his Wife—Editorial in *Western Christian Advocate* on "The Spanish Difficulty," 327

CHAPTER XXV.

Events in the Consulate—Visit of Frigate *Tennessee* to Kingston—Bishop Coxe—Commissioners to San Domingo—History and Description of Jamaica, ... 339

Fifth Period—Work in Ohio.

CHAPTER XXVI.

Return to United States—Secretary American Colonization Society—Residence in Cincinnati—Illness and Death of Mrs. Pearne—Resignation of Secretaryship—Transfers to Cincinnati Conference—Appointed to Grace Church, Dayton—Second Marriage, to Miss McDonald—Dayton District—Unveiling a Painting—Address—Urbana—Wesley Chapel, Cincinnati—Centennial Sermon, ... Page 363

CHAPTER XXVII.

Central Church, Springfield—God in the Constitution—Answer to Ingersoll—First Church, Xenia—Semi-centennial Sermon—Hillsboro District—Hillsboro College—Hillsboro Charge—A Remarkable Event—The Gospel on Horseback—Closing Words, ... 410

ILLUSTRATIONS.

THOMAS H. PEARNE AT THE AGE OF THIRTY YEARS, ... *Frontispiece.*
OREGON PRESIDING ELDER AND HIS FAITHFUL MULE, ... Face Page 134
THOMAS H. PEARNE AT THE AGE OF SEVENTY-EIGHT YEARS, ... Face Page 410

First Period.
BEGINNING ITINERANT LIFE

CHAPTER I.

I WAS well born. Like Paul, I was free born. My birth date is June 7, 1820.

> "My boast is not, that I deduce my birth
> From loins enthroned and rulers of the earth;
> But higher far my great pretensions rise,
> The child of parents passed into the skies."

My parents were, on my mother's side, of the hardy Cornish stock; on my father's side, of Rochester Bridge, Kent County, London. Father was strictly a Cockney; *i. e.*, a Londoner; mother was a Yorkshire woman. The former inherited the culture and keenness of observation of the civic conditions of his birth and early years. Mother transmitted to me the vigor and robustness of her own sturdy constitution. Both lived to a ripe age, each of them dying when about seventy-four. Both were members of the Church of England. Mother's ancestors for two generations had been Wesleyans. Her father and her grandfather were local preachers in Mr. Wesley's Connection. The tradition runs that on mother's side there was a dash of the Wesley blood in our veins.

Yet while both my parents had the forms of godliness by their membership in the Church of England, neither of them knew its power. They had never experienced what is understood, among Methodists, as a change of heart. On their arrival in New York, a Methodist and a relative inquired of father whether he had ever been converted, and how his soul was prospering. It was the first time in his life that such questions had ever been addressed to him. The same person invited them to attend a revival-meeting, then going on in Duane Street Methodist Episcopal Church, New York. In the first Methodist meeting they ever attended they went forward to the altar for prayers, and united with the Methodist Episcopal Church as seekers of religion. I have often heard my father say that he was indebted, under God, for his salvation to the zeal of the New York Methodists, and to this wise provision for receiving persons as seekers of religion on trial in the Methodist Episcopal Church.

The earliest years of my life were spent in New York. When I was five years old—*i. e.*, in 1825—my father moved with his family into Central New York. We settled in a place called New York Mills, a cotton factory village in Oneida County, which employed some five hundred operatives. The place was three miles east from Utica, and one mile west from Whitesboro. Father's family was typically large. It consisted of ten children—seven sons and three daughters. One died in infancy; another in his ninth year. A third died at fourteen. The others lived to adult age. Their names were, respectively, William, Nathaniel, Thomas, Francis, Mary, Harriet, Benjamin, John, and Hester. Hester was called home when fourteen, John Wesley at twenty-three, Harriet at twenty-five, Nathaniel at fifty, and William at seventy-five. His ministerial life began when he was twenty-one, and continued fifty-four years. Nathaniel was a merchant. For many years he was in the wholesale store of A. T. Stewart, New York; and for a few years he kept a retail store on Bleecker Street. Benjamin was a mechanic. John Wesley was a printer, a compositor in the office of the New York *Commercial Advertiser*. Three of the family remain: the writer, sister Mary, and brother Benjamin; the latter, respectively, in Cortland and Oxford, New York. Those who have gone, died in the Lord, after lives of piety and usefulness. All the children in my father's family were converted in early childhood, and united with the Methodist Episcopal Church, most of them before the age of twelve.

In my boyhood, the introduction of instrumental music in the Sunday service created much agitation and violent contention. A maiden lady of some maturity came into the church while the first hymn was being sung. For the first time instruments had been introduced into the choir in the gallery; but as she was under the gallery, directly below where the choir sat, she did not observe the musical instruments, and she sang from the same hymn-book with my mother with apparent zest and delight. After the prayer, and when the second hymn was announced, the instruments sounded the pitch. "What is that?" said she to my mother. "Musical instruments," was the answer given. She was seized with hysterical convulsions, which lasted several days.

Father and mother and my oldest brother, and our hired girl, with three other persons, united with the Methodist Episcopal Church by letter, and were organized into a class by the Methodist minister stationed in Utica, and my father was appointed class-leader. Father held a license as a local preacher. For a time we had meetings in our house, and then the mill company assisted the villagers in building both a Methodist church and a Presbyterian church. In both these churches we had sweeping revivals of religion. In the Presbyterian Church, Rev. Charles G. Finney was the evangelist. In one of these revivals a large number of children were converted. Among these were two brothers and a sister of mine, and also Edward G. Andrews, at present, and for twenty-five years past, one of our honored and beloved bishops. My father was a schoolteacher in England and in this country, and he was also an accountant. For several years he was the clerk and the cashier of the factory. He was a man of large reading, of good education, and of literary tastes and pursuits. He had a somewhat full library. As I was a voracious reader, I soon held its treasures in my possession.

Our home was a bright, Christian home, the abode of content and piety. It was well ordered, full of cheer and comfort. The family were taught to fear and love and honor God. Family worship was kept up morning and evening. The religion of the family was sunny and joyous. Music was much loved and enjoyed. We were a very happy family. We knew and sang the old Methodist hymns and tunes. Mother was a very sweet singer. Father sang some; but his voice was less musical than mother's. Father regularly filled appointments as a local preacher in places not too far from our home.

In 1832 father entered the traveling connection, in which he continued thirty-six years. His death, at the age of seventy-four, was peaceful and triumphant. His last words were, "Happy! happy!" Mother's last words were: "Though I walk through the valley of the shadow of death, I will fear no evil: for thou art with me: thy rod and thy staff they comfort me." At fourteen I was made a class-leader of a large class, mostly of females, some forty or fifty of them. Six months later I was licensed to exhort, and at fifteen I was licensed as a local preacher. In 1836-37 I attended school at Cazenovia Seminary, in Madison County, New York. The principal of the school was Rev. George Peck, D. D., who later filled a large place in the Methodist Episcopal Church as editor of the *Christian Advocate*, New York, and the *Methodist Quarterly Review*.

OLD-TIME VETERANS—PHŒBUS—MERWIN—BANGS.

The writer's feet first pressed the soil of old Oneida Conference in his childhood. In his early manhood he traveled the circuits and ministered in some of the stations of that goodly field. There were giants in those days. He saw them. He heard them. He remembers them. However far his path may have since diverged from those earlier scenes, and however diversified the experiences and events of the later years, memory has emblamed the recollections of those golden times. Those memories reach distinctly to 1828.

One of the well-remembered events of that early period was about that time. It was the presence in my father's home, as guests, of three venerable preachers of the New York Conference. They were men of large stature and fine presence: tall, portly, and of courteous bearing. The third session of the Oneida Conference was held in Utica, N. Y., three miles distant from New York Mills, the place of my boyhood home. These persons were visitors at the Oneida Conference from the New York Conference. New York Mills was then a new charge. Two years before this the first class of seven persons was organized in my father's house; four of them, as already stated, were of our family. The name of the new charge first appeared in the Annual Minutes in 1826, with Charles Giles as pastor. In four years it had grown to three hundred and sixteen members. It was now assisting in sustaining the Conference. The manly guests, already named, were: Dr. William Phœbus, Rev. Samuel Merwin, and Rev. Nathan Bangs.

Dr. Phœbus was then an old man. He had been forty-seven years in the itinerancy. He began his ministry in 1783, the year before the organization of the Methodist Episcopal Church. Thus my association with him in childhood relates me, personally, with the beginning of our organic Church life. Dr. Phœbus was well-preserved, vivacious, and most agreeable in his manners. He was born in Maryland in 1754. After having traveled ten years he located, and after a brief term he re-entered the itinerancy. In 1798 he was again located, and engaged in the practice of medicine in New York. Eight years later he joined the New York Conference. In 1824 he was superannuated, in which relation he remained until his death, in 1831. His mind was vigorous. His knowledge was large and various. In men and books he was well versed, and also in the early records of the Church and in the different systems of Church order and government. He was large in person, and noble looking. His manner was genial. He was quite attentive to children, who in turn loved and admired him. He was fluent in speech, and well stored in racy incidents, which he rendered graphically. Upon my young imagination he made a deep impression, never since effaced. He was a leading member of the General Conferences of 1808 and 1812. He was a strong man in Methodism, aiding effectively in extending her borders and strengthening her stakes during her immature period. He helped to lay broad and deep her foundations, upon which the Methodist Episcopal Church has had a most astonishing growth in numbers, activities, and resources.

The second of these eminent ministers was Rev. Samuel Merwin, who was yet in his vigorous prime. He, too, was genteel and elegant. He was probably a little above fifty, and had been preaching thirty years. He was above average height, of full habit, yet not corpulent. Dr. Bangs was less corpulent than Phœbus, and taller than Merwin. He baptized me in my early childhood, in Duane Street Church, New York—of which fact I still hold a very distinct recollection. As I recall him he was slightly round-shouldered, with his head somewhat inclined to one side. He, too, was a most genial, interesting person. All the early Methodist preachers were specially attentive to the children in the families where they were guests. Dr. Jesse T. Peck, afterward bishop, was also a frequent visitor at our house, and we much enjoyed his visits.

My call to the ministry antedated my conversion. It was very strong and clear, and I even commenced to preach in my eighth year. My entrance into the pastoral work was somewhat peculiar. In the fall of 1837 I was attending the Cazenovia Seminary, Rev. Dr. George Peck the principal. I had no means. I boarded myself, and did odd days' work, and I also did chores in the morning. I lived on bread and milk and potatoes and salt, renting a room and doing my own cooking; my entire living costing me from fifty cents to seventy-five cents a week. A vacancy occurred on a circuit some fifteen or twenty miles away. A junior preacher was needed. The presiding elder came and offered the place to me. I remained on this charge nearly two years. Near the end of the second year I had two offers to go through college. An Episcopalian, who came to my semimonthly services, and whose generous hospitality as a host I often shared, said to me one evening,

"Are you very desirous of getting a classical education?" Upon my returning an affirmative answer, he offered to send me through the Geneva College, an Episcopalian institution in Western New York, and then through the theological school at the same place, defraying all my expenses, and then depending on me to repay the debt as I might be able after graduation. I consulted my father, who said that meant that I would enter the ministry of the Protestant Episcopal Church. I declined, with many thanks. A Methodist layman made me the same kind of an offer. He wished me to go to the Wesleyan University in Middletown, Conn., then our only collegiate institution in the East. We had then no theological school in our Church. That is the offer I should have accepted. I would have done so, only that a presiding elder dissuaded me, urging me to enter the Conference at once, and educate myself while employed in the pastoral work. This wrong advice I followed, and, being recommended to the Conference from the charge on which I had been a supply for almost two years, I was admitted into the Oneida Conference in the early autumn of 1839.

I was then nineteen years of age. I pursued my studies in Greek and Latin and Hebrew, gaining a smattering knowledge in those languages. But it was a mistake not to have obtained a classical education, which has been recognized and regretted through my whole ministry. While perhaps holding an average grade among my ministerial brethren, I am satisfied I would have been much more effective and useful in my ministry if I had more fully prepared myself by education. There was less blame for the wrong counsel of presiding elders sixty years ago than now. Educated young men are waiting every year to enter our itinerancy, and those whose education is incomplete should not be allowed to enter the traveling ministry. And there is now even less excuse on the score of poverty for failing to secure educational preparation than there was in the earlier times; for we have a society in our Church, deserving high commendation for it, which will advance the necessary means for attending school to those who are needy. In this way the children's fund has aided, by loans and gifts, six thousand young persons who were called of God to labor in his work, either as teachers or preachers. In the year 1897 sixteen hundred have been thus assisted. This list for a single year includes persons of twenty-five nationalities. If, with the knowledge I now have, the life I have lived could be begun anew, I would never commit the folly of my early manhood, and omit the opportunities then offered for acquiring an education.

CHAPTER II.

THE first year of my supply on the Onondaga Circuit, James Atwell, of blessed memory, was my colleague; the second year, Benjamin G. Paddock. Both were veterans, and both gave me sympathy, kindness, and abundance of excellent instruction. The early system of our itinerancy, of going out in pairs, was very advantageous to the young ministers. It answered a good part in their training.

After my admission into the Conference on trial, my first appointment was on Truxton Circuit. Lyman K. Reddington was my senior colleague. He died a few years ago, aged over ninety years. Here I spent my first Sabbath after Conference. I preached four times. The plan of the circuit for that day was ten A. M., Truxton, preaching and class-meeting. I led the class here, as also in Cuyler, five miles away, where I preached at two P. M. My plan named the third appointment at Kinney's Settlement, and to stay at Kinney's—class-leader. I reached here at five o'clock. I stopped with the class-leader, Brother Kinney. His wife informed me he had gone on to meeting. So I concluded my plan was wrong, and that five o'clock was the proper hour for my evening appointment. I rode on half a mile. A large congregation was waiting for the preacher. I entered, saddlebags in hand, and at once I took my seat in the teacher's desk, for it was a schoolhouse. The congregation looked at me with apparent curiosity, for I was a total stranger. After a few minutes a gentleman beckoned me to follow him out of doors. He said: "You are a stranger. May I inquire your name?" I gave him my name, and informed him that I was the junior Methodist preacher, sent there from Conference. He said: "My name is Kinney; I am the class-leader. You will stay with me to-night. Our meeting is across the creek at our church, at early candle-lighting. This meeting here is a Baptist meeting. The people are expecting a Baptist minister from Tully. If he does not come, I doubt not the people would like you to preach to them." So we returned into the house, and I began, with some shame, to take a lower seat. The expected minister not arriving, I was invited to preach, which I did, and then at evening at the Kinney Church, making four sermons and two class-meetings in one day and twelve miles of travel.

The next day I hired a buggy, and started for my old circuit to get my books and my clothes. I passed through Cazenovia, where my father was stationed, and where my presiding elder, Dr. Elias Bowen, lived. He changed me from Truxton circuit to Madison station, as the minister who was appointed there was unable to serve them on account of ill-health. The year was a delightful one. Revivals occurred, and some fifty or sixty persons were converted. Here I became acquainted with the daughter of Solomon Root, Esq., Miss Ann P. Root, who, two years later, became my wife, and with whom, for thirty-three years, I lived in happy and prosperous union of hearts and hands. An incident in connection with the wedding will be enjoyed:

I was married, October 5, 1841, by my father, who at the time was stationed in Utica. As I wanted to take a wedding trip to Trenton Falls in my buggy, and return to Utica for the Sabbath, my father exchanged pulpits with me for that Sunday, and he went to Marcellus for me. I reached Utica with my bride on Saturday night, putting up at my father's house. I grew up three miles from Utica, and I knew personally many of the leading members of that Church, where I was to preach. At Church-time my mother and myself, accompanied by my wife, made our way to the church. As we were about to enter I saw Father Swartwout, one of the veterans, standing on the doorstep a little distance away, with others of the Official Board, whom I knew. I told Mrs. Pearne to go in with my mother, and I would go and speak to my friends standing near. Of course, my wedding suit was befitting. A fine silk hat, a white necktie, kid gloves, morocco shoes, etc. Approaching my venerable friend, I said, extending my hand, "How do you do?" Instead of taking my hand, he eyed me from head to foot, and inquired my name. I told him my name. "What!" said he, "are you a son of our minister?" "I am," said I. "Well," said he, "do you call yourself a Methodist minister?" "I do not so call myself," I replied; "but I am one all the same." "Well, well," said he, "you do not look like the fortieth cousin to a Methodist preacher."

It should be remembered that Mr. Swartwout was very plain in his dress. He wore a white, broad-brimmed hat; a single-breasted, straight-collared, cutaway coat, and straight boots—not rights and lefts. They were round-toed as well. He added, "I suppose you have a written sermon in your pocket, which you will pull out and read to us." "No," said I, "not that; I never read my sermons, but I preach them. Come and hear me." He did hear me. I had a fine time. He got very happy under my sermon, and shouted, as did some others. At the close of the sermon he met me at the foot of the pulpit stairs, and shook hands with me very cordially, saying: "I take it all back, what I said to you about not looking like a Methodist preacher. You are one, and I bid you God-speed. God bless you, and make you very useful!"

My next station was Marcellus, in Onondaga County. It adjoined the circuit in which my ministry began. We had two prosperous years, and nearly one hundred souls professed conversion. During this year I formed the acquaintance of a young man and his father—artists, portrait-painters—who occupied rooms in a disused clock factory. They came to Church, and professed great interest in me. I sat for my likeness in crayon. It was not very satisfactory. There was an air of mystery about them, and when I would call they seemed embarrassed. The mystery was afterwards solved by the discovery in their rooms of counterfeiter's implements; and they were arrested for counterfeiting. The portrait-painting was a blind.

During this year I attended a funeral some eight or ten miles away. It was of a lady of nearly ninety years. She was the mother of twelve children, some forty-five grandchildren, and thirteen great-grandchildren. They were Holland Dutch by descent. The old lady came from Holland in her young married life, with some two or three of her children. The family had gone twenty miles to secure a Dutchman to conduct the funeral. He could not serve them, and, at his suggestion, they came for me. They were wealthy people. The funeral was in their house. It was elegantly furnished, and they were evidently luxurious livers. I had not been preaching more than fifteen minutes when they broke out in loud lamentations and grief, which continued for some minutes. Indeed, it seemed uncontrollable. It prevented any further preaching. We rode two miles through a drenching rain to the burial. I returned by request to the house, and dined with the family. The dinner was elaborate. Five or six courses of meat, including beef, mutton and pork, venison, capons, turkey, duck, and goose, and other courses of dessert. The sideboard was laden with liquors of various kinds, of which nearly all partook. I was urged to take some wine or stronger stimulant; which, however, I declined. The hilarity of the dinner festival was fully the counterpart of the demonstrations of sorrow and mourning which had interrupted my preaching. On leaving, I was presented with two dollars for my attendance and with profuse compliments for my sermon, which they averred had been very satisfactory. This funeral will give an idea of the prevalent customs of those early times.

On this station we had a large number of English people, who had come to America a few years before, having been members of the Wesleyan society in England. Among them was a venerable superannuated minister of eighty-four years. He was a fine preacher and a sweet-spirited man. His name was James Jay, a relative of William Jay, of Bath, an Independent or Congregational minister, who had published a valuable collection of Scripture passages and comments for every morning and evening. Benn Pitman, the stenographer, said a few years ago in Cincinnati, "that he was probably the only person in the United States who had seen those who had known John Wesley and had shaken hands with him and heard him preach. Mr. Jay I knew intimately for two years. He often preached in my pulpit. He and his family were members of my Church. He had been for several years one of Mr. Wesley's helpers or assistants before Mr. Wesley died. Mr. Jay knew him well for four years before his death. My grandfather on my mother's side, Thomas Hall, was a local preacher in Mr. Wesley's Connection, and had often heard him preach. Mrs. Lester, a venerable old lady, whom I well knew, and who was a frequent visitor at my father's house in my early teens, was a member of Mr. Wesley's society for ten years before his death. She had often heard him preach, and had been present in his society meeting or class-meeting when Mr. Wesley led the class.

Mr. Jay gave me two incidents of Wesley's life which he witnessed. Mr. Wesley came into his circuit and spent a day. At the dinner, at which were several Wesleyan preachers and circuit officials, there was a little disposition to gossip. One of the preachers remarked that one of Mr. Wesley's preachers had become very gay in his apparel. He had taken to wearing ruffled bosom shirts. "Well," said Mr. Wesley, plucking Mr. Jay's coat, "when Jemmy can not preach without a ruffled shirt, he shall have one if he wants it." After dinner, and following the afternoon sermon, Mr. Wesley started on his journey, accompanied by the ministers, all well mounted. After going about two miles they alighted, and Mr. Wesley sang a hymn with them and prayed. Then they shook hands and parted.

From Marcellus I was sent to Skaneateles, seven miles west from Marcellus. I remained here only one year; but my return was earnestly requested. Here also, as at Marcellus, was a large sprinkling of English people. They were all fine musicians, instrumental and vocal, and there were four of them, each of whom wanted very badly to lead the singing in the Church. Sometimes two of them would hasten to select and start the tune before the other could get in his work. The division of leaders divided the Church into segments of about equal numbers. I announced that I would dispense with the choir and choristers, and I would lead the singing from the pulpit. This gave us pause from friction. I continued it through the year.

In 1864, eighteen years later, I returned from Oregon to attend the General Conference, to which I was a delegate. I spent a Conference Sunday in Skaneateles, where I was made most cordially welcome. I preached in the afternoon from 1 Samuel ii, 30: "Them that honor me I will honor; but they that despise me shall be lightly esteemed." Bishop Simpson had preached one of his magnificent sermons in the morning. The reunion was very pleasant. The year I was pastor in Skaneateles was successful. Large congregations attended upon the preaching and upon the week-night services. Our accessions and conversions amounted to one hundred.

The following year I was sent to Auburn, five miles west from Skaneateles. The stone church was sixty by ninety feet; a large congregation and membership. The Millerite excitement ran very high. I had twelve class-leaders. Six of them had embraced the Millerite delusion, which was that Jesus was coming in March, 1843, in person from heaven to judge mankind, and to set up his millennial kingdom. They converted their class-meetings into Second Advent discussions, and dissensions threatened permanently to disrupt the Church. I took their class-books from them, and gave them to those who would teach a more edifying doctrine. My predecessor had taken a crowd of people of disreputable notoriety into the Church, and for the first six months of the year we were holding leaders' and stewards' meetings weekly, dropping out the unruly and disturbing elements, until we had disposed of one hundred and twenty, by dropping or expelling them. Then we had a powerful revival, and one hundred and fifty were added to the Church.

At the end of the year we were returned to Madison, our first station. Family reasons induced this. My wife's mother was in feeble health, and requested that Mrs. Pearne should return to her home and cheer her closing days. The year was marked by great peace and some ingathering of souls. In Madison, Marcellus, and Skaneateles we made substantial improvements in church and parsonage property. In Madison we built a new church, and introduced into it a pipe-organ, the first one introduced into a Methodist church in New York State west of the Hudson River. It was not dedicated until my successor, Rev. A. J. Dana, was in charge. When the dedication of the church occurred, Dr. Bowen, the presiding elder, was requested to dedicate the Lord's house. He objected to do so, unless the organ was removed. The committee waited upon Dr. Joseph Cross, the stationed minister of Cazenovia, and asked him if he would dedicate the church with an organ in it. He promptly answered that he would, and he would also dedicate the organ with every pipe in it. This statement was announced to Dr. Bowen, and he consented to officiate. This was in his dedicatory prayer: "O Lord, we dedicate this beautiful church-building, with all appropriate and necessary appurtenances thereunto belonging or in any manner appertaining, to thy great name and worship." The circumlocution was his way of avoiding and evading the recognition of the organ. If interrogated upon the subject, he could make answer that the organ was neither "appropriate nor necessary."

CHAPTER III.

DURING the May of the Conference year, 1844, I attended the General Conference of the Methodist Episcopal Church, which met in Green Street Church, New York, as a spectator, and saw and heard all that occurred in that historic Conference on the subject of Bishop James O. Andrew and Rev. Francis A. Harding, as slaveholding bishop and minister. Bishop Andrew was suspended from episcopal functions as long as the impediment of his connection with slavery should remain. The Conference refused to reverse the action of the Baltimore Conference, by which Mr. Harding had been expelled from the Conference for being a slaveholding minister. There were giants in that body on both sides of the great debate, which lasted through several days. That was a very live question in our section of the country, and some twenty thousand of our members in the Eastern and Northern States seceded from the Methodist Episcopal Church, and organized the Wesleyan Methodist Connection.

The whole scene of that General Conference is mapped out in my memory as vividly and strongly as though it occurred yesterday. The great speeches on the side of the North, were by Hamline, Peck, Bangs, Olin, Durbin, John A. Collins of Baltimore, and others. On the South side, William A. Smith, of Virginia; George F. Pierce, of

Georgia; Ignatius A. Few, of Georgia; William Capers, of South Carolina; and John Early, of Virginia. The Ohio Conference delegation impressed me very strongly. It included James B. Finley and Joseph M. Trimble, whose resolution was the one at last adopted, and it included, also, William H. Raper, who impressed me as the noblest Roman of them all. Edmund S. Janes and L. L. Hamline were elected bishops.

In more orderly and elaborate form, a few years ago I carefully wrote up my impressions of that General Conference. It is too valuable as a historical narrative, so detailed, not to put it into these pages. It is as follows, viz.:

PERSONAL RECOLLECTIONS OF THE HISTORIC CONFERENCE OF 1844.

Some months since a call was made through the press to ascertain how many members of the General Conference of 1844 were still living. Six or seven responded to the call. One of them—James M. Jameson, of the Ohio Conference—furnished the *Western* several interesting papers on the subject, giving his recollections of the men and the action of that body. They had rare value as historical contributions. No call has been made for papers from those who were present as spectators only at that memorable Conference. Yet it may add a chapter, not without value, if I shall furnish my personal recollections and impressions of that historic body, not as a member, but as a deeply interested onlooker.

Bishop James O. Andrew had become a slaveholder by marriage with a lady who owned slaves. He had been elected bishop twelve years before as a

non-slaveholding minister. He could not have been
elected bishop if he had been a slaveholder. There
has never been a moment in the history of the Methodist Episcopal Church when a slaveholding minister
could have been elected a bishop. Francis A. Harding—a member of the Baltimore Conference—had
married a slaveholding woman, and so violated a rule
of the Discipline, as the Baltimore Conference held.
For this, as he refused to disentangle himself by manu-
mitting his slaves, the Conference suspended him.
From this decision he appealed to the General Conference of 1844. The decision of the appeal sustained
the action of the Baltimore Conference.

Bishop Andrew's case was finally settled by adopting a resolution offered by J. B. Finley and J. M.
Trimble, which, after reciting the complications of
the episcopacy with slavery, and so marring Bishop
Andrew's acceptability as a general superintendent,
declared "that it is the sense of this General Conference that he desist from the exercise of this office so
long as the impediment remains." This was carried
by a vote of 111 to 69. Before the Conference assembled in New York, and during its session, public excitement had become strong and intense. Abolitionism had become widely prevalent in the non-slaveholding States. Hence the meeting of the Conference, the
action expected to be taken, and the action, as stated
above, actually taken, aroused strong and general
agitation and excitement. The results of that action
in the division of the Methodist Episcopal Church,
and later in the attempted dissolution of the Federal
Union, and also in the bloody Civil War which ensued, have ever since given a wide, living, and permanent interest to the General Conference of 1844 and
its action.

For two weeks, from day to day, with the liveliest

interest in its doings as an Abolitionist, I sat as a spectator in the gallery of Green Street Church, New York, and watched the proceedings. The whole scene was one of vivid, thrilling interest. It made an impression on my mind never effaced. All the incidents and conditions are as distinct in memory as though occurring but yesterday. The grouping of the leading delegations, and also the persons, features, forms, and voices of the chief leaders and movers of thought in the body, as I now recall them, are as distinct in memory as when I sat there forty-eight years ago, and observed them. Upon the left of the pulpit were the South Carolina and Georgia delegations. In the same vicinity, and on both sides of the aisle, were the other principal Southern delegations.

On the right-hand side of the pulpit, and extending up the seats on that side of the house, were the New York, Baltimore, and New England delegations. Across the aisle from them, and extending toward the rear of the house, were the Philadelphia, Oneida, Troy, Genesee, Pittsburg, Ohio, and other delegations. In fact, the Southern Conferences were ranged on one side of the house, and the Northern and Border Conferences were on the other side of the house. This could not have been a coincidence. It must have been designed. I do not claim exact accuracy in the detail of these statements. Substantially, they are correct.

In the Virginia delegation were two noted men— John Early, an elderly man, of coarse features and severely plain countenance. He was afterwards a bishop of the Methodist Episcopal Church, South. He held the office some years. His marked persistence in gaining and holding the floor, and his having his say on nearly all questions, made him conspicuous. One of his colleagues, a brilliant man, was William A. Smith. His fervid eloquence, and bold, almost reckless statements, excited admiration. They utterly failed to move the solid North from their convictions.

Among the many celebrities in that memorable assembly who personally impressed me, I name the following, with the Annual Conferences they represented: From the Georgia Conference were, A. B. Longstreet, Ignatius A. Few, and Lovick and George F. Pierce—father and son—both distinguished men, the latter afterwards a bishop in the Methodist Episcopal Church, South.

Of the ten New York delegates, four were strongly marked—Nathan Bangs, George Peck, Stephen Olin, and Peter P. Sandford. Of the seven from the Troy Conference, Tobias Spicer, a veteran, and Jesse T. Peck, for the first time a delegate, deserve mention. Genesee Conference was ably represented by Gleezen Fillmore, Samuel Luckey, and six others. Silas Comfort and D. Holmes, Jr., and five others, answered from old Oneida Conference. William Hunter, Homer J. Clark, and John Spencer, with their four co-delegates, held up the credit of the Pittsburg Conference.

Ohio Conference had a strong delegation of eight—Charles Elliott, William H. Raper, Joseph M. Trimble, James B. Finley, Leonidas L. Hamline, and others. They were men of very fine presence. This Conference was honored in several ways. Finley and Trimble presented the famous resolution in the Bishop Andrew case. Finley looked the grand old pioneer and chieftain that he was. Trimble was youthful and ruddy. L. L. Hamline made the eloquent argument which carried the Conference as by storm to the adoption of the Finley-Trimble resolution. Philadelphia Conference had Levi Scott and John P. Durbin and four others.

Kentucky Conference had Henry B. Bascom and

Hubbard H. Kavanaugh. Both of them afterward became bishops in the new organization. Tennessee Conference had Robert Paine, afterwards a Southern Church bishop; John B. McFerrin, Book Agent and editor, and later a missionary secretary; A. L. P. Green, and others. William Winans and B. M. Drake were of the Mississippi Conference.

From Baltimore Conference, John A. Collins, Alfred Griffith, and Henry Slicer showed themselves strong men and masters in debate. W. M. Wightman, William Capers, and S. Dunwoody, from the South Carolina Conference, were conspicuous. The two former became bishops in the new Church organization. The personalities of Olin, Durbin, George Peck, Nathan Bangs, H. B. Bascom, and others were strongly marked. These gave them a ready and wide recognition as men of power.

I can not distinctly recall the position in the auditorium of the delegates from the Mississippi Conference. One of them greatly and honorably distinguished himself—William Winans, D. D. He was a native of Clermont County, Ohio. He had been many years in the South. He had taken in slavery by inoculation, as it were. It struck in on him deeply. He was intensely and aggressively pro-slavery, a more vehement and vigorous defender of the "peculiar institution" than were those "to the manner born." A wide Byron collar, buttoned at the throat, and worn without cravat, was the neck-dress; heavy locks of black, flowing hair, worn long. His general dress was somewhat *negligé*. His voice was strong and ringing. I heard him deliver an able and stirring address on "African Colonization." He spoke loud and rapidly. During the speech of an hour his face was flushed; the veins on his forehead stood out like whipcords; his trumpet-tones rang out to the remotest parts of the great Broadway Tabernacle.

A passage between Drs. G. F. Pierce and J. T. Peck will have flavor. They were on opposite sides of the house, and of the question as well. They fleshed their maiden swords on the engrossing question. Neither of them had ever been a delegate. Dr. Pierce said: "We have unity and peace, and seek it because of its effect on the connection; and I believe to-day that if the New England Conferences were to secede, the rest of us would have peace. There would be religion enough left among us to live together as a band of brothers." He also spoke of New England as the prime source of all the difficulty, and that, but for her, he believed the residue of the Church would be the gainer by it.

Dr. J. T. Peck said: "The brother from Georgia says this measure will not save us from secessions. We shall have secession from New England! Sirs, as the name New England struck my ear, I felt a thrill of the most intense interest. But the reverend gentleman proceeded to say, 'They are busybodies in other men's matters! A thorn in the flesh! A messenger sent to buffet us!' And alluding, as I understood him to do, to a certain movement in New England, and certain principles on which that movement was based, he called it 'the foul spirit of the pit, the judgment of perdition,' etc. . . . But my friend from Georgia says: 'Let New England go! I wish in my heart she would secede! And joy go with her, for I am sure she will leave peace behind her.' Let New England go! I can not forget this exclamation. It vibrates in my soul in tones of grating discord. Why, sir, what is New England, that we should part with her with so little reluctance? New England! The land of the

Pilgrims, the land of our venerated fathers in Israel, the land of Brodhead, of Merritt, of the reverend man at my side"—pointing to George Pickering—"and a host of worthies whom we have delighted to honor as the bulwarks of Methodism in its early days of primitive purity and peril. Let New England go? No, sir, we can not so easily part with the pioneer land of the devoted and sainted Jesse Lee."

When the heat of the wordy battle had passed away, apologies were in order for any severe, cutting personalities, which, without intention, might have been uttered. Those of Dr. Peck were profuse and ample. Pierce's reply, in substance, was, that he trusted that he had not said a word which would ruffle a hair on the head of his worthy antagonist. When it is remembered that Dr. Peck's head was completely innocent of hair, the laugh which followed this sally of Dr. Pierce will be easily accounted for.

After the Finley-Trimble resolution had been adopted, and the time had come for the election of two bishops, to the surprise of very many, Edmund S. Janes, not a member of the Conference, was elected bishop. George Peck had been much talked of as the coming man for a bishop. He had been editor of the *Christian Advocate and Journal* and of the *Quarterly Review* for several years. If a bishop had been elected in 1840, he would undoubtedly have gained episcopal honors. There was a genuine disappointment at Dr. Peck's failure to be elected, and, as intimated, a surprise at Janes's success.

Bishop Janes's accession to the office was attributed to the solid vote of the Southern delegates, and probably some votes from some of the Northern Conferences. Three or four reasons were alleged as probably causing the preference for Mr. Janes over George Peck. All through the hot debate in the Conference,

while Dr. Peck had not said severe and pungent things
upon the question in hand, yet he had voted with the
North on all the phases of the case as, one by one, they
reached the voting stage and it was well understood,
South and North, that Dr. Peck was a decided anti-
slavery man, if not actually an Abolitionist. Mr. Janes,
not being a member of the General Conference, he
antagonized no section nor party, and while it was believed that Mr. Janes was a Democrat in his political
leaning, and that his sympathies were with the South
and her institutions, he had, during the winter preceding the General Conference, made the tour of the entire South as financial secretary of the American Bible
Society; and so had visited all the Southern Conferences and addressed them in that behalf, and had also
preached for them. It was also held and talked in
New York and elsewhere, at that time, that the South
would secede, and they were then preparing and providing to do so; and, from the stand taken by Bishop
Soule, it was conjectured and talked that he would go
with them, and, not unlikely, the Southern delegates
hoped that Janes also would go with Soule into their
Church when it should be organized.

My host, Mr. Francis Hall, informed me that Mr.
Janes was present when the Conference voted for
bishops. He sat in a seat near the rear of the church.
The tellers announced and counted the ballots in open
Conference. Mr. Janes kept the tally for his own
vote, and also of that for the other candidates. When
the vote for him had reached and passed the majority
line, he turned to Mr. Hall, who sat next him, and
said, "I am elected a bishop of the Methodist Episcopal Church." Whatever may have been the suspicions of some and the hopes of others, that Bishop
Janes would go with the South when they should
secede, I never heard his loyalty to the Methodist

Episcopal Church called in question nor doubted. Nor did I ever hear of his doing or saying anything then, nor since, to confirm the suspicions expressed by some at the time of his election, that the Southern delegates had an understanding and a hope that he would join the Church South when it should be organized. Mr. Hamline's election was the result of his matchless speech, which carried the solid anti-slavery vote of the Conference. The bishops who were present during the discussion and decision as to Bishop Andrew's case, were Soule, Hedding, Andrew, Waugh, and Morris. During the pendency of his case Andrew sat apart from his colleagues. He presented a paper setting forth his relation as a slaveholder. It was in substance as follows: Several years before an old lady of Augusta, Ga., bequeathed to him a mulatto girl, in trust that he should keep her until she was nineteen years of age, and that, with her consent, he should then send her to Liberia; and, in case that she refused to go to Liberia, he should make her as free as the laws of Georgia would admit. She refused to go to Liberia, and remained *legally* his slave, although he received no pecuniary compensation nor advantage from her. Five years before the date of that Conference, the mother of his wife left to his wife a Negro boy, and, as his wife died without a will, this boy was legally his slave. In the January preceding the General Conference the bishop married his present wife. She possessed slaves inherited from her former husband's estate, and belonging to her. Shortly after marriage he had secured them to her by a deed of trust. The laws of Georgia did not admit of emancipation, so that he was a legal slaveholder in those conditions.

The bishops were, by resolution, invited to speak to Bishop Andrew's case, if they should so desire.

Bishop Soule made a long speech against the adverse action proposed in reference to his colleague, as being lacking in conservatism, and as opposed to the prevailing usage of Methodism. Later the bishops presented a paper to the Conference, signed by J. Soule, E. Hedding, B. Waugh, and Thomas A. Morris, requesting the Conference to postpone further action in the case of Bishop Andrew until the ensuing General Conference, and that, in the meantime, the bishops could assign to Bishop Andrew such work in the slave States as would not be objectionable to them, and would not thus offend those sections of the work where the hostility to a slaveholding bishop presiding in a Conference would not tolerate his presence.

The next day Bishop Hedding withdrew his name from the paper, the others adhering to their signatures. The Conference laid the bishops' paper on the table by a vote of 95 yeas and 84 nays.

I close this paper with a brief account of a most delightful recollection I have of witnessing, while in New York at that time, the début of John B. Gough in his brilliant career of marvelous power and success as a temperance advocate. It occurred in the old Broadway Tabernacle, at the May Anniversary of the National Temperance Society. It was ten o'clock at night. Edward C. Delevan, Esquire, Leonard Bacon, D. D., and another, whose name I can not recall, had held the vast audience of perhaps three thousand souls spellbound by their burning words.

A seedy-looking young man was introduced to the audience as John B. Gough. His name was unknown. He had only been reformed some three or four weeks. He was thin and cadaverous-looking, and unpromising. From all parts of the house he was hissed. I sat in the gallery, near to where he stood on the platform. He took a firm standing position, and closed his lips tightly. I saw his eyes flash, as of a purpose he would not relinquish. He waited until the hissing ceased, and then began thus: "Three weeks ago I was kneeling on the new-made grave of my wife, murdered by my intemperance. I solemnly promised God, that if he would give me help, I would mount this fiery steed of the appetite for strong drink, and I would draw upon the powerful curb-rein until I brought him back upon his haunches." He suited the action to the word with such dramatic power that the audience cheered him with round upon round, and then for an hour he held the vast audience by the magic of his fascinating eloquence, as he has so often done since.

Recurring to that famous General Conference, it was from the sowing of dragon's teeth on that occasion, from the muttering of division and of Church separation, that, seventeen years later, secession occurred, and the battalions of civil war were set in this fair land. Our country ran red with fraternal blood. Then God buried human slavery in the blood-red gulf of war, thus freeing our country from the blight and curse of human slavery, and rendering the Nation homogeneous and united, a free and happy people.

During my second pastorate in Madison, some fifty were added to the Church.

CHAPTER IV.

FROM this term of pastoral labor in Madison, my next removal was to Binghamton, N. Y., seventy miles south. Here were spent two happy years. My father had preceded me in this charge, and later my eldest brother succeeded me. And later still, on my return from Oregon, in 1864-5, I was for six weeks pastor of the same old Henry Street Church in Binghamton, which I had rebuilt during my first pastorate there. The name Pearne seemed a favorite one in Binghamton, for the City Council called a street by our name. Pearne Street is still a full street in that city. Both years were those of gracious awakening and outpouring. Many souls were converted and added to the Church. A very important murder trial was held in Binghamton during my pastorate. From my ability to write rapidly in shorthand, my services were sought in taking down the evidence and the arguments of counsel, especially the testimony of experts on insanity. The man was acquitted. The reason for this was, that the evidence was almost entirely circumstantial, and the jury were reluctant to convict for capital punishment one against whom every particle of the evidence was circumstantial.

Henry Street Church, in Binghamton, when I entered the charge was called, derisively, by the toughs, "the old Eel-pot." It was nearly square, very much like the four-square city described in the revelation of St. John the Divine. It was two stories high, with a gallery on three sides. This, under my earnest and unremitting labor, was transformed into a modern church of due proportions, beautiful, comfortable, elegant. The church edifice was an education. That newly-modeled church improved and elevated the tastes and spirit of the people. It was before the days of the Church Extension Society. The official members of the old Eel-pot Church had purposely nursed and incurred an indebtedness of $250, which they would not pay, that it might be used as a fender against any troublesome Church beggar who might come to them for a collection for a needy Church. That debt was paid when I went into the repair business. That church improvement, costing some $3,000 or $4,000, had a charming effect upon the dear old Church members. It was like life from the dead. The unpaid balance was paid off on the day of dedication. For twenty years after its renewal, its walls, frescoed and beautiful, echoed the songs of a jubilant, glad people, when it gave place to an elegant structure of modern appointments, costing some $40,000 or more. It is doubted that I ever achieved so much for the welfare and life of a Church, as I did in the remodeling of the old Eel-pot Church into a modern and lovely church structure. Binghamton can never fade from my memory. It was, and it still is, a hallowed place to memory dear.

My next move was a great disappointment. It was intended, doubtless, as a punishment from my presiding elder, because I happened to differ with him. I was sent from a second-class station to Wyoming, a circuit, almost in the stage of collapse, without a parsonage and without much promising character as a charge. It required all the nerve and all the manliness I could summon to submit to it, and go to the place to which I was sent. I moved my goods, by pike, seventy-five miles, and they stood in the street twenty-four hours, because there was no place to store them. At last we put them into an attic, and ourselves boarded the whole year in the ladies' boarding hall of the Wyoming Seminary. But it was the best year for results of any in all my ministerial life up to that time. Never since have I had a richer, riper year, nor one more full of Divine power, and of grand, blessed results. In Wyoming, six miles above Kingston, the society seemed to be in a moribund condition. I made two successive attempts to hold a protracted meeting, but both attempts were utter failures. In Hartsough Hollow, Plymouth, and Kingston we had precious revivals.

The fates seemed against us in Wyoming. I sent over the mountains for Elisha Harris, an eccentric local preacher. We entered into a compact to have a successful revival meeting in Wyoming, or die. Instead of dying, we were the liveliest kind of human beings. We visited from house to house over a radius of three miles in diameter. At length the skies gave forth a sound; the slain of the Lord were many. For six weeks the battle raged; the work of God was mightily revived. In the whole circuit three hundred souls were converted. The persons converted were some of them Deists, Universalists, and Newlights. My lieutenant, Elisha Harris, staid right by me and with me until our victory was won and housed.

I should describe him before narrating a scene in which he very successfully wrought. He was entirely unlearned. Beyond reading his Bible and writing his name, he knew and could do nothing. But then he knew Jesus. He knew the Holy Ghost. He knew what salvation meant. He knew men too well to be deceived in them or by them. He was small in stature and spare; with hatchet face and deep-sunken black eyes, which flashed and blazed like orbs of fire when he was under full tension. His eyebrows were shaggy and overhanging. He had the most percussive, piercing shout I ever heard. After the revival was over, he lingered a few days in Wyoming. A Universalist preacher came to Wyoming to preach. Elisha divined his mission. He came to me to say that he would meet that vaunting Go'iath. I advised him to keep away. He said he had to meet him, and God would take care of results. When I found he would go, I advised him to meet him with the Word of God, and to ask God to keep him from making great mistakes. The man came. His sermon was a smooth, smart, moral essay. No one could tell what his distinctive doctrine was from the sermon. Elisha did not like the way the thing lay. When the Universalist preacher was through, he gave opportunity for any who doubted his positions to rise up and call them in question. Elisha sat on the back row of seats, which were higher than the seats in front, which had been made for the smaller scholars. He jumped over the low seats into the middle of the schoolhouse floor, and leaped up from the floor, perhaps three or four inches. Then he shouted "Glory to God!" at the very top of his voice. "I say, sir," said he, addressing the minister, his eyes flashing fire and his voice of piercing power, "how do they come up in the resurrection?" The preacher was dazed and rattled. He did not seem to know what to say. He scratched his head, and repeated: "Come up? Come up? I suppose they get up as a man would get up out of a chair." Then Elisha clapped his hands, and again shouted, "Glory to God! I have got you." Elisha then said: "You prowling wolf of hell, you come here to steal back from God's sheepfold the lambs of Christ's flock whom we have gathered, and you do not know how they come up in the resurrection." Then he read in John v, 28, 29: " 'Marvel not at this: for the hour is coming in which all that are in the graves shall hear his voice, and shall come forth; they that have done good, unto the resurrection of life; and they that have done evil, unto the resurrection of damnation!' And you do not know how they come up in the resurrection?" The minister, seizing his hat, said, "I did not come here to be insulted." "Insulted! insulted!" said Harris: "and you do not know how they come up in the resurrection!" The man started for the door. Elisha started after him sans hat and sans overcoat. The man broke into a trot. Elisha trotted after him, calling him a "wolf of hell," and telling him "he did not know how they come up in the resurrection!" He literally ran the man out of town. The people were in sympathy with Harris, for they knew him to be a conscientious, good man. The man never came back to look after his lambs.

One of the converts was a Deist. He had not been in Church for years. His conversion was very marked. He and his wife joined the Church. They were wealthy. They built a thirty-thousand-dollar church, and a five-thousand-dollar or ten-thousand-dollar parsonage. They sent for me to come and dedicate the church. He died a few years since, after a life of great usefulness. He was a very godly, consecrated man. His wife also became an earnest Christian. They have given blessed proof of the genuineness of their religion, by their wise and liberal gifts of money for benevolent and Christian causes.

During that great revival in Wyoming Circuit, Elisha Harris and I visited all the families, shops, stores, and manufactories and places of resort, where we could find persons, and conversed personally with all we met about their souls and their spiritual welfare. Among others, I visited Payne Pettebone, the person referred to above. I told him that I had called to have a conversation with him, and as there were others present, he took me into his counting-room, and locked the door. I said to him: "First, I wish to invite you to attend meeting. We are holding special meetings, and it would give me great pleasure to see you there." He replied that he had not for ten years attended religious meetings, except at funerals. He did not believe in them. He was a Deist, he said. He believed in God; but not in the Bible, nor in the religion of the Bible; but he was open to conviction, and he would read any books I would furnish him that would refute his ideas of Deism. I told him I could bring him books that had refuted every leading point in Deism; but there was a shorter and a surer way to come to the truth on this subject; and that way was prayer. The God who had made him, if he approached him in prayer would reveal the truth to him as to experimental religion; and then I proposed to him to spend a few minutes, at stated times, twice each day, and I would stop at those times and pray specially for him. It was specified that he also was to kneel down and pray at those stated times. This was on Wednesday. I saw him no more until Sunday, when I preached to a full house on "The Day of Final Judgment." I asked all present who felt their need of preparation for the judgment-day, and who would pledge themselves to ask God to prepare them for the judgment-day, to rise up, and indicate both in that way. All in the audience, including Mr. Pettebone, arose, except one person. He was a very dissipated man. At evening, when I invited seekers of religion to come to the altar, Mr. Pettebone arose, and said he was going forward, but he wished first to make a statement. He spoke of the visit I made him on the Wednesday before, and said that the first time he prayed he was deeply impressed with a sense of God's presence; that every time he prayed that impression deepened; that the result of it all was, he felt himself a sinner in need of a Savior. Then he came forward with many others, and the revival went forward until hundreds were saved.

A letter was received by me recently from Rev. E. W. Van Schoick, one of my successors on the Wyoming Circuit, giving Mr. Pettebone's account of his own conversion, which I introduce here:

COLDWATER, MICH., *April* 28, 1898.

MY DEAR DOCTOR PEARNE,—Have you forgotten the call Brother Pettebone and I made on you in Cincinnati on our way South? We did not stop with you very long, but long enough to recall many pleasant memories of your pastorate in Wyoming, Brother Pettebone's home, where I, too, was pastor in the early seventies. My pastorate there was very pleasant and successful, as it was my good fortune to enter into your labors of years before. William Swetland, Payne Pettebone, Isaac Shoemaker, Daniel Van Scoy, Daniel Jones, and others of great force of character, were my Official Board, having been converted under your ministry there.

Payne Pettebone, as you know, was a remarkable man. He was converted sitting in his pew while you were preaching. As you were discussing the plan of salvation by faith in Jesus Christ, making it very plain and real, Mr. Pettebone said: "Yes, I see it as never before: Jesus Christ alone is the Savior of all who receive him. I receive him. I receive him now as *my* Savior." And right there in his seat he received the evidence, which never left him, that God, for Christ's sake, had forgiven his sins. What a glorious history he made for the Church of his choice! Sincere, conscientious, tried and true, a wonderfully successful business man, his thousands, and even millions, were all laid at the feet of the Master; and how much good he did by his gifts to Wyoming Seminary, Wesleyan University, Drew Seminary, and to hundreds of struggling Churches, eternity alone will reveal. He and his wife gave the beautiful church at Wyoming as a thank-offering to the Lord for the prosperity with which he had favored them. His father-in-law, William Swetland, died before I became pastor at Wyoming, but his memory of good deeds was as ointment poured forth. Mrs. Pettebone, William Swetland's daughter, still lives, and, if anything, goes even beyond her father and husband in the munificence of her giving, having just presented to Wyoming Seminary a gymnasium, complete, at a cost of over thirty thousand dollars. How little you knew, when you won William Swetland and Payne Pettebone to the Church, what you were doing for Methodism and for the world!

And Daniel Jones, one of the most useful men in that Church,—have you forgotten how you captured him? He had the elements of a great character, but was emphatically a man of the world. Before you came he did not attend Church at all. But you had a way of reading men, and said, "There is a man who will be a power in the Church if I can once win him." So, in a wise way, you set about it. He was very fond of a horse, and, as you saw him driving past the parsonage nearly every day, evidently watching his horse with admiration, you said, "I think I have discovered the way to that man's heart." One morning, seeing him start toward Kingston, you found it convenient, an hour or so after, to take a long walk in the same direction. Observing him returning far down the road, you turned about, and trod your weary way toward home. Your walk indicated that you were very tired. You were red in the face. You were wiping the perspiration from your brow. As he came near he could not fail to see how fatigued you were, and, as a man of generous impulse would be supposed to do under like circumstances, invited you to ride. Of course you accepted, and quickly turned the conversation to the subject of horses. You saw that he was fond of a horse, and remarked that you, too, loved a horse, and were so pleased to ride behind such a noble animal as his—did n't know when you had had such a treat. All the way to Wyoming you conversed on the good points of that horse, not even mentioning religion to him. When he drew up in front of your house, you said, as you were getting out of the buggy, "How much I have enjoyed my ride and my chat with you! I do n't know how I can repay you, unless you take it out in preaching. By the way, I do n't remember seeing you at Church since I came." "Well, to tell you the truth, I have n't been to the Church in years, but I think I must drop in and hear you," was his reply. He did "drop in," and not many weeks afterward was converted, and soon became one of the useful officiaries of that Church.

I rejoice that it has been my pleasure to know you. I have watched your work with delighted interest, and am so thankful that, after such a long term in the ministry, both in the pastorate and presiding eldership, your eye is not dim, your natural force is not abated, and you are still abundant in labors and in honors. God bless you!

Very cordially yours,

R. W. Van Schoick.

CHAPTER V.

WHILE upon the Wyoming Circuit I gathered up the items about Bishops Asbury and McKendree which follow, and to these I subjoin a legend of Asbury in Tennessee, from an eyewitness, which enhances the value of the incident. In addition, I furnish the proof of Mrs. Denison's correctness in my narrative of her.

FRANCIS ASBURY—PERSONAL REMINISCENCES.

My father's library, during my boyhood, contained the standard Methodist books—Wesley, Watson, Fletcher, and especially Asbury's Journal. The last, and Wesley's Journal, were eagerly devoured by me for the adventures they recorded. No work of fiction ever so absorbed me, nor was equally interesting to me, as these Journals. Asbury's Journal filled me with the highest admiration for the first American bishop and his marvelous heroism as a pioneer. I often wondered whether I should ever, in any considerable measure, equal his privations and the adventurous incidents through which he so bravely and cheerfully passed. And yet I myself have been in perils of waters and perils of robbers as exciting as those he records.

In my five years of itinerant labor in East Tennessee, I have preached and held quarterly-meetings at the eastern base of the Cumberland Mountains, at a place called Bean Station, where Mr. Asbury and his comrades were accustomed to wait until a sufficient number of travelers would gather to enable them safely to cross the Cumberland Gap into Kentucky. The legends of his sojourns at the station were current when I traveled the Knoxville District, in 1865 and later.

When, in my early teens, I became a traveling minister, sixty years ago, I listened to the folk-lore of the elder Methodists in my charges about the movements of the earlier leaders of the Methodist Episcopal Church. But I was always specially attentive to those which related to the grandest hero of them all. I record in this paper two legends of the pioneer bishop, which have never been published. In 1847, 1848, and 1849, I traveled the first of those years the Wyoming Circuit in Pennsylvania, and the last two in Wilkesbarre. Wyoming Circuit included all the west side of the classic American ground, called the Wyoming Valley, which the pen of Campbell has immortalized in his "Gertrude of Wyoming." On the circuit, near New Troy, as it was then called— Wyoming as more recently known—lived the widow Elizabeth Denison, a lady of more than fourscore years, who still retained her mental powers in full vigor. She was a daughter-in-law of Colonel Nathan Denison, a colonel in the Revolutionary army, detailed at the time of the Wyoming massacre in the Wyoming Valley. July 3, 1783, Colonel Denison and Colonel Zebulon Butler led the forces of the volunteers out from Forty Fort, near the middle of the valley north and south, to the bloody holocaust which overtook them, as the result of an ambuscade into which they were decoyed by the apparent retreating of the Indian and English troops, until those enemies had surrounded them and slain them in cold blood. Of two hundred and thirty persons, mostly boys and young men, and quite old men in that forward movement, one hundred and seventy were slain. Only fifty escaped. Mrs. Denison, who was a member of my Church in New Troy, and who was a girl of only eight years when the massacre occurred, would narrate to me the thrilling events of those perilous times. The monument commemorating those scenes stands just below New Troy. Among other incidents, she related to me the particulars of a prolonged visit to her home, made by Bishops Asbury and McKendree.* She was at the time a young bride, having married the son of Colonel Denison. The two bishops had called there for a stay of some days.

Asbury's Journal records three visits which he made to Wyoming. The first one he mentions, occurred July 2, 4, 7, 1793. He makes these notes on that visit:

"July 2—After preaching at Sunbury, June 28th, on 'The Grace of God, which appeareth unto all men,'

---

* An article in the *Northern Christian Advocate*, April 13, 1898, enables me to fix the approximate date of this visit of Asbury and McKendree in 1814. The article is illustrated by a cut of the barn in which Asbury preached on that occasion. The text from which Bishop Asbury preached is given. This short article is of historic value:

"BARN IN WHICH ASBURY PREACHED ABOUT THE YEAR 1814.

"About the year 1814, Bishop Asbury, accompanied by Bishop McKendree, passed through Brooklyn, Pa., when on their way from a Northern Conference to the Baltimore Conference. They tarried long enough to hold a service in Brooklyn in a barn, an excellent cut of which is herewith given. The text from which Bishop Asbury preached was 1 Sam. xv, 14: 'And Samuel said, What meaneth then this bleating of the sheep in mine ears, and the lowing of the oxen which I hear?'

"That the cut represents the identical barn in which the sermon was preached is fully authenticated, though it does not now occupy the same site that it did at that time. Many years ago it was moved to the place it now occupies, and the we wrought up the hills and narrows to Wyoming. We stopped at a poor house; nevertheless, they were rich enough to sell us a bushel of oats; and they had sense enough to make us pay well for them. We reached Mr. P.'s at about eleven o'clock P. M. I found riding in the night caused a return of my rheumatic complaint through my breast and shoulders. But all is well. The Lord is with us."

"Thursday, 4th—Being the anniversary of the American Independence, there was a great noise among the sinners. A few of us went down to Shawanee (Plymouth), called a few people together from their work, and found it good for us to be there."

"Sunday, July 7th—The Lord has spoken in awful peals of thunder. O what havoc was made there fifteen years ago! [This was obviously a mistake, or a slip

---

addition on the right was constructed. The large open doors show the audience-room in which the service was held.

"In 1888 Edward L. Paine, son of the Rev. Edward Paine, who owned the barn, was a lay delegate to the General Conference from Wisconsin Conference, and was the oldest layman of that body, being eighty-seven years of age. He stated on the floor of the Conference that he heard Bishop Asbury preach the sermon to which reference is made above, and on that occasion, which was a memorable one, though only thirteen years of age, he gave his heart to God and his hand to the Methodist Episcopal Church, of which he remained a faithful member until the day of his death.

"For the picture of the barn and the portrait of Mr. Paine we are indebted to the Rev. G. E. Van Woert, pastor of our Church in Brooklyn, Pa., who will furnish excellent photographs of the barn in two sizes; the larger, shown in the cut, for thirty-five cents, and the smaller for twenty-five cents. Brother Van Woert devotes one-half the profits of sales within his charge, and all the profits of sales outside, to the payment of the debt on the Missionary Society. The picture is worth preserving for its historic associations. Send orders to Brother Van Woert."

of the pen, for the scene to which he refers was the Wyoming massacre of July 3, 1783, ten years before.] Most of the inhabitants were either cut off or driven away. The people might have clothed themselves in sackcloth and ashes on the 3d, if in white and glory on the 4th of July. The inhabitants here are very wicked, but I feel as though the Lord would return."

The bishop must have staid in the valley until the 8th, when he started up the Lackawanna over the twelve-mile swamp. On this trip he must have traveled alone, as there is no account of his having had a traveling companion until later in life.

The second visit he made to Wyoming was July 17, 1807. He says in his entry of that date:

"Once more I am in Wyoming. We have wearied through, and clambered over, one hundred miles of the rough roads of wild Susquehanna! O the precipitous banks, wedging narrows, rocks, sidelong hills, obstructed paths and fords—scarcely fordable—roots, stumps, and gullies!"

Two days later he speaks of ordaining Thomas and Christian Bowman, who were probably ancestral relations of our venerable senior bishop, who was born and reared near Berwick on the Susquehanna, twenty miles below Wyoming Valley. The next visit to Wyoming which he mentions, is in 1812:

"August 4th—We arrived at Father Bidlack's, and went forward to Wilkesbarre. [Father Bidlack was a Revolutionary soldier and a Methodist traveling preacher, who lived across the river from Wilkesbarre, at Kingston, and a mile distant.] The court was sitting, and a sermon was expected. My subject was, 'Knowing the terror of the Lord, we persuade men.' They gave me the court-room.

"August 5th—We came along down by the turnpike, and rough enough we found it. Farewell to

Merwine's. I lodge no more there, whisky-hell, as most of the taverns here are. . . . We lodge with George Custer, Wyoming."

"Friday, 7th—I am still. I abstain. In the evening we had an assemblage of people, and Brother Boehm spoke to them in German."

Henry Boehm was at this time Bishop Asbury's traveling companion. He was nearly one hundred years old, erect, and well preserved when I last saw him. He was present at the dedication of the Metropolitan Church in Washington in the sixties, and took part in the services—pronounced the benediction or offered a prayer.

It is quite evident that neither of these three visits to Wyoming was the one detailed to me by Mrs. Denison, because Bishop McKendree was not with Bishop Asbury at either of these visits, and this is apparent from the journal of the bishop. Asbury was less regular and careful in his Journal as he approached the end of life, and he may have been too feeble to journalize that last visit, which must have been made between 1812 and 1815, the year in which he died, March 31st.

Mrs. Denison said to me that Bishop Asbury was smaller in stature than Bishop McKendree, that he was a great sufferer from the infimities of age and from his lifelong infirmity, the rheumatism. He was neither petulant nor brusque; yet he was somewhat abstract, taciturn, and reserved. He seemed at that time to live apart, and to commune with himself. Bishop McKendree was gentle, affable, and free in his conversation, and very full of wisdom and instruction in his communications. Bishop Asbury was thin and weak from his long and severe journeyings and from his great sufferings. Bishop McKendree was of full habit, apparently in perfect health, exceedingly approachable, putting his associates completely at their ease. He was well informed; a good converser, drawing those in his company to himself by an irresistible fascination of manners, and by a most magnetic personality.

Colonel Denison, who, at the time of the visit of these two bishops, was himself well stricken in years, was greatly charmed and delighted with Bishop McKendree. He said that the bishop was so well posted in all matters that he would elicit admiration in any official public position he might have held. "Indeed," said the colonel to Mrs. Denison, "Bishop McKendree is well-fitted to have been a United States senator. He would have graced the position."

Mrs. Denison said to me that Bishop Asbury impressed all who saw him as being a very devout, earnest, and godly man, who walked in close fellowship with God.

Bishops Asbury and McKendree were scarcely ever absent from the Annual Conferences. I read of but two instances in the West where the Conference was presided over by any one but the bishops. William Burke once presided in the absence of both the bishops. In the Ohio Conference, which met in Cincinnati in 1814, both the bishops, Asbury and McKendree, were present. But Asbury was too ill to preside, and McKendree had been injured by a fall from his horse, and John Sale was appointed by the bishops to preside. In his Journal, Asbury says:

"Monday, 5th (September)—I made an attempt to speak a few words from Philippians ii, 2-5. We have progressed in our business very well, though deprived of the presence of the bishops to preside. . . . John Sale presided with great propriety. John Sale finished the plan of the stations from a general draft I furnished him. We closed our labors in peace. One thing I remark, our Conferences are now out of their infancy. Their rulers can now be called from among themselves. . . ."

From 1865 to 1868 I was presiding elder on the Knoxville District in East Tennessee. During this term I learned several incidents about Bishop Asbury from those who had been eye and ear witnesses of the events described. I give but one of them, as this gives a good, general idea of the bishop's habit in his annual tours over the continent, always by private conveyance, and always sharing the hospitality of the pioneers, which was accorded to him with a regal largeness, freedom, and munificence. On one of my tours near Dandridge I formed the acquaintance of a gentleman who lived there, and who was then a person of seventy years or more. He said that one morning, when he was quite a young man, he was going out through the gate which opened into his father's extensive estate, and upon which his father was yet living, when he met an aged man who had just driven up to the gate in a light carriage. The stranger informed him that he was Bishop Asbury, and he was just about driving in to spend the day and night with the young man's father. The bishop inquired whether the young man's father still lived there, and, learning that he did, the bishop said: "Then I will go in, and stay with him for the day and night." A young man accompanied the bishop, whose name I have forgotten, said my informant. This young man was John Wesley Bond, father of the distinguished Rev. Dr. Thomas E. Bond, who, at a later period, was editor of the *Christian Advocate*, New York. My informant said: "I went back with them. It was arranged to have preaching at our house that evening. I was sent out through the neighborhood to give notice of the meeting, and to invite the neighbors to attend it. A large number of people assembled. The young man preached. Mr. Asbury had retired. The bed was curtained in the old-fashioned way, with high curtains and a canopy. At the close of the sermon, the bishop said: 'Please draw the curtains.' The bishop sat up in the bed, and talked at some length with much freedom, pathos, and power. 'The people,' said he, 'are hungry for the Word of God. It should be dealt out to them in plain, simple, and loving speech. The gospel needs no flowers of rhetoric, no word-drapery. It is God's message of love and peace to a fallen world and to a perishing race. The message should be direct, clear, urgent.' He then exhorted the people in a most tender, pathetic, urgent manner to seek God, and to prepare for eternity. 'This,' said he, 'is probably the last time I shall ever be with you on earth. O, will you not be entreated to be reconciled to God? Shall we sit down together in the kingdom of God, to go out no more forever?' There was a general time of weeping and shouting. All seemed deeply affected by the kindly, tender, persuasive words of the bishop." This was his last visit in that State. On Sabbath, March 31, 1816, he passed through the gates into the everlasting city of God. This visit is recorded in Asbury's Journal. It occurred in October, 1814, and it is thus related in two or three lines:

"Monday, 17th—We came rapidly through Dandridge to William Turnley's. Here are kind souls. I was sick, and soon in bed; but John Bond preached for them."

The foregoing reminiscences are published in this form by the Cincinnati Conference Historical Society, with the permission of the Conference itself. The following incident anent Bishop Asbury in New York, is furnished by the late Asbury Lowrey, D. D. It is, of course, authentic:

"Richard Goodwin, a relative of my father, was a local preacher, living at Goodwin's Point, Cayuga Lake, New York. He was elected to elder's orders, probably at some Conference when he could not be present. He afterwards met Bishop Asbury on the road somewhere. The facts being made known to him, Bishop Asbury dismounted and ordained him an elder, under a tree. Whether there were three elders, or none, to lay hands on the head of Goodwin, with the bishop's, I am not informed. The stream of apostolic succession doubtless forms many eddies as it comes down to us from Wesley and Asbury.

"A. LOWREY.

"P. S.—Richard Goodwin was the father of the Rev. William H. Goodwin, D. D., of East Genesee Conference, of whom, perhaps, you have some knowledge."

The next two years I was pastor of the First Methodist Episcopal Church in Wilkesbarre, then and now one of the richest and strongest Churches of Methodism. It was then the best charge in the old Oneida Conference. My compensation had come in double measure and form, for what I had supposed to be a punishment from my presiding elder. We built a twenty-thousand-dollar church the first year of my Wilkesbarre pastorate. It will assist in understanding the financial conditions of such charges in those earlier times, when the facts are stated. The parsonage was a small, humble dwelling, which could then have been built for six hundred dollars or seven hundred dollars. The salary, all told, was four hundred dollars a year and the parsonage. This was the most they had ever paid. A one-hundred-and-thirty-thousand-dollar church has replaced the brick twenty-thousand-dollar one of forty-eight years ago; an organ, costing thirty thousand dollars, is its latest acquisition, and a parsonage worth ten thousand dollars or more has succeeded the humble six-hundred-dollar house in which I and the men who preceded me had lived. Many were added to the Church by profession during my pastorate in Wilkesbarre. The last month of my stay here my wife was very ill with the typhoid fever. She became well enough for me to remove her to her sister's, in Madison, N. Y., one hundred and forty miles away, while I should attend Conference.

I was appointed from Wilkesbarre to Owego, in New York State. I moved my goods to Owego on wagons, seventy miles. I set up the furniture in the parsonage, and put down the carpets, and then I went up seventy miles to Madison, to remove my wife to my new charge. She was too ill to be moved, for she had had a relapse. On Saturday I returned from Madison to Owego, and slept in the parsonage. On Sunday morning I woke up with a splitting headache. I was unable to eat. But I took a strong dose of pepper-tea, and went into the pulpit to preach my opening sermon for the year. A high fever was on me. I soon became delirious. I preached on incoherently. The brethren took me out of the pulpit, and put me in bed, a victim of typhoid fever, as it proved to be. I lay forty-two days in a state of coma; and as I got better of the fever I was seized with pneumonia, and came very near dying. The year was a broken one. And yet we had a good degree of success. About forty or fifty professed conversion. This was my last charge in the old Oneida Conference.

The Conference met in 1850 at Honesdale, Pa. I was appointed, by request of my host, a Newlight preacher, to preach in his church. I had ascertained that the Church was Arian in belief—denying the Divinity of Jesus Christ, the depravity of men, the personality of the Holy Spirit, and the conversion of sinners by the washing of regeneration and the renewing of the Holy Ghost. My character had passed as approved on Thursday. I went to the Newlight, or so-called Christian, church to preach. I said to myself: "This is your last and only opportunity to free your skirts from their blood, by openly opposing and exposing their doctrinal errors, and warning them faithfully of their delusions." My text was Deuteronomy xi, 16: "Take heed to yourselves that your heart be not deceived, and ye turn aside after other gods, to serve them and worship them." I dwelt upon heart deceptions as the most alarming. I instanced names and doctrines as being well adapted to mislead the unwary, and then said: "You call yourselves Christians, implying that you have a right to that name over your fellow-Christians of other names and denominations; and while deceiving by bearing, as exclusive, a name common to all Christians, at the same time, by your denial of the Divinity of Christ and his atoning sacrifice, you crucify the Son of God afresh, and put him to an open shame." The next morning my character was arrested, the first and only time in my life, for violating Christian courtesy. The case was tried, and then the Conference passed my character, and the affair ended.

I was ordained a deacon in 1841, in Owego, New York, by Bishop Joshua Soule, having concluded my two years of probation in the Conference, and having creditably passed through my Conference examination.

In 1843 I was ordained an elder by Bishop Beverly Waugh, in Wilkesbarre, Pa. The occasion was one of great solemnity and much prayer. The ordination took place in a grove. There was no church that would hold half the people who came out to the services. The sermon was preached by John McClintock, D. D., one of the most cyclopedic scholars in the entire Church, if not in the whole land.

In the Conference, after my first year of probationary Conference life had passed, Bishop Robert R. Roberts presided. He was one of the most noble and manly-looking of men, and withal very saintly in countenance and appearance. He preached from Luke xvi, 31: "If they hear not Moses and the prophets, neither will they be persuaded, though one rose from the dead." In the course of his sermon, he said, instead of persuading men to turn to God, a spirit from the dead would terrify them, and cause

> "Each particular hair to stand on end,
> Like quills upon the fretful porcupine."

This quotation from Shakespeare quite won me, for I was a great admirer of the English poet of Stratford-on-Avon. The congregation was deeply moved under the sermon.

CHAPTER VI.

INCLUDING my two years of supply work before joining the Conference, and the time I spent as a probationer and a member of the Oneida Conference, there were fourteen years of service. As I re-traverse in thought the well-remembered scenes and associations of those early years, the recollection affords me great satisfaction, and I am led to exclaim in gratitude to God,

> "In each event of life, how clear,
>   Thy ruling hand I see!
> Each blessing to my soul most dear,
>   Because bestowed by Thee."

In the work of the ministry, to which my call had been strong and unmistakable, I had a glow, an inspiration, and a joy exquisitely delightful. The call I could not resist if I would, and I would not if I could. While I was deeply conscious of the weakness and slenderness of my resources—educational and otherwise—still there was a charm in my loved work which was wonderfully fascinating.

One of the supremest pleasures of my life has been the abiding conviction that I was in God's hands, as an instrument of blessing to men and of glory to God. In this feeling there was a singular freedom from care and doubt and uncertainty, and from all concern and anxiety. Happy as the lark,

> "My life flowed on in endless song;
>   Above earth's lamentation
> I caught the sweet though far-off strain,
>   That hails the new creation."

The spring season answered to a springtime in my soul, day by day. The summer was sweet and gentle and beautiful, in correspondence with the green pastures into which the Good Shepherd was leading me and the still waters that were flowing about me. The rich autumnal tints seemed to borrow their golden hue from the approaching Beulah-land, and every bush aflame with God. My Decembers were as pleasant as May.

Early on a lovely spring morning, as I well remember, when I was riding on my way to an appointment, the sunshine and showers were alternating, the carol of birds and the sighing of zephyrs in the pine-tree tops above me, made a sort of paradise for the moment, and music filled my soul. The words I sang I had long known, and while singing them my whole soul drank in unutterable bliss. These were the words:

> "Lovely is the face of nature,
>   Decked with spring's unfolding flowers,
> While the sun shows every feature,
>   Smiling through descending showers.
>
> Birds, with songs the air beguiling,
>   Chant their sweetest notes with glee,
> But to see a Savior smiling,
>   Is more soft, more sweet to me."

At this point it will be in order to introduce to my readers some of the strong, brave men with whom I was associated in the old Oneida Conference. I published sketches of some of them in the *Northern Christian Advocate*, of Syracuse, N. Y., a few years ago. There, I speak of them as old-time veterans.

In my childhood some of the earlier ministers of Methodism were guests in my father's home. I was old enough to listen intelligently to their recital of incidents in their early ministerial travels.

MARMADUKE PEARCE

was a marked man. In my young manhood, fifty years ago, he was one of my earliest and best-known friends. He entered the traveling connection in 1811, in the Genesee Conference. After four years on circuits, he was appointed presiding elder on the Susquehanna District, Pennsylvania. Two years more of circuit work within the bounds of the Susquehanna District, and then he was transferred to the Baltimore Conference. Here, also, he was presiding elder on the Northumberland District, some twenty or thirty miles below his old district in the Genesee Conference. After this he filled some of the most important charges in Methodism. He was a delegate in the General Conferences of 1820 and 1828. In 1848, when I was pastor in the Wilkesbarre Station, he was my guest for several days. He was then eighty-four years of age. He was a man of fine presence. He preached in my pulpit on that occasion a sermon twenty minutes long, from Psalm lxxxiv, 11. The effort was a masterpiece of eloquence and power.

JOHN DEMPSTER, D. D.

In his earlier years my acquaintance with John Dempster was slight. Later, I knew him well. He was the son of James Dempster, whom Mr. Wesley sent to America in 1774. James Dempster was a Scotchman, a graduate of Edinburgh University; hence, probably, the marked intellectual power of his son. He did not long remain in the Methodist body. At the age of eighteen, John was the only convert at a camp-meeting in Herkimer County, New York. He nobly complemented the scant service of his father by a long, brilliant career as an itinerant, and by being the father and founder of our theological schools. His ministry began in 1816, and ended with his life in 1875. One year he spent in great exposure and hard service in the wilds of Lower Canada. Six years he was a missionary in Buenos Ayres, South America. Of the remaining forty-eight, eighteen were spent in New York State, and the others in New Hampshire and Illinois. On his return from South America in 1842 I met him often. His transcendent ability and his deep personal devotion elicited admiration. In 1843, during my incumbency at Auburn, N. Y., he was present in my congregation, and listened to a sermon on the Laodicean Church. At evening he was greeted by an immense audience. His sermon was forcible and thrilling. Large numbers of his former admirers, who had listened to his eloquent sermons when he was pastor in that church nineteen years before, were among his auditors that evening. In each of three towns of Central New York—Auburn, Cazenovia, and Rochester—he was for five years a pastor. In Cayuga District four years, and in Black River District three, he was presiding elder. Twenty years later, traveling over parts of the Cayuga District, I found the fame of his great achievements everywhere current. Probably no Methodist preacher has ever, for two generations, more strongly and permanently than he, impressed his personality upon a people. That whole section, including the cities named, was shaken with tremendous awakenings and revivals under his ministry.

Dr. Dempster died November 28, 1863. The writer published this notice of the great and good man:

A great and good man has been translated to his reward. The California *Advocate* of December 10th, announces the death of Rev. John Dempster, D. D., at Evanston, Illinois, on the 28th ult. He was in his seventy-fourth year. More than fifty years ago, Dr. Dempster was converted at a camp-meeting in Herkimer County, New York. He was, we believe, the only convert of the meeeting; yet eternity alone can disclose the measure of good resulting from this achievement of that apparently almost fruitless camp-meeting. Mr. Dempster was poor and uneducated when converted. Grace quickened his naturally vigorous intellect, and roused him, not in vain, to earnest endeavor after high mental and moral acquisitions. From a condition of marked illiterateness, he became an accomplished and profound scholar; from being unpolished, even to positive awkwardness and painful hesitancy of speech, he reached eloquence of the highest order. He was a close, vigorous thinker and writer. In his early ministry, Dr. Dempster was eminently zealous, and successful. Central and Western New York have for forty years borne the impress of his piety and ministerial efficiency. In Auburn and Rochester revivals of unprecedented power and extent attended his labors. The two cities named have ever since felt the moral impulse then and there given. Great as a Christian pastor, mighty as an original thinker, masterly as a pulpit orator, Dr. Dempster early took rank as a leading man in the Church. In the quarterly-meetings which he held as a presiding elder, he was greatly successful in opposing and confuting infidelity. An instance occurred at Marcellus, New York. The leading infidel of the place, himself highly intelligent and especially well read in skeptical doctrines, made the Doctor his guest. They spent the whole night in conversation on the evidences and truth of Christianity, the Doctor grappling and overturning every argument, fact, and theory of the learned infidel against Christianity. This was afterwards admitted by the infidel, who, when pressed for the reason of his adherence to infidelity after all its props had been swept away, stated that where he found one man who could thus refute his cavils, he found ten whom he could confuse and who could not answer his positions, and he would not give up his theory for one man in ten. Dr. Dempster was not only great in defending Christianity against the assaults of infidelity, but also in elucidating and maintaining the doctrines of Christianity against errorists. An example of this was given the writer many years ago by a person who witnessed it. At a camp-meeting in Jefferson County, New York, the Doctor was preaching on the Divinity of Christ. A Socinian, who had listened to him as he advanced argument after argument and fact upon fact in support of the Savior's Godhead, when the Doctor adduced the fact that, by the command of the Supreme Father, the angels bowed in worship before the only begotten Son, forgetting all restraints of time and place, sprang to his feet and exclaimed, "He is God, he is God!" Dr. Dempster was a member of the General Conferences of 1828 and 1832, and also of several of the more recent, and at the time of his death he was a delegate elect from the Rock River Conference to the General Conference of 1864.

For several years he was a missionary at Buenos Ayres, South America, and the Church founded there by his wisdom and zeal, still sheds its light and warmth upon the surrounding gloom of a semi-barbarism. The specialty of Dr. Dempster for the last quarter of a century has been ministerial education in Biblical schools. To him belongs the high honor of inaugurating and founding theological institutions in American Methodism. The Biblical Institute at Concord, N. H., and that at Evanston, Ill., are monuments of his zeal and constancy in this noble endeavor. He had for several years cherished the purpose of founding a Methodist Biblical Institute on this coast. Our contemporary says of this:

"He had long cherished the desire and purpose of visiting the Pacific Coast with the design of establishing such an institution here. If the California Conference had been in circumstances to respond to a very generous proposition which Dr. Dempster submitted to that body some four years since, his last wish in regard to his probationary mission would have been realized. Until very recently—perhaps to the last—he looked to this coast with the deepest concern, intending to visit us the present winter, and, if might be, take initiative measures for the realization of his long-cherished purpose. Summoned to a higher sphere, he leaves to others the inspiration of his earnest wish and the execution of his noble purpose. His name is enrolled among the most eminent of American ministers. His illustrious example of successful devotion to the acquisition of knowledge must powerfully stimulate our rising ministry to enter and explore all the fields of science that lie within the sphere of their high vocation. Dr. Dempster subordinated all his learning and abilities to the Dominion of the Cross."

We have no particulars furnished of the death scene. That, however, is not of material moment. Such a life, one so full of God and heaven and duty, is ample guarantee of the eternal happiness and triumph of its subject, whatever may have been the immediate incidents of the dying hour. The last public testimony we have from the Doctor was given at a Conference love-feast recently, the last he attended on earth. It is as follows:

"Speaking at the Conference love-feast at the recent session of the Rock River Conference, he said that he was converted at a camp-meeting. 'A long night of struggle was my lot—a night whose darkness bordered the world of despair; but on the rise of the natural sun a new sun arose—the sun of eternity. The clouds, the trees, the leaves, the very stems of the trees, were vocal with music, and I joined the great concert. My purpose in half a century has not changed. You all see, brethren, that in the case of John Dempster, the evening shades are lengthening. The day is far spent, the night is at hand, but the path is bright beneath my feet, and bright beyond. I look for the crown of immortality.'"

> "O, may we triumph so,
> When all our warfare's past
> And dying, find our latest foe
> Under our feet at last."

REV. JOSEPH CASTLE, D. D.

Among those well-known by me in the early times was Joseph Castle. He was a commanding figure. Tall, erect, muscular, but not corpulent, he was graceful in form and action. His countenance, while in repose somewhat grave, was expressive, thoughtful, benignant. His sermons were distinguished by clearness and beauty of expression. They were uttered in a full orotund voice. He was quite popular and in large demand. His itinerancy began in the Genesee Conference in 1823. His first appointment was in Augusta, Canada. His next was in Wyoming, Pa. Between these two places there were probably three hundred miles of distance. Four years later he was stationed in Oswego, N. Y. Five years from his joining the Conference on trial he was appointed to Wilkesbarre, Pa., then, as ever since, one of the leading charges in Methodism; then successively in Auburn (two full terms), Ithaca, Utica, Cazenovia, Ithaca (second term), Berkshire District. By transfer in 1839 he became a member of the Troy Conference. His appointment there was Garrettson Station in Albany. Later he went to the Philadelphia Conference. In 1864, when I attended the General Conference which met in Philadelphia, he was present at a service at which my father and brother and myself officiated. He was then presiding elder of the Philadelphia District, although approaching his eightieth year.

REV. GEORGE HARMON.

George Harmon was the patriarch of the Oneida Conference, having entered the Philadelphia Conference in 1808. Charles Giles preceded him one year in his entrance into the same Conference; but Harmon was much longer effective. In 1831, Giles took a supernumerary relation. In 1836, Giles became a member of the Black River Conference, while Harmon lived and died in the Oneida Conference. He was small of stature, silent, reserved, seldom heard on the Conference floor except to answer routine questions. And yet he must have been a man of rare abilities, even among those about him who were justly reputed foremost men. From him the writer learned some incidents about Asbury, which may hereafter be rehearsed. When the writer entered the Oneida Conference in 1839 on trial, Harmon was already a veteran in his thirty-second year. He was yet vigorous. In that year he was appointed to his fourth district, having been presiding elder already twelve or fifteen years. During my acquaintance with him after that, he must have been on districts some eight or twelve years more. He was appointed presiding elder after having been a traveling preacher only five years. His pastoral charges were many of them first grade; as Geneva, Ithaca, Lyons, Utica, etc. After forty-five or fifty years of most honorable, useful toil he was retired.

THE PADDOCK BROTHERS.

Benjamin G. Paddock and his younger brother, Zechariah, held leading positions in their day. The former entered the traveling connection in 1810, the latter six years later. Both were from time to time effective presiding elders. Both filled stations of more than ordinary grade. Benjamin G. Paddock was my second colleague in my first circuit.

DAVID A. SHEPARD.

David A. Shepard was fifteen years my senior in the Conference. For several years he was my presiding elder. He was an able, thoughtful, popular preacher, always thoroughly acceptable and useful. In one place, where the Reformed Methodists were somewhat aggressive in denouncing the bishops and leading ministers of our Church as having and wielding great power, Mr. Shepard made a speech on the subject. He set forth the truth that for a great system, and which was grandly effective, more power was required than for a small system. "As for example," said he, "no one would think of putting a hundred horse-power to turn a coffee-mill." Then, applying the illustration to the Methodist Episcopal Church, which employed so many itinerants and ministered to the spiritual needs of so many hundreds of thousands of people, and comparing the Reformed Methodists, so few in number and with so little connectional form, he showed the inconsistency of caviling at the greater Church for requiring and wielding its greater measure of power.

THE AFRICAN MISSIONARY.

The short, glorious career of Squire W. D. Chase ended at Syracuse, N. Y., in fifteen years after it began, and during, or immediately after, the session of the Conference of which, for some years, he had been a member. His last sermon on earth was preached at the Conference, which met July 26, 1843, in Syracuse. He had been several years a missionary in Liberia, Africa—long enough to take into his system the seeds of death, which, alas! too soon grew to their fatal result. I shall never forget the sermon. He knew and we knew that the seal of death was upon him. Hence he spake as a dying man to dying men. His text was Romans i, 5: "By whom we have received grace and apostleship, for obedience to the faith, among all nations, for His name." It was the supreme and final act of the missionary returning to his home Conference, his farewell to them and to earth. It was the grand enunciation and vindication of his stupendous work as a missionary, that in benighted Africa he had been enforcing "obedience to the faith for His name."

W. W. NINDE.

William Ward Ninde was an orator of great ability and renown. He was an eminent, illustrious minister of Christ, known far and wide for his holy life and his able and brilliant, and all too brief, career as a preacher and pastor. He entered the traveling connection in the Genesee Conference in 1828. The charges he filled were mostly within the present limits of the Northern New York Conference. They were of fair grade: Oswego, Adams, Pulaski, Syracuse, Lowville, Rome. In all of them, except Pulaski and Lowville, he staid the full term. In Oswego and Adams he was stationed two full terms. After a year's work on the Herkimer District, he finished his short but glorious career February 27, 1845. In company with Albert D. Peck, his successor on the district, I visited him a short time before his death. With one or more of his children I saw his son, W. X. Ninde (now a bishop). He was a bright-looking, flaxen-haired boy. The father was fully ready for his departure—peaceful, hopeful, happy. He impressed his strong personality upon all that region. His name is as ointment poured forth.

ELIAS BOWEN, D. D.

I must not omit this grand, colossal figure of the early times. He was twice my presiding elder. Dr. Bowen was a strongly marked man. Of fine form and figure, of commanding presence, with abilities far above the average, he wielded a wide religious influence. He was a strong, aggressive preacher, rather than a popular one. His favorite weapon was a battle-ax. He was a controversialist, rather than an evangelist. He seemed never more at home than when assailing and refuting what he held to be erroneous. In his first district, the Wilkesbarre, he preached a most severe and violent sermon against Hopkinsianism—a form of Calvinism then prevalent. His opposition to what he deemed untrue and injurious was relentless. On one occasion, at a session of the Oneida Conference, when Dr. Dempster was present seeking to enlist the Conference in favor of theological seminaries, Dr. Bowen preached a sermon, by Conference designation and by previous appointment, directly and strongly against theological schools in Methodism as subversive of the true mission and intent of Methodism. During the anti-slavery agitation he became a most violent and radical Abolitionist. Just before the late Civil War he published a book denouncing the complicity of the Methodist Episcopal Church with slavery. The war ended slavery. Dr. Bowen's book was therefore unsalable. At the age of eighty he died, in 1871. In his fifty-six years of itinerant labor he filled the leading charges in New York and Pennsylvania. For twenty-four years he was a presiding elder. He was a grand, glorious man.

CHAPTER VII.

AMONG the early Methodist preachers in the old Oneida Conference, there were none with whom my relations were so pleasant and serviceable as Jesse T. Peck, D. D., LL. D., who later became a popular and useful bishop, and his elder brother, Rev. George Peck, D. D. He was my preceptor and the principal of the Cazenovia Seminary, which I attended for two years successively. He was present when I made my first public declamation, and for which I had no relish. I had been a local preacher some years, and I stated to my principal, and my father's close friend, that I did not want to appear on the stage and recite a speech of somebody's preparation; that if he would allow me, I would get up and make an address prepared by myself; or, if he thought best, I would preach a sermon. But he said the rules of the school would not admit of my doing so; that perhaps it might be well for me to begin in the second grade of declaimers, where the declamations were private. It was the worst advice he could have given me, for it was usual for the lads present on such occasions to have a roystering time in making fun, and laughing at the unfledged orators and their awkward ways. Then he said, "Pay no more attention to the boys that are present than you would at so many cabbage-heads." I went on the stage blowing my nose to show my utter disregard of the presence of the audience; and when I stood upon the stage I paid little regard to posture or to gracefulness of gesture and action. The boys roared, and, to my horror, the principal himself joined in the boisterous, tumultuous laughter. I had recited one verse of several I had learned (nearly all beginners select poetry for their declamation exercises), when the storm was at its height. Then I stopped, and indignantly rebuked the unseemly conduct of the audience, including the principal, Dr. Peck. I apprehend I became quite natural, and the amusement rose to a higher pitch. I was about to leave the stage, when Dr. Peck said it would not do to be written down a failure in my first attempts at speaking in school. I went back and finished my recitation. The scene was written by Dr. Peck to my father, with the assurance that his son would go through, and that he did not need to be concerned as to the outcome. After that I did not any more practice the speaking drill in the second grade declamation class.

Dr. George Peck attained great honors and distinction as editor of the *Methodist Review* and *Christian Advocate*.

GEORGE GARY.

George Gary was one of the finest-looking of men, and one of the best equipped, most fascinating, and effective of the Methodist ministers of his times. Lest this statement, and others which will follow, should be deemed rather excessive and fulsome, as the extravagant estimate of inexperienced boyhood before riper age had lent its more sober and critical judgment, let it be observed: In my boyhood for a year Mr. Gary was my honored and loved pastor; in my early manhood, after entering the Oneida Conference, Mr. Gary for a dozen or more years was my contemporary in an adjoining Conference (the Black River) while he was yet in his full, vigorous manhood. During those years I had many opportunities of seeing and knowing him, at Conference sessions and at camp-meetings, and on other like occasions. A dozen years later I succeeded him in the Oregon Mission, and there I learned incidents and estimates of him which could not be ascribed to the extravagance of youthful and immature admiration of one's hero.

Over one hundred and four years ago—viz., December 8, 1793—George Gary was born in Middlefield, Otsego County, N. Y. He was well born—a Puritan of the Puritans. In 1630, Arthur Gary and his two sons, Nathaniel and William, came from England, and settled in Roxbury, Mass. Arthur Gary and Nathaniel Gary were his ancestors. Nathaniel Gary was his great-grandfather. At the age of nine or twelve years George Gary was converted at the family altar in his childhood home. As the morning prayer ceased, George still remained on his knees by the woodpile in the chimney-corner of the old log-cabin. He was weeping and sobbing. The minister inquired the reason for his grief. He was under conviction of sin. Prayer was offered for him, and by him. Then and there, and once for all, he was soundly converted. His childhood call was, like Samuel's, effectual. It staid with him through a full and very useful life.

As now recalled, Mr. Gary was slightly below the average stature, perhaps five feet eight, or five feet eight and a half inches. He was a blonde, with light, flaxen hair, and blue, expressive eyes. His head was so faultless, and so well adjusted to his body, that a Canova might well have envied it. His form was somewhat full, but not too much so. His pose was admirable. His movement and action were grace itself. His manner was extremely charming. He was altogether a most fascinating man.

In several aspects his life-story was remarkable. On the death of his mother, and while he was yet quite young, he went with his uncle to live with him in Pomfret, Conn. Thus he grew up in the atmosphere of his ancestors, and in their native land he began his ministry. Five years after he began his ministry in New England, he was transferred to the Genesee Conference in New York, the State of his birth; and in the second year of his itinerancy in New York he was preaching to the people among whom he was born. In 1809, when he was fifteen and a half years old, he was admitted on trial into the New England Conference. His first charge was in Barre, Vt., as third preacher on a large circuit. Elijah Hedding, afterward Bishop Hedding, was his first presiding elder. The next four years were spent on great circuits in Maine. In 1814 he was transferred to the Genesee Conference, New York, and stationed on Herkimer

Charge in the Mohawk Valley, below and probably including Utica. In 1815 he was the third preacher on the Otsego Circuit. In 1816 he was on Sandy Creek Charge, near Watertown, yet in Oneida District. In 1817 he was stationed in Utica. In 1818, when he was twenty-four and a half years old, he was presiding elder on Oneida District. His light hair and ruddy complexion and his short stature gave him a most youthful, even boyish, appearance, while at the same time he was bearing great responsibilities. It is not the purpose in this sketch to write a full biography of him, nor to give specifically the list of his appointments. It will suffice to say that for nearly all his ministerial life he was a presiding elder.

From 1844 to 1848 he was superintendent of the Oregon missions, under conditions and for purposes which will be better understood by a brief preliminary recital of facts. Commodore Wilkes had been sent to the Pacific Coast to survey and sound and map our bays and sounds and rivers upon the Pacific. While there he visited Oregon, especially the Hudson Bay Company's posts, which were then under the spiritual direction of the Roman Catholics. He visited, also, the Methodist missions there. By the former of these he was toasted and fêted. By the Methodist missionaries he was shown a cheerful, generous Christian hospitality, and no more. In his reports to the Secretary of the Navy he lauded the Hudson Bay Company and the Roman Catholics; and he disparaged the Methodist missions, as conducting a large colonization scheme, rather than a mission for souls.

Dr. Bond, then editor of the New York *Advocate*, took up the cry, and but too successfully urged the reduction of our material and secular concerns in Oregon. Mr. Gary was sent to Oregon to sell out all our improvements and possessions there, and to reduce the missions to purely religious interests and movements. This he did, wisely and successfully, so far as he was directed; although the whole policy of the movement, as seen from the present standpoint, was the gravest possible mistake. The large establishments were then indispensable to the missionaries remaining in Oregon. The Hudson Bay Company would let the missionaries have no cows, sheep, horses, or hogs to raise flocks from, and Mr. Lee was obliged to go to California, and procure these necessaries to the continuance of the missionaries in Oregon.

On August 14, 1848, Congress passed an Act organizing the Territory of Oregon, in which was a clause granting, severally, to each mission station then being in Oregon six hundred and forty acres of land. Our Church had had six missionary stations in Oregon. But by Mr. Gary's direction, acting under instructions of the Missionary Board, these were sold or given away. But for this we would have had three thousand eight hundred and forty acres of land in the most eligible points in Oregon; a plant which would have been a foundation for schools and churches in all that mighty empire for all after generations. As it was, we lost all that most desirable and deserved means; while the Roman Catholics there, as in other of the frontier Territories, laid the foundations of religious propagandism on the widest scale.

Mr. Gary's early educational advantages had been very limited. Until he became a Methodist traveling minister he had never studied grammar, and yet he spoke and wrote the purest and most correct English. He was a fluent, eloquent, and accurate speaker, never violating any grammatical, nor any of the rhetorical, rules of speech. This skill we attributed to his close observation of the best speakers, and to his reading of the most eminent and correct English authors. If Mr. Gary, after his marvelous pulpit abilities were fully matured, had become a star transfer from Conference to Conference, as has become the usage since his time, he would have filled the finest pulpits in the strongest charges of Methodism. But at that period several things prevented; *e. g.*, he was unambitious for place, position, and honors; in those times there were few star appointments; transfers to special appointments were then rarely made. One of the earlier of the kind was that of R. S. Foster from the Ohio Conference to Mulberry Street Church, New York, in which he nobly vindicated the wisdom of the transfer. As indicating Mr. Gary's modesty and unaffected avoidance of distinction, this example is in point: His friends desired to procure for him the honorary degree of Doctor of Divinity from Wesleyan University. In this they would doubtless have succeeded, and if they had, never would such honors have been more worthily borne. Yet his positive refusal to permit such procurement of honors restrained his friends. He lived and died an untitled Methodist minister.

Reckoning Asbury as the first American bishop, and one of the earliest Methodist itinerants, Mr. Gary, who was ordained by Asbury, was, therefore, of the second generation of those eminent fathers of our Church. This place he has most worthily filled. A volume of incidents of his extraordinary history, which would have living interest, could be written. While Mr. Gary was in some respects a brilliant man and a genius, yet he was a man of unusually strong common sense. In the dialect of these times he would be pronounced a level-headed man. I was present at a session of the Conference of which he was a member and a presiding elder. The character of one of his preachers was under examination. The question was asked officially, "Is there anything against Brother Blank?" Mr. Gary replied, as now remembered: "There are two deaths which a Methodist preacher may die; one, the end of this earthly life; the other, the loss of the respect and confidence of his brethren and of the Church, which means the death of his usefulness as a Methodist minister. The former is infinitely preferable to the latter. I therefore move that Brother Blank be requested to ask for a location." Without further discussion the motion prevailed.

Mr. Gary abounded in humor. Instances decidedly humorous and sometimes peculiarly funny occurred in his ministerial life.

Traditions of amusing incidents in the career of George Gary which display his prevailing genial qualities are numerous. I could furnish many of them, but brevity requires that I should select but a few, and abbreviate them.

He was often an inmate of my father's house, and an inimitable *raconteur*. Three years after he left Oregon I arrived there. One of the first things I heard of him after reaching that country was that he was a man of habitual cheerfulness, who greatly enjoyed relating the incidents of his earlier itinerant life, and whose nature was genial and kindly. It was also current that he was apparently much shocked at the homespun freedom and the rollicksome ways of the Oregon brethren. He was accustomed to admonish them very gravely, when starting out on an equestrian trip, to ride quietly, either on a walk or a slow trot, and never on a canter, and with the dignity becoming Methodist ministers. They gave me the legend—though I had heard it many years before—how on one of his first charges he was well-nigh rejected because he was so young-looking, his appearance making him seem much younger than he really was. This is the legend as heard in boyhood, and as rehearsed to me in Oregon. Mr. Gary was the third preacher on the circuit. The story that the circuit had a boy preacher reached the charge before he did. It preceded him at every appointment. Before seeing him the stewards had laid in objections to the presiding elder that he was too young and inexperienced for the chief appointment, where the competition was sharp and the people were critical. They suggested that the boy preacher should be restricted to the rural appointments, and the chief places be left wholly to the service of the senior preachers. To this the elder objected, that it would be quite unfair to discriminate against the young preacher, especially before having heard him at all. In this sensible advice the stewards acquiesced. When the Sabbath came for the young man to preach in the county town his fame as a boy preacher had preceded him. A full house awaited his coming with no ordinary interest. Punctually he came, and he marched up the aisle with the veritable saddlebags. Ascending the pulpit stairs and conducting the preliminary exercises with becoming words and manner, he announced as his text John vi, 9: "There is a lad here, which hath five barley loaves and two small fishes; but what are they among so many?" In that sermon the boy preacher won his right of way with the people of that chief town, whether the stewards were reconciled to him or not. His sermon was in keeping with the genius which led to the selection of the text. All admired him, and they said he was very mature for such a boy in years and looks.

His immaturity when he acceded to the district was the occasion of some surprise and questioning, in which he vindicated his right to the place accorded him by showing himself fully equal to the great trust reposed in him.

Soon after his incumbency of his first district he visited New York. He called Saturday evening on

Dr. Nathan Bangs, who inquired his name and place of labor. He gave his Christian name, George, and, withholding his surname, he stated that he preached in Oneida, in the central part of the State. Dr. Bangs gave him the freedom of his library, and begged him to amuse himself with books, and excuse the Doctor while he completed his preparation for the next day's sermon. Sabbath morning Gary went with his host to the church, and followed him into the pulpit, taking such part as was assigned to him. At the close of the sermon Dr. Bangs announced a four o'clock afternoon service at some uptown ward and schoolhouse, saying to the audience that a young preacher from the country was in the pulpit, who he hoped would fill that out-appointment, in which case he, the Doctor, would preach there in the church himself. Gary arose and declined the schoolhouse service; but he said if it was agreeable to them, he would preach in that church at the hour named. "Then," said Dr. Bangs, "I will preach uptown and the young brother here." His able and vivid sermon produced a profound impression. Dr. Bangs saw him no more for years; but the fame of his sermon was so great that the Doctor took down the General Minutes, and found that his young guest was the presiding elder of Oneida District. The next time Mr. Gary visited New York, Dr. Bangs, having found out his real rank, accorded him fuller courtesies than on his first visit.

Mr. Gary was a born orator. The instances of his transcendent power over his immense congregations were most remarkable. His great strength lay in his dramatic power in rendering thrilling Scriptural incidents. He was greatly at home at camp-meetings and quarterly-meetings before large masses, who had gathered with high expectations. He rarely, if ever, disappointed them. His voice was clear, musical, penetrating. When animated in preaching, his countenance was irresistibly attractive and expressive. Some of his sermons were masterpieces of skill and power. They can never be forgotten. A few specimens are given. "Daniel in the Lions' Den" is one.

In quiet, deliberate manner he briefly recounts the story of the prophet's sentence. This fixes the attention of all. Then he describes the den as a vault or chamber beneath the surface of the earth. The beasts are eagerly looked for. Their roar is distinct. But when Daniel is committed to the den the lions are as still as death. The sleepless night of the king is set forth, and with the early dawn the royal monarch approaches the den. Suiting the action and voice to the occasion, the preacher advances to the edge of the platform, and looks down as if recognizing Daniel. In the most tender and pathetic tones he cries out: "O Daniel! O Daniel! is thy God whom thou servest continually, able to deliver thee from the lions?" and then, in changed voice and with ventriloquial effect, the answer comes up from the prophet calm, serene, confident: "O king, live forever! My God hath sent his angel and hath shut the lions' mouths, that they have not hurt me; forasmuch as before him innocency was found in me, and also before thee, O king!" The pause, the hushed silence of the vast throng, is almost painful. But when at the king's command Daniel's accusers are committed to the hungry lions, a rustle is heard, and the people recover their breath. If it were anywhere else tumultuous applause would break forth. As it is, many are weeping, and some are shouting over Daniel's deliverance. To eye and ear and heart the whole scene has been most vivid and realistic. In another sermon, but with like manner, the three Hebrews in the fiery furnace were the theme of impassioned words and expressive acting. The audience were carried off their seats, and with mingled tears and shouts the victory was announced.

One of his favorite sermons was on Isaiah lxiii, 1-6: "Who is this that cometh from Bozrah?" etc. After a calm recital of the text and its brief exegesis, he advanced to the front of the platform, and seized the skirt of his coat and emphasized the questions and answers, each in unlike tone and manner, and yet in both thrilling his hearers as though an angel from heaven had been speaking. Besides his vivid impersonations of his characters, Gary's voice when he was impassioned had always marked expression of tenderness and pathos. The other remarkable instances of Gary's power as a preacher are these: The first was at a camp-meeting in the Britain Settlement, north of Syracuse, some fifty years ago. He first drew his audience to their feet in a dense mass around him, tears flowing from all eyes. The sermon was preached at the eight o'clock hour Sunday morning, when many were all the time arriving upon the ground. The external conditions were all unfavorable to marked effect. The sermon was only twenty minutes in length. Text, Genesis xix, 17: "Escape for thy life." The minister was in tears. He depicted the angel urging Lot to great speed and earnestness in escaping from the awful, fiery storm. He then, with signal emphasis, applied the warning to all present, and in piercing tones and with a voice quivering with emotion he uttered the cry of the text, "Escape for thy life!" One hundred or more fell to the ground as though stricken with sudden death. Sinners cried for mercy, souls were converted, and for hours afterward one continuous prayer-meeting was kept up, in which scores of souls were converted. The other instance of his power at camp-meeting was given in the *Advocate*, by V. M. Coryell, in 1879. It occurred in Danby, near Ithaca, seventy years ago. He had just arrived upon the ground from the funeral of his wife. As he approached the end of his sermon his soul became all absorbed in his overwhelming affliction. He was now about for the first time to say good-bye to his children as orphaned of a mother's tender care. He referred to the unprotected loneliness of those dear children. Then with overwhelming and indescribable pathos and with flowing tears he repeated the verse:

> "O, what are all my sufferings here,
>   If, Lord, thou count me meet
> With that enraptured host to appear,
>   And worship at thy feet?"

Then in still more tender tones, he repeated the next lines:

> "Give joy or grief, give ease or pain,
> Take life or friends away;
> But let me find them all again
> In that eternal day."

Then the great fountain of tears was broken up. Men cried like children; others shouted amid tears. Unsaved men and women uttered piercing cries. Multitudes were converted, and many shouts of glory and victory were lifted up.

Thirty-eight years ago this great and good man went up to his crowning. His death was triumphant.

Second Period.

LIFE IN OREGON.

CHAPTER VIII.

MY transfer to Oregon was peculiar and providential. In 1850 I went into Michigan to consider and decide upon the question of seeking a transfer to that Peninsula. I was so well pleased with the country, that I greatly desired to remove there, and I decided to do so if I could get a transfer to the Michigan Conference. Bishop Waugh presided at the Oneida Conference in 1850. I waited on him, informing him of my wish. He said the bishops were favorable to transferring men to Michigan. It was a growing State, and more men than they had were in demand. But it seemed difficult to supply certain places in Oneida Conference for that year. He promised me a transfer to Michigan the next year, if I would stay in my own Conference the pending year. To this I agreed.

In 1851 I went up to our Conference, which met in Ithaca, N. Y., fully expecting to be transferred to Michigan. My goods were all packed in readiness for that removal. Bishop Janes presided at the Oneida Conference in 1851. He wished to transfer me to Oregon, then a foreign mission of our Church. I suppose that wish was pursuant to information he had had, that, in 1847, when a call was made in the *Christian Advocate* for two men and their wives to go to Oregon as missionaries, Rev. Albert D. Peck and myself had offered ourselves in response to that call, with our wives, who were sisters. Our response came too late, as William Roberts, of Newark, N. J., and James H. Wilbur, of Northern New York, had offered and had been accepted before our offer had reached the Board. My heart had always been drawn towards Oregon as a mission field. Jason Lee and his two Flathead Indian boys, in 1839, had been guests at my father's for a week, and I had talked much with him and with the Indians, and had had my sympathies strongly enlisted for Oregon. In the meantime, Rev. Mr. Peck had died. His wife had remarried, and I had given up all thought or expectation of ever going to that country. The call of Bishop Janes made a strong impression upon me; and yet I could not decide the matter alone. Mrs. Pearne must be consulted. The bishop said, "Go and see your wife, and come back as soon as you can." He also said, that if I should conclude to decline Oregon, he would transfer me to Michigan. I went on Friday. I had to go by lake to Cayuga Bridge, forty miles; thence by rail to Utica, ninety miles; and thence by stage to Madison, twenty miles. On Monday morning I was back at the seat of the Conference. Mrs. Pearne had readily given her approval of the measure, and I informed the bishop he might transfer me to Oregon. The presiding elders and the Conference had unanimously approved of my transfer to that distant mission field, the Conference also agreeing that if at any time I might wish to return, the Conference doors would swing open to receive me.

The gold excitement as to California was still

at fever height. The bishop asked me if I thought I could resist the temptation to go to the California gold-mines when I should arrive in California *en route*. I said I could. His transfer ran in the usual form. The letter he gave me with the transfer said in substance: "Go to Oregon, live there and work there for Jesus, and die there for Jesus." It seemed from that letter that I was expected to separate myself, finally, from the associations of a lifetime on the Atlantic Coast, and begin lifelong associations with a country I had never seen. But I had put my hand to the plow. I would not look back.

In three weeks' time we were on the steamer *Illinois*, *en route* for Oregon *via* Panama, Acapulco in Mexico, and San Francisco. The steamer was much crowded with passengers for the new Occidental El Dorado. I think there were over a thousand passengers. Four ministers were on board; two for Oregon, and two for California. Three of the preachers were Methodists, and one was a United Presbyterian. After we went aboard ship, we found that three of our wives had been put into one stateroom, and their husbands into another, with an alcove between the rooms. As we sat in the alcove, before the steamer started, and had made each other's acquaintance, I remarked that while it was inconvenient for husbands and wives to be separated, yet the alcove connecting the rooms was convenient. We could have family prayers without interruption from other passengers. Later, the United Presbyterian minister demurred to my proposal about prayers. He said it was not practicable; for we sang hymns, while in his Church he sang Psalms. But said I, "That need not hinder our praying together and singing together, if you like; for I can sing Psalms with you, and so can the others, and I doubt not they would be quite willing." "That is not it exactly," he replied; "we do n't like to countenance hymn-singing by singing Psalms with those who sing hymns." So we had no family prayers. As will be seen, he was very greatly liberalized by living in Oregon. Ten years later, he returned to the States. He wrote to me, from up the country where he lived, that he was coming to Portland, *en route* for the States, and he would like to be my guest over the Sabbath, and to preach in the Methodist Episcopal Church at night; and the people of that Church could sing their own hymns and use their own organ, and he would preach, and sing a Psalm alone at the end of the sermon. His name was Samuel G. Irvine. He was made moderator of the United Presbyterian General Assembly that year.

We arrived in Aspinwall, at the mouth of the Chagres River, on Sunday morning. The ship anchored in the Chagres Bay, two or three miles from port. The purser had said we might stay on shipboard, if we did not want to disembark on Sunday. So we staid. But in the afternoon the captain ordered all the passengers to leave the ship, as they were going down to Navy Bay, some ten miles away, to coal up. This put us to a great disadvantage, as all the boats from the shore had gone back to port. But we overcame this, by going in the ship's lighter. Reaching port, we found that all the best boats had gone up the river, and we had to take, from what were left, such as we could get. We chartered a sampan; *i. e.*, a boat with a plank roof over it. This, as a protection from sun and rain, was desirable. It was the rainy season; and the flat-bottomed boat was very slow and unsuitable for the river, which was in flood. The river was too rapid for oars, and too deep for poling. We had to cordelle it by the bushes or rope. The bushes were loaded with a small, red ant, whose bite was like fire, and we could not escape it.

We were a week crossing the isthmus; five days to Gorgona, a distance of sixty-five miles; and one day by mule, twenty-two miles, to Panama; and one day in Panama. Our company consisted of Rev. Mr. and Mrs. Irvine; Rev. Adam Bland, wife and child (Brother Bland and William Taylor were brothers-in-law); and Rev. Henry Ercanbrack, myself, and Mrs. Pearne and child. It rained in torrents without premonition, and then instantly the sun would scorch us with its torrid heat—a very hazardous condition to encounter. Several of the steamer's passengers died from yellow fever on the passage up the river. We were in great peril at one time. Our sampan had become wedged under a lateral branch of a tree on the shore, the river was rising every moment, and we were in danger of being sunk in the boiling, roaring flood. Some of the ladies, especially Mrs. Bland, became very nervous and highly excited. In another instance, Mrs. Bland became much alarmed. The practicable; for we sang hymns, while in his Church he sang Psalms. But said I, "That need not hinder our praying together and singing together, if you like; for I can sing Psalms with you, and so can the others, and I doubt not they would be quite willing." "That is not it exactly," he replied; "we do n't like to countenance hymn-singing by singing Psalms with those who sing hymns." So we had no family prayers. As will be seen, he was very greatly liberalized by living in Oregon. Ten years later, he returned to the States. He wrote to me, from up the country where he lived, that he was coming to Portland, *en route* for the States, and he would like to be my guest over the Sabbath, and to preach in the Methodist Episcopal Church at night; and the people of that Church could sing their own hymns and use their own organ, and he would preach, and sing a Psalm alone at the end of the sermon. His name was Samuel G. Irvine. He was made moderator of the United Presbyterian General Assembly that year.

We arrived in Aspinwall, at the mouth of the Chagres River, on Sunday morning. The ship anchored in the Chagres Bay, two or three miles from port. The purser had said we might stay on shipboard, if we did not want to disembark on Sunday. So we staid. But in the afternoon the captain ordered all the passengers to leave the ship, as they were going down to Navy Bay, some ten miles away, to coal up. This put us to a great disadvantage, as all the boats from the shore had gone back to port. But we overcame this, by going in the ship's lighter. Reaching port, we found that all the best boats had gone up the river, and we had to take, from what were left, such as we could get. We chartered a sampan; *i. e.*, a boat with a plank roof over it. This, as a protection from sun and rain, was desirable. It was the rainy season; and the flat-bottomed boat was very slow and unsuitable for the river, which was in flood. The river was too rapid for oars, and too deep for poling. We had to cordelle it by the bushes or rope. The bushes were loaded with a small, red ant, whose bite was like fire, and we could not escape it.

We were a week crossing the isthmus; five days to Gorgona, a distance of sixty-five miles; and one day by mule, twenty-two miles, to Panama; and one day in Panama. Our company consisted of Rev. Mr. and Mrs. Irvine; Rev. Adam Bland, wife and child (Brother Bland and William Taylor were brothers-in-law); and Rev. Henry Ercanbrack, myself, and Mrs. Pearne and child. It rained in torrents without premonition, and then instantly the sun would scorch us with its torrid heat—a very hazardous condition to encounter. Several of the steamer's passengers died from yellow fever on the passage up the river. We were in great peril at one time. Our sampan had become wedged under a lateral branch of a tree on the shore, the river was rising every moment, and we were in danger of being sunk in the boiling, roaring flood. Some of the ladies, especially Mrs. Bland, became very nervous and highly excited. In another instance, Mrs. Bland became much alarmed. The natives who were propelling the boat landed at a grassy bank, and, taking up their machetes, or long knives, they left us, and disappeared from sight. Mrs. Bland insisted they were going for re-enforcements, and then would return and kill us. In a few minutes they came back, each man having a stalk of sugar-cane, which they had brought to chew. So the suspicion of murder was dismissed. Reaching Gorgona, we spent the night there. I was very ill, with strong symptoms of yellow fever. I went to a druggist's, and bought thirty grains of sulphate of quinine, divided into two equal parts. One of them I took at nine o'clock and retired, telling my wife to give me the other at midnight; if I was delirious and refused to take it, to get help and put it down me. The coercion proved unnecessary. My wife awakened me, and I took my medicine. The next morning I was as clear as a bell. But the night-shirt and the sheets were as yellow as saffron. On the route to Panama, on muleback, each lady was accompanied by a muleteer, who carried a child. After traveling on muleback some three miles, Mrs. Bland gave her babe some food. She had the muleteer to tighten the cinch, to make the saddle firmer. Remounting and ascending a rise, her husband, who was following his wife, asked a swarthy Frenchman about the road. He gave a French shrug, and said, "Impassable." He held a rifle. She concluded he was a brigand demanding a passport; and as she knew her husband had none, she supposed the end of life had come for one or both of them. She whipped up her mule. The saddle-girth broke; she came to the ground, and running after me she declared that the Frenchman was killing her husband. This, too, proved a groundless fear.

At Panama we were divided; Ercanbrack and Bland going on the steamer *Republic*, and Brother Irvine and myself going on the *California*. We missed connection with the Oregon steamer at San Francisco, and were delayed a week in California, making our trip from New York to Oregon six and a half weeks. We touched at Acapulco in Mexico. Arriving at San Francisco, we found that the steamer *Republic* had knocked a hole in her hull. Our vessel was sent down to tow her into port. We reached San Francisco Sunday morning. At evening I preached in Powell Street Methodist Episcopal Church to five hundred men and two women. The brethren pressed me very hard to remain in California, and wait until they could communicate with New York, and receive authority from Bishop Janes for me to remain permanently in California, where they alleged we were more needed than in Oregon. We declined.

I ought perhaps to mention that, by the request of Rev. William Taylor, the California street preacher, and later Bishop of Africa, I preached on the Plaza to his street congregation, at two o'clock in the afternoon of the day of our arrival. He sung them up by singing the hymn, "Hear the royal proclamation." The people gathered from all directions. There were probably from five hundred to eight hundred persons present. I preached

October morning, like a silver strip along the coast. Above this, in the distance, was the dense, dark green of the fir-timber on the mountain's side. Above this we saw the snow-covered peaks of Mount Hood, Mount Rainier or Tacoma (the Indian name), Saint Helen's, and Mount Jefferson, which seemed like a setting for the mountain picture on which we gazed. I had never before seen snowy mountains. The view was one of thrilling enchantment. It can never be forgotten. The ship stopped at Astoria for an hour. I went ashore. The first man I met was Mr. Leonard, a gentleman whom I had often seen in Owego, N. Y., my last charge before leaving for Oregon. He addressed me by name, and said he had often heard me preach. We were five hours ascending the river to Portland, a hundred miles distant. The last twelve miles we had been sailing in the Willamette River. In Portland we met Rev. James H. Wilbur, pastor of our Church in Portland, and Rev. C. S. Kingsley, principal of the Portland Academy and Female Seminary.

Mr. Wilbur advised that we should remain at Portland until William Roberts, superintendent of the Oregon and California Missions, could be informed of my arrival, and could appoint me to my work, which, Mr. Wilbur said, might be up the Willamette River or down the Columbia, or possibly over to Puget Sound. My letter of instruction from Bishop Janes directed me to report in person to Mr. Roberts in Salem, his residence. So I pursued my voyage up the Willamette River in a steamer. Thirteen miles from Portland is Oregon City, where we encountered a portage and a fall in the river of some eight or ten feet. Here was erected the first Protestant house of worship on the entire Pacific Coast from Cape Horn to the Straits of Fuca. The distance from Oregon City to Salem, fifty miles, was passed on an upper river steamer, which in winter and spring was able to ascend the river one hundred miles above Salem, the capital of Oregon Territory. Mr. Roberts, by direction of Bishop Janes, appointed me presiding elder on the Oregon District, which included all the United States territory from the Missouri River to the Pacific, eighteen hundred miles east and west; and from the California line in north latitude 39th degree to the 49th degree of north latitude, six hundred and fifty miles; including an area of 1,170,000 square miles. The States now included in the Oregon District as existing forty-six years ago, are Oregon and Washington, Idaho, Montana, and North and South Dakota.

Fortunately, only the western part of this immense area was sparsely settled; and so the actual distance east from the ocean was about three hundred miles. There were from ten to twelve charges, and about six hundred members. The following itinerant ministers were employed in ministerial work: William Roberts, superintendent of the Oregon and California Mission Conference; Portland, James H. Wilbur. In 1847, William Roberts and James H. Wilbur came to Oregon. James H. Wilbur had been connected with the Black River Conference in Northern New York, and Mr. Roberts had been successively a member of the Philadelphia and the Newark (New Jersey) Conferences. C. S. Kingsley was doing a very excellent educational work. His school was well patronized. F. S. Hoyt, a former member of the Newark Conference, was exceedingly popular and useful, both as an instructor and a minister. He was secretary of the Conference, and he joined with me later in offering the Oregon circular resolution on Lay Delegation. A. F. Waller and J. L. Parrish lived in Salem. They both came to Oregon in the good ship *Lausanne* in 1839, reaching Oregon some time in 1840. L. T. Woodward, principal of Santiam Academy, came in 1850; as did also N. Doane, one of the earliest graduates of Concord Biblical Institute. David Leslie was an early missionary, now superannuated. William Helm, of Kentucky, was a veteran. John Flinn, an accession to the ministers, in 1850, Dallas. D. E. Blain and John McKinney were filling Calapooya Circuit. C. O. Hosford, a native preacher. J. F. Devore, an accession in 1850. Joseph O. Rayner, stationed in Clatsop and Astoria. J. S. Smith, Jacksonville. Later came P. G. Buchanan, who preached in Portland a time; B. C. Lippincott and Benjamin Close labored in Puget Sound; G. M. Berry on the Columbia River work; Isaac Dillon came in 1852 from Ohio. The workers who had preceded my coming were earnest and faithful men. Some of them had been in Oregon a dozen or more years. Others, whose coming was later than mine, approved themselves to

God and the Church by their devotion and zeal, Gustavus, J. M., and H. R. Hines, brothers, especially.

The population of Oregon, as given by the United States Census of 1850, was: Of whites, 13,294; Indians, about 100,000; perhaps more. This population of whites was scattered over the western part of Oregon. The vast regions between the Cascade Mountains and the Missouri River were peopled only by wild beasts and savages. In Western Oregon the people were scattered at wide distances apart, on respectively mile sections and half-mile half-sections. There were perhaps six or eight hundred people in Portland, two-thirds as many in Oregon City, five hundred in Salem, a hundred and fifty in Astoria, and twice as many in Vancouver, on the Columbia. In Vancouver there was a United States military post, and perhaps two hundred settlers. Albany, Marysville, La Fayette, Dayton, Eugene City in Willamette Valley, Roseberry in Umpqua Valley, and Jacksonville and Phœnix in Rogue River Valley, were small villages. The number of settlers was very small; so it was in the city of Dalles, where we had also a United States military post. We had long horseback rides, with rivers to ford and swim, making the work hard and perilous. But we had kind, hospitable treatment, excellent meetings, and some success.

In November, 1851, the Oregon Mission Conference was held in Portland, Oregon, by William Roberts, superintendent. He divided the work into two districts: Oregon District, William Roberts, presiding elder; including Salem and all below it to the sea; including, also, Olympia, Steilacoom, Seattle, Mound Prairie, Cowlitz. Mary's River District, Thomas H. Pearne, presiding elder. This included Lebanon, Calapooya, Albany, Marysville, Belknap's Settlement, Eugene City, Roseburg, Jacksonville, Phœnix. Before detailing more at length the progress of our work in Oregon, it may be well to give a few general statements, which will enable the reader to follow more intelligently and with more interest the narratives and incidents which may be recited later.

CHAPTER IX.

AS to the name Oregon, which Bryant mentions in his well-known lines in Thanatopsis—he speaks of persons

> "Losing themselves in the continuous woods,
> Where rolls the Oregon, and hears no sound
> Save its own dashing,"—

there are two theories. One of these accounts for its origin thus: The plains of Oregon are covered with a wild herb, called origanum, or thyme; whence, by a corruption of the word origanum, came the word Oregon. This is much the more probable of the two. The other theory is, that the early Jesuit missionaries who visited Oregon found a tribe of Indians dwelling on the banks of the Lower Columbia, with large, pendent ears, whom, because of this physical peculiarity, they called Auricanes, or large-eared Indians, and that the word Oregon is a corruption of the word Auricanes. But this account is shown to be improbable, by the fact that if those early Indians had this peculiarity, they would have transmitted it to their descendants; whereas, no such descendants are found.

DESCRIPTION OF OREGON.

Oregon, when I saw it in 1851, was a great country, having the boundaries of an empire. It rivaled in beauty many lands, and greatly excelled some others. Oregon abounds in magnificent scenery. Its mountains are fringed with somber cedars and pines and firs, and their being crested with snow-peaks heightens the scenic effects. The prairies are covered with countless sunflowers growing on stalks, perhaps eighteen inches in height, and abundance of daisies and violets carpet the whole country with beauty, and perfume the whole air with their fragrance. My first view of Oregon from the sea produced the most delightful impression. We were near enough to the mouth of the Columbia to trace all the outlines of the coasts; the shore-line was covered by a fog looking like a silver ribbon. Above that were the Cascade Mountains, five thousand feet high, clothed to their tops with fadeless green, which, however, in the distance was slightly empurpled. Above the mountain-line rose Mount Hood to the right, eighteen thousand feet, and to the left Saint Helen's, fourteen thousand feet. As the sun purpled the summits of these peaks, the combination of silver and emerald and purple and white was indescribably beautiful.

The scenery on the Columbia River is simply magnificent. The shores are bold and bluff, piled up with columnar basalt, as clearly outlined as the Giant's Causeway and Fingal's Cave in Staffa, on the shores of Scotland. Grand reaches of water are seen; rocky islands, here and there, with columnar rocks like a stone church-spire; dashing waterfalls adorn the steep river sides,—making up a very lovely and sublime panorama. The ever-present snow mountains lend an indescribable charm to the near or distant view. Along the Willamette River the scenery is more subdued and quiet than on the Columbia. But the beauty of the Willamette Valley is unsurpassed by anything I have ever seen in any other country in the whole wide world. And yet, when in the thirties Senator Thomas H. Benton advocated and urged the acquisition of Oregon, it was decried as a land of barren wastes and fruitless sand-dunes, not worth the taking in. Relatively, Oregon will compare favorably for loveliness, fertility, and productiveness with any other country.

Oregon has three natural divisions—the Western, the Middle, and the Eastern divisions. The Western extends from the sea to the Cascade Mountains. It includes the coast-range of mountains, ranging from fifteen hundred feet in height to three or four thousand feet. Western Oregon again is divided into three parts—the Willamette Valley, running north and south, say two hundred miles long and sixty miles wide. The Willamette River rises in the Cascade and Coast Mountains, two hundred miles south from the Columbia River, and runs north, flowing into the Columbia one hundred miles from the sea. It is navigable, except the small portage at Oregon City Falls, for one hundred and fifty miles, during eight months of the year. On the west side are Tualitin, La Creole, Yamhill, and Mary's and Long Tom Rivers, which rise in the Coast Mountains, and enter into the Willamette River at distances of thirty miles apart. On the east side of the Willamette, Clackamas, Putin, Molalla, Santiam, Calapooya, and Mohawk Rivers flow from the Cascades to the Willamette, at greater or less distances from each other.

The Umpqua Valley lies east and west. It is made by the Umpqua River, which, rising in the Cascade Mountains and flowing westerly, debouches into the sea, after cutting right through the Coast Mountains. This valley is one hundred miles long and fifty miles across. It is very picturesque and productive. The soil possesses great fertility. Rogue River Valley is a repetition of Umpqua, with perhaps wider valleys than the Umpqua.

Washington State, north of the Columbia River, has no considerable east and west rivers traversing it. The Cowlitz River rises in Mound Prairie, and flows southward to the Columbia, debouching into the Columbia thirty or forty miles from the sea. North of Mound Prairie is a comparatively level and heavily-timbered section, separating the waters of the Columbia from the waters of Puget Sound, Hood's Canal, and Admiralty Inlet. North of these is the Gulf of Georgia, with hundreds of islands, and receiving the waters of Fraser River. North and east of this Gulf of Georgia is our northern boundary-line of 49 degrees north latitude, running westerly until it reaches the center of the Gulf of Georgia, thence south by the main ship channel through the Gulf of Georgia, around the south end of Vancouver's Island, through the Straits of Fuca to the sea.

These magnificent inland seas are surrounded by inexhaustible fir forests, suitable for masts, spars, and lumber, and navigable for the largest ships to all their shores, containing twenty-eight hundred miles of sea-line.

Middle Oregon is a high table-land, stretching from the Cascade Mountains eastward two hundred and fifty miles to the Blue Mountains. The rivers which enter into the Columbia from the north in Middle Oregon are, Spokane River and Louis River; from the south, Des Chutes, Baker River, John Day's River, Umatilla, Powder, and Walla Walla Rivers. Eastern Oregon, as the territory was originally bounded, runs eastwardly from the Blue Mountains to the foot of the Rockies.

Oregon has three distinct climates, which are determined by its mountain ranges. The climate of Western Oregon is mild and humid. Roses and strawberries are in bloom, and the grass is green all through the winter. The thermometer is seldom more than 90 degrees Fahrenheit in the summer, nor lower than 20 degrees in the winter. Middle Oregon is high table-land, unprotected from the northern cold. It is intensely cold in winter, and terrifically hot in summer. The climate of Eastern Oregon is like that of the Middle, only more so.

The average summer weather of Western Oregon is 67 degrees, and the winter weather 46 degrees. The isotherm of Portland in latitude 46.20 north is that of Charleston, S. C., in latitude 32.20 degrees, nine hundred miles south.

The cause of this unusually mild climate of Western Oregon is twofold. The Gulf Stream of the Pacific runs close to the shore in Oregon, and the Cascade Mountains protect Western Oregon from the arctic blasts of winter.

Oregon is an exceptionally fine country for camp-meetings. From May to November scarcely any rain falls. In fourteen years' residence in Oregon, I never heard thunder but once, and then that was very distant and light. One season I attended and conducted seven camp-meetings in as many weeks. In all that time I slept in a house but one night, and we had no rain at any of those camp-meetings. Beginning at a certain point in the Willamette Valley on the east side of the river, and descending the valley, I went with my wife to four camp-meetings, and then, crossing over to the west side of the valley, I ascended the river, and held three more. Mrs. Pearne and myself attended all these seven camp-meetings. We carried our tent and clothing, including bedding, in a two-horse open buggy, drawn by two horses. We carried our tent in the buggy, and the tent-pole we fastened to the front and rear axles, the pole extending behind the buggy. We pitched and occupied our own tent. The people furnished us our food, and we furnished the transportation of tent and bedding. The camp-meetings were usually seasons of great power and blessing. Probably two hundred persons professed conversion during the season in which I held these seven meetings described. The people attending and sustaining the camp-meetings were very kind and hospitable. The climate was usually so dry and cool, that quarters of fresh beef hung up in the trees, and protected from the yellow-jackets by cheesecloth, would remain fresh and wholesome for two weeks at a time.

Several peculiar camp-meeting incidents are recorded. On one occasion, when I was preaching at a camp-meeting in Long Tom, in Lane County, on the Sabbath, a man went deranged. He ordered me down from the pulpit, that he might preach. I expostulated with him. He became angry, and plucked off his shoes and pelted me. His aim was so good, and his force in hurling the shoes at me was so great, that I had to do some expert dodging to save my face from mutilation. Then he ran up into the stand to take me out. Strong men seized and bound him, and carried him out. There was no lunatic hospital in Oregon. A log pen was made for him, into which he was put. He was fed and cared for in that pen; but he died in a few months.

Usually, at all our camp-meetings, people of all the different denominations would attend. They seemed to feel as free and as much at home as the Methodists did. One could not determine from general observation who were Methodists, and who were not. At a camp-meeting I held in Rock Creek, Clackamas County, there were a large number of persons other than Methodists present. They were urged by me to make themselves entirely at home, which they appeared to do. One morning I took a walk before breakfast. Half a mile from the meeting I found a man milking in his kraal, or cow-pen, whom I had not seen at the meeting. I entered into conversation with him, about as follows: "I don't think I have seen you at our camp-meeting up above here." "I presume not," said he; "I never go to such places; they are about the last places I would attend." "Why not?" I inquired. He replied, "I don't believe in them." I said, "Perhaps you do not profess religion?" "O yes, I do," said he. "Of what Church are you a member?" I asked. "Of the Baptist Church," said he. "But," said I, "there are several Baptist families camped up here at our meeting." "They are not my kind of Baptists," said he. "What kind of a Baptist Church is yours?" I inquired. He answered, "It is a Two-seed Baptist Church, or a Two Principle Baptist Church, as they are sometimes called." "Explain what you mean by Two-seed Baptists," said I. This was his answer: "The Lord has a seed and the devil has a seed. The devil's seed are goats. The Lord's seed are sheep; and there is no mixing them 'are breeds. The devil has been trying to make goats out of the Lord's sheep for six thousand years, and he has never made a single goat out of a sheep. And at your camp-meetings and protracted-meetings ministers of the gospel have been trying to make sheep out of the devil's goats, and they never made a sheep out of a goat yet." I had never before met that variety of Baptists. I said to him: "I see plainly why you are called Two-seed Baptists; but I think there is another name which would be quite as appropriate. I should call you Hard-shell Baptists. You do not hold Sunday-schools, I suppose?" "No," said he. "You do not try to have sinners converted into saints, do you?" Again he replied in the negative. "Do you," said I, "send missionaries to convert the heathen?" To this the reply was negative. Again I asked him, "Do you have Sunday-schools to teach your children the Bible?" To this he replied, "No." Once more I asked him, "Do you never hold revival-meetings or protracted-meetings?" And as before, he answered in the negative. I said: "My friend, I don't think you have given your Church the right name; you should call it the Hard-shell Baptist Church."

I held a camp-meeting once in the forks of the Santiam. We had been somewhat annoyed by the Campbellites, who denied conversion by faith and the Holy Ghost, and who taught baptismal regeneration, or conversion by baptism. Weeks before the meeting I announced far and wide that I would preach on salvation by faith as being the Bible teaching on that subject, rather than salvation by water baptism or immersion, as held by the Campbellites. My sermon lasted three hours and a half. Beginning at eleven o'clock A. M., I finished my discourse at 2.30 o'clock. Strange as it may seem, I held the audience for all that time without a break. We heard less about salvation by water after that sermon than we had been accustomed to hear before.

At each of these seven camp-meetings there were conversions. The number of professed conversions in all of them was something over one hundred and fifty.

I was once invited to go to Sublimity and hold a service, and baptize the child of the plucky little German class-leader. He also desired that I would preach on the subject of infant baptism; for all his neighbors were Campbellites, who pooh-poohed and ridiculed infant baptism, and he wanted to have a logical justification for his cause. I made an appointment for that purpose. It was announced that I would preach on Infant Baptism, and baptize a child. A large crowd gathered. I preached faithfully and strongly on the subject. Two Campbellite women found it too strong for them. One of them said to her sister present, "Did you ever hear tell of the like of that?" "No," was the reply. "And that is not all," said sister Number 2; "I won't hear any more of that kind of talk." They then both left the church. The house being an unchinked log building, they stood outside and kept up a chattering, which somewhat disturbed the people present. I baptized the child, and then I inquired if any one present desired to make any announcement; for we were accustomed in that country to make announcements at all religious meetings, and announce religious meetings of all denominations at one another's meetings. A Campbellite preacher, who had been accustomed to preach in that school-house, arose, and said, "Four weeks from to-day I shall preach the gospel here, I shall." Said I,

"Brother, you do n't mean to say that you have not had the gospel preached here to-day?" "I say nothing about that," said he; "but I do say that four weeks from to-day I will preach the gospel here, so I will." The class-leader seemed to think it was his turn, and he observed, "If you do, it will be the first time."

CHAPTER X.

MY district required twelve weeks of travel four times a year. I lived in Salem. I had six appointments north of Salem, and as many south. I had one rest-week each quarter, making twenty-two hundred and fifty miles of travel in a year. I traveled on muleback or horseback on the southern half of my district; by steamer, canoe, and horse on the northern half. The work was sufficiently laborious, and quite full enough of exposure, hardships, and peril.

The engraving on the opposite page represents my faithful servant and bearer, who carried me on my long and toilsome journeys for tens of thousands of miles. Her name was Cynthian. My friend, Hamilton Campbell, one of the early lay missionaries, had lost one of his noble span of matched mules. He kindly sold me the surviving animal. I paid him one hundred and sixty dollars. Cynthian was sixteen hands high; young, spirited, yet dependable, docile, fleet, easy-gaited. In the long summer days, lasting from four o'clock A. M. until eight o'clock P. M., I often rode her from seventy to eighty miles in a day. In all my travel on her, on the Oregon District, as presiding elder, I have ridden many thousands of miles. My full equipment for these long rides, in which I never carried an umbrella, and never was wet by the rain, may be thus described: The broad-brimmed hat

OREGON PRESIDING ELDER AND HIS FAITHFUL MULE.

was covered with oiled silk, and so was waterproof. The next piece of top-gear is the poncho, or Mexican scrape, a waterproof shawl, with a slit in the middle, through which the rider's head was put; and this covered his whole body, and fully protected it from wind and weather. The indispensable portmanteau, or saddlebags, is covered from view by the poncho. The pommel of the saddle rises high in front, and the kentil, or rear part of the saddle, is also high; so making a well-fitting seat for the rider. From the pommel is suspended the invariable lariat, a rawhide rope of perhaps forty feet, and by which the mule or horse is staked out for his feed of grass. The large wooden stirrup makes an easy rest for the foot, and the tapidary, or front cover of the stirrup, keeps the foot from going too far through the stirrup, and protects the foot from the rain. The mule and I were close friends. She would always whicker for me when I approached her; and when I lay out upon the plains, with blankets beneath and over me, and the saddlebags for my head, after she had filled herself with the grass meal, she would come and lie down beside me, and bear me company through the night. When I attended the General Conference I parted with her reluctantly; but I sold her, for fear she would be stolen in my absence. I received four hundred dollars in gold for her.

In December, 1852, I had to escort a missionary with his wife and child, and a lay brother and his wife and child, and a sea captain, from Portland to Olympia. We took steamer at Portland in the morning, and went to the mouth of the Cowlitz River. Before starting, I went into the bakery at Portland, and laid in two or three loaves and some crackers and cheese. We also carried our blankets and wraps. It was snowing heavily all the way down the river, and at Cowlitz it had reached a depth of six or eight inches. We chartered a whale-boat and a crew of four Indians, and started up the rapid river, propelling our boat with oars and poles. By dusk we reached a deserted bachelor's cabin on the river bank. We learned by the Indians of a potato-patch near the dwelling. We sent the Indians to dig potatoes, which, with sharp sticks, they gathered. We washed them in the river, and roasted them in the ashes. These, with the stores I procured, made the supper and breakfast for ten adults and two infants.

At noon we reached Gardner's, or "Hard-bread," as he was called, because his biscuits were so hard. I carried home one of his biscuits, which were blue in color because of the blue pod in the wheat, which the screen of the miller did not take out. The biscuits were sodden and heavy and hard. One of them shot from a cannon would kill a man as dead as any leaden or iron ball.

The snow was deep, and deepening. The weather was cold. The hotel was cheerless. It would not do for the ladies and babies to stay at the hotel, for it was too open and cold. They could not go through from Gardner's to Olympia, fifty miles, because the horses were all at the other end of the line. I learned that Mr. Jackson, a farmer settler on the road eight miles towards Olympia, had a comfortable house, and entertained travelers. Three and a half miles away was a factory of the Hudson Bay Company. The chief factor of the company, Dr. McLaughlin, at Oregon City, had often told me, if I was ever in want of anything which the company could supply, to call on them for it, and I should have it. I learned, on inquiry, that they kept some fifty or sixty horses and saddles as well, and I walked out to the factory in company with Captain Harland. The snow was knee-deep and getting deeper, and the mercury was falling. I concluded I would get horses and saddles for the men and their families, and send them to Jackson's, where they could remain until the conditions were more favorable. This was my errand to the Hudson Bay Company's farm. We had gone within half a mile of the place, and were kept in the right direction by a lane or road, which terminated half a mile short of our objective point; and that half mile was prairie, with untrodden snow eighteen inches deep. It was almost dark. The house at the end of the lane was the home of a Catholic priest. I called in to inquire my way. He said it was half a mile in the same direction as the lane. I told him as soon as it became dark we would be unable to see our way, and we were in danger of being lost. I asked him to permit us to stay with him until morning. He declined. We started for the farms; night came down upon us, and we were lost. We wandered in that prairie for two hours. Fortunately, some Indians were passing, whom we hailed. They were going to the farms. We followed their tracks, and reached our destination. We knocked for admittance. The agent of the company refused to keep us, and refused to furnish the horses. I told him we would not leave there, for we had already been lost two hours between the priest's house and the farms. Then he admitted us, and seated us in a cold room. After insisting on the horses for the travelers, we were promised them on payment of sixteen dollars, and two dollars extra for the horses we would ride back to the hotel with. We went to bed supperless; *i. e.*, we lay down on the floor in a cold room and covered ourselves with blankets, and slept till morning, when we left. I sent my guests to Jackson's, where they were comfortable, and in a few days they pursued their way to Olympia. I hastened back home, for the indications were that the rivers would close up.

From Oregon City I went by steamer to Champoeg, the boat breaking the ice. At Butteville the boat could go no farther. With my saddlebags and blankets on my shoulders, I walked through the snow, breaking the roads, twenty-six miles, reaching home at ten o'clock P. M., December 25, 1852, as tired as a man could be. I had eaten nothing since early morning. My weariness and hunger had been very severe.

About a month after reaching Oregon, I had occasion, on one Saturday, to travel thirty-five miles across the country, to hold a meeting at Dimmock's, on the French prairie. I went to the Willamette River, expecting to find a ferry-boat at Champoeg, ten miles beyond which was Dimmock's. But the boat had been washed down the river in a freshet. I had to go back from the ferry and up the river six miles, to find De Gere's ferry. Attempting this, I was lost in a fog. I met a cowboy driving his cows to pasture. He piloted me to the house of a German, named Fulquarts. I inquired of him my way to the ferry. He directed me thus: "Vell, den, you see mine farm down dere in de pottom" (an inclosure of an acre or two for a truck-patch). "You vill take dat farm up on your right hand, und dat vill bring you to von ferry bad slough; dere you had petter get down and lead your horse, or you vill mire down mit him; den you vill take anoder farm up on your right hand, and turn anoder corner down on your left hand, and dat vill pring you to de ferry." The ferryman was a half-breed Indian. I had to inquire my way to Dimmock's. I asked the Indian if he could speak English. I could not make him understand me. I said, "What is your name?" He said, "Icta," which means "what?" I said, "Is your name Icta?" He said, "Wake," which means "No." Then I said, "Your name is Icta Wake?" He laughed at my verdancy. I could learn nothing from him. So I pushed on, traveling three or four miles, fording places of deep water. At last I came to a whitewashed house, surrounded by a peach-orchard. I hailed. An Indian woman came to the door. I said, "Who lives here?" She answered, "Lucy." Supposing she had given me her Christian name,

I inquired, "Is your husband's name 'Lucy?'" "Nawitka," said she. "Then your name is Lucy Nawitka?" She understood me, and she could speak English. She laughed at my blunder, and said, "My husband's name is Lucea." Nawitka is the Indian word for Yes, or Certainly. I asked her the way to some American's house. She said if I kept on I would reach Champoeg in a mile and a half; and then I would find Dr. Newell, an American. Here I staid all night; but I had eaten nothing since morning, and I went to bed supperless. The next day the Doctor piloted me to Dimmock's, which I reached at church-time.

I once attended a quarterly-meeting when the floods were out; for we sometimes had very serious floods there. I was water-bound at Marysville, forty miles from home. Here I boarded a steamer, tied my mule in the bow of the steamer, and rode to Salem. Then I struck out for the hills to head the streams, where I could ford them, on my way to Oregon City, forty miles away. Bear Creek was out of its banks; for twenty or thirty rods each side of the bridge there was water to wade or swim through to and from the bridge. The bridge was the only visible object before me. I took my saddlebags on my shoulders and slung my blankets on my back, and got on my knees on the mule's saddle. The bridge was a pole bridge; *i. e.*, fir poles from four to six inches thick were resting on these string pieces. The water was just up to the cross-poles. I stepped off my mule on to the bridge, and, unfastening my lariat, said to the mule, "Now, Cynthian, you must be very careful, or you will get into the creek, and you will have to swim out." She seemed to understand me, and she did go carefully. Her weight and mine sprung the stringer pieces, and the cross-poles drifted off from under her. She sank down astride the middle stringer. I pushed my foot against her neck, and she fell off her perch into the creek. I gave her rope, holding on to the end of it, and brought her round to me, remounted her, and rode out, and went on my way to my destination.

CHAPTER XI.

I HAVE spoken of sloughs or swales. These were numerous, and sometimes dangerous to cross. I came to one, which looked so formidable that I rode back some distance to inquire of a settler how to cross the slough safely. He said: "It is pretty bad. But you go to the worst-looking part, and you will see the ears of dead mules sticking up. You follow that sign, and ride over on the backs of the dead mules, and you can cross that way." Of course he was joking. Another man came to a bad-looking slough. A boy on the hither side was cutting wood. A dialogue ensued. "Boy, is that a safe slough to cross?" "O yes." "Has it a good, hard bottom?" "O yes," said the boy. The man essayed to cross. His horse mired. He had to dismount and wade out. He was very angry, for he thought the boy had deceived him. He cursed the boy roundly. "Why did you lie to me? Did n't you say the slough has a good, hard bottom?" "O yes," said the boy, and then applying his thumb to his nose, with the other digits erected, he said, "O yes, the bottom is good and hard, but you did not get down to it."

I have mentioned the German's specific directions to me how to find the ferry. They were sufficiently plain. I often found Americans who would direct me thus: "Well, stranger, you will follow this trail you are on a right smart, till you come to where it forks; you will take the right-hand eend, and follow that a right smart, till you come to the second fork; you will take the left-hand eend, and follow that till you come to a cabin, and there you will do well to inquire." Often the cabin would be a bachelor's home, and the occupant absent miles away, and no other cabin in sight. I always carried a pocket compass, but for which we should have had serious trouble in finding our way.

WEDDINGS AND FUNERALS.

Sometimes the character of people can be learned by knowing their customs at funerals and weddings. It will be found amusing, if not instructive, to consider the following Oregon examples, and a few, also, furnished from other periods and places. In Oregon and in the South, from which many of the earlier immigrants had come to Oregon, it was customary for funeral sermons to be preached, months, and even years, after the deaths and burials of the deceased had occurred. In more than a few instances I have conducted funerals when the second wife or the second husband, as the case may have been, sat with the mourners at the funeral of the first wife or husband, respectively. And, really, it sometimes seemed to me that the second wife or husband was the most real and serious mourner of the whole group. This may have been imagination on my part; but I am candidly giving my actual impressions at the time.

The Donation Land Law of Oregon, enacted August 14, 1848, in the Act of Congress organizing the Territory of Oregon, provided for the gift of three hundred and twenty acres to each adult settler in Oregon then being single and living in Oregon at the time of the passage of the law, or at any time after the passage of the law up to December 1, 1851. If married, the law gave to each of the parties, husband and wife, a half section of land, making the donation to both a full section of a mile square. As the time-limit of the land law approached, the matrimonial business was very active; and it was not too scrupulous as to the fitness, in age or otherwise, of the parties marrying. It was not unusual for old bachelors and widowers of forty or more years to be married to girls entirely too young to contract and enter into marriage relations. Reaching Oregon in October, 1851, this feature of the subject was strongly impressed upon my attention. Soon after my arrival in Oregon, I formed the acquaintance of an interesting girl of apparently eight or nine years, whom I caressed and petted as a child. A few weeks later, I saw her in another part of the country from where I first met her. I renewed my attentions to her as a child. I inquired, "Have you left home to attend school?" "La, no!" was her reply; "I 'm married!" Amazed, I let her down from my knee, saying: "I thought you were a child. How old are you?" The answer came, "I am ten, going on eleven." Before that child was eighteen she had been several times married and divorced.

In Washington Territory, near the mouth of the Cowlitz, I married a couple, at a quarterly-meeting held on that occasion, in a Roman Catholic church-building. When I asked the man the usual question: "Wilt thou have this woman to be thy lawful wedded wife, to live together after God's ordinance in the holy estate of marriage so long as ye both shall live?" quick and strong and percussively he replied, "You bet yer!" The explosion and force were terrific. The audience were convulsed at the eager and novel way of his answering. I looked serious, and said, "Did you mean yes by your answer?" He responded affirmatively. The wedding proceeded to its conclusion.

In the fifties I attended a large "swell" wedding. With the parties standing before me, I called for objections, if any could be alleged, why the parties named should not be united in holy marriage. A brother present replied, "I object!" "What," I inquired, "is your objection?" He answered, "I am older than she, and I have a right to be married first." I said to the bride-elect, "Will you wait a moment until I shall have married your brother?" She assented. I said to her brother, "Bring forward your bride-elect, and I will marry you first." (There was no license required then.) He said, "No one will have me." Several young ladies stepped out in a row, and said to him, "Take your choice." He looked at them for a moment, and then said to me, "I withdraw the objection." I said: "You have practically made an offer of yourself in marriage, and have been accepted. Unless you can render a reason for declining to carry out your offer satisfactory to every one of these young ladies, I can not release you." The reason he assigned, and which the ladies accepted as satisfactory, was this: "I fear if I should marry one of them, the others might die of broken hearts." The objection of the brother being withdrawn, his sister's marriage ceremony proceeded to its close. My fee, on this occasion, was a fifty-dollar gold coin. It was octagonal in form, and weighed the same amount in Troy ounces as two and one-half double eagles. It was called a slug.

I attended a wedding in Hillsboro, Ohio, for which I received, constructively, an immense fee. The groom expectant engaged me to wait at my home for him from twelve noon to one P. M. This I did. At one he came, and requested another hour's extension. It was granted. At two, he requested a third hour's extension, which, also, was admitted. Before three he was present with his bride-elect. After marrying him, he requested that we should furnish him some music. We sang for him, the organ leading, "Vain delusive world, adieu," and another piece. He seemed to enjoy it. On leaving, he asked what my charges would be. I replied: "I never make a charge. I leave that to the parties." As he passed out, he said, "Minister, I am ten thousand times *obleeged* to you." In New York, in my boyhood, I had learned that every "thank you" I received was worth eighteen and three-fourths cents. I multiplied the value of a "thank you" by ten thousand. By that rule, applied according to arithmetic, he had paid me in "thank you's" eighteen hundred and seventy-five dollars.

Before going to Oregon, I married a couple in New York State. In doing this, I seriously questioned whether I might not have rendered myself liable for cruelty to animals. At my instance, as the bride was unusually long in dressing her hair, the man to be married said to his espoused, "Sally, the minister would like you to make more haste." With a savage fierceness, she turned to him, and said, "Joe! you shut up, or I will slap you." When it is considered that she was an Amazon, and he a wizened, dwarfish man, the situation can be imagined. Having no personal fear of her power, I said to her, "If you wish me to marry you to this man, you must be ready within two minutes." This was effectual. She put up her long, luxuriant, golden hair, and was married. As the groom accompanied me to the gate, and handed me a dollar for my fee, he remarked: "She does n't handsome much; but the way she has got to hoe my potatoes and corn is a caution." I was relieved. The match was more nearly even, with his grit over against her size and her spirit, than I had feared.

In Binghamton, N. Y., I married my first colored couple. This was an "upper-ten" affair, as a colored wedding. Those present were all mulattoes. After marrying them and wishing them joy, I said to the groom, "Now you may salute your wife." He stepped aside, with a most polite bow, saying, "After you, minister." Of course, I politely declined to avail myself of his offer.

CHAPTER XII.

I HAVE referred to the jargon. It was a dialect common to settlers and Indians and half-breeds. It was easily learned, and very convenient in traveling in Oregon at an early day. A stranger in Oregon could make his way through the country with great difficulty, unless he understood the Chinook vocabulary. Indians and half-breeds abounded in Oregon. The Indian words on the Pacific are far more soft and liquid than the Indian words on the Atlantic; and they are also equally significant. Onon*daga*; Niag*ara*, as pronounced in the days of the Revolutionary fathers; Catta*ra*gus—Seneca words—are harsh and guttural, as contrasted with the Oregon Indian words; as Umatilla, Multnomah, or the broad, open valley; Willamette, or the long and crooked river; Yaquinna, Yakimah, Coquille, Molalla, Yamhill, Spokane, Walla Walla; Wailetpu, pronounced Wa-i-*let*-pu.

Our life in Oregon contained now and then an amusing incident or a perilous adventure. I was holding a camp-meeting on the Callapooya River, forty-five miles from home. A messenger reached the camp-ground on Saturday evening, informing me of the dangerous illness of my wife. On my long ride of forty-five miles I had a rapid, deep, and dangerous stream to cross. I started at nine o'clock P. M. For twenty-four miles my way led me over a pathless, unpeopled prairie. I took a course, steering for a butte beyond the prairie. After I had traveled about six miles a pack of wolves followed me, making night hideous with their howlings, and making din and noise enough for twoscore of wolves. They sometimes came so near that I could hear their breathing. My horse was greatly excited, snorting and sometimes shrieking with terror. Reaching the Santiam River, I tried, by loud and prolonged calls, to arouse the ferryman, who lived on the opposite side of the river; but it was all in vain. I plunged into the river, and my horse swam over in good form. I reached my home about half-past three in the morning, having made the distance in six and a half hours, making my rate an average speed of seven miles an hour. My wife was very ill, and continued so for weeks, during which time I had to stay at home and nurse her.

In a trip from Portland to Yreka, California, in an open buggy, over three hundred miles, with Bishop Simpson, as we were rounding a rocky point in Rogue River Valley, where the river makes a short turn, my horses suddenly jumped forward and sideways, greatly risking our going down a precipice into the river. The cause of this was a sudden, loud rattling by a rattlesnake. The warning noise startled the horses and us as well, for it was very sudden and very fearful. After driving past the point I procured a hazel rod, and, returning, dispatched the snake and cut off his rattle, which I presented to the bishop as a trophy. There were thirteen rattles and a button, showing the snake to be about fifteen years old. He was four feet long, and about two and a half inches in diameter.

In March, 1853, Bishop Edward R. Ames, the first bishop of the Methodist Episcopal Church who came to Oregon, and held our first Conference as a full and regularly-organized Conference of the Methodist Episcopal Church, visited us. He re-arranged the work, making three districts: Willamette River District, Thomas H. Pearne, presiding elder—residence, Salem; Umpqua District, James H. Wilbur, presiding elder; and Puget Sound District, John F. Devore, presiding elder. The bishop also appointed me an agent of the Missionary Society of the Methodist Episcopal Church, to make a settlement of the accounts of the late superintendent, Rev. William Roberts, and to close up the secular business of the mission. We thus ceased to be a mission. We became an integral part of the system and connection of the Methodist Episcopal Church. After fourteen years of tutelage, we were graduated to a full-fledged and fully-equipped synod of Methodism. It was meet, therefore, that the property interests of the Missionary Society should be closed up. These consisted of certain educational plants, which had been nurtured by the Missionary Society, and notably Clackamas Female Seminary in Oregon City, which was sold, and the avails, in part, turned over to the assets of the Willamette University, of which Rev. F. S. Hoyt, a graduate of the Wesleyan University, Middletown, Conn.—a son of one of the veterans of the

New Hampshire Conference, Rev. Benjamin R. Hoyt—was the president.

Brother Hoyt was an able administrator of the school under his care. He was a strong preacher and a wise manager of those things within his prescribed sphere. He was for several years—ten, probably—the efficient secretary of the Oregon Annual Conference. The university grew in means, standing, and usefulness during his incumbency. In 1860 he was elected a delegate to the General Conference, which met that year in Buffalo, N. Y. Rev. Alvin F. Waller was his associate delegate. Dr. Hoyt received from the Ohio Wesleyan University the well-deserved honor of a degree as Doctor in Divinity, which he has ever since worn with marked credit and distinction. His work as a member of the Oregon Conference terminated in 1860. He became a professor in the Ohio Wesleyan University, and a member of the North Ohio Annual Conference. Later, he was elected editor of the *Western Christian Advocate*, an office which he filled with marked ability for twelve years, when he returned, in 1880, to the active, effective ranks of the itinerancy, being presiding elder of the West Cleveland District for six years, and then for six years more on the Sandusky District. From these twelve years of active and laborious itinerant life he returned to the educational work of the Church, by a professorship in the Baldwin University, in the line of pastoral theology. Dr. Hoyt, while conservative in his mind and methods, was also safely and thoroughly progressive and up-to-date. In the Oregon Conference he signed with me a circular resolution in favor of lay delegation, which was known as the Oregon Resolution, and which received a large vote. He conducted the *Western Christian Advocate* with ability and success. Our relations for forty-five years have always been cordial and unbroken. He has never failed to command my respect, confidence, and appreciation.

The episcopal visit of Bishop Ames in Oregon was highly appreciated and enjoyed by the ministers and people of Oregon. His sermons at Salem and Portland were popular and effective. He showed himself a wise counselor. He was clearly a man of affairs, and of large business ability. In Salem he preached a Conference sermon on Faith, from the words, "These are written, that ye might believe that Jesus is the Christ, the Son of God; and that believing ye might have life through his name." (John xx, 31.) The sermon produced a profound and permanent impression. He preached a characteristic sermon in Portland, from the words, "With what measure ye mete, it shall be measured unto you again." When Bishop Ames returned East, I accompanied him on the steamer down the Columbia River as far as to Astoria. Father Broulier, the head of the Jesuit order in Oregon, was a passenger. For some two hours, in the rear part of the dining saloon, I discussed with him the work of the Roman Catholics in Oregon as compared with that of the Protestants. The bishop overheard most of the conversation, although he did not mingle in it. He said I held the Jesuit father to a close and plain showing of the respective merits and claims of the two competing systems respectively represented by the Jesuit and myself.

The organization of the Annual Conference came none too soon. A large overland emigration from the Western States poured into Oregon. These added several thousands to its population. They were found by the Methodist ministers stationed in all parts of the Territory. Enlargement and increase came to our Church. Churches were built, and revivals occurred. Sunday-schools were organized in many places. A lieutenant in the United States army, Mr. Roberts—a Baptist in his Church affinities—stationed in Oregon, personally gave five dollars to every Sunday-school so organized in Oregon. Some twenty or thirty Methodist Sunday-schools were thus assisted by his bounty in Sunday-school requisites and library books. Among the additions to our Church, by the immigrations of that and the following years, we numbered the three Hines brothers heretofore named—Gustavus, Joseph W., and Harvey K. were given to us. They all came from the Genesee Conference. Gustavus, the elder, had been one of the early missionaries. He and his wife had adopted the only daughter of Jason Lee, the pioneer projector and leader of the Oregon missions. She came with them to Oregon, and married in Salem. These brothers were men of marked zeal and ability. Joseph W. removed to California, and died there. Gustavus remained in Oregon, doing heroic work for Christ, and died full of years and honor. Harvey K. still remains a patriarch among his brethren.

A large proportion of the immigration landed from the plains in Southern Oregon. There were two brothers, named Royal, with their families, from Illinois. One of them, Rev. William Royal, was a member of one of the Illinois Conferences. He and one of his sons became members of the Oregon Conference. Rev. James B. Royal, and a nephew of his, T. B. Royal, also became members of that Conference. The latter ran a career of great honor and usefulness, and a few years since preached his semicentennial sermon. His son, Rev. Stanley O. Royal, after a full course in Drew Theological Seminary, joined the Cincinnati Conference in 1877. He has been secretary of the Conference eleven years, and has filled important charges. His wife is a daughter of Bishop Walden. Crossing the Plains in 1852, they were in a large body of emigrants. When the emigrant train reached that part of the Plains where the Indians were becoming troublesome, and where the emigrants found the feed and water scarce, a majority of the party resolved to travel on Sunday for their greater security and welfare. A minority, headed by the Royals, resolved to rest on Sabbaths. They separated. The majority encountered sickness and drought and Indian marauders, and reached Oregon in a disastrous condition, and very late in the season, sans cattle, sans horses, sans wagons, and came into Oregon on foot, and stripped and sore. The division led by the Royals reached Oregon earlier than the majority party, and in better condition. Their stock and wagons escaped the loss and wreck which came to the majority party. It was a marked instance of a Divine vindication of observing the Lord's-day.

The work prospered and prevailed in the year following Bishop Ames's presidency in 1852. In Southern Oregon Mr. Wilbur had built and opened a seminary, called the Umpqua Academy. He had organized and set going in orderly form the work in the Umpqua and Rogue River Valleys. The deserts and moral wastes of Southern Oregon were wearing the bloom and the beauty of the Lord's vineyard. The people were glad for the coming of the messengers of gospel peace. The gathering of the ministers to the next Annual Conference was with rejoicing, and the bringing in of the sheaves garnered in the Lord's house. Brother Wilbur was a very hearty and earnest worker. His spirit was contagious. His associates in the ministry caught the holy flame. They shouted the harvest home over precious souls gathered into the fold of Christ.

In Puget Sound, Mr. Devore had wrought prodigies of valor. New charges had been formed, manned, and worked. In Seattle, Steilacoom, and Olympia the cause had had uplift and enlargement. The North and the South brought their joyful tidings to gladden the center, which, too, had acquired the swing of victory. Portland had received many accessions. The Portland Academy and Female Seminary was largely attended. Oregon City was growing under the able ministry of P. G. Buchanan, and Yamhill was well served by Nehemiah Doane. Astoria and Clatsop were in line. Vancouver Circuit was becoming stalwart. Salem, under the pastorate of William Roberts, was swinging into the line of victory. Lebanon was enlarging. The Santiam Academy was full. Calapooya Circuit was in a flame of revival. La Creole, Santiam Forks, Mary's River, Long Tom, and Eugene City were under vigorous march. Willamette University was magnificently doing its great work. A Bible agent, Rev. L. C. Phillips, had entered upon his blessed service of disseminating Bibles. Isaac Dillon had come from Cincinnati Conference to join the founders of an empire in laying broad and deep the foundations of many generations.

The Conference session of 1854 was held in Belknap Settlement, in Benton County, Oregon, fifty miles south from Salem. Bishop Simpson was assigned to hold it; but he was detained by an accident to his steamer. The writer was elected the president of the Conference. The business of the Conference was well forward by Sunday. The deacons and elders were elected. On Sunday morning the Conference sermon had been preached by me, from Acts vi, 5-8: "And they chose Stephen, a man full of faith and the Holy Ghost. . . . And Stephen, full of faith and power, did great wonders and miracles among the people."

The audience was large. The interest was considerable. I had just reached the peroration of my discourse, when I saw a man, wearing a linen duster and bearing a gripsack, enter the log church and seat himself just inside the door. I had never seen Bishop Simpson, nor had I ever seen a likeness of him; but I said: "If the gentleman who has just entered the house is Bishop Simpson, for whom we have been looking so long, he will please come forward, and I will introduce him to the audience." He came forward, and he was introduced. He delivered an earnest exhortation, announced a discourse by himself for three o'clock, when the ordination of deacons and elders would take place. His sermon was one of great power. In the course of it he quoted the words of Paul to the elders of the Church at Ephesus, when he said: "But none of these things move me, neither count I my own life dear unto myself, that I might finish my course with joy and the ministry, which I have received of the Lord Jesus, to testify the gospel of the grace of God." His rendering of that part of his subject was exceedingly dramatic. The people were intensely interested. Some wept, and others shouted. Many who heard that sermon will probably never forget it in time nor in eternity. Then calling up the deacons-elect, he ordained them. A brief recess was taken. The lunch was eaten in the chapel yard. On reassembling, the bishop preached a marvelous sermon, and then he ordained the elders. The hold which Bishop Simpson had upon the hearts of his frontier audience, in the log church in the Belknap Settlement, was unmistakable. The Conference minute business was concluded on Monday. On Tuesday the session was adjourned. The members felt that they had been through a Jerusalem Pentecost, and were now ready for another year of toil and struggle and victory.

I insert here excerpta from a letter which I published in the *Western Christian Advocate*, July 2, 1884, soon after the death of Bishop Simpson, which occurred June 18, 1884. It will doubtless have interest for the readers of this volume:

THE LATE BISHOP SIMPSON—REMINISCENCES OF HIM IN OREGON AND ELSEWHERE.

When, on Wednesday morning, June 18th last, the chariot stopped at 1334 Arch Street, Philadelphia, for God's faithful servant, a good man, greatly beloved and honored, tried, true, and brave, entered it and ascended to his crowning. Telegraphy had made all the world as real spectators of Bishop Simpson's ascension as Elisha and the sons of the prophets were of Elijah's. As Elijah had asked his colleague and successor what he should do for him, and had promised to grant his request, so the good bishop, standing amid his colleagues and his brethren of the General Conference of 1884, at the close of the session, said: "It is exceedingly gratifying to me, as I feel that the shadows are gathering around me and others, to see young men, truly cultured and devoted to the cause of Christ, able to come forward and take the reins of the Church and guide it so successfully onward. May God be gracious to them, and make them greater than the fathers!"

The purpose of this paper is to give incidents in Bishop Simpson's life which came under my personal notice. They will have interest to his many friends and admirers, because they illustrate the man in his less public and official life. Having never been published, they will have the added charm of freshness. Most of these occurred in Oregon. One of them, and among the most thrilling, occurred in Washington, D. C., on the next day after Mr. Lincoln's reinauguration. Bishop Simpson's first official visit to Oregon was in 1854. Bishop Ames had preceded him there in 1853.

I first saw Bishop Simpson in the Conference room in Oregon. The Conference met that year in Belknap Settlement, Benton County, about a hundred and twenty miles above Portland, the chief seaport. Steamboating on the Upper Willamette was suspended. There were then no stages nor other public conveyances up and down the valley. The bishop had been hindered by an accident to his ocean steamer. He reached Portland on Thursday, the day after the session had opened. He procured a man to take him to the seat of the Conference. But this person, not knowing where Belknap Settlement was, conveyed him to Polk County instead of Benton. He entered the log church on Sunday morning, just as the writer was closing his sermon. No one there had ever seen him. I said, "If the gentleman who has just entered the room is Bishop Simpson, he will please advance to the pulpit." He came forward. I introduced him. He gave the cause of the delay as a shipwreck, through which he had just passed. He said that when in imminent peril, and amid consternation and alarm, he had been greatly comforted by the lines of Henry Kirke White, some of which he repeated thus:

> "Once, on the raging seas I rode;
>   The storm was loud, the night was dark;
> The ocean yawned, and rudely blowed
>   The wind that tossed my foundering bark.
>
> Deep horror then my vitals froze;
>   Death-struck, I ceased the tide to stem;
> When suddenly a star arose,—
>   It was the Star of Bethlehem."

He told how sweetly thrilling the lines were, and how deeply they had moved him, adding:

> "Now safely moored, my perils o'er,
>   I'll sing, first in night's diadem,
> For ever and for evermore,
>   The Star, the Star of Bethlehem."

The effect on the audience was strongly marked. Many wept; some shouted. The bishop spent several weeks with me, visiting different points of interest. One Saturday afternoon, in Salem, he inquired: "What did Bishop Ames preach on last year in Salem?" I replied that Bishop Ames had preached a most memorable sermon on "Faith." The next day, in the same pulpit, and to many of the same people, Bishop Simpson preached his matchless sermon on "This is the victory that overcometh the world, even our faith," and "Have faith in God." The effect was indescribable. Breathless silence prevailed at times, succeeded and broken by sobbing and weeping and shouts. He carried his hearers up in thought and feeling as far as science and reason, and sight and promise, and experience and imagination, could go toward the Invisible and the Eternal. And then, while expectation was keyed to its utmost pitch, he climaxed the thought, by quoting:

> "Faith lends its realizing light;
>   The clouds disperse, the shadows fly;
> The Invisible appears in sight,
>   And God is seen by mortal eye."

Tears of joy and shouts of rapture attested the magic of his eloquence. . . .

The greatest triumph of his preaching power which I witnessed was on the occasion of Lincoln's reinauguration. The inauguration-day, Saturday, was dreary, cloudy, drizzly. Just as Mr. Lincoln took the oath of office, the clouds parted, and sunshine flooded the scene. The next day the bishop preached in the House of Representatives to a most distinguished audience. Senators, congressmen, diplomats, secretaries, judges, generals, admirals, and many others, were present. Floors, galleries, aisles were crowded. In front of the speaker's desk sat Mr. Lincoln. A lady led the singing. Prayer was offered by Dr. Thomas, afterwards killed by the Modocs. The bishop's text was, "I, if I be lifted up, will draw all men unto me." He spoke of the power of Christ to diminish war and promote peace, and then, as if recollecting himself, he referred to the Civil War then flagrant, as though it might be considered fatal to his argument, and he added: "I am not much of a believer in signs and omens; but when, yesterday, just as the old Administration expired and the new one began, the rifted clouds let God's sunshine flow, I could not but regard it as an augury of returning peace, and that the war would soon close, and the new Administration would be one of peace." Instantly, as if by electricity, the audience were stirred; they cheered earnestly; many rose to their feet; hats were thrown up; men embraced each other, and wept and shouted. Mr. Lincoln was vigorously rapping the floor with his cane, the big tears chasing each other down his bronzed face. It was a masterly triumph of human eloquence, set on fire by sympathy and Christian patriotism. He subsequently delivered the same discourse in Chillicothe to the wonder and admiration of the preachers of the Cincinnati and Ohio Conferences. I heard him repeat this discourse in Portland, Oregon. Its effect there was marvelous.

Bishop Simpson impressed me, in a very intimate association with him for three weeks, with his deep spirituality and fellowship with God. He was a man of rich religious experience; as much so as any man I had ever known. Several remarkable incidents of his visit are ineffaceably fixed in my mind. They will remain with me as long as memory shall hold her place. The incidents which follow illustrate certain Scripture statements. They also enforce them; as, "Cast thy bread upon the waters, and it shall be gathered after many days;" and "Your labor shall not be in vain in the Lord;" and especially, "The eyes of the Lord run to and fro in the earth, to show himself strong in behalf of them whose hearts are right with him." A trip to the Dalles of the Columbia was crowded with adventurous incidents, some of which were of thrilling power. The French word Dalles denotes a narrow passage of waters. At the place we were to visit, the whole volume of the Columbia River's waters rush and roar and tumble between perpendicular basaltic walls, a hundred feet below, with a power and a majesty of wonderful sublimity. The passage is so narrow that a boy could easily throw a stone from one bank to the other. This is one of the great wonders of nature. It equals Niagara in its weird enchantment. But it was not alone, nor chiefly, to see the Dalles that we went. Our passage there involved very important business relating to our Missionary Society and our Church. The passage to the Cascades, seventy miles from Portland, was in a river steamer. A portage of five miles obstructs the navigation of the Columbia. Above the Cascades, a small steam-launch plied to the Dalles, forty-five miles. This launch was disabled at the time of our trip, and we were obliged to make the passage by canoe. This was the bishop's first voyage by canoe. The canoe was forty feet long. It contained fish-nets, dogs, three squaws, two Indians, two half-drunken white men, myself, and the bishop, to say nothing of innumerable fleas. The two white men were both drunk on very mean, mischievous whisky. One of them was coarse and brutal in his nature. The other was more gentle, and evidently more educated and refined. The latter, in the conversation the bishop afterwards held with him, admitted that he was a student in Indiana Asbury University when Simpson was its president. They were profane and obscene in their filthy discourse. They were apparently seeking to provoke and exasperate their clerical fellow-passengers. The bishop was mild and patient. After the coarse-fibered one had fallen off into a stupor, his associate ceased talking. After a while the bishop said to him very kindly, "My friend, is your mother living?" "O yes," was the reply. "Where does she live?" "In Indiana." "Did you attend Asbury University?" "Yes," said he. The bishop addressed other like questions. "Is your mother a praying woman?" to which he replied affirmatively. "Does your mother pray for you?" "O yes," said he, "every day. I should have been in hell long ago but for her prayers." Once more the bishop addressed him: "I would not like to seem impertinent; but there is one other question I would like to ask you." "Certainly," said the now serious and thoughtful young man; "any question you please." In a tender, gentle tone, and in a somewhat pathetic manner, the bishop said, "Do you think your mother knows what kind of a life you are leading?" The young prodigal here quite broke down, burst into tears, and said, "I would not have her know it for the world; it would break her heart." The bishop followed this up with other kindly words. Reaching Dog River, on the Oregon side, at dusk, the young man crossed over the river to what is now Washington State, and the bishop saw him no more. We staid in the Indian's tepee for the night. We went to bed—our bed on the sand—supperless. The dried salmon which the Indian offered us, after he had toasted it upon a stick, smelled too rank, and we could not eat it. This occurred in March, 1854.

In October, 1864, I was going down to the Dalles from Umatilla, on a large river steamer on the Columbia. There were many passengers returning from the Salmon River mines. One of them inquired my name, and, after I gave it to him, he recalled the canoe ride from the Cascades to Dog River, and he asked me if I remembered it. He said he was one of those two passengers; that the other one, whom he had then called "Sandy," had been for several years in the State prison; and then, in answer to my inquiries, he said that that day had been a day of destiny for him; the questions of the bishop had led to his reformation. He had ceased his drink-habit, and left off swearing, and had begun a life of prayer. God had converted him. He was a happy man. He had a wife and three children, a half-section of land, and money in the bank, and he was on his way to heaven, and his wife also, and he owed it all to the wise counsel and the kindly treatment of that good man, the bishop; and he desired me, whenever I should have the opportunity, to tell the bishop that his faithful seed-sowing of more than ten years before had brought its harvest in due time. In June, 1868, on the summit of the Rockies, I told the bishop the story of his success in that wayside seed-sowing which he did on the Indian's canoe fourteen years before. It was a notable fulfillment of the promise, "He that goeth forth and weepeth, bearing precious seed, shall doubtless come again with rejoicing, bringing his sheaves with him."

CHAPTER XIII.

AFTER our first day's canoe-sailing and our night at Dog River, we embarked the next day in the same canoe for the Dalles. The wind was blowing a stiff gale up the river. The river being in freshet, the wind caused high waves to roll across the river; but we were plowing through them ten knots an hour. The bishop became nervous, and we went ashore. There was no shelter, and the March wind was bleak and cold. We relaunched our craft, and reached the Dalles in an hour's sailing. After transacting our business at the Dalles military post, we secured Indian ponies, and rode up the river four or five miles to see the Grand Coulee, where the river had once flowed, and to see the Grand Dalles, or narrow passage of waters.

We had to ascend a cañon to find safe crossing of a small but swollen, unfordable stream. We crossed on a log and descended the cañon; we saw the wonderful passage of the great Columbia, which carries nearly as much water as the Mississippi. Returning up the cañon for our log-bridge crossing, we encountered a large, gray wolf, who for a time refused to give us the right of way. By dint of bold riding and loud hallooing and swinging our lariats, we started his wolfship, and proceeded on our way. Emerging later from the cañon into the open, we encountered a large cavalcade of Indians, some two hundred, all mounted and armed. There was a general unrest among all the Indian tribes in Oregon. Several murders by the Indians had occurred, and an Indian war broke out within a few months after this. The procession halted. We were in deadly peril. The bishop said, "Are we not in great danger?" I told him that if the Indians should find us, or believe us to be, Indian agents or traders, or United States military, our scalps would be taken within half an hour; but if I could convince them that we were Methodist preachers, I believed we would not be harmed. We boldly rode up to the head of the column. I addressed one of the chiefs in the Chinook jargon, "Claihaiam six," which is "How are you, chief?" He answered me in English, "I do not talk jargon." "Where did you learn to talk English?" "In Ithaca, N. Y." "How did you go there?" "With Commissioner Parker." I introduced Bishop Simpson to him, and through him to the Indians present, as a great ministerial "Tyee," or chief; and Bishop Simpson introduced me as a great Oregon chief, or minister of the gospel. We rode down together to the Dalles, and had some interesting conversation.

In descending the Columbia, the bishop preferred to sail in a larger craft than a canoe, which, in our ascending the river, had given him so much alarm. I secured passage on a sloop, which was used for shipping wood and other freight up the river. We were much baffled by the persistent up-river winds. In trying to tack we were unable to make progress, and for twenty-four hours we made only three miles. I became restless. I walked back to the Dalles, and chartered a ship's lighter, and secured a crew of six strong Indians. We took the bishop and our baggage aboard, and pulled down some two or three miles further to a bend in the river, where for ten miles the river ran due west, and where the wind had unobstructed sweep. We rowed for two hours, without making any progress. We landed and spent the night on the river bank, under the lee of a great rock, with our feet to the fire. The next morning the wind had changed to the east. We were pulling our boat by oars! The sloop came by and passed us, arriving at the Cascades some hours before us. Entering the Willamette River, we noticed that the river craft had colors at half-mast. Inquiry gave us the information that the steamer *Gazelle* had, the morning before, blown up at the wharf, killing nearly all on board. That was the boat we should have taken, had not baffling winds delayed us. We felt that a sheltering Providence had preserved our lives against our persistent efforts to reach Portland at an earlier moment.

The bishop's visit had been made a great blessing to the entire Church and ministers of Oregon. His counsels were wise. His appointments of the preachers were judicious.

In 1855 we had Bishop Baker to hold our Conference. That year we elected two delegates to the General Conference; viz., William Roberts and Thomas H. Pearne. The General Conference met in Indianapolis, the first time it had ever met so far

West. The session was a somewhat exciting and contentious one. The great issue dividing the Conference was the rule on slavery, which it was thought should be made stronger; and the presiding eldership, which it was claimed should be abolished. The Conference was conservative, and neither of the objects sought by the Abolitionists on the one hand, and the reformers of the polity of Methodism, prevailed. In discussing the slavery question, a somewhat amusing episode occurred. Dr. James Floy and Dr. John McClintock debated in Shakespearean phrase, one of them remarking, in the language of Antony in his oration:

> "My heart is in the coffin there with Cæsar,
> And I must pause till it come back to me."

The other responded:

> "Let all the ends thou aim'st at be thy country's,
> Thy God's, and truth's."

> "To thine own self be true;
> And it must follow as the night the day,
> Thou canst not then be false to any man."

Bishop Morris, who was presiding, said, "Brethren, let us turn our attention from William Shakespeare to the Methodist Discipline."

In discussing the presiding elder question, one of the speakers, Barnes M. Hall, of the Troy Conference, a man of splendid presence and of considerable ability as a speaker, made a statement, which was unguarded and doubtless unwise, to the effect that he had successively filled the office of presiding elder in the Troy Conference on two of the best districts in the Conference. In his judgment, and in the judgment of some of the best ministers and laymen, while he had probably filled it as well as any of his predecessors, neither he nor they believed that as a presiding elder he had earned the salt in his porridge. I reached over to Peter Cartwright, and said to him, "I wish you would shoot him between wind and water, for he has laid himself open, and he can be punctured." Cartwright obtained the floor, and remarked that he had been presiding elder continuously for thirty-six years, and had known all the bishops of Methodism from Asbury down, yet he thought the Episcopal Committee should go for the bishops who appointed Brother Hall to districts for eight successive years; who, in his own opinion, and in the opinion of the best ministers and laymen and ministers in the districts he served, had not earned the salt in his mush. Mr. Hall arose to a question of privilege. Dr. Cartwright had misrepresented him; he had said nothing about "mush;" he spoke of porridge. Dr. Cartwright said he had not misrepresented him at all. In his country it was called porridge; but in Cartwright's the same thing was called mush.

I met Bishop Morris in one of the lobbies of the State House, in which the General Conference was held, on the last night of the Conference—a very hot night in June. the 8th—and asked him if he would visit Oregon during the ensuing quadrennium. He said, "No; would n't I cut a fine figure riding over the hills of Oregon on a mule?" When it is remembered that Bishop Morris was immensely corpulent, his reply will be better understood. Up to that session of the General Conference the statistics of the Methodist Episcopal Church had been limited to but few items. Upon my procurement, the range of the statistics was made to include baptisms, deaths, ministerial support, and the value of Church property.

In 1854 it was determined by the preachers and laymen of Oregon to issue a weekly religious newspaper, to be controlled by a joint stock company. T. H. Pearne was elected editor, and he was directed to procure an office and a six months' supply of paper. But as this had to be shipped by sailing vessel around Cape Horn, it was long in coming. The name *Pacific Christian Advocate* was finally adopted on the motion of Alvin F. Waller, one of the veterans of the Conference. The first number was issued September 5, 1855. On September 5, 1895, the paper celebrated its fortieth anniversary. The issue of that date bears a halftone likeness of myself and successors, Benson, Dillon, Acton, H. K. Hines, W. S. Harrington, and the present incumbent, A. N. Fisher, D. D. At the request of the editor, I addressed the following to the paper, which appeared in its issue of the date last given:

SEPTEMBER 5, 1855—SEPTEMBER 5, 1895.

Between these dates four decades have rolled their events into history. A generation has come and gone. The Northwest has developed into populous, magnificent States. Slavery has gone down; rebellion has been suppressed by a long, bloody Civil War. The world has advanced. The kingdom of Christ has been widely extended. The world has been approaching its glorious destiny of truth and righteousness. The end draweth nigh.

How the flying years have sped after one another adown the swiftly-receding past! How long, and yet how short, seems the term of forty years since the *Pacific Christian Advocate* was launched in Salem, Oregon! Of all who then participated in the establishment and conduct of the paper, and who were its patrons and readers, how few, comparatively, remain! How many of the early Oregonians, who were then active and potential, have since left these mortal shores for the invisible and unknown realm into which all of earth's former generations have entered! All this is the first suggestion of the occasion and the hour. Only survivors of epochs and movements can fully appreciate—if indeed they can—the great change of actors and agents which forty years make. In a new and forming period these changes are all the more impressive. They stand out very vividly and boldly in the receding perspective.

THE CHIEF ACTORS.

In the Oregon Methodist circles of that period, that were active and effective, a few persons stand out prominently in my memory. Foremost and commanding, was James H. Wilbur, the vigorous, self-sacrificing, laborious, popular, and useful man, because he was so manly and noble. William Roberts, the accomplished, gentlemanly minister and superintendent of the mission; Alvan F. Waller, staid, sedate, sensible, good; J. L. Parrish, genial, practical, and of strong personality; David Leslie, the patriarch of the early comers, kindly, thoughtful, devout;

Nehemiah Doane, retiring, unobtrusive; Luther T. Woodward; John Flinn, with his great, Irish soul, full of sympathy and love; Francis S. Hoyt, resourceful, meditative, lovable, president of the Willamette University; Dr. Wilson, one of the earliest of the Oregon missionaries; Isaac Dillon, scholarly, cheerful; Gustavus, Joseph, and Harvey K. Hines, the strong, brave trio; William Helm, an earnest, consecrated man. And of laymen, George Abernethy, ex-governor; Alexander Abernethy, his brother; Alanson Beers; George Holman and his noble wife; James R. Robb; Charles Craft; Hamilton Campbell. Others there were: C. S. Kingsley, John McKinney, Enoch, Joseph, and Abram Garrison, Fabritus Smith, C. Alderson, S. Matthews, J. F. Devore, and others; some of whom may yet be living. Of the thirty-one named, I can recall but nine who yet remain. All of those named were persons of great energy and influence, who left their impress upon the new State. So many of them have gone to their silent rest,—

> "Time, like an ever-rolling stream,
>   Bears all its sons away;
>   They fly, forgotten, as a dream
>   Dies at the opening day."

I forbear this line of somber reminiscences.

ORIGIN OF THE PACIFIC CHRISTIAN ADVOCATE.

In 1854, after repeated talks on the urgent need there was for a religious paper as the organ of Oregon Methodism, the purpose ripened into plans. It was determined to organize a joint stock company to establish and issue a religious weekly in Oregon. It was estimated to cost some three thousand or four thousand dollars to purchase an office and a six months' supply of paper. Articles of agreement were prepared. George and Alexander Abernethy, James R. Robb, Beers, Holman, Kingsley, Waller, Wilbur, Parrish, Pearne, Hines, and perhaps one or two others, subscribed the necessary amounts. I wrote to Francis Hall, Esquire, a relative of mine, who was then the publisher and proprietor of the New York *Commercial Advertiser*, to purchase and forward to us the necessary outfit, remitting to him the funds required. They were nearly six months in coming around Cape Horn to Oregon.

THE NAME OF THE PAPER.

We had considerable study and care in agreeing upon a name for the new paper proposed. The Methodists of California had already projected and started a paper called the *California Christian Advocate*. The California Congregationalists were issuing *The Pacific*. The Southern Methodists of California had started a paper, called, as I now remember, rather indistinctly, the *Pacific Methodist*. The *Oregon Christian Advocate* was suggested, but rejected as being too local and narrow. The *North Pacific Herald* was proposed, but rejected as being entirely too long. At last the *Pacific Christian Advocate* was suggested and adopted. Forty years of history have vindicated the wisdom of the name selected.

PLACE OF PUBLICATION.

The paper was first published in Salem. The office stood back from the river in the sparsely-settled part of the town. The building selected was small, inconvenient, unsuitable; but it seemed to be the only place to be obtained. It was a humble, unostentatious beginning. After a few months the paper was removed to Portland, where it should have gone from the first.

THE FIRST ISSUE.

The first number of the paper was badly printed. The impression was dim, indistinct, and blurred. The ink was not evenly distributed by the roller upon the form. It was difficult to read. The general appearance was unpleasant and unsatisfactory. To me it was especially disappointing, as, also, it was to most of the friends of the enterprise. The selected and contributed articles were of fair quality. These defects were early remedied and soon forgotten in the improved issues which were sent out not long after. The first editorial, or leading article, filled about a column and a quarter or a column and a third of the old style—four pages, blanket sheet. Its subject was an outline of the scope and purposes of the new weekly journal.

CIRCULATION, SALARY OF EDITOR, ETC.

The circulation of the *Pacific Christian Advocate* was at first rather small. It slowly increased, until, in the first year, it had grown to eighteen hundred or two thousand. Many subscribed for additional copies to the one for their own use, and sent them back to the States to relatives on the Atlantic board. Some subscribed and paid for three or four copies to send East, to assist in building up and sustaining the paper. It always had many good friends, who nobly stood by it. The expenses of publishing the paper were so large, and its income was so limited, that we were compelled to use the strictest economy. The editor's salary for several years was seven hundred dollars a year. For this small sum he was obliged to do the labor of two or three persons. His duties were various, including a somewhat wide range. He kept all the books for subscriptions and advertising; he mailed all the papers sent out; he collected all the accounts, and paid all the expenses of the publication; he was publisher, bookkeeper, proof-reader, editor, and general choreboy. For all this overwork and drudgery there was never any extra pay nor specific remuneration. It was often impossible to pay the printers and meet current expenses without borrowing money. This I often did, sometimes carrying a debt of several hundred dollars. As I recall those early times, and the buffet and struggle through which we came, I am surprised that we succeeded as well as we did.

EVOLUTION.

The joint stock company fell through because of the non-payment of subscriptions. I was soon the sole proprietor of the plant, which had cost three thousand five hundred dollars. I had to borrow money to pay the purchase bills and current expenses.

In May, 1856, I was a delegate to the General Conference which met in Indianapolis. William Roberts was my co-delegate. The paper was edited in my absence by Rev. Dr. Hoyt, then president of Willamette University. The Conference bought the plant, and instructed the New York book agents to continue the publication. I was elected editor. In 1860 I was re-elected. In 1864 I declined a re-election.

MISSION AND HISTORY OF THE PAPER.

The paper has fulfilled a high and important mission. When the Constitution of the State was formed and adopted, the paper made itself felt in favor of Oregon as a free State. There was a strong effort made to adopt a slavery clause. The presence of a large part of the population of Oregon as immigrants from slaveholding States rendered it strongly probable that the slavery schedule would be adopted. The paper advocated a free State, and it opposed other objectionable features during the formation of the constitution, so that its mission in that direction was vitally important. Then, when secession was rife, and the Breckenridge and Lane faction of the Democratic party tried to swing California and Oregon into the secession movement, the editor of the *Pacific Advocate* rung the bell loudly for the Union cause, and against secession, adding to his editorials on this behalf his personal influence in the pulpit and on the rostrum for the Union.

The paper has been an important factor in promoting the growth, stability, and usefulness of the Methodist Episcopal Church in Oregon and Washington and Idaho States. It has most amply repaid all it has cost in its effective influence in conserving and furthering the cause of truth and righteousness.

SUCCESSORS.

The honored men who have succeeded me in the conduct of the paper have deserved well of the Church, not only on the Pacific Coast, but also throughout the connection. Noble men, able men, God-honoring men, I love and admire them, and I pray for them every day. I wish and I predict for the *Pacific Christian Advocate* a very glorious future, grander and higher than its past.

THE LATE DWIGHT WILLIAMS.

In the anniversary issue of the *Pacific Christian Advocate* for its fortieth year, the first article on the first page is a hymn written by this modern poet of Methodism, entitled, "Looking Backward." In my first station, after my admission on trial into the Oneida Conference in 1839, as I have elsewhere shown, fifty-nine years ago. Dwight Williams and his saintly mother became members of my charge. He was somewhat younger than I; but our fellowship was very sweet. When my father, some years after my first pastorate in Madison, became pastor there, he found Dwight Williams, then, as always, true and faithful. It was fortunate that the *Pacific Christian Advocate* could include this poetic genius to write up the occasion. He has done it nobly and well. All honor to him and to those who are staying by the stuff! They will not fail of their great reward. But to the poetic lines:

"LOOKING BACKWARD.

"Down to the vale of Long Ago,
That slumbers in the haze below,
We turn as from a mountain tower,
To feel the rapture of an hour,
  As o'er the spaces measured
  With trophies we have treasured,
We mark the iron path of power;
Where rugged toil and bold design,
With hero faith and love benign,
Have led us to this outlook wide
With far-off visions beautified.

Four slow decades—a tale enscrolled,
And by ten thousand voices told,
Enversed in songs of liberty,
Inscribed on temples of the free—
  Romantic years of story,
  And new found fields of glory,
The preludes grand of what shall be;
For ah, the Prince of Peace leaves not
The world beset with evil plot;
Yes, we have seen his charioteers
Along the valley of the years.

Is He not here the 'Light of men,'
To diamond-point the living pen
That writes of Him and his great peace,
Till it shall run with no surcease?
  Not chariots and horses,
  We harness swifter forces;
For evil, too, with dread increase,
Rides sumptuously on paths of power,
Or sits defiant in his tower.
We ride as swiftly, and our star
Leads on to triumph fields afar.

What means it that our King and Lord
Came not to conquer by the sword?
Could he take up so mean a thing
Whose orders take the lightning's wing,
  Whose chariots go with wonder
  From chambers of the thunder
While angel legions he could bring?
Ah no! he calleth heroes of his own
Invincible in him alone!
Look down and see the archways grand,
As on the path of years they stand.

.   .   .   .

All praise to thee, thou lowly One,
Once here, now on thy star-gemmed throne;
King of the present, King of the past,
Lord of the ages, First and Last.
  The vision is before us,
  Thy beauty shineth o'er us;
All power and love are thine, thou hast
The golden scepter evermore;
No boast of ours; thee we adore,
And bless thee as we look below,
Down to the vale of Long Ago."

CHAPTER XIV.

IN 1862, I think, Bishop Simpson made his last visit to Oregon, during my stay there. Three things stand out in my memory in connection with that visit. One was, the bishop's sermon at the Conference, and his address to the candidates for admission into the traveling connection. A second was, his address on the state of the country to an immense week-night audience in Portland, Oregon. The demonstrations were not equal to what I witnessed in Washington three years later, as already described. Nor yet was it equal to what tradition describes as to his discourse at Chillicothe, on occasion of the reunion of the Ohio and Cincinnati Conferences. Yet the effort was recognized by those present as one of the finest and most effectively eloquent of addresses ever heard. The third was, a six or seven days' ride from Portland, Oregon, in my buggy, with Bishop Simpson, to Yreka, California. We usually drove forty or fifty miles in each day. The weather was charming. No rain fell during the whole trip. My two horses carried us the day's trip usually by the middle of the afternoon. A messenger was sent out to invite in the neighbors to a religious meeting. The bishop would give us a sweet, unpretentious fireside, or sitting-room, talk on some previous topic, and the subdued and subduing influence of those meetings I can never forget.

The bishop was in the spirit of genial and blessed fellowship. The people were often moved to tears, and sometimes to shouts, by his kindly and stirring words. I never enjoyed a man's conversation and spirit more than his on that occasion. We never were without interesting and profitable topics, and never was a person more able nor more willing than he to give out his views and his kindly fellowship to his traveling companion. The return trip was beguiled of its loneliness by the memory of the drive from Portland to California. He was always welcomed and hospitably treated where we stopped. I am sure that in all the families where we stopped that visit will be remembered in years to come by those who entertained us. I was led to compare that drive with those which Bishop Asbury and his traveling companion made all over this continent a hundred years ago and later. The social influence of the early ministers in these fireside occasions was one of its most prolific of blessings.

The *Pacific Christian Advocate* started out with a subscription-list of about fourteen hundred. But after a few months, it was found that the paper could be much better issued in Portland; and it was removed there. Its circulation and advertising business greatly increased after its removal. In 1856 the General Conference ordered the purchase of the outfit, and elected T. H. Pearne the editor. In 1860 he was re-elected; but in 1864 he declined a re-election. His salary was fixed at seven hundred dollars, and for this allowance he edited and published and mailed the paper with his own hands for four years. This sum was increased later to one thousand dollars. The paper became a very important factor in promoting the interests of Methodism in its work in Oregon. With varying measures of success, the enterprise has been maintained for forty-three years. It is still a vigorous and potent agency for truth and righteousness in that most interesting and growing field.

The action taken as to the *Pacific Christian Advocate* was as follows, viz.:

Resolved, 1, That the Book Agents at New York be directed to establish a Book Depository, and publish a weekly paper in Oregon Territory.

Resolved, 2, That we advise the Book Agents at New York to purchase, at a cost not exceeding three thousand five hundred dollars, the publishing office already established, and continue the publication of the *Pacific Christian Advocate*.

Resolved, 3, That the Oregon Conference be directed to appoint a Publishing Committee of five, who shall have power to fix the salary of the editor of the *Pacific Christian Advocate*, audit his accounts, and have a general oversight of his editorial conduct, and make an annual report of the same to the Oregon Conference and to the Book Agents at New York.

The same General Conference provided, also, for a Committee on Appeals, to have the handling and decision of appeals. A special committee of not less than fifteen of the members of the General

Conference was also provided for, and their duties and powers are thus defined:

The General Conference may try appeals from members of Annual Conferences who may have been censured, suspended, expelled, or located, without their consent, by a committee of not less than fifteen of its members, nor more than one member from each delegation, who, in the presence of a bishop presiding, and one or more of the secretaries of the Conference keeping a faithful record of all the proceedings had, shall have full power to hear and determine the case, subject to the rules and regulations which govern the said Conference in such proceedings; and the records made, and the papers submitted, in such trial, shall be presented to the Conference, and be filed and preserved with the papers of that body.

Two years later I was appointed by the Oregon Conference to defend its action in the case of one of its members, who had been convicted of traducing the character of one of his fellow-members, and subjected to a reprimand from Bishop Simpson, who presided in the Conference of 1862, and which we were informed had been appealed to the General Conference of 1864. I was a delegate that year in connection with James H. Wilbur, who was employed by the appellant to conduct his case. When the case was called, I made a motion before the court that the appeal should not be entertained, for the following reasons: The appellant had forfeited his right to that appeal (1) by locating from the Oregon Conference, and (2) by his readmission into the Baltimore Conference. Bishop E. S. Janes decided that every traveling minister had the right of appeal, and that my motion was therefore out of order, and it could not be entertained by him. From his decision I appealed, and stated the grounds of my appeal, as follows: The Court of Appeals must take into account the conditions of this case, and must determine, before admitting an appeal, whether the possible results of the appeal would be practicable. For example, suppose the appellant, after locating, had remained a local preacher; or, suppose he had then joined another Church, could the Court of Appeals, in such a case, admit his appeal? By location, he had forfeited his right to appeal; for his right to an appeal lay in his being a Methodist *traveling* preacher. But the appellant had re-joined from location the Baltimore Conference. And supposing the appeal admitted, one of three things would happen: the action appealed from might be confirmed, or reversed, or sent back for a new trial; and, in the latter case, if the case were sent back for a new trial, it would require the Oregon Conference to re-try a person who was not one of its members, but was in fact a member of another Conference. The court reversed the decision of the bishop, so sustaining my appeal.

The General Conference of 1856 greatly enlarged the statistical tables. Up to that date the statistics of our Church were limited to five items as to members, four items as to the number and value of parsonages and collections for Bible and

Tract Societies, collections for Conference claimants and for the Missionary Society.

In response to a resolution I offered, and which was referred to the Committee of Revisals, the General Conference of 1856 added the following questions of statistics, viz.: Number of deaths the past year; number of probationers; number of local preachers; number of adults baptized the past year; number of children baptized the past year. This Conference also provided for missionary bishops, limiting their jurisdiction to their mission fields, and providing that if they ceased to be missionary bishops, or should be removed from their field permanently, they should fall back into the Annual Conference of which they had been members theretofore. The Conference adjourned on the 8th of June. The following action, on motion of William Roberts, was had in reference to the representation of the Pacific Conferences in the General Mission Committee:

WHEREAS, The Conferences on the Pacific Coast are too far removed from the Atlantic States to allow of a personal representation in the General Mission Committee without involving great expense; and

WHEREAS, The domestic missionary work in these Conferences is constantly changing, and requiring modification in its general arrangement, and needs special representation in the said Missionary Committee; therefore,

Resolved, That, in the appointment of the General Missionary Committee, the bishop be directed to constitute corresponding members of the said committee for the Oregon and California Conferences, respectively, who shall have a corresponding relation to said committee, *and shall be allowed to vote by proxy in its annual meetings,* on all subjects relating to domestic missions on the Pacific Coast.

In Oregon I made myself familiar with public affairs, and I criticised somewhat freely what I conceived to be deserving of reprehension. For example, the Legislature of Oregon had projected a Sunday law, which left the subject wide open. A coach and six could have driven right through it, because of the laches it contained. I made an appointment to preach in Salem, the State capital, on a certain Sabbath evening, and to review the proposed Sunday law, which was then under consideration. I expressed myself very plainly and fearlessly on the subject, and I compared the proposed Oregon Sunday law with Sunday laws in some of the older States. The result was, the Legislature was plied with petitions and protests on the subject, until the law was amended, and Oregon took her place alongside of her sister States in a manner creditable to her good name as a young member of the United States of America. Hon. Delazon Smith, one of the first senators elected after the admission of Oregon, was a leading member of the Convention which presented the State Constitution. He was from New York. I conferred with him upon the wisdom of giving Oregon ample size. Referring to New York and Rhode Island, he and I concluded that size and population will give a State more recognition and influence in the Republic than smaller dimensions and fewer people. We both agreed in this as to size; and as to the population we believed it would come in the course of time, and he reported in favor of the present dimensions of Oregon. It is about three hundred and thirty miles east and west, by two hundred and eighty north and south, containing 94,500 square miles. The population has climbed to three hundred and seventy-five thousand. All the Pacific States have followed the example of Oregon. California has 155,000 square miles; Washington, 78,750 square miles; Idaho, 96,150 square miles; Montana, 274,400 square miles; Wyoming, 217,600 square miles; North Dakota has 100,000 square miles, and South Dakota 180,600 square miles. These States combined have an area of 1,275,600 square miles, one-third the area of the entire Republic.

During the pendency of the State Constitution and the admission of Oregon into the sisterhood of the States of the Republic, I attended all the sessions of the State Constitutional Convention, and took down in shorthand the principal discussions and enactments of the Convention, freely discussing in the columns of the *Pacific Christian Advocate* the measures proposed. Among other things, the attempt was made to have a slave Constitution for Oregon; a State the very soil of which was dedicated to freedom by a law of Congress. I vigorously opposed the movement. General Joseph Lane, our delegate in Congress, was stumping the State for re-election to Congress, and in his canvass he would put in arguments in favor of Oregon as a slave State. We defeated the slavery clause, scheduled for us to vote on, and defeated the pro-slavery measure by a majority of over three thousand votes, and the general's majority was cut down from five thousand majority to less than three thousand, as I now recall the result.

Oregon and California were settled, in large measure, by immigrants from the slave States of Missouri, Tennessee, Kentucky, Arkansas, and Texas. Hence the effort to plant slavery upon the State; and hence, also, the expectation of the fomenters of the secession movement of 1860 and 1861, that the Pacific States would join their fortunes with the proposed Confederacy. We were aware of this expectation during the election campaign of Abraham Lincoln as a Republican candidate, and the candidacy of Breckinridge and Lane of the ultra Southern wing of the Democratic party, and of Douglas and Stevens of the Free Soil wing of the Democratic party. It was probably because of this stand which I took in favor of the Free State party in Oregon, that I was sent as chairman of the delegation of Oregon in the Republican National Convention, which met at Baltimore in 1864. The Convention met where the first blood of the War of the Rebellion was shed. When the business of the Convention was advanced enough, Rev. Dr. J. McKendree Riley made the opening prayer. It was deeply affecting. He thanked the Lord that after four years of bloody war we were enabled to hold a National Convention in the city of Balti more. His tones were pathetic. The Convention stood during the prayer. Many of the members wept freely. One man in particular, of the Ohio delegation, which sat next behind us, could not refrain from sobbing and weeping violently. In the preliminaries of the Convention he had been very chatty, and withal quite too profuse in using profane words. After the prayer, and when the Convention was seated, some one challenged the sympathetic man who before had been so full of profanity, thus: "I did not know that you were so —— pious." "Well," said the other, "I do n't cry very much nor very often as a rule; but that prayer was so —— good, it just drew the juice out of me in spite of everything." He rather sobbed this out than said it. It was a singular mixture of religious emotion and profanity.

When the Convention was quite ready for its work, I arose to a question of privilege. I said: "It seems to me it should always be in order to bear good news to a body like this. Yesterday the State election in Oregon occurred. A telegram just received announces the fact that the election was a Union victory by a majority of five thousand. It is the first gun of the campaign. It shows that 'all is fair in the West.'" The news was received with vociferous cheering.

After Mr. Lincoln was nominated, for the nomination of Vice-President there was almost an even race between Senator Daniel S. Dickinson, of New York, and Andrew Johnson. Just before adjournment the evening before, Parson Brownlow made a speech, in which he named his old-time Democratic opponent, Andrew Johnson. He suggested that the Convention should nominate him for the reasons: 1. He is a true Union man; 2. It will enhearten the Union men of the South; 3. It will make the rebels mad. Before the chair announced the result of the vote for Vice-President, I said to our delegation, who had voted for Schuyler Colfax, "If we change our vote to Johnson or to Dickinson, other States will fall into line, and the man we vote for will be nominated." After a brief moment, they said, "Let us vote for Johnson." I arose, and said, "Oregon changes her vote from Schuyler Colfax to Andrew Johnson." The example was contagious. In a few minutes Johnson was nominated. I was one of a committee to inform Mr. Lincoln, orally, of his renomination. He said in reply, that there was no lack of Presidential timber when the Convention met; that there were a hundred men or more as well capable, and as deserving of the honor, as he; "but," said he, "I suppose the Convention was very much in the condition of the Irishman, who was crossing a swimming stream on a mare, with a colt following. The Irishman was unhorsed. He could not swim. The mare soon got out of his reach. He seized the tail of the colt. The load seemed too much for the colt. One on the shore cried out to the man, 'Let go the colt and take the mare's tail,' to which the Irishman replied, 'Faith, sure, and this is no time to be afther shwapping horses when I 'm in the swim.' So," said Mr. Lincoln, "the Convention probably felt that it was no time to be swapping Presidents when we were still in the midst of war."

I have referred to the stand I took in favor of Oregon as a free State. When South Carolina seceded, and State after State was falling into line and swinging out of the Union, I took a very prominent and determined position in favor of the Union. There was a large number of persons who were opposed to coercion to retain States in the Union; others were in favor of the secession of States. The politicians were afraid to strike out for the Union. I took the ground that every true man and true patriot must stand by the Union, even if it came to war. I preached a sermon in Portland on the duty of Christian loyalty, from the words of Jesus, "Render unto Cæsar the things that are Cæsar's, and unto God the things that are God's." An immense crowd heard it. The house was crowded, and hundreds could not get in; but they thronged the doors and windows. One man, a neighbor and an old man of seventy, climbed out over the back seat, and went out swearing that he would like to hang that —— black Republican to the first lamp-post. He had held Federal offices nearly all his lifetime. I made the *Advocate* ring out for the Union, and I took the stump in favor of the Union. The politicians recovered the use of their tongues when they saw the tide setting in for the flag and the Union. It was doubtless owing to my activity in this behalf that attention was turned to me as a proper person to be elected United States senator; and that induced the people to elect a majority in favor of my selection for that high office. It was a great blessing to me that the movement did not succeed. My life has been happier, and probably more useful, as a minister, than it could have been in another line.

CONTRASTS.

A beautiful prophecy in the seventy-second Psalm says: "There shall be a handful of corn in the earth upon the top of the mountains: the fruit thereof shall shake like Lebanon: and they of the city shall flourish like grass of the earth." It is pleasant to see that the season of sowing and planting in Oregon when I was there, has given place to the harvest. The handful of corn is beginning to shake like Lebanon. They of the cities are flourishing like the grass of the earth. The harvest measures of "thirty, sixty, and a hundred-fold" are being realized in that goodly field. The condition of things in Oregon is represented in the highly-figurative words of Amos ix, 13: "Behold, the days come, saith the Lord, that the plowman shall overtake the reaper, and the treader of grapes him that soweth seed." The figurative language of the Oriental Scriptures seems all too pale and weak to describe, adequately, the contrasts of the present days with those in which forty-five years ago I wrought for Jesus in the distant Occident.

The population then was 13,294; now it is 1,200,000. Then there was only one great Territory; now there are eight populous, thrifty States. Then Methodism was small. There were, in 1851,

15 ministers; in 1897, 250; an increase of 166.7 per cent. Churches and halls in 1851, 4; in 1897, 685; an increase of 1712.6 per cent. Value of Church property in 1851, $3,000; in 1897, $2,061,185; an increase of 687.5 per cent. Church members in 1851, 750; in 1897, 40,098; an increase of 534.6 per cent.

In 1851, Oregon was a comparative solitude. It is now populous, having all the arts and elegancies of an advanced civilization. The exports of Oregon, Washington, and Idaho amount to $32,000,000. The agricultural, mineral, and timber products of these three States amount to $40,000,000. In those three States there are twelve hundred miles of railroad.

It is something to have contributed to such stupendous material and spiritual results. A man who devoted the most vigorous and earnest years of his life to aid in bringing about such great harvests of benefaction to man, and such revenues of glory to God, may imitate the self-congratulations of Paul, that he has not run in vain, nor labored in vain, nor spent his strength for naught. Those material and statistical facts may be measured and tabulated. Humanity has no logarithms large enough to compute spiritual results. "He who reapeth receiveth wages, and gathereth fruit unto life eternal." Who can fathom eternity? Who can compute the fadeless glory of the immortal state?

CHAPTER XV.

ON April 1, 1864, we started for the General Conference, which met that year in Philadelphia. We went first to California; thence by overland stage we proceeded to the Missouri River, and from there by rail to Philadelphia, which was reached on the fifth day of the session. Readers will enjoy reading these hurried letters to the *Pacific Christian Advocate*, headings and dates just as they were published at the time:

AN EDITOR'S JOTTINGS.—I.

OCEAN STEAMSHIP PACIFIC, *April 5, 1864*.

DEAR ADVOCATE,—By a good run, we reached Astoria a little after midnight of the 2d inst. At 8 o'clock A. M., crossed the bar, which was quite smooth. Before we had been out an hour, we encountered a very severe southeaster. It was the most so of any the Captain had encountered during the last winter, and it lasted until Monday noon. This hindered us not a little. After being out some thirty hours from the bar, we had made less than a hundred miles. Has the reader ever been on shipboard during a gale at sea? If he has, he can appreciate our condition. The howling of the storm among the shrouds, and the rushing waves, how hungry they look! Waves before us; waves behind us; waves to right of us; waves to left of us; rushing, crashing, foaming, seething waves. Long waves and short waves, reguar and irregular; waves gentle and waves violent. "They that go down to the sea in ships, that do business in great waters, these see the works of the Lord, and his wonders in the deep."

But that our good ship takes the sea well and has but a light cargo, our condition would be critical. But she rides the waves like a duck, and, in the teeth of a bitter head-gale, she makes progress.

There are about twenty passengers in the cabin, and a like number forward. Captain Burns is an admirable seaman, watchful, capable, and attentive, and we feel that if disaster should befall us, it would be through no fault of his.

The ship's officers and hands are well-trained and at their posts. The steward's department is in complete order, both as to quality of food, neatness, and attention. Many of the passengers are suffering much from sea-sickness; but, as the storm has now abated, we shall soon see them convalescent.

On board we have Mr. Pierson and family, and Mr. W. S. Hussey and family, all except Mr. Pierson on their way East. We hope to reach San Francisco to-morrow evening, when, if time allows, I shall add something more to this brief line.

RIVER STEAMER YOSEMITE, *April 7, 1864.*

DEAR ADVOCATE,—We arrived at San Francisco at 5.30 o'clock P. M. of yesterday. The flags at the forts and the Presidio were at half-mast on account of the death of Major Ringgold, paymaster United States army. San Francisco has grown almost beyond my knowledge since 1859, when I last saw it. The North Beach has very much changed in five years, being now densely built up. But the principal change is in the southeastern part of the city, where palatial residences and fine churches, and schools and asylums, give evidence of solid, substantial improvement. Our stay in the city was so brief as to give little opportunity for sight-seeing; but by the kindness of N. P. Perrine, formerly of Portland, I was enabled to see the different parts of this New York of the Pacific. Among other places, we, of course, visited the office of the *California Christian Advocate* and Methodist Book Depository. Brother Thomas, the editor, and Brother McElroy, the agent, greeted us cordially. The depository is a success, and our California brethren are entitled to credit for their far-sightedness and enterprise.

"Mine host" of the International, Brother Weygant, is sharing a fair amount of patronage. His present hotel is much more commodious, and convenient than the Tremont House, which he formerly kept.

Brother Blain, the pastor of the Howard Street charge, has erected a very fine church edifice, and is sharing a good degree of prosperity. His congregation is as large as that of any Protestant Church in the city, and a very interesting work of revival is in progress.

With Dr. Wyeth, pastor of the Powell Street Church, a pleasant acquaintance was formed. This church has been refitted and refurnished, and will be reopened next Sabbath for public worship.

The Russ House, the Masonic Temple, and other stately piles of masonry, are monuments of the enterprise and wealth of San Francisco. The work of recovering the sunken *Comanche* is said to be nearly completed. It will be some time, however, before the ironclad will be ready for use as a means of defense for this port and city. A terrific storm has been raging over the line of the telegraph, between this place and Salt Lake, stopping all communication East. To-day it is resumed.

Rev. Brethren Taylor and Lucas, from British

Columbia, are on their way East, the former overland, and the latter by sea. I hope to overhaul Brother Taylor at Virginia City, and proceed in company with him, East.

The *Yosemite*, on board which I write this, is a beautiful boat. Our number of passengers is not large, perhaps a hundred in all. Among them is a man who is peddling a pamphlet purporting to be a heavenly dispatch by spiritual telegraph. It is a singular compound of Scripture, nonsense, and humbuggery, and, from the way the peddler draws comparisons and illustrations, there is little doubt that he will sell his book, whether the buyers get the worth of their money or not.

I hope to be able to jot a brief line from Virginia City, and another from Brigham Young's country. Mr. Young, readers will observe, is described by Artemus Ward as "somewhat married." Till my next, adieu.

AN EDITOR'S JOTTINGS.—II.

STRAWBERRY, CAL., *April 9, 1864.*

DEAR ADVOCATE,—This is a singular, out-of-the-way place, and would never have figured in public had not the glittering treasures of Washoe tempted the cupidity of the great American people; nor then, except that Strawberry lies in the direct path of travel to the silver-mines of Nevada Territory. There is hope for some places in Oregon from this view of the case. The silver and gold deposits of Idaho and Southern Oregon will equal, if they do not rival, those of Nevada, and who can tell what places, that had seemed doomed to "waste their sweetness on the desert air," shall come up into importance, and yet thrill with the pulsation of active, earnest business, pursued by theorizing multitudes?

Our route from Sacramento was by rail to Folsom, twenty-two miles. Hence we came by Concord coaches to Placerville, twenty-seven miles. Three coaches, each drawn by six horses, were crowded with passengers, carrying, in all, some thirty persons. From Placerville to this place, forty-seven miles, mud-wagons supersede the coaches, and the travel is slower, on account of the mud and the greater unevenness of the road.

California has put on her holiday attire. Verdure and beauty smile from every hillside and valley. The rains have come and gladdened the land, giving good promise of "seed to the sower and bread to the eater." Flour speculators who have counted on a drought in California, and a high price of breadstuffs, may as well abandon their delusive hopes; for the wheat-crop in California, while it may fall short of the usual yield, will yet be a fair one.

We spent a pleasant evening with Rev. T. S. Dunn, from whom we learned that his Sunday-school numbered some one hundred scholars, his Church eighty members, and his ordinary congregation from two hundred and fifty to four hundred persons. The church edifice is large and eligibly situated. It is of brick, and has been costly. Unfortunately, a debt of seven thousand dollars presses the trustees.

The mail is about to close, and this epistle must be abruptly ended. Of the route to Strawberry and Virginia City remark must be deferred until my next.

STRAWBERRY VALLEY, *April 9, 1864*.

. . . My last, from this place, was quite too brief and desultory. In this it is proposed to speak more in detail. The route from Placerville to Strawberry Valley is very mountainous, and the scenery of the grandest. We were twelve hours in making it, the roads being much injured by the late storms. We are now within seven miles of the summit of the Sierra Nevada Mountains, and are six thousand seven hundred feet above the level of the sea. We pass, to-morrow morning, a rocky point some ten thousand feet above the sea-level.

Among our passengers are Professor Whitney, well known as a geologist, and now engaged in making a survey of the State of California, as State geologist, and Professor King, of New York, also a geologist. I learn from the former that Mount Shasta is ascertained to be fourteen thousand four hundred and forty feet in height. It is claimed by some Californians that Shasta is higher than Mount Hood. If Shasta overtops her Oregon sister, Mount Hood is not as high as has been supposed. We are in the midst of winter scenes. The snow on the summit is nearly six feet deep, owing to the recent heavy fall of snow. Had the ground been frozen when it fell, it is supposed the snow would have been ten feet deep. Sleighs are at the door to carry us eleven miles over the snow-belts; the air without is sharp and bracing, and freezing; within, a blazing fire on the hearth reminds one of the good old New York winters. The hotel, kept by Crosby & Swift, is large and well furnished for the place, and yet they have not accommodations for their numerous guests. Last night there were over a hundred. To-night there are nearly as many.

At four and a half o'clock to-morrow the stage leaves for Virginia City, which will be reached, it is expected, by a little after noon.

The silver mines of Washoe are yielding more largely of late than usual, and the excitement is correspondingly increased. Numbers are rushing there from all parts of California. Many of them will return to their homes poorer and sadder than they were when leaving. Till you receive a line from Virginia City, adieu.

EDITORIAL LETTER—TRAVEL ON THE PLAINS.—III.

VIRGINIA CITY, N. T., *April 11, 1864.*

DEAR ADVOCATE,—This morning we are off at six and a half o'clock for Reese River; but, before starting, a few moments are snatched to pen the incidents up to the present, and record such general facts and reflections as they may suggest. From Strawberry Valley to Virginia City the route passes over the summit of the Sierras, through the valley of Lake Tahoe, and thence over mountain ranges to Carson Valley. Crossing the valley in a southeastern direction, and traversing the foothills of the mountains skirting on the east, you ascend a spur of the loftiest peak, Mount Davidson, and pass, in succession, Silver City, Gold Mountain, and last, but not least, Virginia City, probably about the busiest place, according to its population, on the continent, if not in the world.

The sleigh-ride was anything but pleasant. The snow was so deep and the road so poorly beaten that progress was slow and somewhat difficult. To add to our trouble, we were meeting or overtaking pack-trains and vehicles, and to get past them was no trivial matter, detaining us vexatiously. In one instance mula would not give road, and would not travel faster than a walk, and several passengers and the driver had, at last, literally to put him out of the way; but not until he had fallen with his heavy pack. In another, meeting a carriage with a family, all hands were compelled to take hold and lift the carriage out of the road, and afterwards, lift it back again.

The road through the valley of the lake, and from there to this point, is, nearly all the distance, graded, and is an excellent one, as may be inferred when it is stated that the drive over it is, in good weather, at the rate of from six to ten miles an hour. A good story is told of Horace Greeley in connection with this route. He suggested to Monk, the driver, that he wanted to be in Placerville at a given hour. Over the mountains, along dizzy slopes, where craggy peaks majestically frowned five hundred feet above the road, and frightful declivities yawned as many feet below, Monk drove his noble six-horse team in dashing, furious style, until the old philosopher became slightly nervous, and he suggested to our Jehu not to drive so fast; that, if they should be a little late, he would rather be late than to run such hazards. Monk would whip up his horses afresh, and tell his agitated rider, "Hold on to your seat, Horace, and we shall get through all right."

Tahoe is the Indian name for the lake along which we passed. It denotes clear water. The lake is nestled on the summit of the Sierras, and, in the morning sunbeams, surrounded by snowclad peaks, it glistened before us like a bright setting in a coronal of beauty. The lake is twenty-two miles long, by about eleven or twelve wide, and the water is almost transparently clear. Carson Valley, how shall it be described? Viewed from the heights adown which we drove to reach it, the absence of timber or verdure, and the jagged and ruptured mountains surrounding it, made it appear grand; but it was the grandeur of desolation. It was awful. The Carson River is a small stream, fed by mountain lakes, and which evaporates some seventy-five or a hundred miles below. The valley is in places from six to ten miles wide, and in others from half a mile to a mile. Its length is about seventy-five miles. A couple of miles from Carson City is a hot spring, and the penitentiary incloses it; whether to douse the refractory, or scour them from vice and vermin, does not appear. Virginia City, about a thousand feet above the valley, is six thousand two hundred feet above the sea-level. It lies southeast by northwest. Virginia City has sixteen thousand inhabitants, and numerous quartz-mills and various mining operations in this part of the country make these once dreary solitudes vocal with the songs of industry and the hum of business. The discoverer of these mines was a man named Finney, from Virginia, who went by the name of Old Virginia, and hence the name of the city. It is stated that he sold the Ophir or the Gould and Curry claim since, and now worth millions, for a mustang pony and a bottle of whisky. He afterwards became the owner, by discovery, of the Gold Mountain mines, and, as he had fallen in debt for a winter's washing, he commuted his account with the washerwoman by giving her ten feet of his last found claim. This she retains, and it is said it could be cashed for ten thousand dollars a foot. Poor Old Virginia died comparatively poor and prematurely. He parted with his last claim, as he had the first, for a mere song, and lost his life by mounting a spiking pony, which threw him upon his head, inflicting a fatal wound. A jolly fellow, who had come into possession of fifty thousand or one hundred thousand dollars by the sale of "feet," went and had a long and heavy spree over his good fortune. He was a passenger with us from Placerville to Strawberry Valley, and, stepping from the stage while it was in motion, his head being unbalanced by his too free indulgence, he rolled down the mountain side some two hundred or three hundred feet, and brought up against a tree, nearly butting his life out. Poor Charley! the fate of Old Virginia seems to have little warning for him.

Only five years have passed since these Washoe siver-mines were fairly discovered, and now they are adding many millions yearly to the bullion of the world. When these facts are considered, the silver-mines of Owyhee and Bannock and Santiam give promise of a brilliant and not distant future for our part of the world.

Brother Anthony, the Methodist pastor here, has great prosperity. A spirit of revival prevails, and his people cordially and well sustain him. A tasteful, brick church edifice, worth some forty-five thousand dollars, contains a weekly congregation of from two hundred and fifty to four hundred. His membership, all included, is one hundred and fifty. A funded debt of twelve thousand dollars rests upon the property, the interest upon which is paid from the rent of pews. The writer preached last evening to a large and attentive audience. Off now for Salt Lake, from which place another line may be expected.

AN EDITOR'S JOURNEYINGS.—IV.

GREAT SALT LAKE CITY, U. T., *April 16, 1864.*

DEAR ADVOCATE,—At the risk of being tedious and repetitious, attention is again called to the silver-mining operations in this part of the world. Silver ledges have been discovered in the vicinity of Virginia City, and also on Reese River one hundred and eighty miles east, on the Humboldt, and even in the mountain ranges which border on Utah Territory. To-day I examined specimens of silver and lead ore taken from mines only twenty miles from this city.

During my stay in Virginia City I visited the far-famed Gould and Curry mines and their silver milling works. Entering by a shaft at the top, a descent of four hundred feet was made, and the various tunnels, penetrating the mountain seven hundred feet, were traversed. As fast as excavations are made, solid frameworks are constructed to support the pressure of the earth from above.

The milling works of the company are of the finest. They cost about one million dollars. The engine they now have, and which drives their machinery, is of one hundred and fifty horse-power. Another is being erected, the present one being unequal to their demand. The new one is to be of two hundred and sixty horse-power. This mill has a battery of forty stamps, and runs five large and five smaller amalgamators, besides grinding their quartz preparatory to amalgamation. By the kindness of Mr. Frank Parke, the superintendent of the amalgamation and refining departments, the whole process of reducing the ore to bullion was explained, and it is here repeated, for the information of those curious in such matters.

The quartz is first subjected to the action of batteries of stamps, which pulverize it fine. It is then mixed with certain proportions of common salt, copperas, and blue vitriol and quicksilver. When thoroughly amalgamated, the sand is sluiced off, and the amalgam is then subjected to pressure, to strain off the quicksilver, and the remaining quicksilver is separated from the mass by retorting.

The metal, including gold and silver, is melted down into bricks, assayed and stamped, and sent to England to be again refined and the gold separated from the silver, our people not having yet acquired the art of this last process. When it is remembered that the silver-mines and mills already working yield some two million dollars a month, and that new discoveries are constantly being made, this branch of enterprise, it is seen, will become increasingly important.

Our route from Virginia City to this place presented a field of observation and thought wholly new. Mountains, valleys, and plains are the order of successive days of travel, with the invariable accompaniment of sage, prickly pear, and alkali-beds.

Large fields of common salt are being discovered, which must be of exceeding value in this remote inland country. There is an almost total absence of timber, except sage-brush and a variety of stunted cedar. Water, too, is very scarce, and the Overland Mail Company have to transport water a distance of twenty or thirty miles. Carson, Truckee, Reese, and Humboldt Rivers, receiving the melted snows of the Sierras, bear them down the desert only a few miles, when they are evaporated, and the river bed is dry.

It must not be omitted to speak of the total absence of animal life. For six hundred miles, only one prairie-hen, one hare, and a few ravens were seen. Unbroken silence wraps the desert in profound gloom. Fort Crittenden, the last point of importance passed before reaching Salt Lake, is distant from this city forty miles. Here, as at Austin, on Reese River, the buildings are of adobes, a sun-dried brick, which, as it seldom rains here, answer a good purpose. General Johnston caused some two hundred or three hundred of these to be erected here while quartered in Utah.

The prospect of reaching Philadelphia by the opening of Conference is clouded by two facts: first, the prevalence of an unusual snowstorm in the mountains, blockading the roads; and secondly, the news which reaches us by telegraph, of a brush between the Cheyennes and the Colorado troops on the stage road, eighty miles east from Denver. But I hope, in spite of these difficulties, to reach the Conference during its first week. Of Salt Lake, notice will be made in my next.

The following telegram, from the editor to his wife, has been received since our last:

ATCHISON, K. T., *May 2, 1864*.

"Delayed—weary—well. In Philadelphia, Thursday. No interruption from Indians."

AN EDITOR IN THE DESERT.—V.

ROCK POINT, 220 MILES EAST
GREAT SALT LAKE, *April 20, 1864.*

Utah Territory embraces many features which have interest for the public. Our route from Austin to Great Salt Lake lay through an unpeopled solitude, the path being literally strewed with the carcasses of animals, and lined with the graves of emigrants. Of course we saw nothing of the southern part of the Territory, which is said to be fertile and considerably settled by Mormons. From the opportunities I had of observing Mormonism—and they were rather limited—the conclusion is reached that, in point of political economy, it is a failure. The lands susceptible of husbandry are not well tilled, and, while many of the people may be industrious and some of them thrifty, they are generally poor, squalid, ignorant, and degraded. They consist, in large part, of foreigners: English, Welsh, Scotch, Norwegians, and Danes. The polygamy does not tend to social order and comfort, but the reverse. At one place where we stopped, the landlord has two wives, who have not spoken to each other since the second wife was installed. They live in separate houses, within a stone's-throw of each other; and if they do not throw stones at one another, there is no more intercourse between them than between a Turk and a Christian. The husband spends a week with one, and then a week with the other. In another place where we dined, the Mormon bishop, our host, has three wives, *sisters*, and New Hampshire women. They did not appear happy. The children of this arrangement are far from being as comely, smart, and intelligent-appearing as those outside of Mormondom. You find no books in the Mormon houses I entered, except yellow-covered literature, which the female inmates of these houses spend their time in reading. I catechised the children two or three times, and they were nearly as ignorant as horseblocks, and as stupid as unwashed papooses. It may, perhaps, be supposed that the writer is prejudiced, and that, therefore, his statements should be abated somewhat. Let it be observed that he states only what he saw and what he gathered from those who claimed to be informed, and who appeared to be truthful.

The population of Utah Territory is variously estimated at from sixty thousand to eighty thousand, and even one hundred thousand. The latter is the figure claimed by the Mormons. The first is probably nearest the truth. The capital was located, some years since, at Fillmore, one hundred and fifty miles south from Salt Lake City; but the Legislature, from year to year, persists in adjourning to Great Salt Lake City.

Governor Doty being absent from the Territory, the secretary of the Territory, Mr. Reed, is acting governor in his stead. We formed a pleasant acquaintance with him.

Great Salt Lake City lies on a declivity on the eastern slope of the valley, and about two miles east from the Great Salt Lake. The population is estimated at from eight thousand to twelve thousand. The houses are mostly built of adobe, or sun-dried bricks; they are small, unpainted, and with earthen floors, usually covered with ducking or buffalo robes. The streets are regularly laid out, and irrigated by streams running along between the sidewalks and roadways.

Take out the theater, the State-house, and a few other public buildings, Brigham Young's, and a few other private residences, the buildings of this city are small, unsightly, and uninviting.

Brigham Young's residence, tithing-house, and family schoolhouse, are inclosed within strong stone walls, some ten feet high, and the entrances are guarded by an armed sentinel. We did not see Mr. Young, but we learned that he is sixty-three years of age and in good preservation. His food is plain and his habits are regular. He eschews intemperance in the use of intoxicating liquors, and is evidently desirous of living as long as he may.

We inspected the foundations of the great Mormon temple, begun some eight or nine years ago, but not yet raised above the level of the ground around them. They are built of granite, the blocks being from three to four or six feet by a foot thick. The walls are about nine feet thick and twelve feet high. Under each basement window and doorway are inverted arches, and between the windows are erect arches. At the two east corners are circular cisterns about twelve feet in diameter by an equal depth. They are probably baptismal fonts. The building is about eighty by one hundred feet. We did not measure it. It will never be finished. Mormonism can not survive. Already it contains the elements of its own destruction. Faction and strife are at work, and, at Brigham's death, if not before, the whole system will be whelmed in a common overthrow. It is a singular and significant fact that many of the children of Mormon parents are heartily disgusted with Mormonism, and repudiate its sensual, polygamous institutions.

We recommend the American Bible Society to scatter the word of God among the people, and Christian Churches to send missionaries there, and soon Utah shall be redeemed. The Great Salt Lake is a beautiful sheet of water, one hundred and thirty miles long by from thirty to fifty wide. It is fed by the Weber and Bear Rivers, and by other less considerable streams. It is said to have no outlet. The valley of the Weber is fertile and well cultivated. Echo Cañon, through which we pass after leaving the Weber, is about twenty miles long by from half a mile to a mile and a half wide. Here, in 1857, the Mormons fortified against the forces of Uncle Sam. The ruins of their works are yet apparent. Camp Douglas is the military post, now occupied by General Conner and some two regiments of United States troops. It is about three miles from Salt Lake City. Our progress eastward is slow, of which—more anon.

EDITORIAL CORRESPONDENCE.—V

ATCHISON, KANSAS, *May 2, 1864*.

DEAR ADVOCATE,—The trip to this place from Salt Lake would have been a most pleasant one but for two or three drawbacks which greatly mar it. A full load of passengers—*i. e.*, three on a seat, making nine in all—may do for a few miles, or a few score of them, but when this *press* is kept up for one thousand one hundred and fifty miles, it becomes anything but pleasant. When, to this, are added various less discomforts, the journey hither by stage becomes decidedly tedious. If the eastern part of this line were as well constructed and as thoroughly worked as the western, the overland trip would be but an agreeable recreation. But justice to truth compels me to show a different phase of the subject. The stage-line from Salt Lake to the Missouri is badly managed. The stock is poor and slow; many of the drivers are cross and insolent; the stages (mud wagons) are contracted and inconvenient; the connections are not well made, and mails and passengers are laid over without so much as saying, "By your leave, sir." Such, at least, was our experience. At Weber River we were detained three hours; at Green River, twelve; at Rock Point, twenty-four; at Sulphur Springs, eighteen or twenty; and at Fort Halleck, fourteen hours. The reason alleged was that the crowd of passengers from the East, and a severe snow-storm which occurred about the first of April, had deranged the plans of the agents, and had rendered it impracticable to put us forward in schedule time. We, however, failed to see the force of the argument; for when we were laid over, there were animals to take us, and the roads and weather were favorable. Only for about seventy miles of the entire route were the roads in bad condition. In the Park, some fifteen miles east of Salt Lake, and along the Bitter Water Creek and over Bridger's Pass, the roads were heavy from the melting of the snows. In the pass we rode over drifts that were from four to six feet deep. The fare along the line is rather coarse and ordinary than otherwise. It consists of fried bacon and saleratus biscuit and some indifferent coffee, served up in not the most neat and inviting manner. The price for such a meal was usually one dollar. Along toward the Missouri seventy-five cents is charged, and, as you enter Nebraska and Kansas, the food improves in neatness, variety, and wholesomeness.

So far we have traversed three States and five Territories. The general description which was given of the mines and mining interests of Nevada will answer tolerably of Colorado, with this difference: Colorado is a gold-quartz mining country, the climate is more rigorous, and the water is both more abundant and wholesome.

Nebraska is a level, cold country, with a light soil, comparatively little timber, and evidently not well adapted to agriculture, owing to its altitude and want of strength of soil. Grass, however, does well, and it is probably adapted to grazing purposes. The portion of Idaho through which we passed is much the same in its general features as Nebraska.

Kansas is a rolling, open country, with little timber except along the streams. The swells are not high, but they stretch out in length like long sea-waves. The soil is of the best, especially along the Kansas River. The timber is mostly black-walnut, hickory, cottonwood, and oak. Kansas is poorly farmed. The lack of thorough husbandry is quite evident to the passing traveler. The population is estimated at from one hundred thousand to one hundred and twenty-five thousand. The people of the State are loyal, and they have given good proof of the same by furnishing sixteen white regiments, and quite three colored ones, to defend the endangered nationality and suppress the existing rebellion.

Atchison is a thriving town of about three or four thousand resident population. Its chief interest lies in its being the starting point of travel and commerce across the desert. Outfits are here made, and hence depart the emigrants and stage passengers for Colorado, Idaho, Utah, Nevada, California, Oregon, and Washington. This year the emigration westward is much larger than ever before. Some are drawn thitherward by the lure of gold, some by the love of adventure, some by a restless tendency which is chronic among many of the American people, and still others by a desire to escape the draft and evade the consequences of the rebellion in which they have participated. But whatever may be the cause, there can be no doubt that the emigration across the plains this year is immense. The whole of our route from Salt Lake was made lively by the caravans constantly met. Not a day passed in which we did not meet from thirty to two hundred wagons, and we were told that the tide of travel, by the way of Omaha and other points, is little, if any, less than by this route. Most of the emigrants are going to East Bannock and Boise, Idaho.

After reviewing the advantages and disadvantages of the several countries through which we passed, we give the preference to Oregon over any of them. Our climate, scenery, water, agricultural and mineral resources, and our commercial prospects, place Oregon far in advance of her sister Territories and States.

From the best information we could gather, the conclusion is reluctantly reached that large numbers of the present year's emigration are Copperheads and Rebel sympathizers.

I shall be three days behind time in reaching the General Conference; but not through any fault or mismanagement of mine. I started early enough to have reached Philadelphia in season, had not buffeting winds and waves, and the mis-arrangements of those whose actions I could not control, prevented. A letter may next be expected from Philadelphia.

The preceding letters, giving account of my stage journey across the Plains, leave some things unsaid which should be of record. One of these is an account of peril and escape and heroism that our ordinary life does not furnish. I learned of this in Oregon; for I have seen the lady and her children, who escaped soon after her awful experience. Then, also, I learned it on the Plains from the driver, who, when I was present, was driving on the same route where these things occurred; but not on this occasion.

A driver, two male passengers—one of them the husband of a lady and the father of her two children—were present in the stage. As the stage was ascending a narrow cañon, one of the wheel horses was shot. The driver whipped up his team, when he was shot in the breast and his left arm broken. He gave the lines over to the passenger sitting on the boot with him, and plied his horses with the whip in his right hand. The new driver was shot in the breast, and fell from the stage into the road, the wounded driver seizing the lines. Then the woman's husband, on request of the driver, crawled out through the stage window, and took the lines. Soon the husband was shot, and he fell into the boot. Then the driver called on the woman to come out and drive. The children were left in the bottom of the stage, and the mother made her way to the boot and took the reins. The Indians were distanced. The stage arrived at the station; but in what a plight! The wounded horse fell dead, the driver was dead, her husband was dead, and only she and her two children were living. The station was burned. No one was about. Just then the stage came up from the opposite direction. The woman and her children were taken in. The stage returned on the route it came. The mother and children were saved. She was a young woman, not over thirty years.

Our passengers were becoming very uneasy. We were in a section infested by bad Indians. It was in the vicinity of the tragedy just recited. The stage we should have met was ten hours late. Our five-mule team—two on the wheel, and three in the lead—were slowly and wearily making their way through heavy sand. We saw a cloud of dust a couple of miles to the right of our road. The driver seemed excited when he saw it. As if talking to himself, he said: "If that proves to be Indians, and they come to us, I will cramp this trap and the king-bolt will drop out. I will jump on the front axle and yell at the mules, and they will pull me out of it." "What do you think I'll be doing when that happens?" I said. "What will you be doing?" I answered, "I'll be putting daylight through you." The passengers inside heard the chat, and they responded, "We will put some more daylight through him." Fortunately, the alarm was unfounded. We soon met the westward bound stage. Our anxieties passed away.

CHAPTER XVI.

I DEVOTE this chapter to adventures with Indians and wild animals. Some of the incidents I personally witnessed and participated in. The others I can avouch as true. They will at least amuse, and perhaps instruct, some of my young readers.

When I first went to Oregon in 1851, it was sparsely settled. The white population in 1850 was a little above thirteen thousand. These were widely scattered through the Wallamet Valley, now called Willamette, and through the Umpqua and Rogue River Valleys. The Donation Land Law gave to every single man a half-section of land, and if a married man, a full section of land. This induced a scattered population.

Oregon abounded with game and with wild animals. In traveling over the country I frequently came upon bands of deer who were comparatively fearless, and who would remain grazing even after they had seen me. I once encountered a cougar, called also the ounce and the American lion. It was only two miles from Salem, the capital of the Territory. He was crossing a trail or cow-path, on which I was ascending a gentle acclivity. It was in an oak opening, covered with grass. He was not more than two or three rods above me when he crossed my path. After proceeding a few yards he stopped. I had never seen a cougar before, and I did not know what animal he was. I advanced upon him, and swung my lariat as if about to noose him. He refused to move. His head was down to the ground. His teeth were displayed. His eyes turned green, and glared intensely. He spit, growled, and whisked his tail furiously, as though intending to spring upon me. Fixing my eye sharply on him, I turned my horse obliquely and rode away, perhaps a half a quarter of a mile. Then I stopped and looked at him. He was still crouched where I left him, and vigorously slashing his tail. He was apparently about four or five feet long, and of a brindle-brown color. He looked like a giant cat. My feelings in that encounter with the cougar can be better imagined than described. I sweat profusely, and my hair seemed as stiff as a quill. I presume I turned pale; for I was very much excited, and probably not a little bit afraid.

I was stopping with a friend. He came in one morning, and said he had lost a fine, large, three-months' old colt by a cougar. The animal had seized the colt by the withers, carried it bodily across a meadow, jumped a high rail-fence with the colt in his jaws, and *cached* it in a hollow place in the woods, covering it over with leaves. Mr. W—— and I found the dead colt. He cut off a hind-quarter, put some strychnine into it, and hung it to the limb of a tree about two or three rods away from the cache. The cougar, in returning from a cache, makes a wide circle, and then reduces it in his encircling rounds until within jumping distance, and then he jumps upon his dead prey. This he did in the present instance, and so encountered the bait, which he seized and devoured. We found him the next morning, dead. He was eight feet six inches long from his nose to the tip of his tail. We secured the hide, which, in some measure, compensated for the loss of the colt. It is not strange that brave men will dread, and if possible avoid, a passage at arms with one of these huge monsters.

A great fright came to me from simply seeing the fresh tracks of a grizzly bear. I was riding in the Upper Willamette Valley. I lay off at noon to stop at a friend's house and spend the afternoon and night with him. He proposed a deer-hunt. We went down into a large island in the Willamette River, each bearing a rifle. On the sandy shore of the island I saw the fresh tracks of a grizzly. They were large; say, fifteen inches long and seven or eight inches wide. The bear had been clawing in the sand for a mouse-nest or a mole's-nest. His claws made tracks as large as my fingers. The trees were large, and the undergrowth was dense. The size of the trees made climbing to escape from grizzlies impossible. The undergrowth afforded concealment for the bears, and rendered surprises easy. I was terrified, and immediately told my friend I would not hunt deer in that island. My friend insisted on a further hunt. We soon entered an open. I saw a small herd of deer. Taking aim for them, my rifle shook. My companion said: "Do n't shoot; your piece is unsteady, and you will miss." He shot one of the deer, and we returned with our game. The fear was occasioned by my knowledge of the habits of the grizzly, and of the helplessness of man in an encounter with the wild beast.

John Rexford and his two manly sons were noted grizzly bear hunters. On one occasion John's brother William, a Baptist minister, and therefore not much of a hunter, was visiting at John's. All were at dinner, when they heard the hounds baying the game. Looking out, they saw the dogs chasing a she-grizzly with her cubs. The bear and cubs, with dogs in pursuit, were making for the Calapooya River, perhaps for the better chance it would give the bear and her cubs to escape. Each of the four Rexfords seized a rifle, and joined in the chase. Reaching the river bottom, they saw Mrs. Bruin sitting on her haunches in a thicket of vine maples, with her cubs behind her. She was held in this position by the active dogs. On the way from the house, William had requested of his brother John that he might have the first shot, as he had never killed a grizzly. His brother had consented, and he said to William, "Blaze away, Bill; that is a fine mark." William raised his gun to take aim. The moment he did so, Bruin, with open mouth, moved towards him, coming so near him that she had nearly reached the muzzle of his gun. Instead of shooting, William was petrified with fear. He bawled out a strange, unearthly yell, and fell to the ground, fainting dead away. The bear, seeing the man fall and hearing his outcry, left him and went back to her position as before. John put a bullet in the bear's heart, and she died in a few moments. William had now recovered from his swoon, and, seeing the bear dead, he said, "I killed him, did I not?" "I shot him," said John. "No," said William, "it was I." "Look at your rifle," said John. The hammer of the trigger had not been pulled.

In the early days of Oregon grizzly bears abounded. They grew to an immense size and weight. Some of them weighed a thousand pounds or more. They had enormous strength. They could travel very fast, outstripping the fleetest human runners. They never hesitated to attack a man, and especially if surprised or cornered. They fought with amazing fierceness and destructiveness. They have great tenacity of life. It is said they will live on and fight even after their heart has been pierced with a bullet.

A man, in passing through a thicket where he had to stoop in going through, fell over a log upon the prostrate body of a sleeping grizzly. As though he would compel respect for his gigantic strength and resent his rude awakening, Bruin at once addressed himself to the work of doing up that unfortunate visitor, and divesting him of his clothing and flesh. With his mighty claws he tore off his clothes. With his grim, steel-trap jaws, he chewed up his cheeks and limbs, gnawing the quivering flesh from the bones. He ripped off the skin and flesh from the man's arms and limbs and body, and left it hanging in shreds. And as if to make his work more complete and deadly, he hugged his victim with a strong, warm embrace, and squeezed the breath from the body, and then cuffed and slapped his helpless adversary. When the bear's work with that man was over, he needed reconstruction. It seems strange to say, and yet the truth requires that it be said, that man, so lacerated and chewed up, and so incontinently torn up and wounded and mangled and bleeding, actually recovered from his injuries, although there was hardly a spot about him or on him as large as one's hand which was not torn or bruised.

I will give an account of a fatal encounter a famous hunter had with grizzlies. A great wolf-hunter in Southern Oregon made his living and supported his large family by hunting wolves, and obtaining the bounties which the State gave for wolves' scalps. He and his hounds never failed to attack any wild beast which came in their way, no matter how ferocious or dangerous such animal might be. One day his hounds stalled a he-grizzly with his two she-bears in company. The hunter shot the he-grizzly, breaking one of his hind legs. The bear made for him. The brave man held his rifle in his teeth, and climbed a small tree; but not until the grizzly had torn off one of his boots, and laid open the calf of his leg to the bone. The hunter dropped his rifle; but made his escape into the tree. The bear went off a short distance, and watched him. He set the dogs on the bear. While the dogs were baying the bear, the hunter slipped down the tree and began reloading his rifle, which he had recovered. The bear saw him within reach, and made for him. They fought. The hunter was clubbing his bearship with his rifle. The bear knocked his rifle out of the hunter's hands and reach, and embraced him. The hunter drew a hunting-knife from his belt, and began stabbing the bear. The bear knocked the knife from his hand. The hunter reached around for a second knife he carried, which was in a socket on his boot-leg. He used this weapon vigorously, driving it into the bear's body. The bear tore out one of the hunter's eyes, and laid open his breast. The hunter continued his work with the knife until the savage monster fell over in death. The hunter made his way to a cabin near by, called for a drink of water, and died. The combat was fatal to both contenders.

If the Indians were savage and bloodthirsty in their mode of warfare, they have had dreadful provocation. I saw a white man, who was sober, jump on a drunken Indian, and so injure him that he died in two days afterward.

Peo-Peo-mox-a-mox, or Yellow Serpent, a chief of the Walla Walla Indians, had an only son, who went on a mining expedition for gold to California. He was shot down in cold blood. The old chief never forgave that offense. He was a bitter fighter. He was captured, and put under guard. It is alleged he was trying to escape. He was shot and killed. Hence when the war broke out, some of the whites who fell earliest in the war where horribly mutilated.

A stretch of country in Southern Oregon, included in Rogue River and Umpqua Valleys, and extending for thirty miles, thinly settled, was raided by the Indians. Some of the settlers had gone into a stockade fort for greater safety. Others, who had not found such a shelter were killed. A man named Harris, and living two miles from the nearest neighbor's, was assailed in his cabin by a band of Indians. It was near night. The family consisted of a man, his wife, and a daughter of ten years. The Indians fired upon the house. Mr. Harris, who had two rifles and a good supply of ammunition, returned the fire. When he was firing one of these guns, his wife was reloading the other. He fired on his savage enemies through the space between the logs of his cabin. At length he received a fatal wound, and very soon expired. He told his wife to keep on firing until the ammunition was all spent, or nearly so, and then to shoot her daughter and herself, for it was worse than death to be captured by the Indians. Mrs. Harris took his place, the daughter reloading her pieces as fast as necessary. This action was kept up for some time, and she found her ammunition was nearly gone.

Thus it continued until the twilight deepened into night. Then a small body of white horsemen came riding rapidly by. The Indians retired. When the firing ceased, she and her daughter fled into the adjoining forest. The Indians returned to their assault. Their shots remained unanswered. They fired the house, and in the light of the burning cabin they scoured the surrounding woods, several times approaching very closely the concealed fugitives. When the Indians retired, they spent the night in their hiding. The next day they were rescued by a party of white settlers. Mrs. Harris received from Congress a medal and the gift of a mile square of land for her heroism.

In a later Indian war the Indians occupied a very strong retreat among the lava-beds of an ancient volcano. The troops could get into the vicinity of their Indian foes, but they could not find their places of concealment. At length Captain Jack proposed a treaty at a point agreed upon. General Canby, of the regular army; Mr. Dyer, of the Indian service; Rev. Dr. Thomas, of San Francisco, and perhaps others, repaired to the place. The Indians slaughtered them in cold blood, except Mr. Dyer and one or two others, who escaped. The chief leader in this horrible massacre was brought up among the whites. I knew him well.

CHAPTER XVII.

IT is not generally known that Oregon was in some danger of becoming a slave State. A large majority of the earlier emigrants to Oregon came from slave States, chiefly from Missouri, Arkansas, Texas, Tennessee, and Kentucky. There was a strong determination on the part of the Southern politicians, who were eager to extend the area of slavery in the United States, to induce Oregon, when she should assume Statehood, to become a slave State.

When General Joseph Lane, the delegate in Congress from Oregon Territory, ran in 1856 for re-election, he could count on a Democratic majority in Oregon of five thousand. In canvassing for his re-election, he sought to persuade his Democratic supporters to vote also for slavery in Oregon. In his former election I voted for him, because under the conditions I believed he could help Oregon more than his opponent could. During his canvass for re-election, he again solicited my vote. I told him I had heard that, in canvassing for his re-election, he spoke one word for his re-election and two in favor of Oregon's becoming a slave State. If that rumor was true, I said, I would not only not vote for him, but I would also do all I could against his re-election to Congress. I took the field in favor of Oregon as a free State. General Lane's majority was cut down from five thousand to three thousand. The slave State schedule was defeated by over three thousand.

I made the *Pacific Christian Advocate* an earnest supporter of Oregon as a free State, and I also canvassed in the Willamette Valley in favor of free Oregon. As may well be supposed, I encountered opposition, and my course as an editor subjected me to the misrepresentations and abuse of the advocates of the slaveocracy. I was a target for the shafts of ridicule and falsehood by some of the Democratic papers in Oregon and California. The following article, which was printed in the *Pacific Christian Advocate* in the fall of 1859, will show the kind of conflict through which I passed, and through which I carried my paper. It appeared during the pendency of the slave State question in Oregon:

THE PROOF.

"IN FAVOR OF SLAVERY.—The *Standard*, of the 19th inst., contains a long letter of Joseph C. Lovejoy in favor of slavery. It is addressed to his brother, a member of Congress; and while it is written with evident ability, it goes the whole figure for slavery."

The above extract we transcribe from the last issue of the *Advocate*. The man who wrote the same, if it may be taken as his real opinion given after reading the article, should be classed with that other Solomon in ordinary to some Siwash tribe, who, in the plenitude of his wisdom, exclaimed, "O, how good was Nature that placed great rivers near great towns!"

If, on the other hand, he intended to mislead, then while such writing is admitted to its columns, the *Advocate* should drop the prefix *Christian*, and substitute the word Heathen.

We thus speak, because on the 14th inst., four days

previous to its publication in the *Standard*, the letter referred to was published in this paper, and now, for the benefit of the author of the lying paragraph which is quoted above, we will continue to quote from the *Fool's Experience*:

"*Page:* He that's first a hypocrite, and next a knave, the year after is either an arrant fool or a madman.

"*Master:* How came your knavery by such experience?

"*Page:* As fools do by news; somebody told me so, and I believed it."

The above is from the *Times* of the 28th ult. We do not attempt a reply because the paragraph or its author deserves it, but simply for the sake of the cause to which we are devoted, and for the vindication of our veracity, so needlessly and ungentlemanly called in question. We said that Lovejoy's letter is in favor of slavery. Readers will please read extracts from said letter given below, and we are content that they shall determine upon the question whether our statement is a "lying paragraph" or not. Mr. Lovejoy, among other things, says as follows (the italicizing is ours):

But my convictions at the present time are, not only that the slaveholders have a complete vindication of their present position; but they are entitled to be looked upon as *benefactors to the country* and to *the human race*. . . .

The South are impregnable. The Constitution protects them, *the Bible protects them, and the experience of mankind protects them*. . . .

It can not be denied that *the idea of slavery runs through all the Bible;* it was stamped upon the entire history of the Jewish nation, and upon the history of every vigorous nation upon the face of the earth; indeed, I strongly suspect this is the normal condition of large portions of a depraved race, and I can readily believe that a man may sustain the relation of slaveholder, in all good conscience, and with the entire Divine approbation. . . .

American slavery has produced and cultivated more African intellect, more social affection, more Christian emotion in two hundred years, than all Africa (Central or

Southern) for two thousand years. *American slavery is a redemption, a deliverance from African heathenism.* . . .

The best thing that could be done for Africa, if they could live there, would be to send them a hundred thousand American slaveholders, to work them up to some degree of civilization. . . .

So far as Africa is concerned, *the slave-trade was, and is, humane in its operations;* its abolition was the result of sentiment, and not the determination of calm, deliberate statesmanship. . . .

If more laborers are needed for Texas, Central America, parts of Mexico, and Cuba, they ought to be brought, without objections, under such humane regulations as are made in other cases for the comfort of passengers. . . .

As to the influence of slavery on the character of the whites, that is quite another question; but so far as the political history of our country is concerned, it is not easy to see how we could do without slaveholders. . . .

If the author of these extracts is not in favor of slavery, then he is an arrant hypocrite; and if the *extracts* do not sustain our position, then we confess we can not understand language. What connection the previous publication of Mr. Lovejoy's letter in the *Times* has with the conclusions of its new editor, or how that should induce him to "thus speak," it is difficult to conceive. The time is approaching in Oregon, if it has not already come, when men in public stations must evince self-respect and gentlemanly bearing towards others if they would be respected themselves. The predecessor of the present editor of the *Times* commenced a similar tirade against certain respectable citizens in Oregon. *He commenced, too, by quoting Shakespeare.* He soon ran his inglorious race and left the country, fallen beneath the contempt of respectable men. We forewarn the present editor that an equally ignoble but speedier fate awaits him, unless he profits by the example just cited.

It was the expectation of the Secessionists in the Southern States, that Oregon and California would secede when the Southern States drew off from the Union, and organized the Southern Confederacy. Political emissaries from California, who were ministers of the Methodist Episcopal Church, South, and who had organized that Church in California, came to Oregon, and made political speeches in favor of the Breckinridge and Lane ticket, denouncing the Black Republicans as disunionists, and predicting that if Oregon went Republican, and if Lincoln should be elected, the country would be involved in civil war, and blood would run in consequence up to the horses' bridles. The iridescent dream of the Southern fire-eaters and Secessionists, that the Pacific States would join the Southern Confederacy, had some little shadow of probability in their knowledge that a large majority of the emigrants to California and Oregon were from Kentucky, Tennessee, Alabama, Texas, and Missouri. The following editorial was leveled against the untruths of these secession agitators in the issue of June 20, 1863:

MISREPRESENTATION.

While on a recent trip to Jackson County, we learned that the emissaries of the Church South are earnestly and persistently representing that the Methodist Episcopal Church is the *seceding* Church, and that the Methodist Episcopal Church, *South*, is the old organization. It will be remembered that Rev. O. Fisher, when he was in the country two or three years since, represented the same things, which we then denied, and we did not suppose it would be repeated, or, if repeated, believed; yet the old adage, "a lie well stuck to is better than the truth," seems to find support in this instance; for we found persons recently who actually professed to believe that the Methodist Episcopal Church is the *seceding* body, and the Methodist Episcopal Church, South, the *original* one, holding the old organization and rights. We propose to recite a little of the history of the Great Secession of 1844-1845, for the correctness of which we would vouch, and appeal, for those who desire the proof, to Elliott's "Great Secession," and "The Methodist Church Property Case," a stout, octavo pamphlet published by the Methodist Book Concern in New York, in 1851. In the General Conference of 1844, two cases came up for adjudication, viz.: First, the appeal of F. A. Harding against the action of the Baltimore Conference. The Baltimore Conference had suspended him from the ministry for refusing to manumit certain slaves which came into his possession by marriage. From this action Mr. Harding appealed. (See Methodist Church Property Case, pages 57, 58, 59.) After full discussion, during four days, a motion was made by John Early, of Virginia, afterwards a bishop of the Church South, to reverse the decision of the Baltimore Conference. The vote stood as follows: Nays, 117; yeas, 56. The chair decided that this vote virtually affirmed the action of the Baltimore Conference. W. Capers took an appeal from his decision. The decision of the chair was sustained by 111 for, and 53 against.

The other exciting case which came up for action in the General Conference of 1844, was that of Rev. Bishop Andrew. Bishop Andrew was elected a bishop when a non-slaveholder. Some years afterwards, by bequests and by marriage, he became possessed of slaves, and this fact coming officially before the General Conference of 1844, the subject was discussed variously for some two weeks, when the following preamble and resolutions were adopted by a vote of 110 yeas and 68 nays, viz.:

WHEREAS, The Discipline of our Church forbids the doing anything calculated to destroy our itinerant general superintendency; and

WHEREAS, Bishop Andrew has become connected with slavery, by marriage and otherwise, and this act having drawn after it circumstances which, in the estimation of the General Conference, will greatly embarrass the exercise of his office as an itinerant general superintendent, if not in some places entirely prevent it; therefore,

Resolved, That it is the sense of this General Conference that he desist from the exercise of his office so long as this impediment remains.

Various resolutions, *declaratory* and otherwise, and a protest, were offered, and, finally, a committee of nine was appointed on a Plan of Separation. They reported a plan, the very first condition of which was, "That should the Annual Conferences in the slave-holding States find it necessary to unite in a distinct ecclesiastical connection, the following rule shall be observed with regard to the northern boundary of said connection;" *i. e.,* a majority vote of the members of said societies, stations, and Conferences should govern in deciding their relation, whether to the new organization proposed, or to the old one. Provision was also made to submit the Sixth Restrictive Rule to a vote of all the Conferences, as to whether they would sanction a division of the funds of the Church should the Southern Conferences separate from the Church. This last failed to receive the necessary majority to authorize the division of property. The delegates from the South held a meeting in the city of New York on the next day after the adjournment of the General Conference, and called a Convention in Louisville, Ky., for May 1, 1845, thus *forestalling* the action of the Conferences as provided for by the General Conference. The Convention met, having delegates from sixteen of the Conferences in slaveholding territory, and, by a vote of ninety-four yeas to three nays, erected the Annual Conferences represented in the Convention, "into a distinct ecclesiastical connection, separate from the jurisdiction of the General Conference of the Methodist Episcopal Church as at present constituted," adopting "the doctrines and rules and regulations of said Discipline, except only so far as verbal alteration may be necessary to a distinct organization," and "to be known by the style and title of the Methodist Episcopal Church, *South.*" The whole proceedings of the South to obtain what they claimed was their share of the funds of the Church were upon the idea that the Church from which they had separated was the original, old organization, taking date in 1784.

If persons are ignorant or wicked enough to teach the contrary in Oregon, in the year of grace 1863, and there are those here who are weak enough to believe such perversions, without informing themselves, we sincerely pity them, assuring them that the means are within reach, fully to set them right in the premises.

"HOWLING DERVISHES."

One of our Oregon contemporaries, who is "down on the war," alluding to the Copperhead report of the proceedings of the New York Conference, denounces the preachers of that Conference severely for their political proclivities, and calls them "howling dervishes." He says there are some in Oregon who resemble those New York preachers. If to stand up for one's country

— "through storm and night,"

and in every practicable way to defend the fair fame and the just rights of the inheritance bequeathed by our fathers, subjects them to the epithets of such men and such sheets, probably the Oregon preachers alluded to will bear the odium thus cast upon them with meekness, but without abating a jot of their efforts for the good cause.

The following is in the same line as the foregoing. The writer was a transfer from the Baltimore Conference. It will indicate the animus of those who opposed the war for the Union:

Mr. Editor,—As the writer's name appears under the report "On the State of the Country," passed at the late session of the Oregon Annual Conference, and may, without qualification, create a wrong impression upon the minds of his friends, it is deemed proper to beg the indulgence of your readers to say that he voted against the fourth resolution of that report as it now stands, because he thought its adoption might possibly embarrass true Union-loving ministers beyond the bounds of the said Conference. Second, because, as it appeared to him, one Conference has no right to indicate the line of conduct for their equals of another Conference. This last objection is based upon the opinion that the term "ministers," as used in the resolution and connection, embraces ministers generally. For these reasons an amendment was moved so as to make the resolution applicable to the ministers of the Oregon Conference only, leaving those of other Conferences and Churches to act on the subject, without advice, according to their own sense of duty, which the Oregon Conference claim the right of doing for themselves. Had more time for the examination of the sixth resolution been allowed, he would have voted against that also, unless the language of it had been so understood as hyperbolically expressing the sentiment that the Union is worth maintaining at a great sacrifice.

Respectfully, GEORGE M. BERRY.

August 28, 1861.

We regret that Brother Berry has deemed it necessary to bring this subject, in this form, before the public, lest the impression should be unfavorable to him; and also, lest it should be inferred that the Conference was not generally agreed in its action. To prevent misapprehension, we subjoin a brief statement of facts: As a member of the committee, Brother Berry agreed to the report before it was submitted. In the discussion before the Conference, Brother Berry opposed the fourth resolution, and he and one other voted against it. On the adoption of the report as a whole, the yeas and nays being called, the vote was *unanimous*, Brother Berry's name being recorded with the others in its favor. The Conference acted deliberately, the report occupying a considerable portion of two days. Brother Berry, in common with the other members of the Conference, had full opportunity to discuss the resolution, and his privilege was freely used. The report will speak for itself. It is quite unnecessary to re-argue the matter in our columns.

The following editorial, which appeared in the columns of the *Pacific Christian Advocate*, May 3, 1862, needs no explanation. It shows with what tenacity the opposers of suppressing the secession and rebellion adhered to their cause:

"SECESSION—SCHISM."

The April number of the *Oregon Churchman* has an article on "Secession—Schism." The ground taken is that the separations among Christians are really *schisms*, and are generally and properly denominated *secessions*. We quote two passages for the purpose of comment (italicizing is ours):

> Unquestionably the *strongest argument used against permitting a secession from our Republic is, that if allowed in one instance it will probably be repeated in others, until a total disintegration ensue, and thence universal anarchy*. If this reasoning be sound, is it not equally applicable to our ecclesiastical affairs? Nay, even more; for *political separations are necessarily territorial*, while the others are indiscriminate. In the State of Oregon alone, for example, there are at least *fourteen* distinct ecclesiastical organizations, entirely independent of each other. And where is this to end? for if the first secession be justifiable, so is each successive one which has occurred, or may yet occur.

The argument stated is by no means "the strongest used against permitting a secession from our Republic." A much stronger one is that State secession is itself subversive of government and a crime before God, and it is as really so whether one State, or many, secede. The *principle* is radically mischievous and dangerous as well as wicked. The strongest argument against murder, or any other form of disobedience to law, is not that if allowed in one instance "it will probably be repeated in others, until" murders and other felonies are common. That *is* an argument, but not the strongest. Wherein is the reasoning against State secession different from that against other forms of lawlessness? State secession is not a question of policy or expediency; it is a crime.

Nor, again, are "political separations necessarily territorial:" *i. e.*, they are not confined to the seceded portion nor are they necessarily nor chiefly territorial. State secession is such a violation of law as would work territorial and political injury to the portions *seceded from* as well as the portion seceding, and it is a *crime;* it would work *moral* injury to both parties, and, by example, to all nations. This reasoning, therefore, is not sound in political separations, and, if it were, it would not be sound, nor "equally applicable to ecclesiastical affairs," because it assumes that conformity to one particular form of Church order and organization is Scripturally enjoined, and that, therefore, dissent and nonconformity are criminal. We think it will trouble the *Churchman* to establish these positions. Nor yet does it necessarily or logically follow, that "if the first secession be justifiable, so is each successive one which may occur." If "each successive one" were for the same cause or causes, or for equally weighty ones as the first, the first being justifiable, so would be the following ones. That every Church secession is for the same or equal reasons as all others, is assumption. Let it be proved. The second paragraph we quote is as follows:

> Another very grave inquiry suggested by this state of facts is, as to the extent of its influence upon our social and political relations. It is evident that men's religious education and sentiments form the strongest element in their character, and ultimately control all their leading principles of action. Now all will admit that the tendency of our people in ecclesiastical matters has been towards secession, and that their practical training has been in that school. Of all the leading Protestant bodies which existed at the time of the adoption of our National Constitution, one only remained a unit until the beginning of our present troubles. Each of the others has, at different times, been divided, and subdivided by secession. The same is substantially true in England. And the exceptional Church, identical in the two countries, has ever protested against both the principle and practice of separation, as well in her doctrinal teaching as in her constitution.

There is one cogent fact which goes far to weaken this reasoning: The portion of the United States most loyal, and where State secession is most abhorrent, is by far more divided into sects and separate Church organizations, and more afflicted with what the writer calls *schism*, than the seceded portion. How is this? Other facts may be cited. One of the supplications in the Litany of the Protestant Episcopal Church, and to which the congregations, South as well as North, have been responding for generations, "Good Lord, deliver us," is "from all *sedition*, privy *conspiracy*, and *rebellion*." Yet that Church, with all its unity, orthodoxy, and prayers against rebellion, has not prevented its ministers and members in the South from joining the rebellious forces arrayed against the Government, and one of them—Rev. Bishop Leonidas Polk, of Tennessee—is leading armies against the loyal citizens of his own country. If schism be so fruitful of "political separations" and rebellions, and adherence to the only undivided, national Church organization be so potent to conserve the State, as the argument implies, what are we to think of this case?

More of the navy and army chaplains, previous to the rebellion, have been of the Protestant Episcopal denomination than of any, and, we believe, of all others, and that, too, while that denomination is numerically one of the least in the Nation. Yet the army and navy exhibited many sad and sickening examples of perjury and foul treason. If the *Churchman's* reasoning were good, and there were such political benefit to be derived from the influence of a Church which has "ever protested against the principle and practice of separation, as well in her doctrinal teaching as in her constitution," how comes it to pass that some of the most flagrant examples of "sedition, privy conspiracy, and rebellion," have occurred among those who have enjoyed only the ministrations of the Protestant Episcopal Church?

With all the writer's abhorrence of *Church* secession, he has not intimated—he ought, we think—that State secession is inherently wrong, as well as of dangerous tendency. We have no war to wage against the Protestant Episcopal Church. We were born a member of its elder sister. We honor that Church for its fidelity to evangelical truth; for its strong front against infidelity; for its stability; and we glory in the good it has done and which it is doing; but when certain of its "chief ministers," who maintain a marked reticence upon the horrible crime of rebellion as now raging, attempt to asperse those of other denominations as *schismatics*, and impute to their doctrines and practice secession and rebellion, such impertinence demands rebuke. In administering it, we would discriminate, and except those who, like Dr. Tyng, of New York, are truly catholic, and who say, "Grace be with all them that love our Lord Jesus Christ in sincerity."

CHAPTER XVIII.

THE following Thanksgiving sermon was preached by me in Portland, Oregon, November 27, 1862, while the War for the Union was being prosecuted. It was published by request. The texts were Jeremiah xvii, 6, 10, inclusive, and the one hundredth Psalm:

By official Proclamation of the Executive of this State, we are summoned from the ordinary pursuits of life to devote a day to thanksgiving and prayer, to humiliation before God, and to devout gratitude to the Sovereign Arbiter of human destiny, the Lord of lords and King of kings.

The fact that all the loyal States of the Union, with only two or three exceptions, have agreed upon this as a day of public thanksgiving that the morning sun as he sheds his early beams on the Atlantic slope continues in his western circuit, to call successive States—from Orient to Occident—to this delightful and appropriate exercise, until a great and mighty Nation are prostrate before Jehovah, in supplication or adoration, heightens the interest of the occasion, and exhibits a sublime and most encouraging spectacle.

There are two leading thoughts contained in the Proclamation upon which I would fix your attention with somewhat of detail. They are the duties of humiliation and prayer for national sins; thanksgiving and praise for national blessings.

It is atheistic to deny national accountability and dependence. Shall we admit a God in creation and in all the mighty framework of nature, and preclude him from cognizance and supervision of human affairs, whether personal or corporate? This is as irreligious as it is unphilosophical. The Lord sitteth above the floods. He ruleth in the heavens, and doeth his pleasure among the sons of men. While he numbers the hairs of our heads, and not a falling sparrow escapes his notice; while

> "There's not a tint that paints the rose
> Or decks the lily fair,
> Or streaks the humblest flower that grows,
> But God has placed it there,"

it is equally true that by him "kings rule and princes decree justice;" that "He setteth up one and putteth down another;" that he holds ruler and subject alike accountable for human conduct, rewarding and punishing, as that conduct is, or is not, according to his rule of right. Let no man, and no corporation, no community, and no nation think to evade this accountability. God's government, like his presence, is universal. His authority, like his omniscience, extends to all beings.

His moral government is as far-reaching and effective as to moral beings as his physical is as to material objects. As well might a man think to escape the law of gravitation while in the body, or to respire without the vital air, as to avoid the moral control which God exercises over men and nations. These conclusions are inevitable if we admit the existence of God. Even if there were no light of revelation to shine upon the question, doth not nature herself speak with irresistible conclusiveness? Doth not reason concur with nature in proclaiming the sovereignty as well as the existence of God, as really in morals as in physics? Admit God's existence, and his control follows, alike in moral as in material, equally in great as in small affairs.

As God exists the Sovereign Lawgiver and Judge, the dispenser and enforcer of law, national as well as personal, righteousness or sin follows as we observe or disregard his law. No time shall be lost in debating whether that law is written in the Bible or voiced in nature. Nature and revelation agree in this fundamental rule of equity as to persons, "All things whatsoever ye would that men should do unto you, do ye even so unto them." And they also agree in this fundamental condition of national growth or decay, elevation or depression, progress or retrogression. "Righteousness exalteth a nation—sin is a reproach to any people." "The powers that be are ordained of God." They are ordained "as a terror to evil-doers, and a praise to them that do well."

General commercial prosperity has attended our progress through another year. It is true that privateering has somewhat interrupted commerce in some parts of the world, but this has not been general. Our exports have been carried in American ships, and our navy has everywhere covered itself with glory by its victorious career of defense against the rebellious ports and vessels of the Southern Confederacy. The marts of commerce have been open, and the centers of business have been full and active. It was predicted when the rebellion broke out that New York, Boston, Philadelphia, and other great business centers would become wastes; that the grass would grow in the streets, etc. On the contrary, more activity and commercial thrift has been realized than had been known in ordinary periods.

There has been a happy *exemption from disease*. Plague and pestilence have not been suffered to brood over the land, filling it with shadows and tears. Sad it is to think of the havoc of war, and of the sighs and tears of widowhood and orphanage; yet we may well be thankful before the Lord that he has granted us health and plenty in all our borders.

Our progress in science, inventions, and religion has been most gratifying. While the tread of armies and the booming of war's dread artillery have shaken the land, the schools, colleges, and academies have stood open, and the young have been trained in sound learning, while literature and discovery have extended their sphere and multiplied their triumphs. Inventions have elevated us into the greatest of maritime powers in the world. The naval engagements of the War of 1812 proved us then to be more than a match for the proud British Empire, to which for centuries had been conceded the naval supremacy of all the world. The achievements of the *Monitor* excited at first the terror, and then the admiration of other Powers.

Religion has held sway, even during the prevalence of grim-visaged war. Our army is a more religious one than was ever marshaled. The Sabbath is respected, profane swearing is interdicted by army orders. Our generals, and more recently our commander-in-chief, President Lincoln, have issued orders directing the observance of the Sabbath. A thousand chaplains minister to the bodily and mental welfare of our million troops; and when our soldiers fall in battle they afford them amelioration for their bodily sufferings, and point them, when dying, to "the Lamb of God, which taketh away the sin of the world."

Then, too, you will observe that the missionary operations of the Church have progressed without interruption or abatement. Though pecuniary pressure has rested upon the country, yet the flow of voluntary contributions to the channels of Christian benevolence has been constant and undiminished.

Besides, consider with what a generous benevolence the demands of the wounded and sick of our troops have been met. Untaxed by State enactments and unenforced by legal claims, lint, clothing, nursing, luxuries, have been procured, and bestowed with a promptitude and profusion unparalleled in history. Contributions for the Sanitary Commission have flowed in from all parts, from the mountain and the valley, from the forest dell and the broad prairies, from agricultural and mining districts, uniting a thousand rivulets to form a swelling river of benevolence. Silver bricks from Washoe, golden bars from Lewiston, and coin from other places, have gone singing with a merry jingle to their merciful mission.

Another occasion of thanksgiving is the existence and exhibition of the noblest *Christian patriotism* upon the grandest scale.

When the glorious banner was insulted at Sumter, and its brave defenders were beleaguered by swarming thousands of rebels, an electric thrill of patriotic sympathy pervaded the whole loyal States, and seventy-five thousand men rushed at the call of their President to defend the National Capital, and then a half million, and afterwards as many more, ranged themselves on the side of the country, the laws, and the nationality. Brave, "constant as the polar star," valorous, and invincible, a wall of living breasts surrounds the rebel district, to conquer or to die. To say that all this springs from love of country, simply because it is the place of our birth, or because it is a great and glorious land, is to describe an inadequate cause for such an effect.

That is not the brightest type of patriotism. There are other lands as beautiful; other regions where the skies are as serene, where the drapery of mountain and valley, woodland and lawn, is as lovely; where the air is as genial and balmy as in this; and, besides, there are adopted citizens from vine-clad France and from the forests of Germany, from the hills of Switzerland, England, and from Ireland, whose patriotic zeal burns as fervently as that of the native citizen. The patriotism of the American citizen has a higher, nobler source than this. It takes hold of the great principles of democracy. It battles for our institutions, and it intelligently comprehends their exalted character and their inestimable value. It is a *Christian* patriotism, such as that for which the Pilgrims left the soil of oppression, and planted themselves

"On a stern and rock-bound coast."

Our Constitution is Christian. It does not indeed enact Christianity as a State religion. Christianity needs no such support. It is only burdened and injured by such trammels. Christ said, "My kingdom is not of this world." Yet while no clause in the Constitution says that Christianity shall be the established religion, and while we would not upon any account have it so say, it gives free toleration to all sects and opinions and creeds. It lays no edict of restriction nor prohibition upon the creeds and consciences of the people, leaving every man free to elect his own theory, and to worship according to the dictates of his own conscience, and it is pervaded throughout by the principles and spirit of Christianity.

Our Government is based upon the acknowledged rights of the masses. The divine right of kings is the foundation of monarchies; the possession of physical power is the patent of despots; but the Government under whose genial shadow we have been protected and fostered recognizes the rights, God-given and inalienable, of all men to self-government. The ruler and subject among us as to natural rights are equal; in fact, the ruler is the servant of the people, from whom he derives his right to govern them.

The force of this view is not to be broken by averring that while this is the case in theory, in reality the fact is otherwise. The slavery in the United States is such by the force of State laws. "The Declaration of Independence was the germ from which the Constitution grew into a goodly tree. While our fathers who framed the Constitution were from slave States, they were very careful not to allow the words slave and slavery to enter it. They could not say one thing in the Declaration, and the opposite in the Constitution."

See how they resisted the idea of rank and titles and dignities. The South Carolinians, then, as now, the evil genius of the Nation, sought to incorporate slavery into that sacred instrument; but their efforts were vain. The Constitution, so far as the Federal Union was concerned, is the product of a triumphant struggle for freedom. In that struggle three things were accomplished: "1. The foreign slave-trade was doomed, and that before any other civilized power had condemned it. 2. The word slave was not allowed to occur in the Constitution; the allusions to it were circumlocutions such as the pious employ when quoting an instance of profanity. 3. The Constitution was framed with prophetic cunning for the day of universal liberty; and if the whole country should tomorrow, either by the action of the States interested, or as an incident of the war, contain none but free States, the Constitution would not want an amendment to conform it to the new state of things. There would be marks to intimate its history, and to tell what dangerous roads it had been called to travel, but it would want neither piecing, nor patching, nor darning. This, I confess, gives to my affection for my country the sanction of my reason, and enables my religion all the easier to ally itself with and to invigorate and inflame my patriotism. And we may say of the Constitution, in view of the struggles through which it has triumphantly passed, as the dying Jacob said of Joseph: 'The archers have sorely grieved him, and shot at him, and hated him; but his bow abode in strength, and the arms of his hands were made strong by the hands of the mighty God of Jacob.'"

Thus we find that our General Government, now attempted to be overthrown, is in perfect agreement with Christ's doctrines of the freedom of religion and the brotherhood of men. So that not only are we bound to our country by the ties of nativity or cordial adoption, by its physical features, by its history, and by its literature; these are only as a beautiful frame in which is set the living picture of our moral and religious convictions. Our patriotism, therefore, without scruple—nay, with joy—receives into its bosom the element of religion, and feels that, in defending the country, it is defending not merely mountains and rivers, not merely geographical boundaries, but the very cause of God himself.

These facts bring into the present conflict the martyr element, rendering our soldiers heroic. It was the conviction of a high sense of right and duty which nerved their arm in battle and bore them on to noble deeds, which animated them in the dreadful fight and cheered them as they fell under the iron hail of battle. A martyr is a witness unto blood for the truth of God. "The unholy war now waging is waged by the enemies of the doctrine of Christ, that freedom of religious thought and action and universal brotherhood are the rights of man."

The great idea of the gospel is man's right to self-government and religious toleration; and for this not only professed Christians, but the whole loyal portion of the Union are devoting their blood and treasure. They have drunk in this sentiment with their earliest food, and our adopted fellow-citizens have imbibed it as they do our native air. It is a *principle* for which they are fighting, and the result can not be doubtful. Our path as a Nation may lie through fire and storm; long years of trial and conflict may be before us; France and England and Austria may intervene, and the present army may melt away, only to be succeeded by another and another; but through all and beyond all I see the coming certain victory. This Nation will survive; freedom will live; self-government will be perpetuated; and from the present darkness and strife and disaster will emerge the Republic, regenerated by its baptism of blood and fire. Our gallant ship of State, however angrily the surges of rebellion and disaster may dash against her, and through whatever storms and tempests her course may lead, shall not founder. The poetic prophecy shall become history—

> "Her topsails feel the freshening gale;
>   She strikes the opening sea;
> She rounds the points, she threads the keys
>   That guard the land of flowers,
> And rides at last where firm and fast
>   Her own Gibraltar towers!
>
> The good ship Union's voyage is o'er,
>   At anchor safe she swings,
> And loud and clear with cheer on cheer,
>   Her joyous welcome rings;
> Hurrah! Hurrah! it shakes the wave,
>   It thunders on the shore—
> One flag, one land, one heart, one hand,
>   One nation, evermore!"

Has not God said, "I will overturn, overturn, overturn it?" Now such a patriotism, founded in such principles, rooted in such a soil, and contending with such enemies and for such a priceless inheritance, is worthy of our gratitude. We may and we should unite as a people to render praise to God that we live to mingle in such a strife: that we are permitted to feel the impulses of this Divine patriotism, and to share the glory of that inexpressible victory, when, not in theory only, but in deed and in truth, we, as a Nation, shall have wrought out and fought out and maintained, by God's blessing upon our patriotism and our arms, that glorious truth, *"Liberty and Union, one and inseparable, now and forever!"*

The paper still continued to show its patriotism and loyalty to the Government, as well as to promote the spiritual interests of its readers. The following editorials were inserted at the dates indicated:

PATRIOTISM. (MAY 3, 1862.)

"The love of one's country; the passion which aims to serve one's country, either in defending it from invasion, or protecting its rights, and maintaining its laws and institutions in vigor and purity," is defined to be patriotism. It is certainly the "characteristic of a good citizen," and "the noblest passion that animates a man in the character of a citizen." We go further, and aver that we can not see how a man who lacks patriotism can be a Christian. If untrue to his country, how can he be true to his God? "He that is unjust in that which is least, is unjust also in that which is much." If a man be true to his God, he can not be untrue to his country; because the love of country is implanted by the Creator, and fidelity to one's country is enjoined in the Word of God. Yet patriotism is not the whole of religion. The same law which enjoins civil obedience, and the same Lawgiver who denounces resistance to the powers that be, demand that while we render to "Cæsar the things that are Cæsar's," we shall render to God the things that are God's. The former Christians should do, and not leave the latter undone. It is a matter of gratitude and hope that this Rebellion is developing bright and glorious examples of patriotism. What a record is that of Anderson, and Slemmer, and Doubleday, and Hart, and Brownlow, and Andrew Johnson, and Prentice, and the six hundred and fifty thousand men who are laying their lives on the altar of country! There are many unwritten examples. Bankers have freely tendered their money, artisans their labors and inventions; women, amid their tears, and with well-nigh breaking hearts, have yielded their husbands, fathers, sons, brothers, and lovers for the common safety and deliverance. All this has been voluntary; there has been no conscription or impressment. Self-moved and voluntary, twenty millions—with occasional exceptions—have tendered everything sacred and dear on earth for the defense of their country. Who can look upon this remarkable exhibition without thanking God that he is an American citizen? The mind loves to linger upon individual instances and admire them. An old naval officer who had seen a half-century of service under the Starry Banner, was approached by rebels, who sought to seduce him from his allegiance. They offered him money, promotion, honors, if he would desert his flag, and raise the Palmetto standard. He asked them whether, after fifty years of service in the United States navy, rendered under his official oath, they could trust him should he join them. They responded affirmatively. "Then," said the noble, scarred veteran, "if after all that *you* could trust *me*, *I could not trust you!*" and the seducers desisted.

Not less striking is an instance which occurred in Charleston, South Carolina. We submit it as we find it in one of our exchanges:

Poor F—— is dead. Before the fall of Sumter he exerted all his influence, using both pen and voice against rebellion, until he was thrown into prison. At first he was treated as an ordinary criminal awaiting trial; but after the battle of Manassas the Confederates seemed drunk with triumph at their victory, and mad with rage over the vast number of victims who fell in their ranks. I wrote you with what pomp this city mourned for her dead; amid it all, when the Confederate host seemed likely to win, F—— was offered freedom and promotion if he would espouse the Confederate cause. "I have sworn allegiance to the Union," said he, "and am not one to break my pledge." When tempted with promotion if he could be prevailed on to enlist beneath their banner, he said, "I love Carolina and the South; but I love my country better."

Finding him faithful to the flag he loved, he was made to feel the power of his enemies. He was cast into a miserable, damp, ill-ventilated cell, and fed on coarse fare; half the time neglected by his drunken keeper. His property was confiscated, and his wife and children beggared. Poor fellow! he sank beneath his troubles, and was soon removed from the persecution of his oppressors. The day before his death he said to his wife, "Mary, you are beggared because I would not prove disloyal." "God be thanked for your fidelity!" replied the wife. "They have taken your wealth and life, but **could not stain your honor, and our children shall boast of** an unspotted name. My husband, rejoice in your truth." She returned to her friends after his death, openly declaring her proudest boast should be, her husband died a martyr to his patriotism. Who shall say the day of heroism has passed?

We will not cite further examples at the present; but we take leave to suggest that *religion* also has demands upon us as Christians, as ministers, and as men. In the excitements raging around us, and while patriotism summons us to the rescue, let us not be forgetful of the religious duties we owe to God, to ourselves, to our fellow-men. The *Pittsburg Advocate* has a timely article on revival excitements. We give a portion of it, and commend it to our readers:

It is no longer an experiment what effect the war is to have on the institution of Christianity. Ten months of trial has settled the question. At the beginning of the rebellion all seemed uncertain and conjectural, and the outlook into the future was gloomy and forbidding. Now prominent and well-defined landmarks lie all around us. Guided by the lights of the past month, it is easy to take soundings and see whither we are drifting.

Throughout the rebel States religion has greatly suffered. The papers published in the interest of the various denominations have mostly yielded to the pressure of the hour, and suspended. Occasionally a voice reaches us bewailing the desolations of Zion, and pointing to the temples of religion as deserted and silent. Evidences from the South are cumulative, that the history of religion under the incubus of rebellion is a history of gloom and sadness. Societies scattered, ministers without flocks and without support, the benevolent enterprises of the Church paralyzed,—these are pictures of religious life at the South as drawn by their own limners. It is not so with us. Except along the border, religious institutions continue to be observed, and religious enterprises continue to move much as was their wont in times of peace. The religious press is in vigorous operation. Churches are well attended, and the support of the various religious establishments suffer only in proportion with the general monetary interests of the country. Prosperity, so grateful to the religious sense of the Nation, and withal so unexpected, is cause for gratitude to the beneficent Giver of every good and perfect gift. To all this a new evidence of the Divine benediction on the Churches of the loyal States is now to be superadded. Revival notices begin to appear in the most of our religious exchanges, and form, indeed, a considerable department in our own Church papers. At no former period were these "times of refreshing from the presence of the Lord" more grateful and encouraging, since they attest that, amid the din and smoke of battle, God has not forgotten his Church.

But it is a question whether we are enjoying the utmost prosperity that might fall to our lot. Perhaps we have allowed the vast interests of religion to be thrown too much into the shade by the towering and irresistible war spirit that rules in the land. Perhaps we have not talked too much about patriotism and the war; but too little about the salvation of souls. Jesus Christ and him crucified, salvation by faith, and reformations that shall lead to a life of well-doing, are the sublime themes of the gospel ministry. These topics will make the pulpit successful in winning souls even during war times. But they must not be assigned a secondary rank. The welfare of the soul is, beyond all other questions, of infinite moment. Nothing should be allowed to paralyze efforts for its salvation—not politics, nor the pursuit of wealth, nor even patriotism in this hour when the national life is in controversy. It is the one work of the ministry to save men. And it is pleasant to reflect that this work is going on with vigor, though the Nation is involved in all the horrors of a gigantic war. The honored minister of God, favored with success in his work of winning souls, is achieving nobler victories than the greatest military captains. And though a rival excitement has for months engrossed all minds and occupied all thoughts, this is not a wholly unpropitious time to enforce on men the claims of religion. We are a chastened Nation. The hand of God has touched us. And this hour of great national sorrow may furnish a fitting occasion on which to press men to turn to God. Subdued by a sense of helplessness, and admonished by the perils of the times, to whom should the Nation look for help but God, and what better occasion can the Church have for lifting the Nation up to God?

THE REBELLION. (August 30, 1862.)

The great rebellion has been in operation considerably over a year. Has the determination of the loyal people to suppress the rebellion faltered? So far from that, the purpose is constantly becoming stronger, to maintain the national integrity against any and all enemies, whether domestic or foreign, and also to prosecute the war with greater vigor and more terrible earnestness. An immense mass-meeting of loyal citizens was held in New York on the 15th of July last, which was as large as that of April, 1861, if not larger. At the recent gathering the resolutions of 1861 were reaffirmed. Others were adopted expressive of the conviction that this war is waged only for the overthrow of disloyalty; that no claims or privileges beyond those conferred by the Constitution upon our fathers are sought; that the establishment and enforcement of the Constitution in all its vigor, not a line erased or interpolated, is the great object sought. This resolution also was adopted:

Resolved, That we are for the Union of the States, the integrity of the country, and the maintenance of the Government without any condition or qualification whatever; and we will stand by them and uphold them under all circumstances, and at every necessary sacrifice of life or treasure.

These, and others expressive of confidence in the Administration, and of admiration for the valor and prowess of our army and navy, were adopted with entire unanimity; all showing that so far as New York, the moneyed and commercial center of the Nation, is concerned, the great heart of the people beats true to the Government through the darkest and wildest storms of revolution.

This resolution, adopted with the utmost enthusiasm, has the ring of the true metal:

Resolved, That, steadily pursuing the wise policy of our fathers, we never mean to interfere in the internal conflicts of foreign States; but here, beneath this outstretched sky, in the presence of Almighty God, and of one another, we pledge our lives, our fortunes, and our sacred honor, never to abandon this struggle while there remains a traitor in the land, and that any armed intervention by any foreign Power in our present domestic affliction shall prove the signal for the spirit of Liberty to commence its triumphant march through Europe.

While the moderation, conciliation, and wisdom of the Administration have elicited the approval of all conservative men, yet true and loyal men in the border States, the soldiers in the field, and the great mass of the loyal people feel that the war should hereafter be more vigorously and decisively prosecuted; that the day for temporizing and for gentle measures has passed. To this conclusion, it is believed, the President, Congress, and the people are rapidly coming with great unanimity. That noble patriot, Andrew Johnson, uttered the following in a Fourth of July speech at Nashville:

Some professed to entertain a holy horror of coercion. Why, force and error have coerced the South into her present position, and nothing but force and power will bring her back. You were coerced by the violence and force of secession, and the spirit of secession must be subdued and controlled by force. The strong arm of the Government must be bared, and justice must do her work. We may as well understand the fact first as last, and go to work rationally. Without force and power to coerce, we have no Government. How have matters gone on heretofore? Why, when the Union army came, the first to run to it for protection and privileges were Secessionists, who got promises of protection if they would remain neutral. On the other hand, the poor Union men were terrified with threats of vengeance if the rebel army should return. The Secessionist was protected by the Union army, and was equally confident of protection should the rebel army return; so he felt perfectly easy. The Union man dreaded utter ruin should a reverse occur, and was filled with perpetual alarm. So, under this strange policy the rebel had two guarantees, and the Union man but one. It was time this was stopped. The time has arrived when treason must be made odious, and traitors impoverished. These men have used their prosperity to destroy the Government, and fill the land with bankruptcy and distress; they have given their wealth freely to aid rebellion and treason, and drench the land in fraternal blood, and crush out the last vestige of liberty, and their property should be taken from them to defray the expenses of the war. They are the guilty ones; they are the real criminals. The poor have been deluded and dragged into this war, while the authors and instigators, who have kept up the war by their money and contributions, have skulked at home and demanded the protection of the Federal Government. Why, many of these elegant gentlemen rebelled to get rid of paying their Northern debts. If a miserable, crippled Negro, worth five hundred dollars, was stolen, the Government must be overthrown if the Negro could not be recovered; but your polite, fastidious, and chivalrous merchant can go among what he calls, "blue-bellied Yankees," buy their goods on credit, and then, when pay-day comes, tell his creditors in the North, "O, I have seceded!" It is an outrageous crime to steal a Negro; but it is gentlemanly financiering to defraud a Northern creditor of fifty or a hundred thousand dollars.

THE REBELLION. (JULY 5, 1862.)

Three questions force themselves, at this moment, upon the American people; viz., Will this rebellion soon be suppressed? Will its suppression restore union and harmony between the sections now discordant and belligerent? Will the present rebellion leave the Union stronger or weaker than it was before?

The first question hardly needs an argument or a reply. The affirmative answer comes up from millions of loyal men and women. Only the secession sympathizers in Europe, and those in the States whose sympathies are with the insurrectionists, pretend to dissent from the unanimous conclusion of loyal Americans that the end of rebellion and insurrection draws near. Already Southern papers and insurrectionists are full of apprehension and alarm at the gloomy future which spreads itself out like an angry cloud along their horizon. The reasons for the affirmative response may be briefly stated, thus:

(1) The *right* is on the side of the Government. The object of the Government was in the beginning

to defend itself, and suppress the rebellion. To that single purpose, President, Congress, and the army have adhered with unvarying constancy. This fidelity to the one purpose is one of the most marked and remarkable characteristics of the war. True, Fremont and Phelps and Hunter have seemed to deviate from this object, and to convert the war into an emancipation measure; but their acts were disavowed by their superiors, and these instances proved the exceptions and not the rule. Is it not *right* for a Government as good and as beneficent as ours to defend itself against armed assassins? Is it too much to expect that in such a conflict God will be on our side? Has not Providence already shown himself to be in our behalf?

(2) In this case, the right is supported by a large, well-organized, well disciplined and officered army; an army brave, invincible, and fighting intelligently for a principle. Its superior in these respects has never been seen.

(3) The resources of the Government are equal to all the demands of the exigency. Money, men, fertility of invention, are all with the Federal side.

(4) The history of the war thus far gives presage of its early and complete triumph. Missouri, Arkansas, Kentucky, Tennessee, Western and Eastern Virginia, North Carolina, Florida, have been wrested from the polluting presence of treason. Everywhere, in those and other portions of the country, our Starry Banner floats, in proof of past, and in pledge of future, progress and victory.

(5) The momentum of our previous success in the conduct of the war presages the more certain and rapid conquests awaiting our forces. As our momentum increases, in the same or a greater ratio the dismay and demoralization of the enemy are augmented.

The answer of the second question is similar to that of the first, for the following reasons:

(1) The *people* of the South have never, intelligently and at heart, been in favor of this Rebellion.

(2) If they had been, the oppressions under which they have suffered, and which were imposed by the leaders of this horrid conspiracy, such as conscription and the spoliation of their estates, would have detached their sympathies.

(3) The moderation and justice of our armies will undeceive multitudes who were deluded with the belief that "Beauty and Booty" were the design of the "Northern invaders," as the Union army were designated.

(4) The rapturous acclamations of the people, as with tears and shouts they hailed and welcomed the returning flag of our Union, prove that their old love for the national colors was not dead, but only stifled; and that it will burn again as before, except that the patriotism rekindled will be stronger and more incorruptible. Yes, we shall again be *one people*, with a common sympathy, a common patriotism, and a common destiny, the cords of national unity and peace confirmed and established.

These answers to the first two inquiries forestall that to the last. This Nation will be stronger and better than before. Our enhanced Federal consolidation and our success will not only preclude the hope and the attempt of any future insurrection, but it will at once raise the Government above the power of any foreign nation. The United States will not only stand abreast with Great Britain, France, or Russia; she will rank any one of them single, and equal all of them combined. But the great national debt, it is feared by some, will cripple our energies and impoverish our people. The fear is unfounded. The United States were never so strong in the elements of material wealth and greatness as now, while conducting this memorable campaign; and when it is fully over, the Nation will shake off this incumbrance as the lion shakes the dew of the morning from his mane, and start forward upon a career of progress unprecedented in the history of the world. It is sad to think of the tens of thousands of noble lives that have been sacrificed upon the altar of liberty and law, and of the still greater numbers who bear, and who will bear, the scars of terrible battle. Yet these will embalm the more in the affections of a delivered and great people the cause which demanded not in vain such a libation. Dark as has been the stormcloud which has spent its fury upon us, already the bow of promise spans the heavens, and beyond the present hour may be seen the clear azure and the shining sun.

CHAPTER XIX.

BEFORE Oregon was admitted as a State in 1857, even before she was organized as a Territory by Congress, which occurred August 14, 1848, emigrants in considerable numbers from California and the Atlantic States had settled in Oregon. In 1834, Oregon had received an accession to her population, made up of missionaries sent thither by the Missionary Society of the Methodist Episcopal Church. There were Revs. Jason and Daniel Lee, and probably one or two others, who sailed to Oregon by sea around Cape Horn. This action was probably stimulated by the appearance in St. Louis, some years before, of three Flathead Indians from beyond the Rocky Mountains, inquiring for the white man's God and the white man's Bible. The event created great interest throughout the United States. After going to Oregon and surveying the situation, Mr. Lee found it impossible to plant Indian missions in Oregon unless a reenforcement of men and women should be sent, who would be able to procure subsistence in Oregon, and who should have within themselves the power to produce the necessary provisions for sustaining life in that distant and unfurnished country. The Indians could not feed the newcomers. Indeed, it was all the Indians could do, by hunting and fishing, to provide their own means of subsistence, by hunting the game in that country, and by gathering food from the rivers, which abounded in salmon.

The Hudson Bay Company had possession of Oregon, with their stockade forts and trading factories, in which they exchanged goods for peltries and furs. They also produced from the soil, and from flocks and herds of poultry and cattle, some of the means of sustentation, and these they would not share with the missionaries, whereby they might raise those things themselves. It was supposed that the Hudson Bay Company, with these accessions, would be able to maintain by occupation the British right to Oregon, which then included all that was later known as Oregon, Washington, Idaho, and Montana.

Jason Lee returned to the States from Oregon, taking with him two Flathead Indians, with whom he traversed the country, making speeches on Oregon and displaying his Indian boys. His presence and appeals produced a strong impression upon all the people, especially upon the Methodists. Large contributions of money were made, and a considerable re-enforcement of mechanics and farmers and teachers and millwrights sailed for Oregon in the good ship *Lausanne* in 1839, *via* Cape Horn and the Sandwich Islands. They arrived in Oregon in 1840, when the mission colony numbered fifty-two adults and twenty children. It was current rumor that the United States assisted the outfit, by contributions from the secret service fund, and that this was done with a view of furnishing the claim to Oregon, as a part of the national domain, by the argument from occupation. It is generally believed that these early residents, colonists, and missionaries were potent factors in determining the settlement of the north boundary contention in favor of the United States.

A recent attempt has been made to claim for Dr. Marcus Whitman, a Presbyterian missionary to Oregon, the credit for having determined the right of the United States to Oregon. The claim, however, has not adequate support from existing facts. Rev. H. K. Hines, D. D., one of the later missionaries to Oregon, has, in my judgment, fully established the claim of Jason Lee to the high honor which has been sought for Dr. Whitman. Dr. Marcus Whitman and his wife, Rev. H. H. Spalding and his wife, and W. H. Gray, crossed the Plains in 1836, two years after the arrival of Jason and Daniel Lee. Mr. Lee's re-enforcements reached Oregon in 1840. Those of Dr. Whitman four years later. Dr. Hines, in a very able and fair historical article in the *Methodist Review*, and in papers since published in the *Pacific Christian Advocate*, has conclusively supported the superior claims of Jason Lee and his associates over those of Dr. Whitman to the high honor claimed for Dr. Whitman.

The Hudson Bay Company would not furnish sheep or cattle or horses or poultry to the missionaries. Mr. Lee went to California and procured them, whereby flocks and herds and poultry were grown, and thus the missionaries had meat for food. In 1843 the settlers in the Willamette Valley numbered two hundred and forty-two. Steps were taken to secure a Government, by a choice of officers and the organization of a Provisional Government for Oregon. George Abernethy, a layman, and one of the re-enforcement of 1840, was elected the provisional governor. Five years later the United States Congress, August 14, 1848, organized the Territory of Oregon. The Act included the Donation Land Law, by which every white settler in Oregon, being there as such, and afterwards, until December 1, 1851, was entitled to three hundred and twenty acres of land, if a single man; and if a married man, his wife was also entitled to a like quantity. That law also gave to every missionary station then existing in Oregon six hundred and forty acres of land, including the site of the mission.

The northwestern boundary-line was, however, long a vexed question between the two Governments. Great Britain claimed Oregon from the 30th degree of north latitude to the 60th degree of north latitude. The United States claimed Oregon by virtue of the entrance of Captain Gray into the Columbia River in 1792. We also held that Oregon was included in the sale of Louisiana by France in 1803. In 1818 a treaty of joint occupation was made between the two Governments, which left these lines as a vexed question. In 1842 the treaty fixing the northern boundary-line of the United States at 49 degrees north latitude was concluded between the United States and Great Britain, Daniel Webster and Lord Ashburton the commissioners between the contracting powers. It was not ratified until 1846. Great Britain wanted the whole island of Vancouver, which the 49th parallel of north latitude bisected into nearly equal halves. The Gulf of Georgia divides Vancouver Island from the mainland. At the 49th parallel the gulf between the island and the mainland is quite narrow. The boundary-line at the point of intersection of the island is in terms as follows: "Thence (westerly) on the 49th degree of north latitude to the center of the Gulf of Georgia, and thence by the main ship channel to the Straits of Fuca, and thence through the Straits of Fuca to the sea." The part of the Gulf of Georgia south of 49 degrees north latitude is an immense body of water, with very many islands, large and small, and a shore-line of twenty-eight hundred miles. There are two channels through the Gulf of Georgia, viz.: The Canal de Haro and the Straits of Rosario. The former is plain, short, and direct to the sea. It hugs Vancouver Island right around to the ocean. A ship turned loose on the 49th parallel would follow the channel current without guide or pilot out to the sea. The channel called the Straits of Rosario is long, crooked, difficult, and unsafe. It hugs the shore of the bay, throwing all the islands in the Gulf of Georgia south of the 49th parallel into British America; whereas, the object in deflecting the line on the east side of Vancouver Island was to throw that island into British America, the Straits of Rosario line would throw hundreds of other islands south of 49th parallel to Great Britain. We claimed all those islands in the Gulf of

Georgia, maintaining, and rightly, that the Canal de Haro was the boundary-line around Vancouver Island. The Legislature of Washington Territory formed the county of Whatcom, to include the islands in the Gulf of Georgia. The island of San Juan lies on the south and east side of the Canal de Haro, and the island of San Juan was then included in the county of Whatcom.

An employee of the Hudson Bay Company had squatted on the northwest end of San Juan with a flock of sheep. A Yankee settler had taken up his claim on the other end of the same island. His stock consisted of hogs. The hogs had trespassed upon the grounds of the Britisher; or, *vice versa*, the sheep of the Britisher had trespassed upon the lands of the Yankee. Both men were tenacious and plucky; neither would yield. They would enforce their several claims. The Britisher had re-enforced himself with an armed company of marines. Brother Jonathan had re-enforced himself by a company of United States infantry, under command of Captain Pickett, later known as General Pickett of the Confederate army. Thus they confronted one another with shotted guns. The slightest mismove might have precipitated war. This was the situation in the summer of 1859. President Buchanan sent General Winfield Scott to negotiate a truce, until King William of Prussia should decide which of these two channels, the Canal de Haro or the Straits of Rosario, was the true boundary-line between Great Britain and the United States. A few years ago he decided that

the Canal de Haro was the boundary-line. When
I saw General Scott on his visit to Oregon upon
that mission, he was one of the finest-looking men
I ever saw. He was somewhat corpulent, but not
excessively so. He must have been some years
past seventy; probably seventy-three. His expressive blue eyes, and his ruddy, blond complexion,
his style, and poise, deeply impressed me. I published the following sketch of him about the time
when he was retired, by his own request, from active military life. He was brevet lieutenant-general
from January, 1841, to November 1, 1861:

GENERAL SCOTT.

Our readers will have noticed that General Winfield Scott, by his own request, has been placed, by
order of the President, upon the retired list, and thus,
after many years of service and honor, he ceases to be
the commander-in-chief of the military forces of the
United States.

General Scott was born the 13th of June, 1786.
He is, therefore, now over seventy-six years of age.
He studied law in Richmond, Virginia but through
the influence of a friend obtained, May 8, 1808, a cap-
taincy in the light artillery. In 1809 he was ordered to
New Orleans, where he gave offense to his commanding officer, Wilkinson, by his severe military criticisms,
and was tried by court-martial upon a charge of em-
bezzlement, and, second, that he used disrespectful
language towards his commanding officer. He was
acquitted of the first charge; but upon the second he
was sentenced to suspension from rank and pay for
one year. He spent the year at the house of Benjamin
Watkins Leigh in pursuing military studies, and prob-

ably there laid the foundation of his future fame. In July, 1812, he was appointed lieutenant-colonel, and was stationed at Black Rock. On the 13th of October he was taken prisoner at the disastrous battle of Queenstown Heights; not, however, till he had shown of what he was capable when his blood was up. After his exchange he joined General Dearborn as his adjutant, in which capacity he was of great use in organizing the several departments of the army. He led the advance when Fort George was taken by storm, and tore down the British colors with his own hands. In July, 1813, Scott was promoted to the command of two regiments, resigning his adjutancy. In September he burnt the barracks and public stores at Toronto, took eleven armed boats, considerable ammunition, and several cannon. The year 1813, upon the whole, closed disastrously to the American arms. But Scott's name loomed up as the coming man, and in March, 1814, he received the appointment of brigadier-general. The army placed in quarters were drilled for more than three months by Scott himself, and were perfected in all the evolutions of war. On the 3d of July, Scott took possession of Fort Erie, and on the 5th was fought the battle of Chippewa, on an open plain. With hardly equal numbers, our brave army met the veterans of England, and displayed to the world that we were of the old race, and that the blood of Crecy, Poitiers, of Agincourt and of Blenheim, tingled in our veins. Twenty days after was fought the battle of Niagara— the most bloody, determined engagement which ever took place on this continent, and, in proportion to numbers engaged, the most bloody of modern warfare. While Chippewa and Lundy's Lane are remembered, we shall hear of no intervention on the part of England. If Scott had done nothing more than given us Chippewa and Niagara, it should render him immortal.

They were the prelude of future greatness. They settled, quite as much as Webster, the northeastern boundary question, the Oregon question, the Mosquito question, and will have an ever-living, abiding influence in all questions yet to come.

We have not time to mention the services of General Scott from the time he left Niagara, wounded, to the present hour. It is known of all men. His arduous, patriotic toil; his wisdom in the South Carolina troubles, in the various disputes with England; his triumphant march on the capital of the Montezumas, worthy of Marlborough or Turenne; his wise foresight in our present troubles in advising Mr. Buchanan to increase the force in the Southern forts. But in our opinion, the service which he rendered his country, high above all others—higher by far than the glories of Niagara, Cerro Gordo, or Chapultepec; higher, brighter, purer, more enduring than the most resplendent military achievement—was the shield which his great name afforded against the assaults of Confederate traitors, banded together to overthrow our Constitution, to trample on our laws, dissever our Union, and throw the pall of anarchy over the fairest fabric of Constitutional freedom the world has ever known. All honor to the gallant Massachusetts volunteers, who again rendered illustrious the 19th of April; all honor to the New York Seventh, to all the patriotic hosts who rushed to the defense of the beleaguered Capital,—but had Scott not been there to regulate and arrange, to create and discipline, we have little doubt we should to-day have to mourn over the burning embers of our smoking Capitol. Go, then, leader of our armies; thou hast led us to victory and honor; thou hast saved us in the hour of our peril, and as thou descendest into the dark night of the tomb thou wilt be followed by the best wishes of a still great, happy, free, exulting Nation. Your name and ours are forever united. Washington first, Scott second; who shall be third?

When this sketch was written, Lincoln had not yet achieved the glory which afterwards garlanded him. Grant and Garfield were then unknown quantities.

OUR FIRST MISSION HOUSE IN OREGON.

Our missionaries in Oregon having, in September, 1834, selected the spot on which to erect a comfortable habitation, like pioneer settlers, as well as teachers of our holy religion, they began to clear the land and build a log house. They labored under great inconveniences, as must be supposed. Their oxen were but half-tamed, their tools few and needing to be put in order, and their best shelter, after the fatigue of the day, was a canvas tent. To add to their trials, a violent storm of wind and rain visited them in the midst of their labor, wetting their effects and flooding their works. But all this they submitted to patiently, and in a few weeks their tabernacle in this wilderness was set up in the name of the great God, whom this dark corner of the earth had never known, and was so far completed as to shelter them from the approaching rainy season. It was, doubtless, to eyes accustomed to look upon the elegant mansions of civilized society, but a rude hut. Its dimensions were thirty feet in length and twenty feet in width, separated into two rooms by a partition in the middle. Rough doors split from the logs and hung on wooden hinges, a plank floor, a chimney made of sticks and lined with clay, and four windows, the sashes made in part with a jackknife, constituted its finishing. Its furniture consisted of a chair, a table, and stools, all of domestic manufacture. Their cows afforded them milk, and to the provisions of their outfit were added a little flour from Vancouver, and occasionally game from the Indians. Thus provided, they commenced clearing the land to plant for their future sustenance, to teach the natives, and preach to the emigrants, as opportunities were presented.

The Methodist missionaries who went to Oregon in 1834 had much to do in determining the question of Oregon's entering into the national domain. In 1846 the slogan of the Democratic party, when Mr. Polk ran upon that ticket, was "54 degrees 40 minutes, or fight." The treaty between Great Britain and the United States fixed the 49th degree of north latitude as our boundary. But we probably should not have obtained even that if Oregon had not been in possession by the emigrations induced to seek Oregon because the Methodists had pioneered the way.

Third Period.

RECONSTRUCTION.

CHAPTER XX.

IN asking a year's absence from the Oregon Conference, the chief object was, that I might put in some work for the Boys in Blue at the front. I should have been in the service of the country as a soldier, only that I was so situated that I could not well leave the work placed upon me by my election as editor of a religious paper in a new and distant part of the country, however strong my inclination might have been, without unfaithfulness to a trust which had been accepted by me.

When my nine years of service on the *Pacific Christian Advocate* were up, I declined a re-election. I placed my wife and our adopted daughter at a friend's in Madison, New York, and made my way to City Point, in Virginia, in January following, as a delegate of the Christian Commission. The Sanitary Commission and the Christian Commission were kindred voluntary associations for helping the soldiers in the field. The former supplied the soldiers with proper physical care and provision, thus supplementing the army rations with delicacies and comforts, especially in the time of military engagements, and then furnishing nursing and care to the sick and wounded soldiers. The latter also applied physical nursing and care to the sick and wounded men at the front, and added to these physical ministrations those of a moral and spiritual character. While the country was heavily taxed for the war expenses, the people of the United States could not resist the patriotic and philanthropic impulse to send additional provisions and help to the Union soldiers. In this behalf, ten millions of dollars were contributed by each of these benevolent associations to this humane purpose, by means of the ladies and gentlemen co-operating in this behalf. The Christian Commission raised as much in their work for the moral and spiritual welfare and comfort of the Union soldiers.

The two months I spent as a delegate of the Christian Commission, while involving some hardships and discomforts, nevertheless yielded a rich compensation. I preached to soldiers two or three evenings each week, and on Sundays once or twice each Sunday. Many of them heard their last sermon on earth from my lips. Some of the incidents were of thrilling interest, and all of them were sadly enjoyable. The reader will share somewhat in the pleasure I found in ministering to my fellow-patriots in their suffering and sore need on the field, in the amputating-room, and in the hospital, by re-traversing the service as here outlined, or by my adducing of excerpta from my daily memoranda of those weeks and months of this voluntary service.

General Grant extended his left line some three or four miles to Hatcher's Run. This was some five or six miles up the railroad from City Point. Several of us went up the first day of the engagement, and stopped at the railroad station there, to attend upon some soldiers who had been wounded in the battle, and brought down from the lines in ambulances to be placed in cars, if able to endure the trip, and to be transported by rail to City Point hospital. Those unable to endure transportation were to remain in tents for treatment, as their condition might seem to require. It was a stinging cold February night. The wounded boys had been temporarily treated, and sent down to the railroad. We gave them hot coffee and nourishing food, and placed them in the cars. I carried one bright young lad, and laid him gently in the car upon straw provided for the purpose. After laying him down, I saw in his overcoat breast-pocket a small Bible. Said I, "Soldier, may I look at your book?" He nodded consent. I opened the Bible, and read the name inserted on the fly-leaf. The inscription ran: "To my dear son, Edward ——, from his loving mother: My son, make this book the guide of your daily life." I said to him, "Have you complied with your mother's request?" "O yes," was the reply. "Do you love this blessed Book?" He said, "Yes, indeed." "Do you love the Lord?" He made answer: "Yes, I do. He has been with me every day since I left home and came into the army. The Lord is very good, indeed, to me. He has never forsaken me."

I found a man in the ambulance awaiting some one or more to carry him to the car. He had been severely wounded. He had lost much blood, and he was suffering very greatly. I felt his pulse. It was quite weak, denoting prostration. I gave him some hot coffee, and put some cordial tonic into it, hoping to rally and revive him before he should be put into the car. He was an Irishman. He inquired, "Is it a chaplain yees are?" "O no!" said I; "I am a minister, and I came down in the service of the Christian Commission to the field, to help you in your need, and to show you that you are not forgotten nor neglected by us." "Well! well!" said he; "I do n't know much about that society; but I do say from my heart, God bless all the likes o' yees." I heard of another Irishman who was dying, and Dr. M—— told him of Jesus and his love, and prayed for him in his last moments. He gave him his blessing in this form: "May God Almighty bliss ye and kape ye, and whin ye die may ivery blissed hair iv your head be a lighted candle to light your soul through purgatory!"

After the cars were filled and the train had started, I went into one of the tents. A soldier was just brought in, who was shot in the neck. He was unconscious. I assisted in holding him up in the cot until they could get off his clothes to examine his wounds. The tent was quite warm; the smell of the blood and the grasp of my hand by the sufferer overcame me. I called an orderly to take my place, and went out into the cold and lay down upon my back to prevent fainting away. I recovered, and resumed the service for several hours, going from tent to tent and from ambulance to ambulance, to render help as needed. The next day I went up to the battle-field. I took my place in the rear of the lines, to assist with stretchers to carry wounded men to ambulances, to be thus conveyed to the field hospital. The bullets sang in the trees above me, and the leaves clipped by the shots were all the time falling.

In the afternoon I was assigned to duty at the field hospital. We were very busy carrying wounded men on stretchers into and from the hospital. One noble young man, a colonel, had been struck on the knee by an exploding shell, shattering the knee. His limb required amputation well up towards the thigh. His leg was taken off, and he was placed on a stretcher, and carried upon it six or seven miles to the general hospital at the Point by relays of carriers. The case was pathetic. His term of enlistment had expired the day before. Some days after this I went into the hospital at City Point. His wound had sloughed. The artery had lost the ligature. The limb had been again cut off higher up, and again it had sloughed. The orderly was holding the artery closed by his thumb. The soldier was delirious. He was muttering his commands. After holding the artery for some time, the surgeon said, "Let go." In a very few minutes he had passed away.

In the field hospital at the close of the day there was a large and ghastly pile of dismembered legs and arms to be seen. The field hospital was an old-fashioned Viriginia house, with a large hall in the center, and on one side the hall was the parlor, converted into an operating-room. Over the mantel was an engraving of Bishop Porteus's "Court of Death." The floor was slippery with human blood, and that picture was in keeping with the gory scene of the amputating-room. On the other side of the hall was the residence room. At each end of the house, and on its outside, was the inevitable chimney. During the day there was a lull in the fighting, and in which no victims were brought in. The surgeon had opened the piano, which stood in the hall, an old, decayed instrument, whose brassy, tinkling strings were unmusical and discordant. An orderly was found who could play. The women of the family were brought to the door, and treated to Union music. The roar of the cannon had become still. Behind the two white women were the black women of the place, as a setting for the picture. Led by the instrument, the boys sang, "John Brown's body lies a-moldering in the grave," and "We'll hang Jeff Davis on a sour apple-tree." "Well, you'll have to catch him first," said one of the angry women. I learned afterwards that the reason for this infliction was this: A wounded soldier lay in the yard, who had been disemboweled by a shell. His dying agonies were mocked by the woman, as having deserved and incurred this suffering by invading the sacred soil of Virginia. After this musical entertainment the surgeon said he had got even with that inhuman female mocker, and he was satisfied.

During one of those days, Dwight L. Moody and I went together into the Negro quarters, and he conversed with some of the colored women awhile. He asked a Negress, "Aunty, do you think the Lord Jesus loves his colored children as much as he does the whites?" After a slight pause, she replied, "Brother, the Lord Jesus loves all his redeemed children."

My main place of work was in the field hospital. I had charge of a ward of two hundred patients. Some were suffering from wounds, others from fever or pneumonia or some other ailment. I visited them twice a day, and sometimes three times. I conversed with them, wrote letters for them to their friends, and prayed with any of them who desired it. Generally, the evening call was the most impressive, as usually the deaths occurred during the night, and we buried from two to six or eight each morning, burying them with military honors.

One evening I passed the cot of a dear young soldier with whom I had conversed freely, and who had expressed himself as ready to die. I had written for him several times to his parents and sisters. As I was about passing his cot he seemed sleeping. I laid my hand gently upon his head, and let it rest there for some moments. He opened his eyes, and fixed their large, expressive look upon me, and said: "That was so sweet. I dreamed it was my mother's hand upon my head." The next morning his cot was vacant, and I had the sad duty of committing his body to the grave, "Earth to earth, ashes to ashes, dust to dust." I wrote his mother of the safe and beautiful death of her darling son.

I had a chat with a gray-haired Negro about the war. Said I, "Uncle, I hear it said that you colored folks don't want to be free; that you would rather be slaves than be free." "Well," said he, "massa, you shall tie up a dog to a tree, and give him a long rope. He will go this way as far as he can, and then go the other way as far as he can, and then set up a dreadful howl. Now," said he, "if a dog feels that way to be confined, how do you suppose a man would feel to be a slave?"

Chaplain Hunt told me this story about a colored man early in the war, before the Negroes had been enlisted into the army. He said, "Uncle, why do n't you colored people fight?" He replied, "O massa, we 's de bone." "Well, but," said the chaplain, "why do n't you colored folks fight?" He responded: "Masssa, we 's de bone. You see two dogs fighting over de bone; de bone do n't fight."

I attended a colored meeting in the 24th Army Corps. It was a very lively meeting. One person had had some difficulty in getting a chance to tell his experience. He said: "I done left my wife and my two offsprings in Norfolk, on de oder side of our lines. Byme-by, when de cruel war is ober, if we should never meet again on dis earth, we shall meet in heaven. The city up dere have four gates, and if she goes in at one gate, and I go in at another, it will be all the same as if we bof went through the same gate." Another man expressed himself thus: "Brudders! Lub will gib de debil de lockjaw. You think dat am a queer saying, but I will prove him. When Massa Jesus converted my soul, den I prays to him, and I said, 'O Massa Jesus, convert Massa Tom, for he used de lash on me heavy because I pray.' Den Massa Tom he was converted. He say to me in de mawning, 'Now, Jem, it is time to get up and come in to prayers.' Befo' it was a crack of de whip and a bitter curse; now de whip is done gone, and Massa Tom he prays instead."

I once went through Grant's lines before Richmond without a pass. George H. Stuart, the president of our Christian Commission, sent a number of Philadelphia gentlemen down to the Point, who were greatly interested in the work of the Christian Commission, and they wished to go through Grant's lines. Rev. Erastus Smith, the gentleman in charge of our work at the front, desired me to take the company through the lines. But our passes had all been sent up to General Ord's headquarters for renewal, and none of us had the password. We entered the Christian Commission ambulance, which had our name painted upon it in large, white letters; and then, besides, I carried the badge of all delegates of the Christian Commission upon my right coat lapel. When we reached the sentinel he demanded the password. I told him the situation: "These gentlemen must go back to Philadelphia to-day. They are great contributors to our funds, and brimming over with loyalty. You see this badge, and you see that is the Christian Commission ambulance." "Well," says he, "it is in violation of my orders." Said I, "Can not you speak to your chief, the officer in command?" He did so, and we went through without interruption. He said, "You must take the risk about getting through when you return." When I returned another sentinel was on guard. He refused to let me pass, and we could not get through until a messenger was sent to General Ord's quarters. Then, when I gave him the password, we got through.

My service in the army was exceedingly fascinating. I would not be without it upon any consideration. I was in only the one battle I have described. War is a dreadful scourge. Patriotism and philanthropy have large scope and verge when war lifts its horrid front. These virtues shine conspicuously on the wrinkled visage of bloody war. They show that, dreadful as war is, it has its offsets in the charities which keep step with the army, and display and dispense their divine, angelic healing and help amid the shadows and bloody orgies of war. I shall ever be thankful for the opportunity which God gave me to minister for him to my fellow-citizens in the field of strife and death. And I shall all the more appreciate the sterling patriotism displayed, both in the field and by the citizenship of the country generally, in sustaining the army.

CHAPTER XXI.

THIS chapter opens with a new departure. My transfer to East Tennessee seems to me quite as providential as any other part of my checkered life. My intense sympathy with the Union cause during the war led me greatly to admire the patriotism of the people in this Switzerland of the United States. The heroism of the Waldensians and the Albigenses on the southern slopes of the Alps, during centuries of bloody papal persecution, always kindled my liveliest admiration. To them I likened the East Tennesseans and the Bridge-burners, who took this method to impede the transportation of Confederate troops and munitions of war. This they did deliberately and fearlessly on peril of their lives, and at the cost of their lives. I have often wept while reading the story of their intensely loyal deeds, and the dreadful work they so bravely, and even cheerfully, accepted.

I decided that if Providence would so direct, it would give me great pleasure to serve them as a minister. I had tempting offers to stay in Oregon. I was offered the editorship of the *Pacific Christian Advocate*. I was invited to become the pastor of Union Methodist Episcopal Church in St. Louis, and to re-enter my old Conference, and become pastor of some of my former charges there: Binghamton, N. Y., and Wilkesbarre, Pa. I decided to come East, and get nearer the Hub. Oregon was on the periphery. All my relatives and those of my wife were three or four thousand miles away. I could not return to visit them, without incurring several hundred dollars' expenses. During the war my heart was with the flag and the Union it represented. I chafed under the inexorable conditions which compelled my stay so far away from the center of things. When my eight years of General Conference editorship on the *Advocate* were up, I declined a re-election, as already stated, so that I might be more nearly in the midst of events.

Coming East, many tempting offers were made me. Bishop Clark presided in the Oregon Conference, when, in October, 1864, I left on a year's leave of absence, the first object of which was that I might put in service in the field as a delegate of the Christian Commission, a purpose which I executed at my own expense the last two months of the war. Bishop Clark expressed the hope that he could place me in the South in Church reconstruction. Thus things were urged upon my attention. I attended the session of the Wyoming Conference. The other calls were not yet imminent. I was readmitted among my earlier Conference associates where I began my ministry. I took an appointment in Binghamton, where a new and elegant church was to be built in one of the last charges I had filled before going to Oregon. Thus and there I wrought for six weeks, telling the Binghamton friends that my heart was in the South, and that if the call came I would have to obey it. Bishop Clark wrote to me, inviting me to accompany him in June to East Tennessee, from which an urgent appeal had come from a large laymen's and ministers' Convention, asking the bishops of the dear old Methodist Episcopal Church again to extend over them their sheltering wing. I laid his letter before my Official Board, and obtained their approval of my going and a three weeks' leave of absence. They expressed the hope that, however urgent the call for my transfer might be, I would decline it, and return to them. I went. The spirit of the men was contagious. Their story of the sufferings and sacrifices they had endured for the dear old flag set my heart all aflame to enter into their joy, and assist them in their high endeavor. I reported their experiences in the *Western Christian Advocate* within a few days after they had so feelingly rehearsed it in the Conference love-feast. This report I here insert. I am sure this history will give my readers great pleasure, and I therefore insert it in full.

ORGANIZATION OF THE HOLSTON CONFERENCE OF THE METHODIST EPISCOPAL CHURCH.

ATHENS, EAST TENNESSEE, *June 1, 1865.*

An eventful day for East Tennessee is this first day of June, in the year of grace 1865. It was scarcely less so when the loyal East Tennessee Methodists met in Convention at Knoxville, on the 7th and 8th days of July, and determined to separate themselves from a Church which had been the apologists and defenders of slavery, and the fomenters and supporters of treason, secession, and rebellion, and connect themselves with the Methodist Episcopal Church, which had always stood loyally by the Government of the United States, and which had also been that of their early choice, and upon which God had continued to put honor. A large audience assembled to-day in the Methodist Episcopal Church at Athens, East Tennessee, at nine o'clock. Rev. Bishop Clark opened the services by reading the one hundred and twenty-sixth Psalm and the fifteenth chapter of St. John's Gospel. The hymn

"And are we yet alive?"

was sung, after which prayer was offered by the bishop. The hymn,

"How beauteous are their feet,"

was sung, and Rev. James Cummings and Dr. Adam Poe addressed the Throne of Grace. .

Bishop Clark then remarked in substance:

"BELOVED BRETHREN,—I am not insensible of the responsibilities of this hour, nor of the solemnity of the occasion that has called us together. Indulge me for a few moments in reference to sundry matters, that we may more fully understand ourselves, our relation to the work before us, and the work we have to do. On referring to the records of the Church, I find that the Holston Conference was organized in the year 1824, with a membership of fourteen thousand nine hundred and thirty-four, and forty-one ministers. From that time forth there was a gradual increase of members, till, in 1840, there was a membership of forty thousand and sixty-three, and a ministry of seventy-three. Twenty years ago the last entry in the Minutes of the Methodist Episcopal Church of the Holston Conference was made. But, since that time, what scenes have transpired! The division of the Church, or, rather, the separation of a large number of its members from its communion. Strange coincidences, or rather providences, sometimes occur. I see that twenty years ago, according to those Minutes, the Holston Conference was to have assembled in this place. Before the time arrived the separation had occurred. But here, in the very place where it disappeared, we meet to reorganize it. I do not know whether it was designed [a voice: "It was"]; but the coincidence is marked. I remember with what reluctance the old Holston Conference went out of the old Methodist Episcopal Church; how tenacious the Quarterly Conferences were for adhering. And, in connection with this, let me say, that not only the whole Methodist Church, but the whole country, has had its eye upon East Tennessee. Your love of country was well in harmony with your love of the old Church. And we felt deeply that it was not in the power of the Government to afford you the protection you needed, and that you suffered so much from your devotion. But, thanks be to God, deliverance came to the Nation, and I trust deliverance will come also to the Church, and, as you have taken your place under the Stars and Stripes, that you will also take your place under the old banners of the Methodist Episcopal Church. [A voice: "We will."]

"Why am I here at this hour? Last year, after our General Conference was held, a Convention, largely representing your laity and ministry, was held at Knoxville, and there and then you announced the purpose to reunite with the Methodist Episcopal Church, and invoked our aid. During the last year we have done what we could to aid you in your work, and I am here to organize your Conference.

"I touch upon a point which I had not intended

to name; but it seems proper, from facts which have come to my knowledge, with regard to this organization. The question has been asked, 'Why reorganize?' The plan that has been suggested is that it would be better to leave the Southern Church territory undisturbed. Let us leave this ground untouched, and hold a General Conference of both Churches, and reunite the Church South, by a simple act, to the Methodist Episcopal Church. I do not say the proposition has been made in a formal manner; for no Conferences have been held in the Southern Church to make it; but it has been made by prominent members and ministers of the Methodist Episcopal Church, South, with singular concurrence and unanimity.

"I cite one reason why I think this proposition, that we should stay out of the South, can not be entertained. If we refuse to respond to these calls from East Tennessee and elsewhere—for the calls are from different parts of the South—the effect would be to leave to the men, who have not been with the Government of the United States in its fearful struggle against rebellion, the work of reorganization of the Church. Now, if there is any class of men in the South who should take part in the rebuilding of the Church and the State, it is the loyal portion. I do not feel that we should subject them to this deprivation.

"The division of the Methodist Episcopal Church had one single ground, and that was slavery. You can not find any other. No man under heaven can find any other. We preach the same gospel, have the same organization of Conferences and districts and circuits, and the same allotments of labor, and no man on the face of the earth can fasten upon any other fact than slavery, and that is being taken out of the way. What reason, then, is there for keeping apart? There is none. I can conceive of no other than pride of position; pride of place and power; the maintaining of power in hands that have wielded it, other than for the peace and prosperity of the Government.

"Why, again, am I here to organize the Holston Conference? At our last General Conference, held in May, 1864, provision was made especially for the reception of ministers of the Church South into the Methodist Episcopal Church. It was provided that they should be received on the same conditions as those on which we receive those from the British and Canadian Wesleyan Conferences, with the proviso that they should give assurances of their loyalty to the United States, and of their agreement with us on the subject of slavery. The old Methodist Episcopal Church has been, all through this struggle, loyal to the United States. All her influences have been unmistakably in this direction. Conferences, ministers, and members, almost without exception, have all cast their influence on the side of the Government. And it was the purpose that, in the reorganization and extension of the Church, as we foresaw its extension, no element should enter into the Church that should disturb its harmony on the question of slavery, or of loyalty to the Government. We have no doubt that thousands, all through the South, have been led into this rebellion by the influences, well-nigh irresistible, thrown around them, and that, perhaps, tens of thousands have been led into it conscientiously. But I believe that, with the dawning of the signs of the times, there must come a conviction that they were mistaken, were in the wrong, and, with that conviction, if they are good men and true men, that they will be with us in these matters of loyalty and slavery.

And I can not see any other reason for their remaining aloof from our Church, unless it be the want of loyalty, or adhesion to a system now nearly defunct.

"In addition to the provisions for receiving ministers, the General Conference authorized the organization of Conferences in the South, when, in the judgment of the bishops, they should deem it important or proper; and at a meeting of the bishops they saw that the time had fully come to organize a Conference in East Tennessee.

"In pursuance of these facts I am here. I recognize the following ministers as comprising the Holston Annual Conference of the Methodist Episcopal Church: W. C. Daily, G. A. Gowan, R. H. Guthrie, transferred from the Kentucky Conference; T. S. Stivers, transferred from the Ohio Conference; Thomas H. Pearne, transferred from the Oregon Conference; and J. F. Spence, transferred from the Cincinnati Conference."

The bishop then announced that, in determining the status of the ministers applying for admission, he should take as his guide the published Minutes of the Holston Conference of the Methodist Church, South, for 1862. Since then no Minutes had been published, nor had any session of the Conference been held, other than a gathering of the treasonable portion of it within the rebel lines.

Profound interest and considerable sensibility were manifested during the address of the bishop. Brother Spence, at the request of the bishop, acted as temporary secretary.

The following brethren were severally admitted by the vote of the Conference, each one making a statement, as his name was presented, of his agreement with the Methodist Episcopal Church as to loyalty and slavery; namely, E. Rowley, James Cumming, James A. Hyden, W. H. Rogers, John W. Mann, W. C. Graves, W. H. Duggan, William Milburn, J. L. Mann, R. G. Blackburn, T. H. Russel, J. B. Little, Andrew J. Greer, and John Alley.

Dr. E. Rowley said he had been a slaveholder; did not consider himself so now; regarded slavery as removed by the war, and accepted the fact as a blessing for the whites, whatever its effect might be on the blacks.

J. Albert Hyden said that he had been educated to believe that slavery was religiously right; on that subject he gave himself no uneasiness or trouble; but that he had come to see differently. He believed, with the former speaker, that the removal of slavery would be a great blessing, the greatest blessing since the gift of Christ, to us and to our children's children. Let slavery go. He was never suspected of being loyal to the Confederacy. He remained quiet during the rebellion, and, as soon as practicable, he went into the service of God and his country as a chaplain.

W. H. Rogers said: "It may have been my misfortune that I never was a slaveholder. I was taught to hate the institution of slavery. In 1828 I joined the Methodist Episcopal Church. When the question of secession came up, my mind was made up at once. I was among the first in East Tennessee to put my name to a card in favor of allegiance to the Government. A few months afterward, nine gentlemen, fully armed, came to my house. One of them, a young man, said, 'I presume you will take the oath?' I replied, 'You presume too much. What oath?' He answered, 'That of allegiance to the Confederacy.' I replied, 'No sir! I do n't "cuss."' I was taken to Knoxville, and thence to all the Southern prisons; was in the penitentiary. I had heard of the palaces of the South. I did not find them palaces except in the sense of the poet:

> 'Prisons would palaces prove,
> If Jesus would dwell with me there.'

I had an opportunity 'to preach' Christ 'to the spirits in prison'—the Union soldiers imprisoned. Many of them were converted. I closed their eyes in death, and they took their flight from prisons to the palaces of light and glory. They went home. I returned, and, when put on trial before an ecclesiastical court, adhered to my loyalty."

John W. Mann said: "I am ready and willing to take a place among you. As far as slavery is concerned, my skirts are clear. I never owned a Negro. My wife owned one or two, but they were sacrificed on the altar of my country. I was arrested in this town, and required to take the oath or go to prison. Through the entreaties of my wife, I reluctantly took the oath of allegiance to the bogus Confederacy. I was called 'Lincoln' in this town; was proscribed and persecuted. I left here, and since then have preached in Louisville one year; afterward, in Kentucky, Ohio, and Indiana."

A venerable brother, William Milburn, remarked: "I was never connected with slavery; was not raised up to believe it was right; was taught, from boyhood, to believe it was wrong; there never was an hour in which I approved it; I do n't expect there ever will be. Have tried to be loyal to God and loyal to my Government; I have suffered much for my loyalty; was three times arrested by the authorities of the would-be Confederacy; I have had a saber presented to my throat, and, with oaths, have been required to take the oath. I said to the youth who made the demand, 'Young man, your mother has taught you better than this.' I was trotted off, lame as I was, to Greensboro. My guard all sleeping, at about one o'clock I arose, slipped off, and moved homeward, and at daylight found myself five miles from my prison. I had to remain concealed until John Morgan was killed. I united with the army, and have been with it ever since. I was ordained a deacon by Bishop Roberts, and an elder by Bishop Morris. I love the Church next to my life. I was arrested four times by the Methodist Episcopal Church, South, for my loyalty; but they always had to write, 'We find nothing immoral against him.' I understand that I was expelled by the Abingdon Conference for my loyalty. I would sooner live and die out of the Church, and be unburied, than to be in connection with the Church South. But for the clergy of the Church South this rebellion could never have occurred. The power of politicians was comparatively circumscribed; but when the clergy undertook, in co-operation with them, to rend the Nation, an influence was wielded which reached to every hamlet and fireside. I would rather have the artillery of a Bonaparte and the guns of a Wellington directed upon me than the groans and tears of the widows and orphans which have been caused by the influence of those preachers. I want to live in this Conference and to die here; and I shall do so, unless an element of treason gets into it with which I can not, and will not, associate myself. I can not describe my feelings when I first saw, in a gap of the mountains, the honored flag of my country. Have been forty-one years a member of the Church."

J. N. S. Huffaker said he had been a Union man until it seemed that secession was an accomplished fact. The State had gone out, and it looked as though the Confederacy were established. He had then taken the oath of allegiance. In this view and course he was mistaken. But when the Federal Government afforded protection to loyal men, he went to headquarters at Knoxville, and stated his desire to be a loyal man, no oath being required; that, as soon as it was required, he took the amnesty oath. He was a conservative man, was opposed to the proceedings of the Holston Conference of 1862 touching the rebellion. He believed the organization of the Holston Conference of the Church South would be required, by the force of public opinion, to disband.

J. L. Mann said: "It was my fortune or misfortune to be born in Tennessee. I was reared among all the influences of Negro slavery, and efforts were made to make me believe it was right. But I have ever been an original, unmitigated, simon-pure Abolitionist. I consider it my misfortune that I was ever connected with the Church South. I joined this Conference in 1860, at the brewing of the rebellion. I remained in the northeast corner of the State two years. The Conference of 1862 was not a Conference; it was a political inquisition presided over by that embodiment of treason, Bishop Early. I found it was too hot for me. I went to the Federal army. I took my saddlebags, and went to the Federal army, and for sixteen months I served God and my country in the army."

R. G. Blackburn said: "I was a member of the Holston Conference. My heart is with this movement, and it has been from the beginning. As this is my country, and where I have been between the gates, I may perhaps say, that I took the stand that politics and religion should be separate, and that it was not the business of a Conference to inquire into a man's sentiments, and certainly not to require him to support or favor a disloyal organization. I regard it as the duty of every Methodist in this country to give a hearty support to this movement. I regard it as the blackest treason to attempt to keep up the Methodist Church, South, in this country. Rebellion has been crushed; but to keep up another Methodist organization like that of the Church South, it is in danger of rising again, and efforts would be made to divide the country. And, if we expect to remain one people, we must have one Church in this country."

Some of the speeches, which differed little from those given, are omitted for want of room. T. H. Russel, J. B. Little, John Alley, made similar statements, and were received.

This occupied the forenoon session, constituting one of the most interesting meetings I ever attended. Tears and sobs, shouts and responses, were intermingled with the exercises.

In the afternoon, fast-day services were held in the Church, Bishop Clark and Rev. T. H. Pearne making addresses. A large audience was present.

SECOND DAY'S PROCEEDINGS.

Conference was opened with the usual services, conducted by Brother Hyden. P. H. Read, Augustus F. Shannon, S. D. Gaines, E. E. Gillenwater, Samuel B. Harwell, and David Fleming were received from the Church South. H. B. Burkitt, a probationer of the Kentucky Conference, was transferred by the bishop. Brothers G. M. Hicks, T. S. Walker, T. P. Rutherford, Joseph P. Milburn, and John Forrester, probationers in the Holston Conference of the Church South, were received. Joseph Milburn, a located elder, was recognized and readmitted. Pending the reception of several, a warm discussion arose touching the loyalty of applicants, the Conference carefully guarding against admitting those who had been active aiders of rebellion, and receiving those who had taken the oath of allegiance to the Confederacy only upon full confession and promises of amendment.

Chaplains Drake, Bowdish, and Black, and Brother Webb, of the Minnesota Conference, and Rev. Dr. Poe, were here introduced to the Conference.

SATURDAY'S PROCEEDINGS.

These were opened with customary exercises, conducted by W. C. Graves. The session was occupied in the work of examining candidates for admission into full connection, and answering the questions, "Who are admitted on trial? Who remain on trial? Who are the deacons? Who are the elders?"

The following series of resolutions, touching the principles to govern the Conference in admitting persons to the Conference who had been tainted with disloyalty, was adopted:

WHEREAS, It is expected by the loyal Methodists of the South, and especially of East Tennessee, that in the reorganization of the Holston Conference of the Methodist Episcopal Church strict inquiry will be made touching the opinions concerning, and relations to, the late rebellion, of applicants for admission and recognition as accredited ministers, and that said opinions and relations will shape, to a greater or less extent, our official action in these cases; we therefore deem it necessary to state briefly the general principles controlling us in the premises; therefore,

Resolved, 1. That it is the sense of this body that those who entered into the late rebellion, and imbibed the spirit thereof, are guilty of a crime sufficient to exclude them from the kingdom of grace and glory, and must not be admitted into this Conference, save upon full confession and thorough repentance.

Resolved, 2. That those ministers who abandoned their work and their homes, and absconded the country upon the approach of the national flag, have so far forfeited claim to our confidence and Christian fellowship, that they should not be recognized by members of this Conference as accredited ministers till they shall have been restored by the proper authorities of the Church.

Resolved, 3. That in the reception of preachers into this body constant regard will be had, not only to their personal qualifications and claims upon our Christian kindness and charity, but also to the opinions, feelings, and wishes of our people, and none ought to be admitted whose conduct, during the late rebellion, has been such as to make them odious to the masses, and whose usefulness as ministers of the gospel has been sacrificed to the unholy cause of treason and rebellion.

Resolved, 4. That, while we feel constrained thus to indicate what is now the necessary policy of this Conference, we, with hopeful hearts, look forward to the time, and hope it is not far distant, when general confidence, friendship, and good-will shall be restored, and when, as in better days, we shall be one in heart, one in purpose, and one in our great work and labor of love.

The report on the State of the Country was adopted, as follows:

Your Committee on the State of the Country respectfully report:

The Holston Conference of the Methodist Episcopal Church, in resuming the place she occupied among her sister Annual Conferences up to 1844, takes a decided position of loyalty, and heartily agrees with them in their outspoken antagonism to slavery. Our people have given costly proof of their devotion to the National Government, and by their votes slavery in Tennessee has been buried beyond, as we trust, a hope of resurrection. In assuming this position, this Conference makes for herself a very different record from that of the Holston Conference of the Methodist Episcopal Church, South, touching these questions. That Conference, held in this place in 1862, expelled one of its members "for joining the enemies of his country;" that is, for being a loyal citizen and aiding his Government in suppressing rebellion. It suspended another of its members for a similar cause. In an elaborate report, presented by John N. McTyeire, on these cases, and others similarly accused, "the continued agitation of the subject of slavery" by the Churches North is falsely assigned as the cause of the late wicked rebellion. We say "falsely," because it was not the agitation of the slavery question, but the ineradicable tendencies and vices of the system itself, which brought about the unhappy events which have transpired.

That report also openly avows and advocates the rightfulness of the late attempted disruption of the United States, and gravely urges "the duty of the Methodist Episcopal Church, South, alike because of her historical antecedents and her doctrinal peculiarities touching Southern institutions generally, and this institution—slavery—especially, to be found arrayed side by side with the great masses of the Southern people in religiously contending in part for the same rights—political, civil, and religious—for the security of which they were compelled, in 1844, to adopt measures for a separate and independent ecclesiastical organization." . . . "But now that these questions—*abstract* political questions of secession and rebellion—have assumed a concrete form, and under the inspiration of Abolition fanaticism, have kindled the fires of the most brutal and ruthless war ever known in the history of man, involving every interest, political and religious, held to be most sacred and absolutely vital to the present and future weal of our people, it is the deliberate conviction of your committee that no patriot, no Christian, and, least of all, no Christian minister who claims to be a citizen of the Confederate States of America, and who is presumed to be even partially acquainted with the merits of this unhappy controversy, can throw the *weight of his opinions, words, or acts into the scale of our enemies against us* with moral impunity, or with a conscience void of offense toward God and his fellow-countrymen."

Such *treasonable* deliverance, by a body of ministers in the nineteenth century, and in the United States, as well as the apparent spirit in which they were adopted, and the intolerant, relentless, and bitter persecutions of dissentients by which they were followed, justly produce surprise and astonishment; for they present a most humiliating fact in the history of a religious organization—a fact from which it would seem all good, true, patriotic, and Christian men must turn away with ineffable shame and regret.

In view of the foregoing facts and considerations, it is therefore

Resolved, That we hail, with intense, inexpressible pleasure and profound gratitude to God the triumph of the national arms over a gigantic, unprovoked, and wicked rebellion; the dispersion of the rebel armies which crimsoned the land with the blood of our sons and brothers, swept our homes with desolation, and filled our hearts with anguish; the established unity and integrity of our country and Government; and also the assured future of our priceless national heritage of peace and liberty, civilization and religion.

Resolved, That, as contributive to these results, we cherish with liveliest interest the hope, and we will labor with earnest zeal to realize its fruition, that soon the banners of true Methodism, loyal to country, to freedom, to right, and to God, shall wave in triumph over the whole country, from east to west, and from north to south, as now waves the banner of the Republic.

It was stated by Brother Spence that Brother Fitzgerald had been waylaid by guerrillas, marched to the woods, and robbed of watch, clothing, and money, on his way to the Conference, and that he was expecting to be appointed to North Carolina, and had no money to go with. A collection of fifty dollars was raised for him.

After the report on the State of the Country was adopted, Brother Drake, of the Ohio Conference, and other brethren, sang the Battle Hymn of the Republic.

CONFERENCE SUNDAY.

An immense audience crowded the church during the entire exercises of the day. At nine o'clock a Sunday-school meeting was had, under the direction of Brother Spence. Brethren Black, Hyden, and Gibson, army chaplains, and Pearne and Spence, addressed the meeting, the children singing sweet hosannas. Bishop Clark preached, at 10.30 o'clock, an effective sermon. At times the audience seemed quite transported by the eloquence and fervor of the bishop. At the close of the sermon eight deacons were ordained. At three o'clock P. M., Rev. T. H. Pearne, of Oregon, preached, at the close of which six were ordained elders.

MONDAY.

The Conference finished its session this morning at 10.30 o'clock. Greeneville was fixed as the place of holding the next session. Several preachers additional were received from the Church South this morning. Among them was Rev. L. W. Crouch, a prominent member of the Holston Conference.

The Conference has received forty-three, including probationers, making, with those transferred, fifty in all. Besides these, there are eighteen appointments left to be supplied. The Conference has preachers stationed in Tennessee, North Carolina, and Georgia. The statistics show a membership of 6,494, including probationers, 51 Sunday-schools, 336 officers and teachers, 2,425 scholars, 55 local preachers, and 101 churches. What a glorious result from the labors of about a year spent in hunting up the sheep scattered in the wilderness! What a precious, glorious future may not, shall not, follow this wonderful beginning!

The following are the appointments of the Conference:

KNOXVILLE DISTRICT—*Thomas. H. Pearne, P. E.*—Knoxville, J. F. Spence. Knox, Joseph P. Milburn. Rogersville, E. E. Gillenwater; supply, G. M. Hicks. Sneedsville, F. D. Crumley. Tazewell and Powell's Valley, J. B Walker; one to be supplied. Maynardsville, Thomas S. Walker. Rutledge, Philip Chambers. Jacksboro, John Forrester. Clinton, John Mahoney. Dandridge, Andrew J. Greer. Sevierville, Daniel Carter.

APPOINTMENTS.

ATHENS DISTRICT—*J. Albert Hyden, P. E.*—Athens, John W. Mann, L. W. Crouch. Athens Circuit, John E. Moore. Decatur, Joseph W. Peace. Philadelphia, J. B. Little, J. M. Stamper. Madisonville and Jellico Mission, to be supplied. Marysville, Thomas H. Russel. Louisville, T. P. Rutherford. Little River, to be supplied. Kingston and Sulphur Springs, Samuel B. Harwell, supply; one to be supplied. Montgomery, to be supplied. E. Rowley, President of and Agent for Athens Female College, and member of Athens Quarterly Conference. W. H. Rogers, Conference Agent for Sunday-schools, educational institutions, and embarrassed Churches, and member of Louisville Quarterly Conference.

CHATTANOOGA DISTRICT.—*William C. Daily, P. E.*—Chattanooga, T. S. Stivers. Cleveland, J. L. Mann. Cleveland and Benton, A. F. Shannon; one to be supplied. Hamilton and Washington, M. H. B. Burkitt, G. A. Gowan. Pikesville and Jasper, John Alley; one to be supplied. Ducktown, to be supplied. Harrison and Lafayette, two to be supplied. Dalton, to be supplied. Rome, to be supplied. Atlanta, to be supplied.

JONESBORO DISTRICT—*L. F. Drake, P. E.*—Jonesboro, to be supplied. Jonesboro Circuit, to be supplied. Elizabethtown and Taylorsville, Harmon J. Crumley. Blountville and Bristol, to be supplied. Kingsport, S. G Gaines. Rheatown, Joseph Milburn. Greeneville, to be supplied. Morristown, W. C. Graves. Fall Branch and Kingsport, to be supplied. St. Clair, to be supplied. Newport, James Mahoney. North Carolina Circuit, A. R. Wilson, J. B. Fitzgerald. William Milburn chaplain in the army, and member of Rheatown Quarterly Conference.

CHAPTER XXII.

ON the last day of the session of the Holston Conference, just before adjournment, Bishop Clark made the following closing remarks, which were phonographically reported by Rev. C. G. Bowdish:

BRETHREN,—Though the time for the departure of the train which must bear us away is at hand, indulge me in a few remarks at this closing hour.

And, first, allow me to return thanks for the kind mention you have made of my services, and the generous expression of confidence and affection made by you in the resolution just passed. Next to the approval of God and my own conscience, I hold that of my brethren in highest honor. If my official services among you, in the new and anomalous state of affairs in which we have been placed, have received your approbation, I am glad. And truly thankful shall I be if they are approved by the great Head of the Church, and shall tend to promote the great ends of a pure Christianity among you.

The uniform kindness and courtesy that have characterized your intercourse throughout, the harmony of thought, and purpose, and feeling, are worthy of all commendation. We came together strangers to each other. You were without organization. Everything was in a chaotic state. You had to become acquainted with each other's views, and feelings, and purposes. You had to learn, to a great extent, who among you could be relied upon, and how much reliance could be placed upon the movement as a whole. To see you, then, blending together so harmoniously, becoming one in feeling, plan, and purpose, and giving shape to your movement with as much system and order as an old-established Conference, was not only a sight beautiful to the eye, but a cause of profound gratitude to Almighty God, who has given you this will and purpose. But into this you have been schooled, in a great measure, by the common perils through which you have passed, and the common sufferings you have endured in this ruthless war, which has swept over and desolated so large a portion of this land. From questions which have been proposed to me, I judge it may not be amiss to repeat the explanations which have already been given on one or two points: First. With regard to the specific conditions upon which ministers coming from the Methodist Episcopal Church, South, are received among us. You will observe these conditions are the same as those required of ministers coming from the Wesleyan Connection in England, with the addition that they are to give satisfactory assurances to the Annual Conference of their loyalty to the National Government, and also of their hearty approval of the anti-slavery doctrine of our Church. This was not designed as a reflection upon any individual minister; but you are aware, brethren, that while the old Methodist Episcopal Church has been intensely loyal to the Government, the Church South has, in every department, been tainted with treason. So, also, in regard to slavery; while the old Church has been developing into clearer and more decisive forms of practical application the anti-slavery doctrine she held from the beginning, the case has been widely different with the Church South. The cause of her separation from the old Church, the corner-stone on which she built, was slavery, and, as a result, she has not only received "*the great evil*" as a great good, but has become stained all over with the crimes of oppression and treason. I repeat it, then, that it is not a reflection upon any individual minister, but to guard against the possible creeping in again of either of those two elements, that the old Church has placed these two sentinels at the door of entrance. No true man will wish them removed. No one true to his allegiance to his country or his Church would hesitate to assume the obligation.

Brethren, on going forth from this place to engage in your work, I am aware that you are going forth to a very delicate, as well as important, mission. There is no Annual Conference in all the bounds of Christian labor where the work is environed with so many difficulties, and where so much wisdom, so much gentleness of spirit, so much patience under provocation, will be required as here in this work.

I do not say that we are utterly and entirely to ignore the past, or that you can obliterate from your minds the scenes through which you have been called to pass. Those of you who have been called to suffer, who have been fugitives from your homes, seeking hiding-places among the mountains, whose substance has been wasted, whose sons have been slain on the battle-field, or foully butchered in the presence of beseeching mothers and sisters, I do not say that you can obliterate these sufferings from your memory; I do not say that, without hearty repentance and amendment on their part, you can associate on familiar or brotherly terms with those who have assisted in bringing on this fearful state of things. And yet, brethren, it does appear to me that you are placed precisely of all others in the bounds of the Church, where, in all her history, you can best exhibit the magnanimity of Christianity; where you can exhibit that forgiveness and that love that rises above every injustice and wrong. I pray God you may go forth bearing this spirit in your heart, and may manifest it in all your labors in the vineyard of your Lord and Master. Wherever you go from this place, let it be seen that you bear this spirit with you. See to it that the precious seed you sow be not rendered unfruitful. Your provocations are great, but the indwelling spirit of Christ will make you superior to them all.

Upon the point of reconstruction I will add another word. If you wish to lay deep and broad the foundations of the Church here, you can not do it by excluding all who have been in any way connected with this rebellion, as some propose. You can not lift up your banner, and say, We will have no member nor minister that has been swept away in this fearful tide of secession, this whirlwind of desolation that has passed over this land; but it appears to me that when such persons become convinced of their error, that they were mistaken, that they were led astray by the leadership of others; when men come feeling thus, with open arms and Christian love, you should receive them and press them to your breasts, and bid them Godspeed in the way to heaven.

The announcement of the appointments of an Annual Conference is always an hour of oppressive sadness, and my feelings have ever shrunk from this duty, as a burden I should never have willingly undertaken, had not God, in his providence, placed it upon me. I am aware that all my brethren here can not be satisfied, that their views and their feelings can not always be met; their convenience, their comfort, sometimes, must be sacrificed, and the comfort of their families. The social relations of our itinerants, the comfort of their wives and children, are to be considered. I do hold that the wife of an itinerant should not be forgotten, but that her feelings and her interests should be taken into account in the adjustment of these appointments. These women, who share in the labors of the itinerant, and do their part in carrying forward the great work of an itinerant ministry— all honor to their devotion, and the blessing of heaven rest upon them!

My brethren, your mission may sometimes seem hard and uninviting, but you will remember that it is the same mission that brought the blessed Redeemer from heaven to earth. O, when you view it in this light, when you remember that this work was considered of such transcendent importance as to bring the blessed Redeemer to earth, how it swells into grandeur and importance! You go forth to-day upon the same mission, and to work in the same vineyard. You will remember that he came not here to enjoy the palaces of ease and luxury. He came not here to enjoy the comforts of home or the conveniences of life; but he came to be a homeless wanderer, that fallen humanity might be blessed, redeemed, and saved. You go forth to the same mission, and in all your joys, in all your privations and toils in the vineyard of your blessed Master, remember your Savior trod in the same path, endured the same toils, shared in the same triumphs, and reaps the same rewards. As you bow at this sacred altar, in these closing services, take of the same love that was in the heart of your blessed Master, let that spirit be kindled in your hearts, go forth bearing this spirit, and God will bless you and your labors in his vineyard.

I must now leave this work with you and with God. O, may his blessing be upon you! As your beautiful country is just beginning to recuperate from the desolations of war, and gives promise of returning beauty and prosperity, so may the spiritual heritage you cultivate "bud and blossom as the rose." May the

Great Master go with you, may you be armed and equipped as good soldiers for your work, and the blessing of God be upon you, upon your families, upon the Churches over which you have the oversight, and through your instrumentality sinners be brought home to God! And if you should fall in the work—and this may be the case—it may be that some of these fathers, full of toils and labors in the past, may cease to live, and go to their reward; or it may be that some of the middle-aged, in the strength of their manhood, and bearing the burden and heat of the day, will pass away; or it may be some young man, just rising in the morning of life, and girding himself for the work, may be called; *whoever* it may be, God grant that he may pass away with the light of heaven shining all around, and go from these scenes of toil to the immortal rewards at God's right hand!

Through all my life, down to my dying hour, shall this session of the Holston Conference live in my memory. I shall cherish with fond recollection the thought that I have been permitted to come among you, and that here the banner of the old Church, after an interval of twenty years, has been again unfurled; that Church that has won so many victories in the past, that is spreading her agencies all through the land; that is following up the tide of life along our Western frontier; that is prosecuting her missionary work all over the golden plains of the interior of our country, and spreading along the Pacific Coast; that is raising her standard in India and China. I rejoice to come among you, and, here in the South, to raise up the fallen standard of the old Church, where so many victories have been achieved in the past. Amid these scenes of former toil and triumph may that standard be lifted up forever, and onward may it be borne to still greater victories in the future!

In the *Western Christian Advocate* of August 20, 1891, I contributed the following personal recollections of the events referred to in the last chapter, with some additional particulars. As this was the beginning of our new work in the South, they will be of special interest to the reader.

BISHOP CLARK IN THE SOUTH.

The one feature of Bishop Clark's episcopal administration which will most distinguish it is the leading part he took in replanting our Church in the South, from which, twenty years before, slavery had banished it. Hundreds have said, since reconstruction, that the division of the Church in 1845 had given them great dissatisfaction. Hence they hailed the return of the old Methodist Episcopal Church with the liveliest satisfaction. In this movement Bishop Clark was a chief actor. In conducting it he displayed rare qualities as a leader and organizer. He was prudent, yet wise, bold, resourceful. He showed good judgment of men, and he handled men with skill. In twelve years' experience as a presiding elder I never sat in cabinet with a bishop more careful and wise; and in the special work of reconstruction he displayd these qualities in a marked degree. The great scope and growth of the Methodist Episcopal Church since 1865 prove his far-sighted sagacity. They show that he was divinely led. I was intimately associated with him from the beginning of his work in that Southern field. It is therefore fitting that I should detail such events of that period as will best display his characteristics in that delicate, difficult, and most significant movement.

My personal acquaintance with him began in the General Conference of 1864. Previous general knowledge of him, as a successful educator and editor, had prepossessed me in his favor. The later and closer official and personal relations I had with him confirmed my impressions. Hence I voted for him, for bishop in 1864, when he was elected.

In June, 1865, at his request, I accompanied him to Athens, Tennessee, where he reorganized the Holston Conference of the Methodist Episcopal Church. Some months before a Convention was held in Knoxville, Tennessee, consisting of local and traveling ministers and laymen of the Methodist Episcopal Church, South. The members of that Convention had been loyal to the United States during the then recent war. They also expressed the views and wishes of some thousands of other laymen, who also had been thus true. They had suffered greatly because of such loyalty. Some of them, for this reason, had been proscribed, tried, and suspended by the Holston Conference of the Methodist Episcopal Church, South. Some of them had been in rebel prisons for their devotion to the national cause. All this was duly set forth in the resolutions adopted by the Convention, and which also declared their unwillingness longer to recognize the pastors of the Methodist Episcopal Church, South, as their pastors.

The Convention also requested the authorities of the Methodist Episcopal Church to reorganize the old Methodist Episcopal Church in East Tennessee. In pursuance of these facts, Bishop Clark proceeded to Athens to organize the first Methodist Annual Conference in the late slave States since the division of the Methodist Episcopal Church in 1845. Dr. Adam Poe, then one of the Western Book Agents, was of our party. The railroads in Tennessee were yet under military control. We traveled over them on military passes.

In Nashville, Rev. J. B. McFerrin, D. D., of the Methodist Episcopal Church, South, sought and obtained an interview with Bishop Clark. By the bishop's request, Dr. Poe and myself were present on that occasion. I am the only survivor of the four persons then present. Dr. McFerrin earnestly urged the bishop to desist from, or to defer, his purpose to reorganize the old Church in the South. He hoped to see an organic union of the two Methodist Episcopal Churches after the passions and animosities of the war had subsided. He thought the reorganization of the Methodist Episcopal Church in East Tennessee would revive the smoldering embers of sectionalism, and defer for a long time, if not forever, the fulfillment of his hope of such reunion. He pleaded that the old pastors of that section could better serve the people there than new ones imported from the North.

The bishop replied, in substance, that most of the East Tennesseans had been loyal; that some of their ministers had been deposed for their loyalty, and had been otherwise ill-treated; that the large Knoxville Convention, including many preachers and laymen, and representing thousands of others, had urgently requested the re-establishment of the old Church; and that, in this request, the laymen were more strenuous than the ministers. The bishop also showed that the pastors he would appoint would be chiefly those who had served that people as pastors before and during the war; and that, if the petitioners could not have the ministry of loyal preachers of their own denomination, they would go to other Churches, and not to the Methodist Episcopal Church, South. The bishop said the Methodist Episcopal Church could not ignore the Macedonian cry coming from those sheep without shepherds and a fold; and that, finally, to provide for these and any others in the South who might ask or need such provision, would not, in his opinion, retard, but, on the contrary, would hasten, the organic unity desired, whenever the hour for it should really strike. Dr. Poe said but little, and I said nothing. I detail this conversation thus minutely as an act of justice to Bishop Clark, and because it seemed to me like a turning of the hinges of destiny.

I was transferred to the new Conference, and assigned to Knoxville District. Amid tears and shouts, Bishop Clark organized the new Conference as the Holston Conference. Four districts were formed and manned. Carefully, wisely, and thoroughly the bishop tended these new charges. He presided in two or three Conference sessions during that quadrennium, because, better than a stranger, he knew the needs of the work. How wonderfully the planting of twenty-six years ago has grown and multiplied, is demonstrated by our Church statistics. In church-building there, with suspended Church Extension drafts, he strongly and kindly re-enforced his ministers in the South with counsel and pecuniary relief, until we all came to regard him more as a father and a friend than as a leader and organizer, although he excelled in both these latter qualities.

CHAPTER XXIII.

In the *Western Christian Advocate* for June 7, 1865, appeared the following contribution from my pen:

LETTER FROM NASHVILLE.

This has been a day of special interest in Nashville. McKendree Chapel is occupied by us under a military order. The *title*, I am informed, is in the Methodist Episcopal Church. The building is seventy-five feet by one hundred. The audience-room is therefore spacious and comfortable. A basement, with class and Sunday-school rooms, is under the entire building. The congregation worshiping in old McKendree is perceptibly changing, in the diminishing number of soldiers who attend, and the greater proportion of civilians, including ladies. The parsonage premises are held and occupied by Brother McGee in similar manner as the church.

Yesterday McKendree Chapel was crowded to listen to Rev. Bishop Clark, of your city. His sermon was heard by the immense audience with profound attention. Rev. Dr. Poe, of your Book Concern, assisted in the services. They also attended and addressed the large Sunday-school which preceded the public worship. In the afternoon the sacrament of the Lord's Supper was observed, and nearly sixty communicated. At evening, Rev. T. H. Pearne, of Oregon, preached. Owing to a sudden thunder-shower, the attendance was less than in the morning, yet a good degree of interest was apparent. This is a memorable day for Nashville and Tennessee.

"There are signs in the sky that the morning is near." The Methodist Episcopal Church takes no backward steps. The *Daily Press and Times*, of this city, thus noticed the interview of Bishop Clark and others with Governor Brownlow:

INTERESTING MEETING.—Calling in at the executive room of the Capitol Saturday morning, we found Governor Brownlow in conference—we might say *Methodist Conference*—with the distinguished Bishop Clark, of the Methodist Episcopal Church, of Cincinnati; Rev. Dr. A. Poe, of the Methodist Book Concern, of the same city; Rev. T. H. Pearne, of Oregon, late editor of the *Pacific Christian Advocate*, and some three or four other Methodist clergymen, among them some of our most active chaplains. The first three named are on their way to attend the Holston Conference, which will meet in Athens, East Tennessee, on the 1st of June next. We learned that their purpose is, if possible, to effect a reunion of the Methodist Church of this State with the Church, North, so that the grand old denomination may once more be a national organization. May God speed the reunion! It will be the welding of another of those golden links whose breaking hastened our Civil War. The first was an involuntary meeting of the rebel preachers of this city, summoned by Governor Johnson in 1862, to inquire into their purposes and feelings toward the Government. Governor Johnson presided with the dignity of a bishop; but the rebellious pastors looked as sour as a barrel of pickles.

The editor is slightly incorrect as to the purpose of Bishop Clark's visit. It is not exactly to effect a union of the Methodist Church of the State with the Methodist Episcopal Church, for in Middle and Western Tennessee the Methodists have not generally indicated a desire for such reunion; but in East Tennessee some five thousand laymen and nearly thirty ministers have dissolved allegiance to the Methodist Episcopal Church, South, and propose to unite with the Methodist Episcopal Church.

On next Thursday Bishop Clark is to preside at

the reorganization of the Holston Conference of the Methodist Episcopal Church, and he will appoint pastors over the scattered Churches of East Tennessee. These pastors will be mostly those who have remained true to the Nation through the storm of rebellion, and they and the laymen to whom they will minister, prefer a Church which has never faltered in its loyalty to the National Government. Of the Conference I will write you more fully hereafter.

This place was the headquarters of the Methodist Episcopal Church, South. Here was their Book Concern and Publishing-house. The building and its machinery were converted—rumor says with the approval, if not at the instance of the agents—into an official engineery for manufacturing munitions of war for the now defunct Confederacy. When Nashville was occupied by our troops, the house was employed for holding military supplies. The building looks desolate and dilapidated.

Rev. Drs. J. B. McFerrin and A. L. P. Green, whose inflammatory speeches helped to "fire the Southern heart" in this region, and gave impetus to secession movements here, followed the Confederate army as chaplains, or otherwise, until it disbanded. They have lately returned, and taken the oath under the Amnesty Proclamation. It is said they have become convinced by events that the overthrow of rebellion and slavery is according to the will of God. Their optics must have been very obtuse not to have seen it long since.

Considerable is said here of a union of the two Methodist Churches. The plan favored by leading ministers of the Church South is for us to take the Methodist Episcopal Church, South, back as a whole, with its editors, book agents, bishops, and missionary arrangements entire. How would that be relished in the North? Bishop Soule resides six miles north of this place, on the Gallatin Pike. He is in failing health, both of mind and body.

There is a good deal of latent Copperheadism here. Secesh ladies say "The South is conquered, but not subdued," and the love for the Union is not as general nor as strong as it should be. There is considerable of the Copperish element in the Legislature, which is now in session. Negro suffrage will not be allowed at the present session. The same members will meet next fall. They may provide for it then. It is their only protection against the prevalence of anti-union, anti-freedom, pro-slavery politics in the State of Tennessee. If the Legislature does not give the Negroes the protection of the elective franchise, it will not be accorded in a generation without riots, and perhaps serious disturbance of the peace and order of the State.

Speaking of Governor Brownlow, he is in very feeble health, and I shall not be surprised if he does not live long. But his iron will and his inflexible loyalty are quite as evident as ever. A characteristic incident occurred the other day at the State-house. Dr. McFerrin, on his return from Johnston's army, called upon his excellency. The governor, recognizing him, remarked, "Well, Mac, you know what the hymn says,—

> "And while the lamp holds out to burn
> The vilest sinner may return,"—

and God knows you fill the bill."

The governor, in his correspondence with the president of the East Tennessee and Atlanta Railroad, who proposed to return the road to the governor for the stockholders, after wasting and injuring it in the service of the Confederacy, recites the wrongs and wickedness of the disloyal, rebellious president and stockholders, and assures him that, instead of receiving indemnity from the State of Tennessee, or from the Union, for damage to the road by the United States military, the stock of disloyal men will be sunk for the repairs the road may need. In his controversy with Judge Trigg, the governor is clearly right, and will be sustained.

Nashville is a queer city. It has a very fine natural site. Its State-house is one of the best, if not the best, in the Union. Some of its dwellings are elegant; many of them are small and unsightly. Mrs. Polk's residence and Mr. Polk's tomb are much visited. Her loyalty is said to be slight. Nashville is a filthy city. The hotels are mean, the fare indifferent, and the prices exorbitant. But the South, *free*, shall yet assume other and better aspects, and this city may yet rival Cleveland, in Ohio, or Syracuse, New York, for thrift and elegance. Meanness, affluence, and poverty, refinement and boorishness, are in close propinquity. An incident is related that transpired here when the news of Mr. Lincoln's assassination was received. A female rebel was exulting over the event in hearing of a wounded soldier who was traveling on crutches. Seizing one of them, he commenced cudgeling the virago, who fled from him across the street. As he could not follow her, he stooped down to the gutter, and threw mud at her, soiling her costly dress. A man came to the soldier, as her friend, to take up the quarrel for her. The soldier drew his revolver, and professed his readiness to settle the matter then and there. The defender of the rebel in crinoline, evidently deemed discretion the better part of valor, and retired from the contest.   OBSERVER.

NASHVILLE, TENN., May 29, 1865.

The following editorial in the *Western Christian Advocate* for June 14, 1865, accompanied my report of the organization of the Holston Conference, which I have already inserted in this volume:

THE HOLSTON CONFERENCE.

We again consume our first page with a single report, but so important that we think the length may well be excused. By one means and another, it seems that, all through the border region, information had been given of a proposed reunion of the two great organizations, North and South. The proceedings clearly indicate with how little favor the proposition met. Indeed, we are assured that a prospect of the success of any such measure would have materially affected if not defeated, the organization of the Conference. We can now see clearly that there was no needless delay in forming this Conference. The body is now twice the size that it could have been a year ago, and starts off with a prestige and power that augur well for its future. Bishop Clark has been as wise in his delay as he has been outspoken in his sentiments and prompt in execution. We have now fifty men in that field, with plenty of places to be supplied, where heroic ministers can find a field for all they will do and endure. Our brethren there ought to have the prayers of the Church, and its contributions, too. We adopt them heartily as our brethren, and shall be glad to make the *Western* their voice to the universal Church. We shall yet circulate through their territory, and labor together with them for the common good and the Redeemer's glory. Only think of a North Carolina Circuit! God bless the preacher! This indicates the true way to union. Here is a theory, and practice too. Let the truly loyal antislavery sentiment of the South unite with us, and let us wait for the others till they can see their folly. There will yet be but one Methodist Episcopal Church, from the Lakes to the Gulf, from ocean to ocean; but the vision may tarry. Let us wait for it; it will surely come; it will not tarry. Not one word of bitterness for any; but the world is our parish, and our unrestricted commission is to preach the gospel to every creature. Let us obey the Master, and our glory as a Church, our numbers, and all else, will take care of themselves. Nothing we could publish would be more read than these very proceedings. The place of meeting, as Bishop Clark states, was interesting for the reason assigned; the place of their next session will be scarcely less so as the home of President Johnson.

I traveled the Knoxville District the first four years of my work in the Holston Conference. The district was large. It required travel by pike for the most part. The country was traversed by mountain ranges and by large creeks and rivers, so making the labors of the incumbent severe. Yet the loyal people were kind and hospitable. We had some precious revivals each year of my incumbency on that district; but the country was in a distracted condition. The rebels were coming back to their old homes, and the loyal boys who had worn the Blue and fought under the flag of the Union, and who remembered the way the Confederate authorities had treated some of the Union people of that section during the war, did not treat them very hospitably. The Church South preachers were, in some instances, treated very roughly by their former neighbors and acquaintances. They were whipped, and perhaps otherwise maltreated. I never heard of any of them being tarred and feathered, although this might have been done. They were shot from ambuscades. All this tended to hinder the gospel. I wrote and published my deep regret at this violence and private revenge as being demoralizing, and I spoke openly and strongly against this bloodthirsty spirit. I scarcely ever held a public preaching or other service without opposing violence towards any person for past opinions or actions. I had heard that Captain Sizemore—a captain in the Union army—had threatened to kill a certain presiding elder of the Methodist Episcopal Church, South, if he came about near him attempting to preach or to hold public religious services. I went many miles out of my way to dissuade him, if possible, from carrying his threat of murder into effect. I spent nearly the whole night in urging him not to use any violence, and certainly to refrain from visiting murderous violence upon the presiding elder aforesaid, as it was an example that might have found imitators in dealing with loyal Tennesseeans. I prevailed on him to promise me that he would not molest that presiding elder in his work. The reason he assigned for his purpose to shoot the Confederate presiding elder if he should come into his neighborhood was this: He said that that presiding elder had wantonly caused the death of his young brothers while he, the United States captain in the Union service, was absent from his home. For this conservative position I fell under the disapprobation of many loyalist people in East Tennessee, and I came near losing my life because false statements appeared in the public papers incriminating me, and of those who had been in the Confederate service, for my alleged complicity with the molestation of Southern Methodist preachers.

I had occasion to attend the session of the Holston Conference of the Methodist Episcopal Church, South, in Asheville, North Carolina, in 1866, the first one they held after the close of the war. The year before the Conference had not been held, because the ministers of that body were in the rebel lines. I was set upon by several ruffians in the Conference rooms, who sought to provoke me into a wrangle, and then take my life. I was informed, when I narrated the facts to a bookseller in Asheville, that these toughs had been informed that I was aiding and abetting the proscription and abuse of Southern preachers in East Tennessee, and that this was the cause and the inspiration of the concerted onslaught made upon me. I was fired upon in Knoxville before I had been there a month, and when the murderer saw I did not fall, he ran away as fast as he could. The way I came to believe that the shot was intended for me, was because I wore a peculiar kind of hat, unlike all others worn in Knoxville. As showing the animus of the ex-Confederate Methodists in the Holston country, this incident will be in place. I went up on a freight train from Knoxville to hold a quarterly-meeting a mile or two back from the railroad. The train did not stop at the station called Strawberry Plains, but some half mile above it. The night was very dark. In going down to the station, I fell into a cattle-guard, and seriously wounded myself. The only Methodist living there whom I knew was a Mr. ———. He was a leading member of the Methodist Episcopal Church, South, and he had been an active sympathizer and worker in the Confederate cause. I think he had been in the Confederate army. I called on him with my disfigured and bleeding face, and requested him to lodge me and care for me for the night. This was refused, and I had to walk in darkness and over a strange road two miles to get entertainment and care. He knew me very well, and his was the only residence near the station affording the conveniences and care I required. I told him my situation, and said that I did not know the way to the place where my meeting was to be held, nor the name of any one there to apply to for lodging and care; but he declined my request in a rude and brusque manner.

On another occasion I went to a place to hold a quarterly-meeting on Saturday and Sunday. In that neighborhood there were quite a large number of ex-Confederates. On reaching the church, a friend took me aside, and informed me that threats had been freely made in the community that I would not be allowed to preach there, and he feared that if I attempted to hold a meeting there I would be injured, and perhaps killed. I thanked him for his due and timely warning; but stated that I would hold the meeting there, whatever the personal consequences to me might be. I entered the church and kneeled down as usual to offer a brief prayer; and then I stated to the large audience assembled that I had been informed that I would not be allowed to hold a religious service there; but that I hoped the information was not true. I had no other purpose than kindness in coming; and that freedom of speech was a right I was not willing to surrender. I should hold the meeting I said, and, if molested, I was prepared to defend myself. I displayed my revolver, and laid it down before me. I then proceeded with the meeting without interruption. I received many anonymous letters, containing pictures of coffins and skulls and crossbones, and warning me that unless I left that section of the country I would be done up by the dagger, and find my way into the coffin without further notice. These missives were very alarming to my wife; and yet she would not let me see any trepidation nor apparent alarm. They were generally signed "Ku-Klux."

My brother, Rev. William Hall Pearne, was engaged in the work of reconstruction in West Tennessee at the same time that I was operating in like lines in East Tennessee. He informed me that he repeatedly received Ku-Klux letters, and that he never referred to them, so that the senders could know his thought or feeling in regard to them. On one occasion his train was held up by the Ku-Klux. He had that day shaved off his mustache, and he thinks his life was saved because of that fact. He said the men who came into the sleeper where he was lying, drew aside the curtains, and examined every cot and the occupant. When they came to him he feigned sleep, and they did not waken him. The porter told him afterwards that he heard them say the Northern minister they were in search of wore a mustache; but that as there was no one in the sleeper who had a mustache, the man they were after they were unable to find, and he probably had not taken that train, as they had supposed. The passengers were not further molested; and after the sleeper had been searched, the train was permitted to proceed. Incidents of that nature are not particularly reassuring to the victims of such treatment. It is to be hoped that the day for conduct so barbarous has gone by forever in our country. It was designed to frighten the colored people, and to put Northerners, who, for any reason, might be obnoxious to them, in such dread that they would leave that section of the country. In repeated instances white persons were subjected to brutal treatment, and were driven away by their terrific methods.

In 1867 I went down to Atlanta, to attend a meeting of the Georgia Conference. I was returning from meeting on Sunday morning to my hotel, and met a man and a woman who seemed to want to show a hostile spirit towards me as a Northerner. As I was about to pass them they crowded as far from me as possible, and the woman said to her companion, in a loud and whining voice: "I've no patience with the Northern people, who come down here where they are not wanted; let them stay in the country where they belong." As though he did not hear her, but really because he wanted the affront repeated, he said, "What did you say?" She piped out the same remark. When I saw her evident effort to put distance between her and myself, I was strongly tempted to blow my nose significantly, and then, too, came the impulse to resent the insult by some stinging remark; but I had the grace to keep silent. If I had made any sign, or spoken any word which would have been severe or sarcastic, the Southern press would probably have made a sensational and scandalous note upon the affair, charged me with some indecent or outrageous allegation of my maltreatment of a lady in Georgia, and I could not have sent telegrams fast enough to set myself right against her story of wrong and violence.

The use of tobacco was very general. Not only the men used it by smoking and chewing it, but the women as well. Not only the boys chewed and smoked, but the girls and young women also did. The women, many of them, were snuff-dippers. They would chew the end of a stick, and when the part so chewed was soft and wet with their saliva, they would dip it into snuff, and then lay the stick, full of snuff, into their mouths. This stimulated the saliva, and the expectoration of the snuff-dippers was far more excessive than that of the men. I would hold quarterly-meetings in East Tennessee, where the amen corner occupied by the women would seem clean and sweet enough when the meeting began, and the women could kneel on the hardened tobacco spittle without soiling their silk dresses; but after the meeting had lasted one or two days, no persons could kneel there without ruining their dresses or clothes. I have seen young ladies bite off the mouth end of their cigars, and request the lighted cigar then being smoked, with which to light their cigars, and the same is true of cigarettes.

The old-fashioned large families of the earlier days of our Republic are still seen quite frequently in the South. As a rule, the families are large. I ate a Thanksgiving dinner in East Tennessee with a most remarkable family. The husband was not much, if any, above fifty, and the wife was not over forty-five, with her youngest child yet unweaned. And these persons were the parents of twenty-four children, and of several grandchildren. They were all present on the occasion named. Apparently in perfect health, they were robust, vigorous, and stalwart. The people of East Tennessee were very earnest and pronounced in their religious life. They were demonstrative. They were not timid, nor backward in making manifest their rapturous shouts and hallelujahs. It is refreshing to witness their zeal for the Master, and the matter-of-fact way in which they live their religion. They display much sensibility. They are quite emotional.

# Fourth Period.

AS UNITED STATES CONSUL.

CHAPTER XXIV.

MY appointment as United States consul came about in this way. I was under very severe strain during my five years of toil in reconstruction work in the South. My nervous system and my digestive organs gave way under the pressure. I ran down in flesh and in strength, until the impairment became very serious. The physician pronounced me incurable, unless, by a change of climate and a sea voyage and absolute rest, the decay could be arrested. Senator Brownlow procured my appointment to the consulate at Kingston, Jamaica, by President Grant. The appointment was immediately confirmed by the United States Senate.

As an experiment, I took passage at New York on a schooner, and I was upon the sea nearly three weeks. During the voyage I became so much worse, that it seemed unlikely that I should live to reach the island. I made all possible preparations for the event, and gave the paper of directions for the captain's action when the vessel should arrive at Kingston, if in the meantime I should die at sea. Providentially my life was spared. As soon as I landed I called a physician, who pronounced me curable. His prescriptions were few and simple. They were strictly followed. In a few weeks an improvement was obvious. In a short time it was apparent that the climate and the rest, together with the treatment, would result in recovery. I returned by steamer for my family, and we were soon domiciled in my new field, learning the details of the office, and arranging for my official consular residence in Kingston.

There is no secular calling which a minister could follow that is less objectionable than that of a consul of the United States. On the application of the Secretary of State, through the United States Legation at the Court of St. James, in London, an exequatur was given by the Queen of England, authorizing my official residence in Kingston, Jamaica, as a consul of the United States, so long as my conduct should meet the approbation of the British Colonial Government and that of Great Britain. The duties are light. They would not require more than an average of an hour's time for each secular day, if they could be regularly distributed; but sometimes there would be a rush, and there would be crowded into three or four days work enough for a week, and then there would be an idle period of two or three weeks, when there would be absolutely nothing to do.

The duties of the consulate relate almost exclusively to maritime affairs—the care of American ships which come into port. The vessels arriving require to be officially certified by the consul, and he gives them, when leaving, a clearance certificate. The American seamen in a foreign port are under the care of the American consul. Complaints of ill-treatment are looked into by him. Sick seamen are sent to a hospital, and proper nursing and care, clothing and board, are furnished by the United

States for all destitute American sailors arriving in American or in foreign vessels into the consular port. Ship's dues are paid into the consulate for the Seamen's Relief Fund, and the consul is the official guardian of all American sailors while in port. If the vessel has been impaired by weather or other misadventure, the consul may appoint a Board of Survey, who shall determine whether any, and, if any, what repairs shall be put upon the disabled ship; and whether the vessel is seaworthy or otherwise. All this is necessary for the protection of American shipowners and underwriters. The consul charges certain specified fees for consular service of any kind, and these are paid by the ship, or by consignees or consignors of the vessel. In addition to these duties, the consul would naturally be expected to look after any American citizens sojourning in the island for a longer or shorter time. He has no funds at his disposal to relieve destitute Americans in port; but he would, of course, give them such needed attention and counsel as he might find practicable.

The salary of the consul at Jamaica was two thousand dollars per annum. The perquisites were notarial fees for such extra copies of official papers as might be demanded by shippers or consignees or consignors, and also captains or others. These might amount to two hundred and fifty dollars per year. In addition to notarial fees, the consul has the power to appoint consular agents in other shipping ports of the island besides his own port, one-half of the fees of which go to the consular agents, and the other half to the consul as perquisites. There were seven ports of entry on the island, and I appointed to these consular agents. The fees from them amounted to several hundred dollars. All of them increased the salary of the consul perhaps nearly or quite one thousand dollars. In the event of serious injury to an American ship coming into port, the Board of Survey appointed and the necessary processes required involve considerable expense. But all the service demanded is furnished at the expense of the shipowners or consignees for original copies, which belong to the office of the consulate. Then if certified copies are demanded, these are paid for as notarial fees.

Sometimes, as the result of a survey, the ship is condemned as unseaworthy, in which case the ship is sold for the benefit of all concerned. It sometimes happens that collusion between the captain and the consignee is suspected or charged. Then the case becomes seriously complicated. Not seldom, in such an event, suits are entered against the suspected parties by the owners or underwriters. In my consulate I found an American captain, who had been sued and cast into prison. He had been confined there for over a year, at his own cost for board and expenses. After considerable correspondence and delay I procured his release, and he was returned to his own country.

During my consulate many of the natives of Cuba were, as they are now, struggling for their independence against the tyranny of Spain. Sympathizers in the United States would assist them, and furnish them transportation of war supplies and ammunition. American steamers would come to Kingston for shipping supplies, or for refuge, and obtaining these, or perhaps finding Kingston a safe harbor or refuge from pursuit by Spanish cruisers, they would remain in my port for weeks. The *Edgar Stuart*, a small steamer, was several times in the harbor of Kingston, Jamaica, and remained there for longer or shorter periods. In the autumn of 1873, the steamer *Virginius* also came into my port for escape from Spanish pursuers. The captain was chased into our waters by a Spanish war-vessel. The captain was so sorely beset, and his escape from capture was so narrow, that on his arrival he forsook his vessel, and made his way back to the United States by English steamer to Aspinwall, and thence by the Pacific Steam Navigation lines to New York. I found the ship was duly registered as an American vessel, although her history was not altogether regular and assuring. During our late Civil War the *Virginius* was engaged in running the blockade of the Southern ports. On one of her trips she was captured by the blockaders, and condemned as a prize by the Government. After the war she was sold in the port of Mobile, February, 1866; but shortly afterwards she was again acquired by the United States. In 1870 she was resold to John F. Patterson. Patterson was reputed to have been an agent of the Carlist rebellion in Cuba. It was alleged that he purchased the *Virginius* for the sake of Quesada and Bambetta, well-known Cuban patriots. Bambetta was a passenger on the ill-fated ship when captured, and he was the first one shot at Santiago. Patterson obtained an American register from the port of New Orleans, duly authenticated by United States officials. In 1870 she sailed from New York, with the right, as against all other nations, to carry the American flag. When she sailed she cleared for a port in the Caribbean Sea, to which she went. She did not appear ever to have regularly cleared from any port in the United States. The capture of the captain, Joseph Fry, Bambetto, and many others of the crew and passengers followed.

As the *Virginius* was left in the port of Jamaica without a captain, it became my duty to appoint a commander of the ship upon the nomination of the consignees of the vessel. The law required, however, that he must be an American citizen, and of experience and nautical ability and skill to navigate a ship safely over the seas of the world. Captain Fry was in Kingston at the time, and he was often in the consulate. During this time the United States frigate *Tennessee*, a war steamer, was in port; and at one time when he was present the commander and some of the officers of the *Tennessee* came into my office, and I introduced them to Captain Fry. Their greeting was respectful; but not apparently very cordial. They spoke of having known Captain Fry when he was an officer in the United States navy. After they retired, Captain Fry wept freely over the great mistake he had made in resigning from the naval service of the Republic, and in accepting a place in the Confederate navy. "What a fool I was," said he; "I could have been in a good position, honored and comfortable; but I lost all that, and now I am poor and forsaken." He was nominated by the consignees of the *Virginius* to be appointed to her command. I told them that I thought he was lawfully ineligible, for the law requires that masters of American ships should be American citizens, and I supposed he had lost his American citizenship by engaging in the service of the Confederacy; but he submitted to me his pardon papers from President Andrew Johnson, which restored him to citizenship. After some expostulations with him in view of the dangers he incurred, and the sufferings his family might be obliged to endure if mishap attended his sailing, I appointed him captain of the *Virginius*. He said he had considered it all, and yet he must take the risks involved to gain bread for his wife and children. His case was very pathetic. I felt great sympathy for him, and when I learned that he had been captured and shot the news deeply affected me. His bearing during his trial and execution was honorable. He personally shook hands and said farewell to his comrades of the ship. Before his execution, he addressed the following letter to his wife:

CAPTAIN FRY'S FAREWELL LETTER TO HIS WIFE.

On Board the Spanish Man-of-War Tornado,
Santiago de Cuba, *November 6, 1873.*

Dear, Dear Dita,—When I left you I had no idea that we should never meet again in this world; but it seems strange to me that I should to-night, and on Annie's birthday, be calmly seated, on a beautiful moonlight night, in a most beautiful bay in Cuba, to take my last leave of you, my own dear, sweet wife, and, with the thought of your own bitter anguish— my only regret at leaving.

I have been tried to-day, and the president of the court-martial asked the favor of embracing me at parting, and clasped me to his heart. I have shaken hands with each of my judges, and the secretary of the court and the interpreter have promised me, as an especial favor, to attend my execution, which will, I am told, be within a few hours after my sentence is pronounced.

I am told my death will be painless. In short, I have had a very cheerful and pleasant chat about my funeral, to which I shall go a few hours from now; how soon, I can not say yet. It is curious to see how I make friends. Poor Bambetta pronounced me a gentleman, and he was the brightest and bravest creature I ever saw.

The priest who gave me communion on board this morning, put a double scapular around my neck, and a medal, which he intends to wear himself. A young Spanish officer brought me a bright, new silk badge, with the Blessed Virgin stamped upon it, to wear to my execution for him, and a handsome cross, in some fair lady's handiwork. They are to be kept as relics of me. He embraced me affectionately in his room, with tears in his eyes.

Dear sweetheart, you will be able to bear it for my sake, for I will be with you if God permits. Although I know my hours are short and few, I am not sad. I shall be with you right soon, dear Dita, and you will not be afraid of me. Pray for me, and I will pray with you. There is to be a fearful sacrifice of life, as I think, from the *Virginius*, and, as I think, a needless one, as the poor people are unconscious of crime, and even of their fate up to now. I hope God will forgive me if I am to blame for it.

If you write to President Grant he will probably order my pay, due when I resigned, to be paid to you after my death. People will be kinder to you now, dear Dita; at least I hope so. Do not dread death when it comes to you. It will be God's angel of rest—remember this. I hope my children will forget their father's harshness, and remember his love and anxiety for them. May they practice regularly their religion, and pray for him always. Tell ——— the last act of my life will be a public profession of my faith and hope in Him of whom we need not be ashamed; and it is not honest to withhold that public acknowledgment from any false modesty or timidity. May God bless and save us all! Sweet, dear, dear Dita, we will soon meet again. Till then, adieu for the last time.

Your devoted husband, JOSEPH FRY.

The following article on the subject of the *Virginius* and our strained relations with Spain appeared in the *Western Christian Advocate*, December 31, 1873:

THE SPANISH DIFFICULTY.

The war fever against Spain on account of the *Virginius* affair has entirely subsided. The Fish-Polo protocol has been promptly and honorably carried out by the Spanish Government. The *Virginius* has been returned, and the remaining passengers and crew have been surrendered. There is no reason to doubt that the remaining provisions of the treaty will also be observed. All this is matter for congratulation.

In the meantime, upon the showing of the case before him, the Attorney-General has transmitted to the Secretary of State his written opinion upon the questions, whether or not the *Virginius*, at the time of her capture by the *Tornado*, was improperly, and without right, carrying the American flag. Referring to the provisions of our laws as to the ownership and registry of American vessels, the Attorney-General finds that the registry of the *Virginius* was fraudulently obtained; that, instead of being owned by Americans, as the law requires, the ship was, in fact, owned by foreigners; that only by false swearing was a registry obtained; and, moreover, that the usual bond required in such cases was defective in having no sureties upon it. At the same time, the Attorney-General maintains "that she was as much exempt from interference on the high seas by another power, upon that ground, as though she had been lawfully registered." The right of Spain to capture a vessel of American register, and carrying the American flag, *if found in her waters, assisting, or endeavoring to assist, the insurrection in Cuba,* is admitted by the Attorney-General, who says: "But she has no right to capture such a vessel on the high seas, upon an apprehension that, in violation of the neutrality or navigation law of the United States, she was on her way to assist said rebellion. Spain may defend her territory and people from the hostile attack of what is, or appears to be, an American vessel; but she has no jurisdiction whatever over the question as to whether or not such vessel is on the high seas in violation of any law of the United States. Spain can not rightfully raise that question as to the *Virginius*; but the United States may, and, if I understand the protocol, they have agreed to do it, and be governed by that agreement; and, without admitting that Spain would otherwise have any interest in the question, I decide that the

Virginius, at the time of her capture, was, without right and improperly, carrying the American flag."

The opinion of the Attorney-General as to the wrongfulness of the seizure of the *Virginius* upon the high seas is so fully in accordance with international law, as held by nearly all civilized Governments, including Spain, that we can not see how it can be successfully called into question. The fraud in procuring the register of the *Virginius*, and the unrightful carrying of the United States flag, were offenses, not against Spanish law, but against American law. Of such offenses, not Spain, but the United States, is to be the trier and punisher. To allow for a moment that, under the apprehension that the *Virginius* had not regular papers, and did not lawfully carry the American flag, Spain had the right to seize her upon the high seas, adjudge, and condemn her, is utterly absurd. Such an admission as to any foreign power whatever, would place our commerce, our citizens, and their property, at the mercy or the caprice of any meddlesome Government which, with or without reason, might choose to annoy us. The American flag, when the right to carry it is covered by the usual papers, entitles the vessel so bearing it to as much immunity from assault as the soil of the United States is entitled to freedom from invasion by a foreign power. To all legal intents, the deck of an American ship is American soil. Spain has no more right to invade that soil on the deck of an American ship when in neutral waters than she would have to invade New York or Baltimore. It is granted that inconvenience may sometimes result by vessels procuring papers by fraud, but not half the wrong and injury which the admission of the right of search and seizure upon the high seas would work. The illegal bearing of the United States flag is a violation of American law. When the United States Government is unable to compel the observance of its own laws, or to punish their violation, it may choose a guardian, and ask for assistance. Until our Government reaches that unhappy condition, the assumption that Spain may adjudicate for the United States is simply monstrous.

CHAPTER XXV.

THE war steam-frigate *Tennessee* was sent by President Grant to Samana Bay, in the island of St. Domingo, with a select company, acting as a Commission, to make observations in that bay, and learn whether or not the President had violated any law, or had compromised the Government of the United States in his administration of the affairs of that grant from the Haytians of the use of the bay as a coaling station. The persons composing that Commission included, Manton Marble, of the New York *World;* A. D. White, of the Cornell University; Frederick Douglass; Senator B. F. Wade, of Ohio; and perhaps others. Bishop Arthur Cleveland Coxe, of the Western Diocese of New York, was a passenger from Hayti to New York by that vessel, as I now remember. The ship remained in Kingston Harbor a week or more.

An incident connected with Frederick Douglass interested me somewhat. On Saturday, as we were riding about Kingston, Mr. Douglass inquired of me where he could study the question of color-caste to the best advantage. I told him Wesley Chapel, and I tendered him the use of my pew in that church, explaining that, as I was to preach in another Wesleyan church on that day, I regretted my necessary absence from Wesley; but telling him to inquire of the janitor for the American consul's pew, and to occupy that, because from that he would have a good view of the situation. The next day after, I was with him again. He said he was delighted with his attendance at Wesley. There was a congregation of twenty-five hundred or more. The seats were occupied by the same family; the white father at one end of the pew, and a black wife at the other end, with the children between them of various shades of mahogany; and *vice versa*, the black father at the one end of the line, and a blue-eyed English blonde at the other. He said the singing, led by a powerful organ and a chorus of two thousand sweet voices, more resembled his ideal of heaven than any other he had ever had. As for the mingling of bloods and of races, he described it as a mingling together of pepper and salt all over the house. "Why," said he, "there was not the faintest scent of color-caste about it."

I greatly admired Bishop Coxe. He was genial, frank, refined, intellectual, and intelligent, and, withal, a man of large catholicity. His father was Rev. Samuel Hanson Cox, the once renowned celebrity of Brooklyn, as a Calvinistic divine of the Presbyterian denomination; and yet his son was an Arminian in doctrine and of prelatical Church proclivities. This he explained by saying that his mother was a Churchwoman of pronounced Arminian views. He expressed a high respect for the ministers and work of the Methodist Episcopal Church. He said they were providentially God's great breakwater to save this country from going through Unitarianism, as a half-way house, into open infidelity. Long before he was elected a bishop, when he was rector of a wealthy Church in Baltimore, he had planted a mission in Santo Domingo, which he had ever since maintained, and to which he had been accustomed to go as often as once in a year, or once in two years, to study the growth and the work of that Christian plant, which he had established among the blacks of that island.

My residence of three years in Jamaica with my family afforded me very great pleasure. I traveled with my family all over the island, preached and made addresses in all the chief cities and towns, shared in the generous hospitality of the people, recovered my health, and I have ever since held in delightful remembrance my three years of sojourn as a consul in that "beautiful isle of the sea." It would be an almost criminal omission not to speak of my relations with the Wesleyan ministers and their familes, who made us welcome to their homes and chapels, and to the quarterly-meetings and breakfasts and teas, which were quite frequent— Rev. George Sargeant, the chairman of the district; Samuel Smyth, Henry Bunting, George Geddes, and many others. William West succeeded George Sargeant as chairman of the district. He was a veteran who had seen much service on the gold coast of Africa. He and the other Wesleyan ministers and official laymen united in a beautiful and highly appreciated testimonial, expressing their respect and esteem for me, as did also the Masonic bodies of Kingston. My relations with the ministers of other denominations were very pleasant and enjoyable.

I must not fail to speak of John Martin, principal for many years of the Lady Mico School—a normal school for the training of teachers. He was a fine scholar, and a wise and successful governor and teacher in the institution of that name in Kingston. I am not sure that he graduated; yet I think he did. Upon my representation, the Athens College conferred on him the degree of LL. D., a dignity and honor which he richly deserved.

These recollections of the three years of my stay in Jamaica will always be a green oasis in the memories of life. I give the principal facts which I learned of its history and condition, for the entertainment and instruction of my readers.

Jamaica is an interesting island, whether viewed as to its history, population, climate, soil, or productions. Lying adjacent to our Republic, under the very shadow of our country, and within four or five days of steamboat sail of our chief Atlantic seaports, she is related to us by important present and prospective conditions.

Except the Bahama Islands, all the West India islands are sometimes called the Antilles. Those forming, like a string of pearls, the eastern boundary of the Caribbean Sea, are called the Lesser Antilles; and those on the western rim of the Caribbean Sea, including Cuba, Jamaica, and Santo Domingo, are called the Greater Antilles. The Lesser Antilles stretch away eastward, from the

Gulf of Mexico to the meridian of Paria in South America, say sixteen hundred miles. The name Antilles was given by mistake to the West India Islands. Before the discovery of America by Columbus, a tradition existed, that lying west of the Azores, which were west of Africa, there lay a land called Antillæ, whose position was faintly shown on the early maps of the cosmographers. Nearly eight months after Columbus returned to Europe, it was held that the islands he had discovered were the fabled Antillæ, and Cuba and Hayti were known as the Antillæ before a single link of the Caribbean chain had been discovered.

In the Greater Antilles lies Jamaica. There are in the Lesser Antilles thirteen British islands, scarcely five thousand miles in area, all of them of much less than the area of Jamaica, and relatively of far less importance. And so I am sure my readers will have interest in my facts and descriptions of that beautiful island. Those facts were gathered from personal observation in a three years' residence in the island. Jamaica has been styled, "The brightest jewel in the British crown." Its peerless beauty has never been traced by the most skilled painter. No statist has yet computed its undeveloped resources. Its geographical position and its remarkable history have been the theme of able writers. But there is a still more potent cause for appreciating this singularly beautiful island. It is my profound conviction, that all America, including, also, its adjacent islands, should properly belong to the United States, and they are necessary to her fullest and destined development; and for these reasons I am deeply interested in all that relates to the West Indies. Four hundred and six years ago Columbus discovered America. Four hundred and three years ago Columbus, probably on his second westward voyage, sailed into Saint Ann's Bay, on the north side of the island. In a part of Saint Ann's Bay is a cove, called yet "Christopher's Cove," where he anchored his ships and wintered and where he lay in infirmity and suffering and mutiny, the gentle natives supplying his wants.

Jamaica abounds with woods and streams, and from the sea-line to the loftiest mountain summits, eight thousand miles above the sea-level, the surface is clad in richest livery of grass and flowers and shrubs. Its vivid green and gorgeous flora gained for it at the earliest of its settlement the name, Xamaica—the land of springs and verdure and forests. This aboriginal name, Anglicized to Jamaica, it has ever since borne. Discovered by Spaniards, it became a Spanish colony, and remained such for one hundred and sixty-one years. In that time the gentle natives, who had welcomed the great discoverer and had ministered to his needs, fell victims to the ruthless rapacity and violence of their conquerors. Like frostwork in the sun, these natives melted away from a half million to one hundred thousand or less. In 1655, Oliver Cromwell, then Lord High Protector of England, sent General Venable and Admiral Penn to the West Indies, ostensibly to make reprisals in the

Spanish main for injuries done to British commerce; but really, to capture and subject Santo Domingo, and all this without a formal declaration of war. The expedition failed. The commanders disagreed. It is alleged that one or both of them were suspected of disloyalty to their chief. Feeling, perhaps, that they should not return without having achieved anything to add to their luster, they attacked and conquered Jamaica, and planted upon it the Cross of St. George, which has stamped an immeasurable impress on the civilization of the world. From that day to this, for two hundred and forty years, Jamaica has been a British colony. For two hundred and ten years she was a charter colony; *i. e.*, a self-governing colony. In 1865, during a momentary panic from an alleged uprising of the Negroes, she surrendered her charter, and requested Great Britain to make her a crown colony altogether, without self-governing power, having even no authority to elect either a constable or a police officer.

Venable and Penn were cast into the Tower of London. They were tried by court-martial for their treasonable failure to do something more signal. Vexed at the smallness of their acquisition, Cromwell offered Jamaica to the Colony of Massachusetts. This historical fact is not in the books. It is not, however, any the less true. I give it as authentic. My voucher is the Rev. Professor E. S. Starbuck, of Berea College, in Kentucky, formerly a missionary in Jamaica in the service of the American Missionary Society. He claims to have discovered documentary proof in Jamaica of the truth of the statement. Whatever we have since become as an expansive, acquisitive Nation, adding Florida, Louisiana, Texas, California, and later still the icebergs and seals—aye, and the gold-fields of Alaska—we were then but callow fledglings. Cromwell's offer was declined. Had Massachusetts accepted the largess of Cromwell, the history of England and of the United States might have been far different from what it has been.

Jamaica lies centrally in the Caribbean Sea, between north latitude 17 degrees and 39 minutes, and 18 degrees and 34 minutes. It is one hundred and seventy-five miles long, by sixty-five miles wide. It contains six thousand four hundred square miles, and four millions and eighty thousand square acres. Ohio is six times as large as Jamaica. Jamaica is more than half as large as Maryland, three times as large as Delaware, and five times as large as Rhode Island in area, and six times as large in population. On a clear day, Cuba can be seen from the mountains of Saint Ann's, directly north of Jamaica, ninety miles distant, and Santo Domingo about as far east. Jamaica occupies a very central position geographically. It is fourteen hundred and sixty miles south from New York, and five hundred miles from the Isthmus of Darien. It is in the direct line between England and Australia, and directly on the line between New York and Rio Janeiro, South America. Its geographical position and commercial importance are easily shown.

It is not accidental that three-fourths of the world's surface is water. The oceans of earth are the highways of commerce. Intercourse and commerce are important factors in the civilization and progress of the world. The distribution of the oceans is peculiar. There is less land in the Western than in the Eastern Hemisphere, and far more north of the equator than south of it. The land is distributed into four grand divisions. North and South America, with their adjacent islands, make the western division, or hemisphere. In area, this division is 14,766,336 square miles. The continents of Europe, Asia, and Africa, with their systems of islands, have an area more than twice as large as the Western Hemisphere, or 32,500,000 square miles. The area of the West India Islands is one-sixteenth that of the Western Hemisphere; i. e., 922,896 square miles. If now one should take two maps of the world, say Mercator's projection in duplicate hemispheres, and lay them alongside each other, it will be seen that North America lies between Europe, Asia, and Africa in the east, and Asia on the west, with broad oceans on each side of her. One of these oceans separating them is five thousand miles wide, and the other three thousand miles. No other continent in the world is so situated. This is not accidental. Its importance to North Asia and the West Indies can not be overestimated. With the single exception of Suez, one hundred miles wide, in the Eastern Hemisphere, and Darien in the Western, fifty miles wide, God has made water communication around the world, on its most populous zone. Commerce has compelled the opening of the Suez Canal. It will compel a like canal in the Western Hemisphere, and then the waterway of commerce and travel around the world on its most populous zone will be complete; and, by the way, Jerusalem will be on that line. There is now a railroad from Joppa to Jerusalem, and it will be soon extended east to the Gulf of Persia.

There is still another fact. Jamaica is in the midst of a remarkable sea, directly on the waterline of travel and commerce around the world, on the zone of the world's greatest populations, and therefore on the line where the business and travel of the world will be the greatest, and it also lies right on the line of the north and south commerce and travel of the world between New York and South America. In the earlier times, Washington and others of the fathers of the United States held that this separation of our country from all other lands was a Providential fact, insuring us from harmful contact with all other nations, so indicating segregation and isolation from all other nations as the wisest policy. But steam and electricity and commerce have forbidden us longer to indulge in this dream. If we were disposed to hide within our shell and avoid contact with other peoples, we could not if we would, and we should not if we could. Other nations would not let us, and our aggressive nature and the demands of commerce and travel and the world's progress would forbid. We must intermeddle and intermingle with all other peoples, or fall into the rear, while other nations lead the van; or, asserting our vim, vigor, and victory, we must lead the procession, and we must have virtue enough and wisdom enough to profit ourselves and the race by this intermeddling and intermingling.

There are two most remarkable seas in the world, twin seas. One of them is in the Eastern Hemisphere, and the other in the Western. They are both so nearly alike in area and conditions and relations, as to seem almost like twin seas. On the shores of the one sea the cradle of science was rocked. On the shores of the other, the moundbuilders and the Mexicans, if they are not one and the same, roamed and hunted and offered their human sacrifices. On the waters of the one, Solomon's ships carried peacocks, ivory and gold, and myrrh and spices. On the waters of the other, the mound-builders propelled their bark canoes. On the shores of the one sea dwelt Cadmus, the father of letters, and Priam and Socrates and Seneca, kings of men. The shores of the other sea were traversed by unknown races. One of these seas divides Europe from Africa. The other divides North and South America. As on the shores of the one sea the cradle of the infancy of science was rocked, so on the shores of the other sea shall the highest, grandest, and most glorious results of science and morality and religion be reached and illustrated.

The northern boundary of the great western sea are the Bahama Islands and the United States.

The southern and western boundary are South and Central America. The Windward West India Islands, or Lesser Antilles, like a setting of pearls, are the eastern boundary. The western sea is 1,970 miles long by 560 miles wide. These seas have practically a like area. The Mediterranean Sea has an area of 1,000,000 square miles. The Caribbean has an area of 1,100,000 square miles. In the eastern sea there are sixty-four islands, large and small, some of them of great historic fame. These islands have an area of 32,000 square miles, and a population of 4,000,000, or 130 persons to the square mile. There are seventy-five islands in the Caribbean Sea, with an area of 86,000 square miles, or nearly three times as many square miles as in its sister sea, and a population of four million persons, or forty-five to the square mile.

As America is centrally located between the other continents, so is Jamaica to the other islands in the Caribbean Sea, and also central to North and South America. Jamaica is nearer to the Isthmus of Darien than any other islands in the Caribbean, and therefore it holds the key position of the isthmus. Hence its incomparable commercial value. When commerce and travel in largely increased ratio shall take their way around the world, Jamaica is on the direct line of that movement. When the United States does tenfold its present business with South America, Jamaica will be its principal stopping-place. Populations that are touched and connected by rivers and seas are most important, and are soonest and most perfectly civilized. Secluded peoples come on very gradually. The East Indies are more important than Central Asia or Central Africa. Insular countries, for the same reason, are more advanced than continental countries. And then, moreover, peoples lying in the paths of the world's commerce and travel acquire wealth and elegance and civilization. All this applies to Jamaica.

By the census of 1871, the population of Jamaica is 506,154, as follows: Whites, 13,100, a decrease of 715 below the census of 1861; mulattoes, 100,346, an increase of 19,281 over the showing of the census of 1861; blacks, 372,707, an increase of 46,333 over the showing of the census of 1861. The total increase of population, 64,890, an increase for the decade of 15 per cent, or an increase of $1\frac{1}{2}$ per cent per annum. The whites decreased $\frac{5}{8}$ of one per cent; the colored (or mulatto) people increased 23 per cent, and the blacks 13 per cent. By the census of 1881, the whites were 12,315, a decrease of nearly one per cent. The whole population in 1881 was 585,000, an increase of 79,846, or 16 per cent; mulattoes, 128,468, an increase of 28 per cent; blacks, 444,217, an increase of 13 per cent. In the decade ending in 1881, the whites had decreased 6 per cent, the mulattoes had increased 24 per cent, and the blacks had increased 13 per cent. This showing proves two things: 1. The healthfulness of Jamaica; 2. The greater virility and fruitfulness of the mulattoes over the blacks, and also the greater vigor of the mulattoes than of the blacks. It has usually been thought that the mulattoes were more sterile and the blacks more fruitful than the mulattoes. These figures prove the contrary.

Educationally, the people of Jamaica display creditable conditions. All the primary schools are parochial schools. Each religious body has parochial schools. Forty per cent of the population can read and write, and are attending school. Seventy-one thousand are able to read and write. Eighty-one thousand can read. Attending school, forty-one thousand. In all, 194,000, or one in three of the population can read or write, or both. There are four hundred and forty schools under Government inspection, and therefore receiving money from the Government. The Government pays $78,000 per year, $2.36 for each scholar. There are two hundred endowed, or private, schools, making one school for each ninety-nine of the school population. Total sum annually expended for education, $200,000, an average of five dollars for each enrolled scholar, and $3.25 for each one of the school population. The branches taught are primary. In studies requiring imitation and memory, the blacks excel the whites and mulattoes. In all others the blacks are little, if any, behind them. Many of the blacks and mulattoes are thoroughly educated. Some of them are graduates of Oxford, Edinburgh, and Dublin. Some of them, both of men and women, are of commanding presence, graceful in form, and refined in manners. The public offices are effectively filled by the colored and black people; lawyers, editors, physicians, and ministers. Richard Hill (mulatto) was an accomplished *Belles Lettres* scholar and naturalist. Edward Fraser, a Wesleyan minister, was both learned and eloquent. So was Samuel Smyth, under whose ministry I sat for three years.

A current but mistaken idea "held by foreigners visiting Jamaica," is that the Jamaicans are people of lax morals. Persons passing through the island have seen only the coal-stokers and street gamins, and have formed their conclusion as to the whole people from the specimens they saw. The rural population and very many of the townspeople own their homesteads. The Churches administer rigid moral discipline. One-half the people either attend Church, or are members of Churches. There are four hundred churches, or one church to every three hundred and forty of the population. In the United States the proportion is one church to each five thousand of the population. There are seventy-five thousand Church members, or one to seven of the population. There are two hundred thousand Church sittings, and one hundred and fifty thousand regular attendants upon Divine worship. Surely these facts prove that the Jamaicans are neither vicious nor degraded. Eighty-eight thousand of the people are married. There are six thousand widowers and seventeen thousand widows. One-fifth of the whole population either are married, or they have been married, and are widowers and widows. Two-fifths of the whole population are born in wedlock. Surely such a people are virtuous and happy.

Violent crimes are unknown. I have traveled by night and by day all over the island with my family, without the slightest fear of interruption. The sugar estates have to send messengers on foot and alone to bring money from the banks to pay their hands, carrying upon their persons from $1,500 to $3,000. They are never molested or robbed. One instance occurred in half a century where a messenger with money was robbed. In 1870 over $500,000 were deposited in savings banks. When it is remembered that labor wages are from twenty-five cents to thirty cents a day, these deposits are wonderful. There are 18,000 Wesleyans, 90 churches, 20 parsonages, and Church property valued at $500,000. In 1871 these Wesleyans raised for religious uses $50,000, an average of three dollars per year per member. Other denominations approximate the Wesleyans in these figures. There are $2,500,000 in the savings banks. Only two-thirds of the island are under cultivation. On estates where sugar-cane has been grown on the same land for a hundred years, the yield is still undiminished.

Kingston has a population of forty thousand. There are a dozen other towns with populations varying from one thousand to ten thousand. The products of Jamaica are sugar, coffee, pimento, ginger, arrowroot, sago, indigo, oranges, limes, shaddock, grapes, guava, figs, mangoes, mangosteens, sour-sop, cherry moyer, sweet-sop, star-apples, nutmegs, mace, cinnamon, yams, sweet potatoes, achey, honey, cocoanuts, bread-fruit, senna, pine-apples, bananas.

The woods are, logwood, fustic, ebony, brazilitis, fiddlewood, lignum-vitæ, sandalwood, cedar, sanders-wood, mahogany. Mangoes make a large part of the food of the islanders. During the mango season, the consumption of flour falls off one-half. Cinchona and tea are successfully cultivated. Bananas are largely exported.

The flora of Jamaica is gorgeous. The night-blooming cereus is abundant. The Victoria Regia is one of the largest flowers I ever saw. The leaves are varnished green, on stems capable of supporting a man. The leaves are two feet by five feet, and the flower, which opens only in the night, has a disk eighteen inches in diameter, of wonderfully brilliant hues. The palm-tree is indigenous. There are ninety species. The baobab, or silk cotton-tree, deserves special mention. It grows immensely large. It is found in all tropical regions in the world. Its roots and branches are lateral or horizontal. A baobab-tree, near Kingston, casts a shadow at noon of two hundred and fifty feet in diameter. It has singular habits. One-third of the tree is in bloom, one-third in fruit, and one-third in leaf only. The *Ficus indicus*, wild fig, is a parasite, which has great affinity for the baobab. It fastens its tendrils at the ground and surrounds the trunk, winding itself in close coils around every part of the tree, until the tree is literally choked to death; and then, as the lateral limbs, when dead, could not bear the suspended horizontal coils of the fig, unless supported, the fig drops lines to the ground from the limbs, which take root and support the overloaded limbs; and when the tree, which furnished a scaffolding for the wild fig, is dead, the parasite is supported by a hundred additional trunks, and the wild fig becomes the banyan-tree of the Indies. The cedar-tree of Jamaica, unlike its kindred tree of the north, has open, spreading branches and large leaves like those of the lime, and yet the three varieties of tropical cedar, the red, white, and yellow, have the perfume and colors of the cedars of the north.

The climate of Jamaica is delightful. It is not so hot at any time as the summer climate of Maine or of Oregon. The trade-winds reduce the heat to a comfortable degree. Its insular condition prevents the heat from becoming insufferable. In May and October, the rainy season, the trade-winds cease, and then the temperature becomes extreme and unpleasant; but by ascending the mountains the heat can be graduated to the climate of the temperate zone, at the pleasure of the person.

Hurricanes are of rare occurrence. Every twenty or thirty years furnishes an occasional wind storm, which sweeps with great fierceness and destructiveness. The tropical rains are most abundant. I went once from my office to my hotel in a rain. The streets in five minutes were deluged, requiring me to wade in several inches depth of water, and an umbrella was of little more protection than an old-fashioned sieve. I have known the best climates of the different parts of North America. I have breathed the dry air of Mexico and of Lower California; I have scaled the Sierras and the Rockies; I have traversed the deserts of our interior; I have felt the bracing air of British Columbia and of Alaska; but I have never, anywhere, found a climate so delicious and agreeable as that of Jamaica. The climate of Cuba and Santo Domingo is almost precisely like that of Jamaica. Earthquakes are common. Some of them are very destructive. Mountains have been riven from summit to base. Enormous fissures have been made by them. Mount Sinai, a few miles east from Kingston, was riven, and a slice of the mountain was cut down for two thousand feet as smooth as a knife could cut through cheese, and thrown off, covering a large penn,* and burying houses, men, and animals. The mountains of St. Thomas in the vale were severed to the base, and a river winds its way through the cleft made by the earthquake. In 1692 the great earthquake buried the larger part of Port Royal in the sea, with the dwellings and the thousands of people. In places the earth opened, and then closed again. I read of Robert Goldy, on his tombstone, that he fell into a crevasse, and then was thrown out of that into the bay, and escaped by swimming and survived the accident many years. The bodies of the dead filled the air with the noisome pestilence. Jamaica has no dangerous beasts of prey. There are no venomous ser-

---

* Penn is the word for a ranch or an estate.

pents. But there are lizards in plenty. Centipedes, scorpions, and tarantulas abound; but these are not fatal in their sting. Chigres, or a species of vermin, will pierce the skin, and deposit their eggs under it, which must be extracted, or serious injury will follow.

Jamaica has a fine system of roads, well graded and ballasted, across the mountains and around the shores. The health of the island is widely celebrated. The yellow fever sometimes visits the cities and becomes epidemic; but this results from the filth of the larger cities. The island is beautiful beyond description. Approached from the north side, the land swells from the sea in gracefully-rounded hills, between which streams and waterfalls are born. On the south side the surface is more irregular and craggy. The irregularities of surface, and the serrated, comb-like appearance of the mountain profile cut against the blue sky, are of thrilling majesty and power. Here a chasm, there a bold outline; here the gentle slope, there the sharp acclivity; forest, and field, and tilth, and meadow,—make up a perspective never surpassed, and, once witnessed, never forgotten. Mr. Trollope, quoting Christopher Columbus's description of Jamaica, describes it, as seen from the southern approach, as resembling a sheet of writing paper crumpled and compressed, and then left with all its creases and folds upon it.

The nearer view is none the less enchanting. Take a buggy-ride through the famous Bog Walk, rived by the earthquake from mountain summit to base, through which meanders the Rio Cobra; cross Mount Diabolo, three thousand feet high, on a grade so easy that your horses can trot up the whole ascent; through the parish of Saint Ann's, and see the well-inclosed meadows waving with luxuriant guinea grass, and coffee-walks and orange and pimento groves, redolent of the most exquisite perfume, or gold and purple with their ample fruitage and foliage, and see the flocks and herds,—and you have such a vision of beauty you are ready to say with the delighted Queen of Sheba, "The half has never yet been told."

… Fifth Period.

WORK IN OHIO.

CHAPTER XXVI.

RETURNING to the United States from consular service in October, 1873, from which I had long before resigned, I accepted the position of corresponding secretary of the American Colonization Society, with headquarters at Cincinnati, Ohio. I was elected to this position by the managers of that Society, upon the recommendation of Bishop Simpson. I removed to Cincinnati with my family late in October of 1873. I attended the annual meeting of the managers and members of the Colonization Society, the same fall, in Washington, D. C. I preached on the colonization of Africa from the colored freedmen of the South, in Foundry Church, on the Sunday of my stay in Washington. Soon after, I made a trip to Savannah, Georgia, from which place I shipped some thirty or forty freedmen and freedwomen from Hawkinsville, Georgia. All went off in high spirits, except one, who was told by some meddlesome person, that they would be taken away from New York, and then, when out at sea, they would be sent as slaves to some slaveholding country, probably Cuba. His suspicions got the better of his wishes, and he declined to go.

Reaching home, I found my wife's health so much worse that I resigned my secretaryship, to spend all my time in caring for her. Her disease was *Angina pectoris*, disease of the heart. In May,

1874, after six months of distressing illness, her gentle spirit passed away from earth to be with God. Her disease caused her intense suffering, and it superinduced dropsy. For nearly six months she was unable to lie down. She described the pain in her heart to be as torturing as though a thousand needles were piercing it. When the council of doctors pronounced her case hopeless, in answer to her inquiries, she said to them: "It is well. I am not surprised. I am ready." When they had retired, she sang two verses—the first and the last—of the hymn:

> "When I can read my title clear
> To mansions in the skies,
> I'll bid farewell to every fear,
> And wipe my weeping eyes.
>
> Then I shall bathe my weary soul
> In seas of heavenly rest,
> And not a wave of trouble roll
> Across my peaceful breast."

When the end came, and for which she had prearranged, it was morning. She said, "I think the time has come for our responsive reading of the twenty-third Psalm." She sat propped up in bed, and she was leaning against me, every now and then pressing against me, as if to escape the torturing pain of her heart. I began, "The Lord is my shepherd." She responded, "I shall not want." I continued repeating, pausing at each comma for her voice. When I read, "Yea, though I walk through the valley of the shadow of death," she once more and feebly added, "I will fear no evil." A moment after she peacefully expired. As the last breath ceased, her face, which had been drawn in lines of agony, relaxed, and a smile overspread her features. Her eyes were upturned, and a look of surprise and delight illuminated her countenance. It seemed as though the new scenes unfolding to her were enrapturing.

For more than thirty-three years she had been a faithful, loving wife. Our hearts were wonderfully knit together in love. The honeymoon had never gone down. For ten years she had shared, unmurmuringly, the trials and crosses incident to the itinerancy in New York and Pennsylvania. For another fourteen years she had cheerfully accepted the rigors and privations of frontier life in Oregon. Five years, without a complaint, she was under the heavy strain of the reconstruction work in Tennessee. Part of the time in Oregon I was able to spend, each quarter, only one week in thirteen at our home, and she had remained almost alone the other twelve weeks. She said to me, after we had gone from Tennessee, that I had never left her to go on my district there, that she did not have a shuddering fear that I would be assassinated and brought home dead. Three years we had lived together in Jamaica, and nearly all the last year of her life she was an invalid. In her last illness she advised me to re-enter the active work of the itinerancy, saying she believed I would be more useful and happy in that service than in any other. Noble woman! Heroic and brave! For all the years of our union my home was the dearest and brightest spot on earth. We bore her remains to Cortland, N. Y. In the beautiful cemetery of that lovely village sleep the ashes of my mother and father and of my child. There her dust will slumber until the trumpet of the archangel and the voice of the Son of God shall break the long silence.

The Methodist Preachers' Meeting of Cincinnati had been very kind to me during the year of my residence in that city. They unanimously invited me to become a member of the Cincinnati Conference, which I did, by transfer, in September, 1874. The session that year was held in Wilmington, Clinton County. Bishop R. S. Foster presided. Bishop Ames was present most of the session. He strongly urged me to go with him to Minnesota, and take work in a leading Church in Minneapolis. I should probably have done so, but for the invitation of the Cincinnati Preachers' Meeting. Then, moreover, I had for ten years been intimately associated in Oregon with Rev. Francis S. Hoyt, D. D., who, in that new country, had been the efficient president of the Willamette University, and who was at this time living in Cincinnati, and editing most effectively the *Western Christian Advocate*. Then, also, I had become pleasantly acquainted with the brave old hero, Rev. R. S. Rust, in the years of reconstruction. For ten years our fellowship had been edifying and delightful. It is not strange, then, that under these conditions I should prefer remaining in the Cincinnati Conference, to adventuring again in the new Northwest. I was stationed in Grace Church,

Dayton. I went there without seeking the appointment. Indeed, I did not personally know a single member there, nor had I ever preached in that church, nor seen it to know it.

When I went up on Saturday to enter upon my charge I went to the hotel, the Beckel House. After supper I walked out, and, drawn by the lights and the music, I went into the Public Square, where the Woman's Christian Association were giving a social entertainment. Here I met Rev. W. A. Robinson, stationed that year in Raper, Dayton, with whom I had had a Conference room acquaintance, and he introduced me to several of my members. Thus began my itinerant ministry in Ohio. Grace Church had a lovely and elegant church edifice, which cost one hundred thousand dollars, and a membership of six or seven hundred. Here were spent three happy, prosperous, and, I trust, useful years. Some of the friendships formed in this charge were among the most delightful I have ever known. Two changes were effected during this pastorate, which, I have no doubt, were conducive to the welfare and usefulness of the Church. The first was to change the Sunday-school hour from afternoon to morning. It had been an afternoon school for many years, perhaps nearly fifty, and it was not a very easy thing to change it; but I assured the brethren that if they would keep the morning hour for a year in their Sunday-school the change would vindicate its wisdom, and it would remain permanently the chosen hour. And so it has done. The other innovation was even greater, and more difficult to effect; but it succeeded. That was for the Church to bear the expense of the Sunday-school, and train the scholars in Christian giving. I argued that to induce the children to bring their offerings simply to pay their expenses, the training would inculcate only business justice and self-dependence; but it would not cultivate the grace of giving; and then, moreover, I urged upon the Official Board that the Sunday-school was an arm of the Church's working, and its expense should be borne by the Church as really as the salary of the janitor, the organist, or the choir. This change, too, has vindicated its wisdom by the experience of many years. The missionary collections in this Church the year before I was pastor were: From the Church, $131.88; from the Sunday-school, $486.68. The last year of my pastorate missionary collections were: From the Church, $298.68, an advance of $9\frac{1}{2}$ per cent; from the Sunday-school, $546, an increase of $12\frac{1}{2}$ per cent; whole amount, $844, an increase of 30 per cent.

The first year of my pastorate in Grace Church Bishop Foster spent a Sabbath with me, preaching morning and evening. His preaching produced a profound impression. He found that, wherever he and I went on the streets, all the children greeted me personally. He said it was a beautiful sight to see this respect and love for a pastor among the children. During my second year Bishop Andrews spent a Sunday in my charge.

In our boyhood he and I were Sunday-school mates, and we grew up together in the same village, New York Mills, Oneida County. His preaching was very edifying and helpful to the Church. He has proved a wise and faithful bishop. I was in the habit of preaching five-minute sermons to the children of my charge, before preaching the sermon to adults. The children quite generally attended the preaching service in the forenoon. The short children's sermons proved a genuine attraction and blessing to the children.

During my second year's pastorate I had a visit of nearly a week from a former Oregon associate, Rev. David Rutledge, who was ten years in Oregon, filling some of the best appointments we had. He was a very popular and useful pastor. I esteem him as a very faithful friend. He advised me that I could be much more useful, and really more safe in my reputation, and he believed more happy, if I were to re-marry. I had not then given the subject a serious thought, and I so informed him. I did not know of a person towards whom I had felt drawn as a suitable person for a wife for me. He advised me to visit Bishop Janes, and consult with him on the subject. I took his advice. The bishop recommended me to visit Miss Caroline McDonald, a lady whom he had known from her birth. She was a maiden lady of some thirty-five years, of good mind and manners, and of high Christian character, who was an efficient Church worker, a lady of excellent judgment, and at the same time of such domestic qualities, that he judged I could not fail to appreciate and love her. He said she was in the city, he thought, and that if I saw her and wished a correspondence, I might refer her to him as to my character and standing in the Conferences. I learned that Miss McDonald was in Baltimore visiting a friend. I procured the address, and went to Baltimore. I saw her for an hour or two, and proposed a correspondence. In July following, I attended Round Lake Camp-meeting in New York, and preached. Here, again, I met Miss McDonald. We entered into a marriage engagement. October 12, 1875, we were married by Bishop Janes, in Sand Street Methodist Episcopal Church, Brooklyn. Our marriage has been a happy one. God's blessing has been upon it. I have no doubt my ministry has been very largely more successful because of this union than it would otherwise have been. She has been a faithful and earnest helper in all Church work. Her exercises have been helpful to very many persons, young and old. The marriage has doubtless added years of useful labor to my life, and gladdened my path by its fellowship and by the children she has borne me. A son died in infancy. My daughter still survives, and gives promise of being a useful woman if her life shall be prolonged.

The great iron wheel of the itinerancy rolled me into Hillsboro, Ohio. The first Sabbath of my pastorate here I raised a collection of $1,500, to assist in repairing and furnishing the Hillsboro **Fe-**

male College, which for many years had been doing most efficient service in educating young women in classical and literary lines. Hillsboro Charge was an old and large station, one of the oldest in the Conference. In 1840, Rev. Randolph S. Foster was upon the Hillsboro Circuit, before the station was organized as a separate appointment. In 1841 he was the first stationed Methodist minister in Hillsboro, bringing to the charge his young bride. The small hired house in which he lived while here is still shown. His subsequent illustrious course, as a popular city preacher in New York, and later as president of the Northwestern University in Chicago, and afterwards a most efficient professor in Drew Theological Seminary, from which, in 1872, he was elected a bishop of the Methodist Episcopal Church, is too well known to need more than a mere mention. I learned some interesting personal incidents in his pastorate in Wesley Chapel in Cincinnati, which have probably never been published until I published them, and which will be found in another part of this book in the Centennial Sermon I preached in 1888. Hillsboro Station has had some of the strong men of Western Methodism as pastors. The charge has always ranked as a large and strong society.

I was removed at the end of the first quarter of my second year's work in Hillsboro, and placed upon the Dayton District, to fill a vacancy that had occurred there, and James Kendall, an eloquent and able minister, was my successor. I shall always hold delightful memories of this charge. I was removed in the midst of the year by Bishop Wiley, and appointed to Dayton District, January, 1879. The district contained twenty-six appointments: Dayton, with three charges, Grace, Raper, and West Dayton; Piqua, with two charges; Troy, Tippecanoe, Middletown, Miamisburg, and Franklin, were considerable villages or cities. The other charges were, Addison, North Hampton, Concord, Lewisburg, Gordon, West Elkton, Lockington, Casstown, St. Paris and Lena, Brandt, Red Lion, Fairfield, New Carlisle, and Monroe. William Herr was secretary of the Preachers' Relief Society. The preachers on the district wrought in precious unity and fellowship with one another and with the presiding elder. I was reappointed to the district by Bishop Simpson, in September, 1879; by Bishop Peck, in 1880; by Bishop Wiley, in 1881. They were years of hard but happy toil. The record made has gone up on high, and it rests with God. Of those who were effective ministers when I took the district, as well as I can ascertain three have died, two have located, thirteen have superannuated, eight have remained in the effective ranks. Of the twenty-six who were effective when I left the district, two have died, fourteen are effective, two have located, and eight have superannuated. So the laborers come and go.

My residence during the term of the Dayton District was in Dayton. I was called on to make an address on occasion of unveiling a portrait of Daniel J. Rouzer, who was the president of the

Good Samaritan Society, and a very benevolent, humane man. The following is the address delivered on that occasion:

ADDRESS.

We are met to unveil a portrait. Something which has been obscured is to be disclosed. The obscurity will soon be removed. Death has veiled from human sight the loved form of our friend, Daniel J. Rouzer. The sun had painted him while he was yet among us. The artist has reproduced, on canvas, his visible form and features. You will soon look upon them. You will judge for yourselves how correctly the original has been reproduced. While your eyes behold the lines and lights and shadows that make up this beautiful portrait, another unveiling of him will take place in your minds. Memory will recall those acts of his life, and those traits of his character, which made him loved and lovable. This is being done by those whose acquaintance with him was comparatively slight, but who saw in the glance of his eye, who felt in the pressure of his hand, who beheld in the out-acted kindness of his inner heart, something which they admired. Those who held near relation to him are recalling his generous, unselfish kindness, manifested so variously and so often, and also his manliness of nature. His fellow-compositors are recalling his kindness and trueness in the intimacy of daily office life. One who was connected with him in business relations, says of him:

> In the death of Brother Rouzer the temperance people of this section have lost one whose place can not soon be filled, if ever, and the cause at large an earnest and zealous worker. A reformed man himself, he could feel and appreciate the difficulties under which men labored in trying to redeem their fallen manhood, and his eloquent and burning

words for God and temperance will long be remembered by the thousands who heard him, and hundreds who, by his exertions, were led into the right way will ever cherish his memory.

From long and intimate intercourse with Brother Rouzer, as partner and friend, we learned to love him, and knew more of his inner nature, and his terrible struggle against appetite, than any others outside of his family. While battling against himself, he was ever ready to help others; his hand was ever open to assist the needy, and his heart ever beat in sympathy for the fallen.

Farewell, brother, partner, friend! Your memory will ever be green in the heart of him who has stood by your side in the great battle of right against wrong, and who will still continue to fight on until victory crowns **our banners**, or he is called hence by the Master.

This is not the time nor the place for a eulogy. Many good things can be said of our friend. Of his faults—and who has none?—it is not my duty nor my pleasure to speak. Nothing so sanctifies a name as to write one dead. The society of Good Samaritans, of which the departed was a member, a founder, and its president, the National Christian Temperance Union, to which he belonged, and also those who bore a still nearer relation, are unveiling the man as he was, to their conception. They are re-looking on what has passed from human sight, but on what still lives in human memory, in loving hearts—an unselfish, earnest life; a life full of struggles and conflicts—sometimes winning, sometimes losing, but always honest, always genuine. They are recalling what we admired while he lived, and what is remembered, with loving reverence, now that he has gone away.

Men are measured and estimated for what they are, and not for what they seem; for what they do, and not for what they profess. Men rise or fall in the estimation of others, not as they are brilliant and talented, or rich, or mighty, or exalted in station, or learned, but as they are good and unselfish. This position has the suffrage of the representative men of all classes and of all times and countries. George Herbert says, "A handful of good life is better than a bushel of learning." Walter Scott says, "It is not great learning which awakens men's respect, but the nobler, truer qualities of goodness and truth." Shakespeare says:

> "How far that little candle throws its beams!
> So shines a good deed in a naughty world."

And so, also, shines the faithful, earnest doer of the good deeds. The largest funeral I ever saw, of a private individual, was that of Mr. Marshall, in this city, some two or three years ago. You remember the crowds that gathered in all the streets, and that followed in long, sad procession to your beautiful Woodland Cemetery. It was the spontaneous tribute of a whole people to unostentatious, genuine goodness—goodness in the common walks of life.

These elements of truth and honor and nobility may exist and shine in those of lowly lot, as well as in those of higher station. Pope has very well said,—

> "Honor and shame from no condition rise;
> Act well your part, there all the honor lies.
> Worth makes the man, and want of it the fellow;
> The rest is all but leather or prunello."

This was the thought of Burns, in the well-known lines—

> "The rank is but the guinea's stamp,
> The man's the goud for a' that."

The Scotch bard came honestly by this truth, for his father had inculcated the same in the forming period of Robert's life. Burns thus speaks of the lessons taught by his honored parent:

> "He bade me act a manly part,
> Though I had ne'er a farthing;
> For without an honest, manly heart,
> No man was worth regarding."

The merit is not in place nor surroundings, but in the man himself. The elegance and beauty of a circle lies not so much in its size as in its perfect roundness. At the summit of their influence in their respective lines, Luther and Knox and Wesley and Cowper and Burns were comparatively poor. They owed nothing of their greatness to the distinctions of wealth and place. It is not the clothes men wear, nor the stations they fill, which give human immortality.

When a man does some act with which humanity is, for the time, in close, strong, wide sympathy; when he strikes some chord which vibrates in human hearts extensively, that act will bring recognition and immortality. The passengers on a steamship are startled by the cry, "Man overboard!" Instantly the ship is put about, the life-boat is lowered, a dozen men offer to man her; but before the boat is lowered, a man from the deck, who has had his eye on the strong man struggling with the waves, doffs his coat, and plunges in after the imperiled one. The one for whose rescue he has risked his own life is a stranger to him. He helps him into the life-boat; but, before he himself has entered that life-boat, a shark has seized him, and he perishes; the rescuer is lost. Whose heart, of all those passengers, does not thrill with profoundest sympathy at this self-sacrifice for a life? A nation is in peril. Invaders or revolutionists have arrayed armies against the nation's life or liberty. A man enlists for its deliverance. The nation honors him. A multitude enlist. In bivouac, and march, and bloody field, and deadly hospital, they sacrifice themselves on the altars of a lofty patriotism. Those who return from the wars are recognized and cherished by their grateful fellow-countrymen. Those who fall, sleep in honored graves. Flowers are strewed upon their hallowed dust.

> "How sleep the brave, who sink to rest,
> By all their country's wishes blest!
> When Spring, with dewy fingers cold,
> Returns to deck their hallowed mold,
> She there shall dress a sweeter sod
> Than fancy's feet have ever trod.
>
> By fairy hands their knell is rung;
> By forms unseen their dirge is sung;
> There Honor comes, a pilgrim gray,
> To bless the turf that wraps their clay;
> And Freedom shall awhile repair,
> To dwell a weeping hermit there."

Luther drew the world to his side because he was struggling with giant antagonists to free the world from the most cruel superstitions and utter bondage. Wesley moved the great masses toward himself and to a higher, better life, because he was unselfishly teaching the world of rivers of blessings flowing for them, and to be had without money and without price. Wilberforce and Clarkson, Garrison and Phillips and Lincoln, live in human hearts to-day, shrined and crowned, because they took sides with the oppressed, the weak, or the unfortunate. This practical sympathy with some intensely-absorbing thought or need of humanity, something which humanity believes urgent and important—this being equal to some great crisis or to some felt emergency will always secure fame and following, and earthly immortality.

Why is the memory of the martyrs so green? They died for the truth which to-day enriches the world. Their firmness and constancy, amid martyr fires, and flood, and sword, to maintain and preserve for us truth and freedom, have given them their name and their glory.

> "They lived unknown,
> Till persecution dragged them forth to fame,
> And chased them up to heaven; their ashes flew,
> No marble tells us whither."

It was a like unselfish consecration to the cause of country, and home, and altars, which has made the patriots, reformers, and confessors of all ages the world's great heroes to-day.

We should never forget that the crowning of these is as certain, even amid apparent defeat, as that day succeeds to night.

> "They never fail who die
> In a just cause: the block may soak their gore;
> Their heads may sodden in the sun; their limbs
> Be strung to city gates and castle walls—
> But still their spirit walks abroad. Though years
> Elapse and others share as dark a doom,
> They but augment the deep and sweeping thoughts
> Which overpower all others, and conduct
> The world at last to freedom."

The world respects and loves honest men, who have energy of will and steadiness of purpose to work their own way, though mountains and oceans lie between them and their goal; strong men, mailed in truth, and standing up for the right, as they see the right, against overwhelming numbers. "Energy of will—self-originating force"—as one has said, "is the soul of every great character. Where it is, there is life; where it is not, there are faintness, helplessness, and despondency. The strong man and the waterfall channel their own path. The energetic leader, of noble spirit, not only wins a way for himself; he carries others with him." Thus it has been from the beginning. Washington, Napoleon, Cromwell, Bismarck, Wesley, and Whitefield and Moody, are examples in point.

The world respects and loves men of deep, strong convictions—not senseless, graceless, sentimental fops, sprigs of a windy, fleshless, fishy aristocracy, with gloved fingers and soft clothing; but men of faith and power, with convictions that are living, burning realities; men who dare to speak the truth, even when it is unpopular; men who recognize duty and honor and right, and who follow them, constant as the polar star. Such men are a power while they live, and the world will never let them be forgotten, even when they are dead. Such a man in a workshop will give tone to his fellows, and exalt them to a better life. Franklin is said to have reformed the manners of an entire office in London, while he wrought there as a printer. Such were the men whom Cromwell chose for his armies, and whom he styled "Ironsides" and "Invincibles." John Brown, whose "soul goes marching on," once said to Emerson that, "for a settler in a new country, one good believing man is worth a hundred—nay, worth a thousand—men without character."

"Tell me," said a French writer, "whom you admire, and I will tell what you are as to your talents, tastes, and character. Do you admire mean men? Your own nature is mean. Do you admire rich men? You are of the earth, earthy. Do you admire men of title? You are a toad-eater or a tuft-hunter. Do you admire honest, brave, and manly men? You are, yourself, of an honest, brave and manly spirit." Washington and Franklin, Roger Sherman and Havelock and Lincoln, and others, might be cited as examples and illustrations of the view I have given. They were not brilliant, showy men, but they were true men, honest men, solid men, men of integrity, who would rather be right than to win a throne.

Lord Bacon said, "I would rather believe all the faiths in the legends, the Talmud, and the Alkoran, than that this universal frame is without a mind." He said this when men were clamoring that he was heterodox. Brave men, men of courage, this world approves.

> "If thou canst plan a noble deed,
> And never flag till it succeed,
> Though in the strife thy heart should bleed,—
> Whatever obstacles control,
> Thine hour will come—go on, true soul!
> Thou 'lt win the prize, thou 'lt reach the goal."

Two thousand years ago, Aristotle drew a portrait of the magnanimous man; that is, the gentleman. It is still true to the life.

"He will behave with moderation under good fortune and bad. He will know how to be exalted, and how to be abased. He will neither be delighted with success, nor grieved by failure. He will neither shun danger nor seek it, for there are few things which he cares for. He is reticent and somewhat slow of speech; but he speaks his mind openly and boldly when occasion calls for it. He is not apt to admire; for nothing is great to him. He overlooks injuries. He is not given to talk about himself or about others; for he does not care that he himself should be praised, nor that others should be blamed. He does not cry about trifles, and he craves help from none."

Self-sacrifice and devotion for the good of others give men immortality. The plague was making a desert of Marseilles. It baffled all medical skill. The physicians determined, in council, that a corpse must be dissected. One of the number solemnly promised that he would devote himself for the safety of others, and that he would dissect a corpse. He made his will. The next morning he redeemed his promise— carefully made all the surgical and anatomical examinations required, wrote down his observations, threw the papers into a disinfecting vase, left the room, went out, and died.

The cry of "mad dog" aroused the attention of the blacksmith. He saw that unless he grappled the animal his wife and children would be bitten and die. He seized the dog; was again and again bitten; but he held him until the dog was dispatched, and his family were saved. He then chained himself to the anvil, and met his awful death.

John Maynard, the pilot, remained at the wheel of the burning ship, guiding the vessel to the nearest shore, when the flames had surrounded and scorched him, and where at last he died; but every passenger was saved.

John Howard devoted his fortune and his life to the relief of suffering humanity, and at last he fell a victim to the fever contracted in his visit to a fever-stricken patient. His name is illustrious. His chaplet grows greener as the years roll away. The thousand forms of beneficence which now bless humanity owe their origin and inspiration to his example, and to the grace of the Lord Jesus Christ, which burned in his heart.

And Good Samaritan societies, and National Christian Temperance Unions, and Red Ribbon and Blue Ribbon brigades, and all other organizations for helping humanity, are the outflow of the grace of the Lord Jesus Christ. It was this which suggested the publication of the *Life-Boat*, in which our lamented friend and brother was so forward and so effective. His life, his portrait, his memory, all enforce devotion to the work of helping the needy, and rescuing the perishing, and raising up the fallen. How much of this needs to be done.

> "There are lonely hearts to cherish,
>   While the days are going by.
> There are weary souls who perish,
>   While the days are going by.
> If a smile we can renew,
> As our journey we pursue,
> O, the good that we may do,
>   While the days are going by!"

The rule of John Howard in his beneficence was this: "Our superfluities should give way to other men's convenience. Our conveniences should give way to other men's necessities. Our necessities should give way to other men's extremities." How much sunshine and gladness would come to homes and hearts of sorrow if only these rules were adopted! How much this world needs Good Samaritans!

Thomas Carlyle says: "The whole world calls for new work and nobleness. Subdue mutiny, discord, widespread despair, by manfulness, justice, mercy, and wisdom. Chaos is dark—deep as hell. Let there be light, and there is, instead, a green, flowery world. O, it is great, and there is no other greatness! To make some work of God's creation a little fruitfuller, better, more worthy of God; to make some human hearts a little wiser, manfuller, happier, more blessed, less accursed,—it is work for a god. Sooty hell of mutiny, and savagery, and despair, can, by man's energy, be made a kind of heaven, cleansed of its soot, of its mutiny, of its need to mutiny; the everlasting arch of heaven overspreading it, too, and its cunning mechanisms and tall chimney steeples as a birth of heaven; God and all men looking on it well pleased."

A dismantled hull was discovered on the ocean. She was boarded. They found the skeletons of starved men on the deck. One man they found still alive. They took him off to their ship, nursed and revived him. As soon as he could speak, he whispered, "There is another man." They returned and found him, and rescued him. Our brother and friend manned the life-boat, and went to the rescue of perishing ones. His mute lips on yonder canvas would say, if they could speak, "*There is another man.*" Go for him, brothers; seek him; rescue him; save him.

And never forget, in your need and weakness, Him who is the Good Samaritan from heaven; your brother, my brother; who never passes by on the other side; who supplies wine, and oil, and transportation, and attendance, and nursing, and healing. Put yourselves in his hands, and let him apply the balm of his mercy to your weak, tempted, weary, despairing souls.

In 1882, Bishop Thomas Bowman appointed me to Grace Church, Urbana. Here were spent three happy, useful years. I have never had a more pleasant, appreciative, and well-ordered officiary and membership than I served in Urbana. Here, too, were formed friendships of enduring value. It is one of the best charges in the Cincinnati Conference, for its complete record in all lines of members, Church support, Sunday-school, and benevolent collections. Urbana is a most delightful city of six or seven thousand persons. The people are intelligent, refined, prosperous, hospitable. Urbana has a college under the care of the Swedenborgians.

From Urbana, I was sent in 1885 to Wesley Chapel, Cincinnati, where, also, I remained three years. The people desired and expected my return for the remaining two years of my possible stay; but I was removed from Wesley to Central Methodist Episcopal Church, Springfield, in 1888. We had three years of revival work in Wesley. The two most notable events in the Wesley pastorate were the thorough renovation of the church, costing about three thousand dollars, all of which was paid when the church was reopened. The other event was the preaching of a sermon, June 17, 1888, on occasion of the celebration of the one hundredth anniversary of the founding of Cincinnati. As this contains much historic information in reference to early Methodism in Southwestern Ohio, and especially gives a carefully-prepared history of the Methodist Episcopal Church in Cincinnati, it is presented here complete:

CENTENNIAL SERMON.

"Remember the days of old, consider the years of many generations: ask thy father, and he will shew thee; thy elders, and they will tell thee. When the Most High divided to the nations their inheritance, when he separated the sons of Adam, he set the bounds of the people according to the number of the children of Israel. For the LORD's portion is his people; Jacob is the lot of his inheritance. He found him in a desert land, and in the waste howling wilderness; he led him about, he instructed him, he kept him as the apple of his eye. As an eagle stirreth up her nest, fluttereth over her young, spreadeth abroad her wings, taketh them, beareth them on her wings: so the LORD alone did lead him, and there was no strange god with him. He made him ride on the high places of the earth, that he might eat the increase of the fields; and he made him to suck honey out of the rock, and oil out of the flinty rock; butter of kine, and milk of sheep, with fat of lambs, and rams of the breed of Bashan, and goats with the fat of kidneys of wheat; and thou didst drink the pure blood of the grape."—DEUT. XXXII, 7-14.

At the ripe age of one hundred and twenty years, about to cease from being the leader of Israel, Moses is giving his parting words to the people of the Lord. This address contains memories and warnings. Moses teaches them, in a most affecting manner, the duty of remembering what God had done for them and for their fathers. He urges this duty by several considerations:

1. They would learn, thus, the true way to greatness, honor, and success. In "the days of old," when they were obediently under God's direction and care, this prosperity was real and grand.

2. To recall God's kindly and wonderful dealings with them in "the years of many generations," would be to excite living gratitude to God.

3. To remember the former times would assist them in correcting any existing irregularities, or deviations from rectitude. By these back-sights the crooked line could be straightened, and the future advance in the way their fathers had walked, when God led them in the wilderness, would be in right lines. Paul teaches the philosophy of this when he says: "Whereunto we have already attained, let us walk by the same rule, let us mind the same things."

From this text, then, we gather several lessons, viz.: God's people are his portion and the lot of his inheritance; and God takes care of them. God sets bounds to his people's times and habitations. He gives them the lot of their inheritance—when men recognize that they dwell safely and in content. The review in the case of Israel presents such an advance that the former times and these are in contrast. He found them in bondage; he brought them into liberty. He led them through the wilderness; but he brought them and planted them in a land of corn and wine. God led them; compassed them about; treated them as an eagle treats her young in teaching them to fly. God made them ride upon the high places of power, that they might share the increase and fatness of the land. As they remembered all this, they would be kept in right lines. When surveyors are running straight meridian lines they sometimes, with great profit, take a back-sight, and compare that with their fore-sights, so that the continuous line shall be undeviating. And if all this was profitable for those of the olden times, it will also be profitable for us to "consider the years of many generations."

History must be studied as a whole, and not in detached parts. All things and all people are parts of a great system. If there had been no settlement of Cincinnati a hundred years ago, there could be no centennial now. If there had been no Wesley Chapel, the civilization of Cincinnati would have been different from what it is. Go into all the departments of a cotton factory, and they all bear relation to one result— the making of cloth. If Oliver M. Spencer had not been rescued from the Indians, his life would have had nothing to do with the progress of civilization in our city.

A hundred and fifty years ago John Wesley went up and down through England preaching of Jesus and salvation. The civilization of this world of ours feels the pulse and throb of John Wesley's life, and it will continue to feel them to the end of time. The influence of Christianity on civilization is shown in several ways: Christianity forbids habits of conduct fatal to a high civilization, such as idleness, profligacy, dissipation, loose social relations. Christianity inculcates and induces industry, energy, and the production and accumulation of property. Christianity prevents strikes, and promotes harmonious relations between labor and capital. While the showing of Cincinnati Methodism is not what we could have wished; while, as will be seen, it has not kept pace with the population, yet what would the civilization of Cincinnati have been to-day if there had not been, all through the last hundred years, the presence and the power of an active, earnest Christianity?

This is Cincinnati's centennial year. Our Exposition opens on the coming Fourth of July. In noting the various lines of progress made in a hundred years, the Exposition Commissioners request pastors to preach historical sermons, and all Churches to send up to the Exposition halls photographs of their several churches and of deceased ministers, and this department is expected to contain the evidences of moral and religious advancement. The Churches and their history will be there. We can note their advancement "that we may tell it to the generations following." As we point to these monuments, we may well take up the refrain, "This God is our God forever and ever. He will be our guide, even unto death."

Within a hundred years the hills and forests around this region echoed the strokes of the woodman's ax. Now, in six thousand manufacturing establishments, the hum of industry makes music every secular day of the year, and the smoke from thousands of chimney-stacks rises toward heaven.

The capital brought here a hundred years ago was limited to the barest necessaries of life. The taxable personal property of Cincinnati is assessed at $130,000,000. The real estate is $50,000,000, yielding a revenue of four millions of dollars. Ninety-five thousand persons are employed in manufactories. Eighty millions of dollars cash capital and fifty millions of dollars in real estate are invested and employed in manufacturing plants, yielding an annual product of two hundred millions of dollars. The property of the State of Ohio amounts to $3,198,062,000.

Then we had no churches and schools. Now, churches are in all parts of the city, and every child here can attend schools of various grades, from elementary to collegiate, while two large libraries, and a full law library, afford the means of acquiring knowledge. To gather and tabulate these astounding facts of material progress is comparatively easy. Dollars, and stocks, and farms, and houses, and bank circulation can be counted without serious difficulty.

But moral results can not be measured nor tabulated. They are intangible. A man receives a moral impulse which sends him up and on in the path of progress. A thousand, ten thousand, multiplied by tens or scores, receive like impulses, and they in turn communicate them to others. Moral influences curb and restrain evil passions and criminal purposes, prevent vagrancy, and promote industry and thrift. You can see some of the effects of them; some of the achievements started or impelled by these moral influences; but you can not measure nor weigh the forces themselves. Let us to-day look over this field of moral action, and see what we can gather of inspiring truth, of encouraging precedent, and of stimulating motive; and let us pray that God may assist our inquiries and bless our discoveries.

Other denominations will trace the lines of their history and achievements. It will be ours to follow up the history of our advent and progress, as Methodists, in this part of the Ohio Valley.

Ninety-five years ago the first Methodist sermon was preached in old Fort Washington, by a local preacher named Francis Clark, from Kentucky. A Methodist sermon was preached near Cincinnati, on the road to Hamilton, two years later, by James Smith. His theme was the angel's announcement to the shepherds of Bethlehem. His text was, "Behold, I bring you good tidings of great joy, which shall be to all people."

Eighty-four years ago, John Collins, a local preacher living in Clermont County, came to Cincinnati to buy salt. He made his purchases of Thomas Carter, on Main Street, near the river. He then inquired if there were any Methodists in the town. "Yes," said Mr. Carter, "and I am one." Overjoyed by this news, Mr. Collins embraced Mr. Carter, and wept upon his neck. Mr. Collins proposed to preach if a place could be found. Mr. Carter offered a room in his own house. That night Mr. Collins preached with marked interest to twelve persons. In that house, that evening, were gathered all the Methodists Cincinnati then contained.* That was the second Methodist sermon in Cincinnati. Yet Methodist preaching had been heard and Methodist societies had been formed at Milford and at Pleasant Hill.

In 1804, John Sale was appointed, by Bishop Asbury, to the Miami Circuit, which then included nearly or quite all the territory now within the bounds of the

---

*A writer in the Cincinnati *Commercial Gazette*, July 21st, claims that Philip Gatch preached the first sermon in Cincinnati in 1798. This is obviously a mistake. Judge McLean, who had access to the papers of Mr. Gatch, and who wrote his biography, and also that of Mr. Collins, ascribes the honor to Mr. Collins and not to Mr. Gatch.

Cincinnati Conference. Miami Circuit had been in the list of Methodist charges since 1800, with a varying membership of from one hundred and fifty to five hundred members.

Mr. Sale visited Cincinnati. He found a Methodist class of eight persons not yet regularly enrolled. He preached in a hotel kept by George Gordon, on Main Street, between Front and Second Streets. After preaching, he formed the members present in the first properly-constituted Methodist class in Cincinnati. James Gibson was appointed leader. The other members were: Mrs. Gibson, Mr. and Mrs. St. Clair, and Thomas Carter, his wife, a son, and a daughter. That son became a judge of one of the Cincinnati courts. The daughter became the mother of Ex-Governor Dennison.

A Methodist Discipline of 1812 was found recently in Dayton, with this inscription, in substance:

To JOHN SALE.—This Discipline got into my hands in some way. It belongs to John Sale.
        (Signed,)   FRANCIS ASBURY.

From the time of Mr. Sale's first sermon in Cincinnati, in 1804, it was made one of the regular preaching places on the Miami Circuit, being visited by one of the circuit preachers every two weeks. There was no fixed place of meeting. Sometimes it was held in a log school-house under the hill, sometimes at Brother Newcome's, on Sycamore Street, sometimes at Thomas Carter's, and sometimes in a barn, near the foot of Main Street. The number of the Methodists steadily increased. In 1806, or in 1807, probably in the former year, the first Methodist church was built in Cincinnati, a stone edifice, on the present site of Wesley Chapel, Fifth Street, between Sycamore and Broadway, on the north side. It was a small, square, one-story building. Soon, needing enlargement, this was afforded by building unsightly brick additions on the east and west sides.

The lot for the church and burying-ground was deeded by James Kirby to five trustees, "for the use of the Methodist Episcopal Church in the United States of America." The lot was originally two hundred feet square, extending from the alleys, cutting the block centrally north and south and east and west to Broadway and Fifth Streets, and from Fifth to Sixth Streets, being the entire southeast corner of the block.

In 1805 there were 734 members in the Miami Circuit. Of these there may have been twenty-five or thirty in Cincinnati.

In 1806 the enrollment was 893, of whom there were perhaps thirty or forty in Cincinnati.

In 1807 the Minutes show Miami Circuit 757 members; Mad River Circuit, 332 members—1,089 members in all. Of the members on the Miami Circuit, there may have been fifty or sixty in Cincinnati. There was no separate enrollment nor designation of members in Cincinnati until 1814, when 226 members are reported.

In 1809 the name Cincinnati first appears in the Minutes. It obviously included a large part of Miami Circuit. Twelve hundred and eighty-two members are reported for that year, of whom perhaps one hundred and twenty-five were in Cincinnati. In 1807, Benjamin Lakin and John Collins were appointed on Miami Circuit. Probably the stone church had already been erected. It was small, square, and unsightly. Three services were held on the Sabbath—morning, afternoon, and evening. There were also a Sunday-school and class-meeting held each Lord's-day. Class-meetings have always been a special feature of Wesley Chapel. Mr. J. P. Kilbreth, of a later day, attended a sunrise class-meeting, in a small, frame building, used also for an office, and which stood on the spacious church lot. There he met Judge McLean, who regularly attended, and who may have been the leader.

Wesley and its predecessor have always been conspicuous places in Cincinnati. About the time of the War of 1812, General Hull and his staff passed through Cincinnati, and attended divine worship in Wesley.

When Wesley was built it was often opened for general purposes, because of its size. It was for many years the largest audience-room in the city. Fourth of July and Masonic celebrations were held in Wesley; the same was true as to school anniversaries; and notably those of the Cincinnati Wesleyan College. In 1843, when Mt. Adams Observatory was publicly opened by John Quincy Adams, his address was delivered in Wesley.

Nearly all the Cincinnati Methodist Churches sprang from Wesley. One of the first colonies from this goodly mother of Cincinnati Methodism was the Old Brick Church, Plum and Fourth, commonly, for years, called Brimstone Corner. After some years, the members of the Old Brick bought land on the west side of Western Row, now Central Avenue, and built Morris Chapel. Twenty years ago they moved to the corner of Smith and Seventh, and erected the elegant and commodious structure known as St. Paul Church. Later offshoots from Wesley were McKendree, Asbury, and Trinity. For a long time Asbury and McKendree buildings were rented for day-schools, Asbury for four dollars a month, and McKendree for thirty-two dollars a year. Around the old Stone Church the native trees were still standing, the worshipers being accustomed to tie their horses to them during divine service. But these soon disappeared, to make way for the buildings and streets.

December 25, 1829, the Official Board of Wesley decided to build a new church edifice. Josiah Lawrence submitted a plan of a church drafted by Caleb Williams. That board consisted of Matthew Benson, Robert Richardson, Christopher Smith, Isaac Covalt, Josiah Lawrence, Benjamin Stewart, William Bateman, Oliver M. Spencer. Mr. Spencer was father of the late Henry E. Spencer, ex-mayor of Cincinnati. The church was to be built of brick, ninety-five feet long by seventy feet wide, two stories high above ground, and a basement story; a vestibule in the main story; a gallery on the sides, supported by pillars, but no pillars in the gallery. The cupola was to have a foundation carried to the roof. The house was to be in rear of the stone church. O. M. Spencer, Isaac Covalt, and Matthew Benson were the building committee. F. Hand was to superintend the carpenter-work at one dollar twelve and a half cents per day. I. Covalt superintended the brick-work. The plastering was done by Ezekiel Thorp. During the erection of the building, religious services were held in the court-house and in different churches of the city.

Among the honored names of the early members of Wesley, besides those I have given, were those of William Burke, a superannuated preacher, and, for several years, city postmaster; Adonijah Peacock, John and William McLean, John Elstner, James and John Walls, Arnold Truesdell, William Wood, and others.

After the church was built, the Official Board decided that the women should occupy the seats to the right of the aisles leading from the front down to the pulpit, and the men the seats to the left of the aisles. It was also provided that, if the men and women were found sitting together, the sexton or the trustees should separate them.

May 31, 1833, the trustees passed an order forbidding persons from leaving the house in time of public worship, crowding into the pews past those who were sitting in them, and slamming the doors in going out of the house. The order declared that such conduct showed disrespect for the worshipers, and for the worship of God, and was a mark of ill-breeding. They also passed a resolution recommending that respect was due, and should be paid, to aged persons, and providing that the front row of seats should be reserved for those of advanced years.

The lecture-room was erected in 1859, in part from the proceeds of a bequest of one thousand dollars left for that purpose by some deceased member of the church.

The building of Wesley Chapel was begun December 25, 1829. It was dedicated December 25, 1831. It is a very plain, substantial building, resembling, in its main features, City Road Chapel, built by Mr. Wesley in London. In its day it was one of the best churches in the country. It cost about twenty thousand dollars. It has been the birthplace of many hundreds, perhaps thousands, of souls. Grand sermons have been preached here by some of the noblest and most renowned of ministers. Displays of Divine power were witnessed here at times which were wonderful. A lady is now living who saw, in Wesley, scores lying prostrate and unconscious, overpowered by religious influence.

For years Wesley was one of the finest and costliest churches in Cincinnati. On that memorable Christmas day, in 1831, three renowned and eloquent ministers preached the three sermons. Bishop Soule, then living in Lebanon, Ohio, was to have preached the first sermon and dedicated the church. He failed to appear. E. W. Sehon, one of the pastors, preached the morning sermon. In the afternoon, Burr H. McCown, a professor in Augusta College, preached. At night, H. B. Bascom, also a professor in Augusta College, officiated.

In the summer of 1858, under the pastorate of Asbury Lowrey, Wesley Chapel was thoroughly refitted and improved at a cost of three thousand dollars, and on the 18th day of July, 1858, the reopening sermon was preached by Rev. E. W. Sehon who, twenty-seven years before, had preached the dedicatory sermon. At a like expense the Sunday-school room was erected. In December, 1858, the lecture-room, in the rear of the main building, was dedicated by Bishop Morris. In these reopening services many were present who witnessed the first dedication in 1831. One was present, when the church was reopened in 1887, who attended the reopening in 1858, and also in 1876. Under the pastorate of Sylvester Weeks, in 1876 or 1877, the church was put in repair, and was reopened with appropriate services. A somewhat fuller account of the repairs and improvements put upon Wesley, in the spring of 1887, deserves notice.

The improvements, which began the previous year by the granite pavement fronting the church and parsonage, at a cost of about seven hundred dollars, consisted of replacing the windows with beautiful cathedral glass in elegant designs, those on the west side being protected by wire screens on the outside. The walls were refrescoed in terra-cotta tint and with suitable inscriptions about the pulpit walls, including the Apostles' Creed and the Lord's Prayer. The pulpit was projected from the rear wall, sufficiently to admit of a choir and organ platform behind the pulpit.

Triple gas-burners replaced the old, dim, and dingy double ones. The wood-work was repainted and varnished. The vestibule was covered with hemp matting. The audience-room was recarpeted with well-adapted carpets. The whole involved a cost of about three thousand dollars. The improvements were conceived and carried forward by the Wesley Chapel Beneficent Society, whose members, male and female, displayed great energy and liberality in promoting the enterprise. It would be unjust not to make special and honorable mention of William G. Roberts, James G. Rutter, Charles R. Martin, Newton B. Collord, J. A. Jones, I. F. Tunison, S. M. Martin, and their ladies, who were active and effective in advancing the work.

On the first day of May, 1887, the pastor, Rev. Dr. Pearne, by special request of the Wesley Chapel Beneficent Society, preached the reopening sermon. The basket-collection amounted to some three hundred and fifty dollars. In the afternoon a union love-feast was held, conducted by the presiding elder, Charles W. Ketcham. Dr. Isaac W. Joyce called for subscriptions, and some five hundred dollars were presented. The debt for the improvements was all provided for, and the elegant audience-room of Wesley is as comfortable and inviting as that of any church in Cincinnati. Of the notable subscriptions toward this expense, from those not members of Wesley, should be mentioned those of Mrs. Jane Banks, $100; Mrs. Bishop Clark, $50; a brother in Indiana, $50; R. M. Moore, of Elizabeth, New Jersey, $50; and Payne and Mrs. Pettibone, of Wyoming, Pa., $100.

Since Wesley was erected, how marvelous has been the growth of this goodly city! The population of Cincinnati in 1831, when Wesley was built, was perhaps twenty-five thousand. There were five Methodist churches, as many Methodist ministers, and one thousand two hundred and forty-two members of the Church.

When Wesley was dedicated, there was not a single Methodist in Chicago, nor anything else, except a small hamlet hovering about the United States military post existing there. The next year Jesse Walker, who went there and wrought as a missionary, returned ten members. Now Chicago has far outstripped Cincinnati in population, and commerce, and churches.

In 1858, when Wesley was reopened, the population of Cincinnati was given at one hundred and sixty-seven thousand. There were twenty churches, as many ministers, and nearly four thousand members. Now, after twenty-seven years, Wesley was again reopened. Including the suburbs on both sides of the river, which are really a part of Cincinnati, the population has probably doubled itself in those years. It is a city of solid wealth and substantial dwellings, warehouses, and manufactories. There are twice as many Methodists ministers and churches now as then, and some eight or nine thousand members.

From 1801 to 1809 eleven different preachers were stationed on the Miami Circuit, which included Hamilton and Clermont Counties, and seven or eight counties north of them. From 1810 to 1834 thirty-five ministers in all were stationed in Cincinnati. From 1834 to 1840, when Wesley, McKendree, and Morris Chapel (Fourth and Plum) were the only Methodist Churches in the city (Wesley and McKendree were either called Wesley or East Charge), eleven pastors were stationed in Cincinnati. Since 1840 Wesley has been a distinct charge, and twenty-six pastors have succeeded each other, one of them, J. T. Mitchell, serving two terms. Of these pastors, thirteen have ascended. Those remaining are Bishop Foster, M. P.

Gaddis and J. L. Grover, Drs. Trimble, Miley, Lowrey, Dustin, Weeks, Pearne, William I. Fee, A. N. Spahr, G. W. Kelly, and T. J. Harris.

Of members of the Methodist Church in Cincinnati, including probationers, in the early years of the century, the list is as follows, viz.:

1814,	226	1819,	633
1815,	264	1820,	608
1816,	310	1823,	633
1817,	318	1825,	785
1818,	462		

In Wesley and its predecessor thirty-one different ministers have been stationed, one year each. Seventeen have been stationed in Wesley and the old stone, each two years. Four have preached four years each in the old stone and in Wesley. These are John Collins, E. W. Sehon, J. M. Trimble, and John T. Mitchell. Fourteen have preached in Wesley or the old stone three years each. The last eight pastors in Wesley have been three years each.

Wesley has been a station since 1841. The first four years of that term the station included Asbury and McKendree. The last forty-three years it has been a separate charge or a station by itself. Since 1845 twenty-one different pastors have ministered here. Of these, four served only one year each. John T. Mitchell served four years. Eight pastors staid two years each, and eight three years each. This is an honorable record, creditable alike to the pastors who served and the Church which shared their abundant and acceptable ministrations.

What has Wesley been as to its membership?

From 1841 to 1851 the average membership was	518
" 1851 " 1861 " " " "	304
" 1861 " 1871 " " " "	315
" 1871 " 1881 " " " "	325
" 1881 " 1888 " " " "	406

Until the present pastorate, the largest number of probationers and members reported was in 1844—five hundred and thirty.

What has Wesley effected? Of course, in answering this question, only proximate facts can be given, and these can not be measured in the sweep of their influence. An average of forty conversions a year in Wesley and its predecessor would give the aggregate of three thousand and forty conversions. The average is probably much higher than is here named. Under seven pastorates, selected from personal knowledge or reliable information, there were two thousand and seven hundred conversions, leaving fifty-five pastorates, which would doubtless average thirty-five each, adding nineteen hundred and twenty-five conversions, making nearly five thousand and two hundred conversions in this God-honored Church. An average of thirty deaths a year would give an aggregate of two thousand four hundred, who, since this Church was organized, have ascended to their crowning.

What Wesley has given for missions has been tabulated in the General Minutes for only thirty-one years. Prior to that, whatever was given can only be conjectured, as no publication was made of it.

From 1857 to 1867 Wesley gave for missions, $5,692; average per year of $570. The average per year, per member, was $1.74.

From 1867 to 1877 Wesley gave for missions, $5,519; average per year of $552. The average per year, per member, was $1.85.

From 1877 to 1888 Wesley gave for missions, $3,256; average per year of $296. The average per year, per member, was 90 cents.

It will be seen that the contributions for missions for the past eleven years have perceptibly shrunk. The explanation is found in the fact that Wesley has been depleted of wealthy members by the Churches of the city and suburbs, and that, up to the last decade, the missionary collection was the principal and almost the only one. Since then the Church Extension, Freedmen's Aid, and other Conference collections, if added to that for missions, would probably swell the aggregate annual contributions of Wesley up to the figures from 1857 to 1867.

In 1844, under the pastorate of J. M. Trimble, the parsonage was built. Dr. Trimble himself dug the vault for the cistern, which still remains, a mute witness to his industry.

It will be interesting to consider, with some attention, the names and characters of some of the grand old ministers who have served as pastors in Wesley Chapel. Among the honored names of those who have ministered in the old stone church is that of John P. Durbin. His senior colleague was the revered and immortal William H. Raper. They succeeded the almost equally eminent Russel Bigelow and Truman Bishop. The next year, 1826, Mr. Durbin was a professor in Augusta College. His first charge, to which he went from the cabinetmaker's bench, was Greenville Circuit, which covered a large part of Darke and Montgomery Counties, and nearly all of Preble. In his first year he took rank as a vigorous thinker and an eloquent man. He possessed rare dramatic genius. Richard Brandriff, of Piqua, a member of the Cincinnati Conference, joined the traveling connection in 1821. He died in 1887, aged eighty-five years. He was a contemporary of Mr. Durbin. He knew him intimately. Mr. Brandriff has narrated to the writer repeated instances of Mr. Durbin's early development as a man of recognized pulpit power. In the Eastern States he gave a lecture on St Paul as man, irrespective of his greatness as an inspired apostle, which the press of the time highly commended. His national fame as an orator continued for many years. A member of Wesley Chapel is still living who sat under Mr. Durbin's ministry in the old stone church. He always had large and admiring audiences. The membership in the city in 1825 was seven hundred and fifty; colored, thirty-five. Dr. Durbin's career affords a fine illustration of the opportunity this country afforded and affords earnest and gifted young men for reaching eminent positions. L. L. Hamline, afterward a bishop, was a minister in Wesley in 1835 and 1836. He has probably never been excelled in Ohio as a brilliant, clear, forcible thinker and an eloquent divine. Some of his passages, as now recalled, had surpassing sweep of thought and diction, and overwhelming pathos. James Quinn, John Collins, and W. B. Christie were men of wide fame and usefulness. Of the three, Christie excelled in invariable pulpit effectiveness. Even when he was far gone in consumption, he would astonish and overpower his audiences by vehement and eloquent passages. John Miley, of a period of ten years later, has always been a superior preacher. He still retains the mental fire and power of the earlier times. He is the live and popular professor in Drew. It was while Bishop Foster was pastor of Wesley that he had the controversy with Dr. Rice, on Calvinism. During his incumbency the cholera made its second appearance in Cincinnati. He was with the sick and the dying, never flinching nor shirking his duty to the stricken members and families of his flock. In one instance, a lady member of the Church, living on Sycamore Street, called at the parsonage to solicit Mr. Foster to visit her husband, who was very ill with the cholera. He went, found the man in collapse, ministered to him, and remained with him until he died, smoothed his pillow, and laid him out decently upon the bed. Returning, he found the man's wife dying of cholera. The man, before dying, called for his bank book, found a balance of one thousand five hundred dollars, for which he gave Mr. Foster a check as a personal gift, which, however, Mr. Foster, with the self-sacrifice and generosity characteristic of the early itinerants, gave to Wesley, to assist in paying off a troublesome Church debt.

During this pastorate Mr. Foster had his famous controversy with Dr. Rice on Calvinism. Lyman Beecher, then a professor in Lane Seminary, came to hear his sermons on Calvinism, and rendered him valuable assistance by the loan of books of reference upon the subject under discussion. More than twenty years later, Bishop Foster met, in South America, a thrifty Scotchman, who had been rescued from infidelity, caused by his difficulties with Calvinism, by reading the bishop's book, entitled, "Objections to Calvinism."

John Collins had much to do in molding and directing Cincinnati Methodism. As already seen, he visited Cincinnati in 1804, and preached to twelve persons. In 1807 he joined the traveling connection, and, with Benjamin Lakin as his senior colleague, he was stationed on Miami Circuit, which then included Cincinnati. He was then thirty-eight years of age. In 1821 and 1822, at the age of fifty-two, he was stationed in Wesley Chapel, Cincinnati. Again, in 1834, he was pastor of this Church. There is a lady—Mrs. Kierman—still a member of Wesley, which she joined under Mr. Collins's pastorate. He was evidently, and with good reason, a great favorite with the people of Wesley.

John Collins was presiding elder here from 1826 to 1829. He was small of stature, compactly built, with an expressive, mild blue eye, and possessing large sensibility. He seldom preached without weeping, in which his audiences almost always participated. He was the honored instrument in the conversion of Justice John McLean, of the United States Supreme Court. Mr. Collins's death was as peaceful and triumphant as his long life had been useful and beautiful. His sun-setting was without a cloud. His last words were, "Happy! Happy!! Happy!!!" and all was still. His history is identified with that of the West. His usefulness as a preacher is unsurpassed in Southwestern Ohio. As a successful pastor he had no superior.*

At the age of twenty, William H. Raper was a captain in the War of 1812, in which he distinguished himself as a brave and successful soldier. In 1816 he joined the Methodist Episcopal Church. In 1819 he became a member of the Ohio Conference. In 1825-1826 he was stationed in Cincinnati, which then included Wesley and all the city. In 1837 and 1838

---

* Maxwell P. Gaddis, in his "Footprints of an Itinerant," credits John Collins with having preached the first Methodist sermon in Ripley, Ohio. He was passing through Ripley, on his way to an appointment, and passed a funeral procession on its way to the grave with the deceased wife of an infidel. After the burial services at the grave were concluded, he requested the people to remain, and he preached to them a sermon from the words, "I am the resurrection and the life." (John xi, 25.) Many were in tears. The infidel was converted. Mr. Collins, in 1811, appointed the trustees and made arrangements for building the first Methodist Episcopal church in Urbana, Ohio. In the same year, John Collins, then preaching on the Mad River Circuit, raised a subscription to build the first Methodist Episcopal church in Dayton, Ohio. In 1840, in the great revivals under J. N. Maffitt, in which seven hundred were converted in Wesley, and many hundreds in Maysville, Ky., Father Collins is described as working effectively in a blaze of glory.

he was stationed in Wesley. In 1841 he was a presiding elder in Cincinnati. He died in 1852, at the age of sixty-one. He was remarkable for his refinement, his rare conversational powers, and his great ability as a preacher of the gospel. Noble, honored man! After thirty-two years since his death, his personal impress is still felt.

William B. Christie was born in 1803. He was a proficient student in Augusta College, giving promise then of his distinguished career. In 1830 to 1832 Mr. Christie was pastor in Wesley Chapel. In 1836 he was associated with L. L. Hamline as pastor of Wesley. In 1837-8-9 he was presiding elder in Cincinnati. In 1841-1842 he was stationed in Urbana. In 1842, he died in this city, at the house of his brother-in-law, Dr. M. B. Wright. When dying, he said to E. W. Sehon: "Tell the brethren of the Conference that I have not preached an unknown nor an unfelt Christ. The gospel I have preached to others sustains me now. Tell the brethren to preach Christ and him crucified; tell them my only hope, my only foundation, is in the blood of sprinkling. O, the fullness, the richness, the sweetness of that fountain! I am almost home. God is good to me. Jesus Christ is my salvation." His funeral, from this church, was attended by an overflowing crowd of all classes of people. Persons attended who were never before nor since within these walls. Bishop Morris preached on that occasion. He says, while he had seen many happy Christians die, he never saw a more signal victory than that of William B. Christie in his death.

Bishop Morris was several times a pastor of Wesley. In 1832 and 1833 he was pastor of Wesley, and from 1834 to 1836 he was presiding elder in Cincinnati.

Having spoken of some of the distinguished ministers of Wesley, it will be proper to make reference also, to some of the eminent laymen who have been honored members of this Church.

Josiah Lawrence, a native of Boston, was born April 19, 1791. Early in the century he came to Cincinnati, by way of South Carolina. For very many years he was an active, useful member of the Official Board of this Church. He possessed large wealth, which he liberally used in sustaining the Church and in its benevolent causes. His life was pure; his example was godly; his business integrity was proverbial. He was a merchant and banker in whom everybody had confidence. His portrait adorns the walls of the Chamber of Commerce. One of the oldest members of Wesley said to me: "Josiah Lawrence was a pillar in this Church, active, devoted, liberal, loved by all the Church."

William Neff was for many years an official member of Wesley. He was reared in the Episcopal Church. But he formed a strong attachment for J. B. Finley, under whose influence he was converted, and he became a zealous and devoted Methodist. From his birthplace, in Philadelphia, he came west by the way of Savannah, Georgia, where he spent the earlier years of his life. Like Lawrence, Neff was wealthy and liberal.

Another eminent member of this Church was a man whose early and thrilling history I read in my childhood in a Sunday-school library book. Oliver M. Spencer, in 1790, when a young lad, was brought, by his parents, from New Jersey to Cincinnati. At first they settled in Columbia, where several years were spent. By permission, he came down to Fort Washington, with his parents, on foot, to attend a military drill and parade, which was to continue several days. After the first day Oliver tired of the parade, and, with the consent of his parents, he started back, on foot, and alone, for Columbia. On his homeward way he saw a boat with persons in it, ascending the river. He signaled the boat, hoping to obtain a ride to Columbia. Some concealed Indians captured him, and carried him to their own home, in the Wabash or Michigan region. He had all the experience of Indian life, sleeping at night on the ground, and faring in their rough, irregular way. He was taken by them to Pennsylvania, Indiana, Michigan, and New York. Through the offices of a friendly Indian, he was reclaimed while yet a captive in New York. After his rescue he remained a few years in New York, attending school, and then returned to Cincinnati. Spencer was a leading member of this Church, at times president and secretary of the trustees. He took an active and leading part in the erection of Wesley Chapel.

Mrs. Bell, one of the oldest members of Wesley, bears testimony to the excellent character and piety of Christopher Smith, whom she described as the salt of the earth. One of his daughters, Mrs. Edward Sargent, died a year or two since. Another daughter still lives on Walnut Hills. Brother Truesdell, a teacher, was Sister Bell's class-leader. He was faithful and effective. His widow became the wife of Bishop Hamline. She died a few years since in Evanston. She was a noble Christian woman, of cultured mind and highly-refined nature.

Judge McLean, the distinguished jurist, was a steady-going, earnest, consistent, and faithful Methodist. He was always found in his place, right here on the right-hand side of the pulpit, on the front seat of the amen corner, just there next to that gallery post. His piety was genuine; here he sat; here he testified, by his life and his words, for Jesus. He was a class-leader. J. P. Kilbreth, who came to this city when the century was young, frequently attended his sunrise class in the little, one-story, one-room frame building, called the church office, and which stood on the church-lot near where the parsonage now stands. Judge McLean wrote very beautiful sketches of the lives of John Collins and Philip Gatch, pioneer preachers of Southwestern Ohio.

But we may not overlook the women of Cincinnati Methodism. In this city, fifty years ago, from woman's wise forethought, came the Cincinnati Wesleyan College, which has been graduating trained, godly women for all the middle West. They have filled the land with their blessed influence. Here, too, more recently, was launched the Woman's Home Missionary Society of the Methodist Episcopal Church. The Cincinnati Branch, Woman's Foreign Missionary Society, has been behind none in liberal, effective doing for Christ. Under the ministry of some of the ablest men of American Methodism, came into our Cincinnati Methodism some of its grandest women: Mrs. Judge McLean, Mrs. Josiah Lawrence, Mrs. Benjamin Stewart, Mrs. Christopher Smith, Mrs. Logue, Mrs. Ezekiel Thorp, Mrs. Arnold Truesdell, afterward Mrs. Bishop Hamline, Mrs. Collins, Mrs. Jemima Peacock, Mrs. Sarah Mills, Mrs J. P. Kilbreth, Mrs. T. W. Bakewell, Mrs. Sacker Nelson, Mrs. William Neff, Mrs. Oliver M. Spencer, Mrs. Mary Coner, mother of our own Aunt Jane Banks. Mrs. John Elstner, one of God's own, the Lord's prisoner, still remains. In her prime she was an active manager of the Home for the Friendless. In her age and feebleness she does not lack for friends. Nearly all of these were members of Wesley; some belonged to the old stone church.

In the old brick church, Plum and Fourth Street, next after the old stone church, there grew up, prior to the last half century, a class of noble Methodist women, among whom may be named Mrs. Dr. Jesse Smith, afterward wife of Rev. John F. Wright, and of equally blessed memory. Mrs. William McLean, Mrs. John Reeves, Mrs. Thomas B. Anderson, Mrs. Moses Brooks, Mrs. John Dubois, and her sister, Miss Susan Lanphear. Most of these women had homes of plenty and luxury, which were always open to the ministers of Christ. The few surviving Methodists of those early times recall the domestic delights of those well-nigh apostolic days as a pleasant dream.

Nine years ago, at the ripe age of eighty-three, Ann Davis, mother of the two doctors, John and William B. Davis, went home, after seventy-two years of Christian life. For fifty years she had been honorably connected with Cincinnati Methodism. Fifty years ago she effectively aided Dr. Nast in planting German Methodism in this city. In this roll of honor belong Mrs. Samuel Lewis, Mrs. Gamble, Sr., mother of James Gamble, who is still with us; also Mr. Gamble's sisters, Media Gamble and Mrs. Rizer. Mrs. Gamble had seen Wesley and heard Coke. Of those yet remaining, Mrs. Bishop Clark and Mrs. Glenn, of St. Paul; Mrs. Stewart and Mrs. Perkins; Mrs. Wood, of Walnut Hills; and Mrs. Gamble, of Trinity, and so many more, loved and cherished, I could say much.

I wish to give you some figures showing the actual and relative progress of Methodism in Cincinnati. It has been slower and smaller than in the whole State, and as compared also with Methodism in other cities. Yet it has had peculiar hindrances here not known in other cities and sections. Considering these, its march has not been discreditable.

The population given for 1860 is an approximate figure. The Methodist figures for 1880 and 1888 are approximate, yet they are substantially reliable. They include the German and colored members, and also members in suburban charges.

ACTUAL AND COMPARATIVE INCREASE OF MEMBERS BY DECADES.

1800-1810.—Members, say 130; increase, 130 per cent. Methodists to the population, one in nineteen.

1810-1820.—Members, 608; increase, 375 per cent. Methodists to the population, one in sixteen.

1820-1830.—Members, 1,142; increase, 87 per cent. Proportion, one in twenty-two.

1830-1840.—Members, 2,686; increase, 138 per cent. Proportion, one in sixteen.

1840-1850.—Members, 3,223; increase, 20 per cent. Proportion, one in thirty-five.

1850-1860.—Members, 4,461; increase, 39 per cent. Proportion, one in thirty-seven.

1860-1870.—Members, 4,932; increase, 10½ per cent. One Methodist to forty-four of the population.

1870-1880.—Members, 7,000; increase, 42 per cent. One Methodist to thirty-six.

1880-1888.—Members, say 8,000; increase, 14½ pr. ct. One Methodist to forty-two of the population.

POPULATION—ACTUAL AND RELATIVE INCREASE BY DECADES.

Decade.	Numbers.	Increase Per Cent.
1800-1810	2,510	230
1810-1820	9,242	280
1820-1830	24,831	58
1830-1840	44,338	79
1840-1850	115,403	165*
1850-1860	167,378	45
1860-1870	216,139	35
1870-1880	255,139	18
1880-1888 say	333,000	3

* Notwithstanding 4,832, one in twenty-four, or four per cent of the population, died of cholera.

CHAPTER XXVII.

I WAS sent from Wesley Chapel, Cincinnati, to Central Methodist Episcopal Church, Springfield, Ohio, at the Conference of 1888. I had been in Wesley only three-fifths of the possible length of the pastorate. It was the judgment of all the members of the Official Board of Wesley that I should fill out the full term, and in this view of the case I was in full accord with them. Yet Central Church was deemed to be in a peculiar condition. It was the opinion of Bishop Warren and all the presiding elders of the Conference that I should be sent to Central Church, Springfield. I went there, and while the conditions were somewhat unique, I was never the pastor of any Church where I had more fully the confidence of my officiary and the appreciation of my congregation. All things considered, they were very successful years. We had almost a continuous revival. This is a working Church—a people's Church. During my two years' pastorate in the Central Church, I wrote and published a paper in reply to Colonel Robert G. Ingersoll's article on "God in the Constitution." His article appeared in the first number of the *Arena*, a Boston review. I wrote a reply, and sent it to the editor, who had promised me that my paper should appear in the next number of the *Arena;* but when I sent it the editor returned it, saying that a Roman Catholic bishop and a Con-

THOMAS H. PEARNE, D. D.
(At the age of 78 years.)

gressman had sent him replies, which he deemed it better to publish than to print my article. I then published and circulated my own reply. It was printed in pamphlet form in Cincinnati in 1890. I here insert it as still opportune:

GOD IN THE CONSTITUTION.

"A REVIEW."

Colonel Robert G. Ingersoll has published, in the *Arena* for January, a paper on "God in the Constitution." It holds the place of honor, being the first article. While ostensibly opposing the insertion of God's name in that instrument, he speaks one word for his avowed theme, and three or four for the old hobby he has been riding for the last fifteen years; namely, venomous, unscrupulous attacks upon God, the Bible, and the Christian religion.

The Colonel's article is characteristic. It is a singular mosaic of venom and fun, argument and declamation, hyperbole and reasonable statement, satire and sober truth. Bald assumptions and malignant invective are indiscriminately commingled.

The stale chestnuts of Thomas Paine, who issued a hundred years ago a ribald book, falsely named "The Age of Reason;" the unworthy denunciations of the Bible and religion by Thomas Hertell, a member of Congress, some fifty years since; and the rhetoric, wit, sarcasm, and exaggeration of the Colonel himself, are freely and loosely thrown about in promiscuous, bewildering profusion.

He reminds one of the acrobat in the circus ring, called Dandy Jack, who, after feats of ground and lofty tumbling, pulls off his red cap, and waits for the applause.

The Colonel's production is a rare specimen of intellectual vaulting and leaping, causing the gaping crowd to stare and applaud, we may imagine, much after the manner of those of the olden time, who wondered at the marvelous exploits of the village schoolmaster of the poet,—

> "And still they gazed, and still the wonder grew,
> How one small head could carry all he knew."

With the dogmatism of a pope, the Colonel asserts, as though he believed his absurd proposition:

> As to the existence of the Supernatural, one man knows precisely as much, and exactly as little, as another. Upon this question, chimpanzees and cardinals, apes and popes, are upon an exact equality.

The Colonel puts the jabbering monkeys and the priests into the same category. Such assumptions disclose astounding arrogance. In some of the paragraphs there are more assumptions than lines. They are used as though he considered his assertions arguments, and as though the more extreme and bald the assertion, the more utter the discomfiture of his opponent, and the more certain and triumphant the maintenance of his own propositions. Many of his assumptions have no apparent probability, yet he repeats them as though he believed them axiomatic. Consider

I. Examples of Colonel Ingersoll's Bold Assumptions.—This is one of the opening paragraphs:

> In 1776 our fathers endeavored to retire the gods from politics. They declared that "all governments derive their just powers from the consent of the governed." This was a contradiction of the then political ideas of the world; it was, as many believed, an act of pure blasphemy—a renunciation of the Deity. It was, in fact, a declaration of the independ-

ence of the earth. It was a notice to all Churches and priests that thereafter mankind would govern and protect themselves. Politically, it tore down every altar, and denied the authority of every "Sacred Book," and appealed from the providence of God to the providence of man.

In ten lines here are a dozen assertions, each one of which is unfounded, some of which are untrue, and all of them misleading.

So far as known, the fathers of 1776 did *not* "endeavor to retire the gods from politics." Nay! If the author did not "know enough to know this," he is more obtuse than he has generally been considered. Unless grossly ignorant, he knew that the signers of the Declaration were not idolaters—were not believers in gods many. They were not pagans. Three of them, at least, were ministers, and perhaps others. Yet he sets up a row of imaginary gods, and then employed "our fathers" in 1776, in knocking them down and out by a decree, a declaration shall we say, a constitution? He implies a constitution.

Their utterance as to the derivation of the powers of government was not intended (so far as can be seen) to strike out one god, not many. The signers believed in God, the Creator, in his providence, and in his justice and omniscience as well; for they appeal to the Supreme Judge of the world for the rectitude of their intentions. In the first sentence of that immortal document, they speak of "Nature's God" and "Man's Creator." In the very last sentence they say, "For the support of this Declaration, with a firm reliance in the protection of Divine Providence, we mutually pledge to each other our lives, our fortunes, and our sacred honor."

In view of these facts, what are we to think of the candor and veracity of Colonel Ingersoll?

When he used the statement that our fathers of

1776 "appealed from the providence of God to the providence of man," he uttered what he must have known was false.

Equally improbable, unsupported, and untrue, are other statements in the same paragraph. Let us see:

> This was, *as many believed*, an act of pure blasphemy, a renunciation of the Deity.

Necessarily, this act, and the believing concerning it, were contemporaneous. The act is patent, as we have seen. It was neither blasphemy nor a renunciation of the Deity; because, in the Declaration, four times they recognized and named God. If many so believed, they must have had some basis for their belief outside the Declaration, and they must have felt some statements of their thus believing, or the Colonel could not have known that they so believed. What are those statements, and where can they be found? Come forward, Sir Champion, and produce them, or stand impeached of attempting to palm off, upon an intelligent public, an unproved and improbable assertion.

> "Optics keen it takes, I ween,
> To see what is not to be seen."

Examine another remark:

> It was, in fact, a declaration of the independence of the earth.

It was not so in fact. It was not so, even in form. The signers declared for themselves and their constituents, and for no others, their renunciation and independence of Great Britain. At the same time they recognized their dependence upon their Creator. It was a great document. It declared basal principles; but it was not a declaration of the independence of the whole earth. Our fathers of 1776 declared that "all men are endowed by their Creator with certain inalienable rights." This proved their faith in God and their reverence for his authority.

Equally unwarranted and untrue is the statement that the Declaration "was a notice to all Churches and priests that thereafter mankind would govern and protect themselves." There is no reference here, expressed or implied, to Churches and priests. Nor is there anything in the contemporaneous history of the Declaration, or of the times, to support the gratuitous assertions.

"Politically," says the Colonel, "it tore down every altar, and denied the authority of every sacred book, and appealed from the providence of God to the providence of man."

All and singular these averments are proved false by the witness the Colonel himself has introduced and placed upon the stand. He may not, in any form or to any degree, discredit his own witness. He is bound to abide by what his own witness, fairly construed, says. He can not escape this conclusion by saying that he is talking about the Constitution and not about the Declaration of Independence. He designates the latter by the date of its birth, 1776. He quotes from it words found in the Declaration but not in the Constitution. The Constitution was not framed until thirteen years later. By his own witness, therefore, Mr. Ingersoll is convicted of dense ignorance or of gross fraud and falsehood.

And is such a man, hurling malignant invectives against God and his religion and ministers, to go unchallenged?

Is he to be virtually accredited, by the silent acquiescence and non-protest of Christian people, in his ruthless, fraudulent assaults upon the religion of the great mass of the American people? Finding these glaring perversions and untruths in one of the first paragraphs of the Colonel's paper, it would be fair to conclude that the remainder is also untrue and misleading. We might, therefore, forego further examination, since it is a safe general conclusion that what is false in one part is false, also, in all. And yet it may be best to pursue our inquiries further. Let us consider, then, that

II. IN THE COLONEL'S PAPER THERE ARE NUMEROUS EXAMPLES OF BITTER PREJUDICE, WHICH RENDER HIS CONCLUSIONS SUSPICIOUS, UNRELIABLE, AND MISLEADING.—The following specimen is pertinent.

And if there is to be an *acknowledgment of God in the Constitution*, the question naturally arises as to *which God is to have this honor*. Shall we select the *God of the Catholics*—he who has established an infallible Church presided over by an infallible pope, and who is delighted with certain ceremonies and placated by prayers uttered in exceedingly common Latin? Is it the God of the *Presbyterian*, with the Five Points of Calvinism, who is ingenious enough to harmonize necessity and responsibility, and who in some way justifies himself for damning most of his own children? Is it the *God of the Puritan, the enemy of joy—of the Baptist, who is great enough to govern the universe, and small* enough to allow the destiny of a soul to depend on whether the body it inhabited was immersed or sprinkled?

What God is it proposed to put in the Constitution? Is it the God of the Old Testament, *who is a believer in slavery, and who justified polygamy?* If slavery was right then, it is right now; and if Jehovah was right then, the Mormons are right now. Are we to have the God *who issued a commandment against all art—who was the enemy of investigation and of free speech?* Is it the God who commanded the husband to stone his wife to death because *she differed with him on the subject of religion?* Are we to have a *God who will re-enact the Mosaic code*, and punish hundreds of offenses with death? What court, what tribunal of last resort, *is to define this God,* and who is *to make known his will? In his presence, laws passed by men will be of no value.* The decisions of courts will be as nothing. But who is to make known the will of this supreme God? *Will there be a supreme tribunal composed of priests?*

No intelligent person holds that the God of the Romanist is a different being from the God of the Protestants, or the Calvinists, the Puritans, the Baptists, or the Jews. The Colonel distorts and arrays the extreme views of each to discredit them all, and to make it appear absurd and impracticable that the Constitution should recognize God.

The assertion that the God of the Old Testament was a believer in slavery and justified polygamy, is an unsupported and misleading one. How does the Colonel know what God believed? How can he unless God has told him? And how can a myth, a mere matter of opinion, believe or communicate? Where is the proof that God believed in slavery and justified polygamy? Because he permitted them? Then God believed in sin, in murder, and idolatry, and adultery; for God permitted them to exist. That God believed in neither is shown beyond cavil, in the fact that the moral law cuts up slavery and polygamy by the roots. "Doth the same fountain send forth both bitter water and sweet?"

The attempt to show that if God were recognized in the Constitution, some authoritative tribunal to explain and interpret God's will would be necessary, is prejudiced and sophistical.

The inquiry, "Will there be a supreme tribunal composed of priests?" discloses the old bitter hate against ministers, which, in the Colonel, seems a ruling passion. The criminal codes of all civilized nations are based upon the moral law as revealed in the Bible.

The common law of England, and which, also, is the foundation of our judicial system, expressly recognizes Christianity as a part of the English common law.

There is not a civilized nation on the face of the earth that does not recognize God in its laws. Blackstone, section 2, says: "On these two foundations, the law of nature and the law of revelation, depend all human laws; and where there is no revelation, then the human laws depend upon the laws of nature and on God for their source."

All this is not only as true in our country as in others, but it is more so. Does our brother—who knows these things as well as any one—find any difficulty in that fact? Are priests therefore needed to stand at the elbows of courts to teach them what is and what is not criminal?

III. COLONEL INGERSOLL BETRAYS A SUSPICIOUS ANIMUS AGAINST A CERTAIN CLASS OF HIS FELLOW-CITIZENS.—He says:

Of course all persons elected to office will either swear or affirm to support the Constitution. Men who do not believe in this God can not so swear or affirm. *Such men will not be allowed to hold any office of trust or honor. A God in the Constitution will not interfere with the oaths or affirmations of hypocrites.* Such a provision will only *exclude honest and conscientious unbelievers. Intelligent people know that no one knows whether there is a God or not. The existence of such a being is merely a matter of opinion. Men who believe in the liberty of man, who are willing to die for the honor of their country, will be excluded from taking any part in the administration of its affairs. Such a provision would place the country under the feet of priests.*

To recognize a Deity in the organic law of our country would be the destruction of religious liberty. The God in the Constitution would have to be protected. There would be laws against blasphemy, laws against the publication of honest thoughts, laws against carrying books and papers in the mails in which this Constitutional God should be attacked. Our land would be filled with theological spies, with religious eavesdroppers, and all the snakes and reptiles of the lowest natures, in this sunshine of religious authority, would uncoil and crawl.

In this remarkable passage several things are obvious:

(1) We see the usual, sweeping sneer at religion. In this instance it is that those who profess it are ignorant. The Colonel says, "Intelligent people know that no one knows whether there be a God or not." What about Chancellor Kent, Isaac Newton, Herschel, Strong, Marshall, and Chase? Were they intelligent?

(2) We see here a denial of God's existence. "The existence of such a being is merely a matter of opinion." This is unmixed atheism. If God's existence is only a matter of opinion, then there is no God; then the claim that there is a God—nay, the existence of God—is only a myth. A mere matter of opinion about God is not a fact as to God. In this averment Colonel Ingersoll denies the consciousness of universal Christendom—hundreds of millions of people. That God exists, that he fills human souls with his light and presence and power, is not opinion at all, but fact—a fact attested by millions of people, who have lived in past ages, and by millions who are now living.

(3) These statements contain, also, a malignant snarl against priests and ministers. But this is as usual as the Colonel's restlessness when the subject of hell is named, so that the editor of the Cincinnati *Gazette* described him as "the man afraid of hell." I would not say that the Colonel is afraid of priests, for probably he is not; but if any one should swear that the Colonel does not hate ministers, he would be quite likely to perjure himself. His hatred of them

is unconcealed, unappeasable, and morbid. It survives all accidents and changes. It is irrepressibly, offensively obtrusive. On all occasions, and with no amiable smiles, it ambles to the front, and, like a vicious horse, is snaps its teeth at all within its reach. These outbursts of rage and hostility abound throughout the entire paper; and how unkind! how untrue! Among the signers of the Declaration was a Presbyterian minister—president of Nassau Hall, Princeton, afterwards Princeton College. Among the framers of the Constitution was an eminent Lutheran minister, and perhaps other ministers. During our Revolutionary struggle, in repeated instances, ministers preached and fought. The loyalty and courage of ministers in the late Rebellion were exemplary. Ministers are orderly citizens. They pay taxes quite as honestly and as cheerfully as any other citizens. They obey the laws, and live useful, benevolent lives. Why should the Colonel pursue them as he does? Take the following specimens: "Will there be a supreme tribunal of priests?" . . . "What of the priest, the cardinal, and the pope, who wrest from the hand of poverty 'the single coin thrice earned?'" . . . "For many years priests have attempted to give this Government a religious form." . . . "We have tried the government of priests, and we know that such governments are without mercy." . . . "The priest was no longer a necessity." . . . "There is a suspicion that the priest, the theologian, is not satisfied with this; he wishes to destroy the liberties of the people."

I pause to inquire, What means this unappeasable, ferocious malignity against priests? What is the matter with our choleric, atheistic brother? When a person dwells exclusively, continuously, intensely, upon one line of thought, the fact naturally suggests mental unbalance, want of mental equilibrium; examination is in order. Inquiry as to sanity or otherwise is at once deemed the fitting thing.

This reiteration to weariness against ministers, these suspicions and innuendoes and direct attacks upon them as a class, painfully indicate a want of filial respect and duty. They ominously denote a willful, unfilial disregard of the Fifth Commandment, "Honor thy father and thy mother." "It is an ill bird that fouls its own nest." For be it remembered that the man who so berates ministers is himself the son of a priest. Does he derive his unforgetting dislike of ministers from his early associations as the son of one of them? Was he relating a chapter from his own life when he wrote, "We have tried the government of priests, and we know they are without mercy?" Must we then conclude that he was indeed so bad a lad that his father's rule had to be "without mercy?" or, was the father such a monster of cruelty that the best thing the son could say of him, long after he had passed away from earth, was that his "rule was without mercy?" In either case, we commend to our unhappy, blatant brother the Scripture which saith: "He that is unfaithful in least, is unfaithful also in much." A son who goes back on his earthly father, is quite likely to go back also on God.

IV. THE COLONEL ABOUNDS IN UNJUST, UNFAIR REASONING.—This is a specimen:

To recognize a Deity in the organic law would be the destruction of religious liberty.

His assertions being groundless, his fears are unnecessary. We already have a great deal of Christianity in our civilization. Of our citizens, forty millions are believers in Christ's religion. Besides these, twelve or fifteen millions are children; of the remaining five or eight millions, probably not one in fifty is of Colonel Ingersoll's unbelief.

The informal, incidental pressure of Christianity upon the civil life of the country, and the infusion of its genius and spirit into our laws and institutions, are everywhere and every day seen. They can not be denied nor repressed. They will be seen and felt. It is inevitable.

God is recognized and Christianity is recognized in every piece of gold and silver and paper money issued by the Government, bearing a date; in our religious and secular holidays established by law, in our conveyances and charters, in our court and congressional and legislative records, in the *Anno Domini* which dates our time, in our diplomacy, and in all our legal instruments and chaplaincies. And if, in all these ways, God and the Christian religion have been recognized without materially marring our religious liberties, two things must be admitted: (1) That the term God in the Constitution would not much imperil our liberties. (2) That our brother need not lose sleep through his concern for the safety of our religious liberties. The Colonel makes a discovery, which, however, does not turn out to be true. He says:

> There has been in our country a divorce of Church and State. This follows as a natural sequence of the declaration that "governments derive their just powers from the consent of the governed." The priest was no longer a necessity. His presence was a contradiction of the principle on which the Republic was founded. He represented, not the authority of the people, but of some "Power from on High," and to recognize this other Power was inconsistent with free government. The founders of the Republic at that time parted company with the priests, and said to them: "You may turn your attention to the other world—we will attend to the affairs of this." Equal liberty was given to all. But the

ultra-theologian is not satisfied with this; he wishes to destroy the liberties of the people; he wishes a recognition of his God as the source of authority, to the end that the Church may become the supreme power.

He says, "There has been, in our country, a divorce of Church and State." This statement is not true; there has been no such divorce; there can not be a divorce where there has been no marriage; the Church and the State have never been united in this country. Possibly, in some of the New England colonies, and, perhaps, during their early Statehood some of them may have drawn from the public treasury moneys to support the Churches, as they did also, and still do, to support the schools. But there has been properly and really no union of the Church and the State established by law, as is true in Great Britain and Russia.

France and Belgium both contribute from the public chest for the support of religion, and yet in neither of those Governments is there a formal, legal union between the Church and the State. If the Colonel had said, "The union of Church and State in this country has been prevented," that statement would have been more exactly correct.

The Colonel says, "The priest was no longer a necessity." The priest has never been a necessity, politically considered, in this country. As a citizen he has equal right with the lawyer, the politician, or any other class, and, so far as known, he may be equally useful.

We note, in the following paragraph, like hostility to ministers, and like false assumptions:

> For many years priests have attempted to give to our Government a religious form. Zealots have succeeded in putting the legend upon our money, "In God We Trust,"

and we have chaplains in the army and navy, and legislative proceedings are usually opened with prayer. All this is contrary to the genius of the Republic, contrary to the Declaration of Independence, and contrary really to the Constitution of the United States. We have taken the ground that the people can govern themselves without the assistance of any Supernatural Power. We have taken the position that the people are the real and only rightful source of authority. We have solemnly declared that the people must determine what is politically right and what is wrong, and that their legally-expressed will is the supreme law. This leaves no room for national superstition, no room for patriotic gods or supernatural beings, and this does away with the necessity for political prayers.

It is not true that for many years priests have tried to give this Government a religious form. They have never tried to do so. It is true that some of them have sought to have God recognized in the Constitution; but to accomplish this would not give this Government a religious form; and that fact achieved, would not be a union of Church and State. To insert God's name in the Constitution would be a recognition of a fact already existing, that this is a Christian Nation; and it is such because made up of Christian people, and because its civilization is a Christian civilization. Chaplaincies in our Legislatures and hospitals and barracks and navy do not give our Government a religious form; nor is the fact contrary to the genius of the Republic, the Declaration of Independence, or the Constitution of the United States; for while the first article declares "Congress shall make no law establishing religion," it also declares, it shall make no law "prohibiting the free exercise thereof." Congress does not make a law establishing religion when it has opened its sessions with prayer, and when it employs chaplains in army and navy and in our eleemosynary institutions. If

Congress should refuse to make provisions by law for such religious services, it would, thereby, be "prohibiting the free exercise thereof."

V. COLONEL INGERSOLL MISCONCEIVES THE NATURE OF OUR CIVILIZATION AND THE TRUE SCOPE AND SPIRIT OF OUR INSTITUTIONS.—The following paragraph, while true in some of its positions, is as to others untrue and misleading:

> The Government of the United States is secular. It derives its power from the consent of man. It is a Government with which God has nothing whatever to do—and all forms and customs, inconsistent with the fundamental fact that the people are the source of authority, should be abandoned. In this country there should be no oaths; no man should be sworn to tell the truth, and in no court should there be any appeal to any Supreme Being. A rascal, by taking the oath, appears to go in partnership with God, and ignorant jurors credit the firm instead of the man. A witness should tell his story, and if he speaks falsely should be considered as guilty of perjury. Governors and Presidents should not issue religious Proclamations. They should not call upon the people to thank God. It is no part of their official duty. It is outside of and beyond the horizon of their authority. There is nothing in the Constitution of the United States to justify this religious impertinence.

It is true the Government of the United States is secular, but it is not therefore pagan, Mohammedan, Brahmin, Confucian, or savage. Yet it can not fail to recognize and protect the religious rights and obligations of its Christian citizens. To fail to do so would be to violate the very first article of the Constitution, as we have seen. The Colonel says the Government of this country "derives its powers from the consent of man." This is not true; its powers are "derived from the consent of the *governed.*" The governed, in this case, are, for the chief part, Christians and citizens. They are to be governed, not as pagans, nor by means of a pagan civilization, but as Christians, and by a Christian civilization.

Nor again, is it true that ours "is a Government with which God has nothing whatever to do." From the beginning of our history God has had very much to do with us. He still has; he will continue to have much to do with our Government and people. In the infancy of our existence, he gave victory to our army. He aided our fathers in founding our institutions and in framing our Constitution. Our Nation owes its integrity to the Christian loyalty of its brave defenders, to whom God gave victory in the late Civil War.

It is a non-sequitur to affirm, as Colonel Ingersoll does, that "in this country there should be no oaths," and that "no one should be sworn to tell the truth;" *i. e.*, these conclusions do not follow from the nature and genius of our Government, and certainly not from the Constitution. Article 6 requires that "all senators and representatives and the members of the several Legislatures, and all executive and judicial officers of the several States, shall be bound by oath or affirmation to support the Constitution."

The expedient by which Colonel Ingersoll would get testimony without administering oaths is impracticable and deceptive. He says, "A witness should tell his story, and, if he speaks falsely, he should be considered as guilty of perjury;" *i. e.*, he should be punished as having committed perjury when he had not committed perjury, and, indeed, could not have committed perjury, because he had not taken an oath at all.

In his wish to avoid an appeal to God by a witness, he would enact a fraud into law, and use a trick, and punish people for a crime not committed and not possible to be committed. His objection to an oath is peculiar. "The rascal, who appeals to God by an oath, appears to go into partnership with God, and ignorant jurors credit the firm instead of the man."

This is a shallow device to justify atheism in practice. It is implied that "the ignorant jurors" hold evidence higher, in cases when the witness appeals to God, than when he does not. Here is another characteristic sneer at Christians. The jurors who believe in oaths are "ignorant jurors." It is implied, also, that the men who appeal to God in an oath, appear to take God into partnership, and that, in doing so, they adopt the policy of the rascal.

The safer way, the surer way to get the truth from a witness, is to have him sworn. There may now and then be a rascal who commits perjury; but I would rather trust men who appeal to God than trust men who discard God, and who, instead, form a partnership with the devil. As at present advised, it is safer, all round, to trust the firm of God and Company than the firm of the devil and company.

It is no infraction of the spirit and intent of the Constitution as it is; and, if it were, then the Constitution should be changed so that it would not be held, and could not be held, unconstitutional for presidents and governors to issue proclamations, appointing thanksgiving-days, and calling on the people to thank God. This policy is in line with all the declared purposes and objects of the Constitution, to recognize the moral nature of the citizen and the God to whom that moral nature holds relation, and whose providence is in the thought and moral consciousness of nine-tenths of the citizens. The objects of the Constitution are "to establish justice, to form a more perfect union, to insure domestic tranquillity, and the common defense, the general welfare, and the blessings of liberty." These objects are all subserved by exalting the sense of moral dependence and of moral obligation to God. Thanksgiving-days and fast-days, chaplains in army and navy, in Congress and Legislatures, and in eleemosynary institutions, have this tendency, and therefore, in a high degree, they are constitutional.

The Christians, who sustain this Government, and who from time to time administer it, certainly have as much stake in it, and as intelligently apprehend how great that stake is, and they are certainly quite as able and as well entitled to judge of the best way in which the objects sought by the Constitution can be subserved, as a man can be who declares that "the being of God is a mere matter of opinion."

"One man should not be allowed to interfere with the liberty of another," says our atheistic friend, and so say I, and therefore I say to him, "Hands off." His liberty is license, as seen in his advocacy of the rights of D. M. Bennett to liberty after he had been convicted of a crime against society.

The Colonel's by-play on God's ability to take care of himself, and therefore as not needing our help to get himself in the Constitution, is too flippant, after he has reduced God's existence to "a mere matter of opinion." Certainly God does not need our help so much as we need his. He can better afford to be non-recognized in the Constitution than we can afford to be non-recognized by him.

The Colonel's account of God's government of the nations, and of his tyranny and injustice, are gross perversions and caricatures. It is proper to add as to the Colonel's paper, that some parts of it, in which he describes the nature and uses of an organic law, are well enough and true enough taken by themselves, but he has marred and weakened their force by his gratuitous and vitriolic objurgations against the Bible and God and Christianity.

We are not tenacious for placing the name of God in the Constitution. This is a Christian Government, administered by Christian people and upon Christian principles, whatever may be in, or not in, the Constitution. If it were not a Christian Government, it would not long survive; and it is a Christian Government, none the less, that it is not declared to be in the organic law.

VI. THE IDEAL GOVERNMENT OF COLONEL INGERSOLL IS A LOGICAL ABSURDITY AND IMPOSSIBILITY.— I raise the question as pertinent, in view of the passionate efforts of Colonel Ingersoll to make our Republic atheistic. Where is there to be found, on the face of the earth, where has there ever been found, a nation of infidels or a civilization of atheists? What kind of a Government would that be? Nobody knows. Nobody can conjecture. It would be a monstrosity the earth has never seen. There would be no controlling authority, no cohering vitality in it.

Chaplain McCabe some years ago gave, as a dream, a picture of Ingersollville, a city from the civilization of which God was excluded, and the city was walled to keep God out. Lust and profanity and crime and robbery and violence and disorder prevailed, until the better class of atheists themselves fled from it in dismay, as they would from a pest-house. Infidels can not deny the existence, in our world, of death, and grief and tears, and disappointment. What remedy do they propose for the sorrows of earth, which, sooner or later, come to all? What alleviation does atheism or agnosticism offer?

Christianity presents a balm for every wounded heart, a cordial for our fears. It is effective, it has been proved adequate by millions of our race, by vast numbers of our fellow-countrymen. Why seek to knock that prop down, until another, and at least an equal support, is found? Then, moreover, this Republic is to-day the richest and most potent on the face of the earth, and in culture and learning and intelligence and morals and civilization it excels every other. And to what shall we ascribe it? All the other nations who approximate us in power and resources are Christian nations, and they are strong and prosperous as they are Christian.

What a terrible catastrophe it would be if Colonel Ingersoll's ideas should become prevalent in this country and world of ours! Joy thus cut off from human hearts and lives by a blank atheism, or a blanker agnosticism, and the great Republic, so honored and so exalted and prosperous, relegated to the dull stagnation and collapse which an atheistic control of its affairs would superinduce; we should resemble that dead, ruined planet, the moon, upon whose lifeless, waterless, treeless, verdureless surface the fructifying light and warmth of the sun fall in vain. Mr. Ingersoll, himself, is what he is, not as an atheist, nor an agnostic, nor as the product of either, but as a *man* of brilliant powers, the product of the Christian civilization under which he was reared. He can not produce a civilization of atheism anywhere; nor a man that was ever raised up under an atheistic civilization. He was not himself. He has not the power, thank God, to make of himself, because environed by Christian influences, what he would be if raised up exclusively under the power of his own principles.

The Colonel's vaporings against the religiousness of our civilization proceeds upon a false and vicious theory of our institutions. Our Government is a representative one. It should represent the Christian civilization of its constituents. It must do this, or it is not truly republican. Its constituency are not chimpanzees, apes, idiots, or atheists. For the most part, they are people of brains, good morals, and Christian lives and characters. As already stated, forty millions of them are such; fifteen millions more of them are minors; of the remaining five millions, not the fiftieth part are of Colonel Ingersoll's peculiar atheistic views. In its laws and administration our Government should reflect and represent the better qualities of the sixty millions of its constituents, and it should not punish them in the way Colonel Ingersoll and his hundred thousand atheistic associates would propose. In other words, the dog should wag the tail, and not the tail the dog. A republican government which does not represent the learning, culture, brains, morals, and religion of its people, is a mockery, a usurpation, and a fraud. For the Colonel, himself, we have profound sorrow and pity. He has abilities which, properly wielded, might be greatly serviceable to his country and his race; abilities which would qualify him to govern men and guide the State. But these abilities perverted, as he seems bent on perverting them, may gain him the applause of libertines and base men, who want religion shorn and debased, so that their pollution and wrong may receive less rebuke and hindrance.

He may gain the plaudits of shallow thinkers and surface men, and he may wreck the faith and the lives of, here and there, a young man; but let him, as to himself, remember:

> "One self-approving hour whole years outweighs
> Of stupid starers and of loud huzzas."

Central Church, Springfield, numbered over one thousand members. I deemed it too large, and requiring too much labor to serve it longer, and having received an earnest application from the

First Methodist Eipscopal Church of Xenia to become their pastor, I was appointed to that Church by Bishop Harris from the Conference of 1890. This is one of the oldest and most honored of the charges in the Conference. It has had some of the strongest and most eminent ministers in its long list of pastors. It would have been gratifying to have filled out the full term here. With this dear people and in this most delightful charge three very happy and not fruitless years were spent; but the presiding bishop, J. F. Hurst, and the Cabinet thought otherwise. Among the pastors who had served the First Methodist Episcopal Church in Xenia were Raper, Latta, Ancil Brooks, William Herr; J. F. Marlay, who has served the Church acceptably three full pastorates of two, three, and five years, and he would be current for a fourth term; Lucien Clark.

Great revivals have occurred here. The present pastor, 1898, is John J. McCabe, who completes his fifth year the present September. His great revival the first year of his term was a glorious work, indeed. Some three hundred souls professed conversion. The present membership has increased from some four or five hundred to eight hundred. During his fourth year a large Church improvement has been projected and carried to completion. It increases the seating capacity from six hundred to twelve hundred. The appointments are all of the most modern type. They include church parlors, Sunday-school class-rooms, and committee-rooms, electric-lights, sheds for the country members' horses and carriages; complete steam-heating arrangements are furnished. The outside is finished in dark-brown and light-brown stone for foundations and front elevation, and the side walls in Milwaukee pressed brick. A new church with all these appointments would not cost less than thirty thousand dollars. The acoustic quality is perfect. The ventilation is of the best. The expense is all provided for.

The Cincinnati Conference of 1890 has the following entries on the third day of the session:

The following paper, offered by F. G. Mitchell, was adopted:

"WHEREAS, Our brother, Thomas H. Pearne, will close, in 1891, fifty years of connection with the Methodist itinerancy, during which time he has passed through exceedingly varied and interesting experiences; therefore,

"*Resolved*, That we respectfully request Dr. Pearne to preach a semi-centennial sermon at some time during the next Conference session. F. G. Mitchell, George H. Dart, J. P. Porter, Thomas Lee, W. I. Fee, R. H. Rust, W. L. Hypes, J. T. Bail, J. F. Marlay.

"On motion of J. F. Conrey, the time for the service was fixed for the evening preceding the Conference."

On the fourth day of the same session, on motion of J. F. Conrey, the time for Dr. Pearne's semi-centennial sermon was changed from Tuesday evening to some morning hour. During the year, by correspondence with Bishop Foster, who was to preside at the Cincinnati Conference in 1891, the time was fixed for the morning of the opening session, as a part of the opening exercises.

In the opening Proceedings of the Conference, it is stated:

"By request of the Conference, at its last year's session, Thomas H. Pearne, D. D., preached a semi-centennial sermon."

On the second day of the session, Dr. J. F. Marlay presented a resolution as follows, viz.:

"*Resolved*, That, having listened with great delight and satisfaction to the semi-centennial sermon of Rev. Thomas H. Pearne, D. D., at the opening session of our Conference, we do earnestly request its publication in pamphlet form, as a part of the permanent historical literature of our Church. Signed by William Herr and J. F. Marlay. The motion was adopted by a rising vote."

I have been advised to reprint the sermon in this volume, and I do so for the following reasons: 1. Much of the matter in it is not found in this book; 2. There is no provision for issuing subsequent editions of the sermon; 3. The first edition was long ago exhausted.

SEMI-CENTENNIAL SERMON.

Dear Fathers and Brethren:

In attempting a special sermon like this, I can not escape a feeling of timidity and shrinking, lest it should seem too much like self-appreciation. Pray, dear brethren, that self may sink from view,

and that Christ may be exalted. I trust I can say—
I know I want to say—most sincerely, in the words
of Charles Wesley's hymn:

> "Whate'er in me seems wise or good,
> Or strong, I here disclaim;
> I wash my garments in the blood
> Of the atoning Lamb."

And so we are brought to the chosen theme of this
discourse, which is: "The supreme aim of all true
Christians is, that God may be honored and magnified." This being the fact as to Christians in general,
it is pre-eminently so of those who have for a long
term, and in God's higher ministries, shared his abundant mercies.

The following Scripture texts illustrate and enforce this duty:

> "I will bless the Lord at all times; his praise shall continually be in my mouth. My soul shall make her boast in the Lord: the humble shall hear thereof, and be glad. O magnify the Lord with me, and let us exalt his name together!"—PSALM XXXIV, 1–3.

To magnify the Lord is to recognize him continually by praise; to boast in him; to exalt his name
of wisdom, power, and grace as shown to his servants.

> "Let all those that seek thee rejoice and be glad in thee: let such as love thy salvation say continually, The Lord be magnified."—PSALM XL, 16.

Those who seek the Lord rejoice and are glad
in him. Those who love his salvation have no other
desire but that God should be magnified.

> "I will praise the name of God with a song, and will magnify him with thanksgiving."—PSALM LXIX, 30.

> "And this was known to all the Jews and Greeks also dwelling at Ephesus; and fear fell on them all, and the name of the Lord Jesus was magnified."—ACTS XIX, 17.

"According to my earnest expectation and my hope, that in nothing I shall be ashamed, but that with all boldness, as always, so now also, Christ shall be magnified in my body, whether it be by life or by death."—PHILIPPIANS I, 20.

This service of magnifying the Lord is due for personal and official blessings; for the pleasure God has in the prosperity of his servants; for God's saving strength, and for the work that God does in men and by men, and especially by means of consecrated men, and for the honor God confers in making us "workers together with him."

I.

I find abundant reasons, in my personal experience of God, for all these years of blessing in his service, for magnifying the Lord. For the zeal and constancy God has given me through a long and diversified career; for his providential care in all the remarkable conditions of a life of more than an average of incident through which I have come; for enabling me to learn and love and practice, to some degree, Mr. Wesley's golden maxims; namely, "Do all the good you can, by all the means you can, in all the ways you can, in all the places you can, at all the times you can, to all the people you can, and as long as you can"—for all this I magnify the Lord.

A few weeks ago, I received a letter from a presiding elder in one of the largest and most influential Conferences in the connection. He stands in the front rank of the men of power among us, although he is nearing his threescore and ten. His district has over seventy-five appointments, on a string one hundred miles long and no width, with a growing city on one end. He writes, with typewriter, fourteen hundred letters in a year on the business of his district.

Such a man, with such a capacity and success, should magnify the Lord. His life does. And yet there were preachers who, after he had preached twenty-five years, advised him to retire and give the young men a chance. He replied, in substance: "I will not stand in your way. If you want my place, prove your better right to it by your doing, and the Church and God will give it to you." I magnify the Lord's name that this noble, glorious man had the grace to decline to step down and out until God should clearly so direct him.

Some one has well said that the union of age and youth in Church-life—the fire and energy of the one and the chastened caution of the other—should ever be blended in the work for Christ. We do not retire bishops and college presidents and professors when they reach a ripe age. Our cause suffers no harm in consequence. On the contrary, it is subserved. The same writer adds: "Young ministers and laymen who are full of the Holy Ghost are charged with enthusiasm as a battery is charged with electricity. They have had no defeats and little experience in Church work. It is well that there are always some in the Church who have not had much experience. Inexperienced Christians have their mission. To balance and guide this youthful energy, there are the conservatism and caution of the older members. Let not the young become impatient of the counsels of the old, and let not the old despise the zeal and hope of the young. Separate them, and neither will prosper. Unite them, and let the love of God blend them into perfect harmony, and the Church will be 'fair as the moon, clear as the sun, and terrible as an army with banners.'"

As a preparation for the life God has enabled me to live, he gave me, for three generations, a godly

Methodist ancestry, and a holy father and mother, in a beautiful Christian home. That is to say, I was well-born. For forty-two years my father was a Methodist traveling preacher. My maternal grandfather and great-grandfather were local preachers in Mr. Wesley's connection. They doubtless received their licenses to preach from his hands.

My eldest brother, who went to his reward last November, answered the Conference roll-call for fifty-five years; my own name has stood on the list fifty years; making for my father and his two sons one hundred and forty years of ministerial work, an average for each of forty-six and one-third years.* At eight years of age, during a great revival among children in my boyhood village, in Central New York—New York Mills—I was graciously saved. I knew the renewing and adopting grace of God. Rev. Bishop Edward G. Andrews was also converted in the same revival. After a year or two, I declined in piety; but at thirteen I was powerfully reclaimed. At fifteen, in the same village, I was appointed a class-leader, with a class numbering forty members. Six months later, I received a license as an exhorter from Rev. Schuyler Hoes, preacher in charge of New York Mills Station. At sixteen I was licensed as a local preacher. From that time forward I have been engaged in the blessed work of the Christian ministry.

For the grace, which has cheered and sustained me through a long and happy life, and which, for the last seventeen years, has kept me under the power

---

* This was printed several years ago. It should be corrected thus: Father's ministry as an itinerant extended from 1832 to 1874—forty-two years; my brother's, fifty-five years; and my own, sixty-one years; in all, one hundred and fifty-eight years, an average of fifty-two and two-third years.

of the cleansing blood of Christ, and which, as junior circuit preacher, preacher in charge, presiding elder, missionary, and Christian editor, has kept me going, and given me success, I magnify the Lord. Twenty-eight years I have served as a pastor. Twelve years I have been presiding elder, and ten years editor of Christian journals. Mr. Wesley requested one of his preachers to write an account of his life. He was reluctant to do so. Mr. Wesley said: "I really think you owe it (in spite of shame and timidity) to God, to me, and to your brethren."

II.

After having passed my threescore and ten years, and more than two-thirds of them in the ministry, I present this brief sketch to the honor of God, and upon the call of my brethren.

God makes honorable mention of the aged. Of Moses, when he had reached sixscore years, it is said: "His eye was not dim, nor his natural force abated." At eighty-five, Caleb said he was as strong as at forty-five. When Joshua was five and a half score years old, God commended his piety, fidelity, and success.

God requires respect to be shown to the aged, and especially to those who have grown old in his service. He recognizes the value of the experience and wisdom which age should gather and dispense. By a wise provision, God links different generations to each other by a few long lives. These gather and transmit historical truth from the earlier times to the later; and for this we have warrant in the following: "Remember the days of old, consider the years of many generations: ask thy father, and he will shew thee; thy elders, and they will tell thee." (Deut. xxxii, 7.) Between Adam and Noah, there was but one life, and that life was his father's. When Adam died. Noah's father was fifty-six years old. Noah may have seen and conversed with those who had known Adam.

Abraham was born fifty-eight years before Noah died. Methuselah, Noah's grandfather, lived two hundred and fifty years before Adam died. He was contemporary with Noah several hundred years. Really, Noah's, Lamech's, and Adam's lives spanned the years between Abraham and the creation. Abraham may have talked with some of his ancestors, who had seen and talked with some of Adam's contemporaries.

III.

During the present year we observed the anniversary of John Wesley's death. Blessed man! honored of God, and revered by millions on earth and in heaven, for the work he did for God and man! Yet in Wesley's ancestors of three or four generations, God connected Wesley's times with those of Luther, Zwingli, Melanchthon, Knox, and Calvin.

Through my ancestors I touch the generation that touched the great reformers of the fifteenth century. Benn Pitman, the stenographer, claims to be the only man in the United States who has shaken hands with one who has shaken hands with John Wesley. I challenge this statement. Mrs. Lester, of New York Mills, N. Y., where I grew up, had often heard Mr. Wesley preach, and had shaken hands with him. I have repeatedly shaken hands with Mrs. Lester. In 1840 and 1841, Rev. James Jay was a member of the charge I filled during those years. Mr. Jay had been a member of Mr. Wesley's Conference for years before Mr. Wesley's death. He gave me many touching and beautiful incidents of Wesley. He had often shaken hands with Mr. Wesley, and I have, not seldom, shaken hands with him. Thus long lives connect not only distant generations, but great historic events. The Wyoming massacre occurred July 3, 1783. I have shaken hands and conversed with a lady in that valley, who was present when Brandt and General Butler entered the fort after that bloody killing. In the same valley, a matronly lady, Mrs. Dennison, daughter-in-law of Colonel Dennison, who commanded the United States forces on that dreadful day, entertained Bishops Asbury and McKendree in her house for over a week when she was a bride. She gave me interesting incidents of that memorable week. My father saw and heard Bishops McKendree and George. He also heard the eminent John Summerfield, who, at twenty-five, was deemed one of the most eloquent preachers in America. My personal acquaintance with Methodist bishops began with Bishop R. R. Roberts, who presided at the Conference when I was admitted on trial. Bishop Roberts was the first married man who filled the office of a Methodist bishop in America. He was elected in 1816. He was tall and elegant in form and bearing. I heard him preach a sermon of great power on Luke xvi, 29, 30, 31: "They have Moses and the prophets, let them hear them," etc. He remarked that a visitant to our world, sent from the place of torment to warn men against going there, would be much more likely to terrify them than to persuade them to be saved. In that connection he quoted the well-known lines of Shakespeare, thus: "Causing

> 'Each particular hair to stand on end,
> Like quills upon the fretful porcupine.'"

Except Roberts and Burns, Bishops of Liberia, I have personally known all the bishops since elected. Soule, who ordained me a deacon, had dignity, amounting almost to hauteur. Hedding was the Webster of the

Episcopal College. He was well stocked with judicial sense. Waugh ordained me an elder. He was courteous and refined. Emory was scholarly. Janes was brimming with authority. Morris, like the great West whence he came, was large, strong, sensible, and kindly. Hamline was one of the most eloquent of preachers. At times his preaching was overpowering. I have seen audiences swayed under his eloquence as trees of the forest in a mighty wind. Of the bishops later elected, I need not speak more specifically. The rank and file of this Conference have seen the most of them. They will soon see and know the remainder and their immediate successors.

I personally knew some of the earlier celebrities of our Church, who, while not reaching episcopal honors, were not a whit behind the chiefest of our bishops in talents, in pulpit power, and in wide, far-reaching influence. Of these I name William Case, the missionary to the Indians in Canada. Dr. Nathan Bangs entered the New York Conference in 1802, only eighteen years after our Church was organized. He was often in our home in my early childhood. He baptized me in Duane Street Church, in New York. Rev. Dr. William Phœbus, who entered the traveling connection 1783; Samuel Merwin, Daniel Ostrander, Billy Hibbard, Marmaduke Pearce, Benjamin Bidlack, George Lane, George Peck, Alfred Griffith; Henry Boehm, Asbury's traveling companion; John A. Collins, John P. Durbin, Elias Bowen, and so many more, laid their hands in blessing on my head in my boyhood.

IV.

George Gary was a man of marvelous eloquence and power. Fifty odd years ago I heard him preach a sermon at a camp-meeting, which first drew his audience to their feet in a dense mass around him, and then I saw probably a hundred or more of them fall senseless to the earth as though stricken with death. His sermon was preached at the eight o'clock hour, Sunday morning. Great numbers were gathering to the service, and the conditions under ordinary circumstances would have been unfavorable to marked effect. His sermon was only twenty minutes in length; the text, Gen. xix, 17: "Escape for thy life." There was no more preaching on the ground that day. Prayers and conversions and shouts and songs were continued all over the camp all day long.

I cite another example of "the falling exercise," as it was called. It was in the midst of a sweeping revival. Many had been converted. A great snow-storm made the attendance on this occasion small. Not over forty persons were present. The previous night five hundred were in the church. My father, the pastor, was talking in a subdued tone. The meeting was very quiet. No apparent excitement was seen. All at once, as the people sat listening to the preacher, they began to fall over, and became unconscious. Some of them at once fell to the floor. Others fell on the seat. There was no outcry, no shouting, no demonstration except the falling. Only three maintained an upright position—my father, another, and myself. All others were unconscious. Some of them remained thus for twenty-four hours. Some became conscious in a few minutes. Some recovered silently, others awoke shouting, and still others were singing. Some of them were rigid. Some were limp.

V.

In my childhood days my father's library was well supplied with Methodist biography and history. These to me were very fascinating. They kindled in me a love of adventure in Christ's work, and sent me, later, as a missionary to Oregon. I read Wesley's and Asbury's Journals with great avidity. As I read Asbury's adventures in crossing the Alleghanies in West Virginia, and the Cumberland Mountains in Tennessee, and of his having to wait at Bean's Station for his party to become numerous enough to make the crossing into Kentucky safe from Indian assaults; of his escapes from Indian ambuscades and attacks; of his perils by flood and field,—I wondered whether such heroism could ever again be repeated. But frontier life has been quite as full of exciting passages since Asbury's time as it was before. In my fourteen years' sojourn in Oregon I had probably as many intensely thrilling adventures and experiences as he had in his early ministry in the West. I often swam rivers on horseback. I have been pursued and fired upon by bandits. I have had stirring passages with hostile Indians. I have slept under God's stars in the open prairie, with saddlebags for my pillow and my faithful mule as my only companion.

In March, 1854, in company with Bishop Simpson, I slept on the banks of the Columbia River, under blankets, our camp being behind an immense rock, on a cold night, a rousing fire at our feet to keep us warm and protect us from ravenous wolves and cougars. I give two or three other incidents with Bishop Simpson.

We ascended the Columbia from the Cascades to the Dalles in a large Indian canoe. In the canoe were nets and squaws and dogs, innumerable fleas, and general discomfort. Two drunken white men were in the canoe. Their speech was coarse, profane, and obscene. They were more degraded than the Indians and their dogs. One of them was a graduate of Indiana Asbury University. Gently and kindly the bishop spoke to him, making tender reference to his mother and her prayers. We parted company at night at Dog River. The two white men crossed the river. The bishop and I slept in the Indian's wigwam. Ten years and a half afterward, on the Upper Columbia River, I met the Indiana student of the canoe incident. He was well-dressed and well-looking. He told me he was then a married man, with three children, having a good Christian home, a fine farm, himself and wife Christians, on their way to heaven. He owed it all to the timely words of Bishop Simpson.

We were much baffled in descending the Columbia by strong up-river winds. Repeated attempts to go down the river were vain. The bishop chided my impatience, remarking that it was doubtless a providential detention for some good purpose. It was on this occasion that we slept on the river bank. Reaching Portland we found that the steamer, which contrary winds had prevented us from getting to in time, and on which we should have been if unhindered, had blown up at her wharf, instantly killing twenty-nine of the thirty passengers on board.

On another occasion, the bishop and I suddenly came upon a cavalcade of several hundred Indians, all well mounted and armed. The Indians were hostile. Among them we found an Indian who could talk English. Through him we were introduced to the other Indians as Methodist preachers, and we were safe. If they had believed us Indian agents, Indian traders, or United States military, and we could not have convinced them to the contrary, we should have been killed.

VI.

In the golden age of memory, those earlier times have a rich autumnal tint. If too free a rein be given to fancy, the glamour may be distorting and misleading. There were many excellencies then. There were also serious defects. In many ways the present period shows a marked superiority over the former.

The refinement of to-day puts to blush the ruder coarseness of the past. The impure jest, the profane word, the seclusion and inferior lot assigned to woman, the lack of comfort in hospitals and infirmaries, the brutal treatment of the insane, idiots, and paupers, were common to that earlier period.

Political partisanism was harsh. Public manners were coarse. Drunkenness was open and shameless. Ignorance and prejudice were conspicuous in many ways, in comparison with the present more general diffusion of education. All these prove that the former times were not better than the present. They were much worse.

Fifty years ago I conducted a funeral service. The deceased was a very aged lady. Twelve children, fifty grandchildren, and twelve great-grandchildren—in all, seventy-four descendants of the deceased—were present. After the burial, all the family, and other relatives and guests, repaired to the mansion and dined. Costly viands tempted the appetite through eight courses. Wines and all the various kinds of distilled liquors were on the sideboard.

The dwellings and churches of the fathers were severely plain and rude. Woman was accorded less respect and freedom than now. Fewer occupations were open to her for earning a living. In the home, on public occasions, on the rostrum, in legislatures and courts, and in general intercourse, there was less of refinement than now. The schools and colleges were less advanced in grade than at present. As to the comforts and luxuries and refinements of life, in all lines, the present is far in advance of the former period.

Members and ministers of the different Churches, our own included, bought and sold slaves, and held them for gain. More, they defended slavery from the Bible. But for the sturdy resistance which conscientious Abolitionists in our Church, lay and ministerial, made to the encroachments of the slave-power, slavery would have captured and dominated all the States and Territories of the Republic. The fidelity and firmness of our fathers of half a century ago, and more, caused the Church secession of 1845. From that came, sixteen years later, the Rebellion of 1861, and so the Nation was saved to liberty. In Christian homes was the sideboard, with intoxicating beverages. Treating at elections and at raisings was prevalent. The license system tolerated and protected the drink-traffic. It would be difficult to-day to find any Church in the Nation with moral hardihood enough to tolerate the traffic. All intelligent Christians regard the licensing and taxing of the system as of the nature of a bribe to induce compliance with the infernal traffic, and as a moral complicity with the sin. Taxing the drink-traffic, as in Ohio, is a clever dodge of the politicians working in the interests, and possibly in the pay, of the venders and manufacturers of intoxicants. Against this form of complicity with the infernal business, as well as that of the license system, our Discipline very properly levels its prohibition.

In resolute, unflinching hostility to the drink-habit and the drink-traffic, and in favor of the total prohibition of both, the Methodist Episcopal Church has led the way; and as surely as that God lives, and right is stronger than wrong, the American saloon will become a thing of the past. As surely as slavery has disappeared from our Nation, so surely will the deadly, Satanic liquor-traffic disappear. Political parties will be smashed, and slates will be broken, and contention and bloodshed may be seen—aye, even riot and war may precede that victory; but come it will;

> "For right is right, since God is God,
> And right the day must win;
> To doubt would be disloyalty,
> To falter would be sin."

In large measure the honor of the grand achievement will be given to our beloved Church. May the Lord hasten the day of its utter overthrow! How I would like to witness its annihilation, and to join in the bannered procession which shall celebrate the abolition of the American saloon!

Zealous as were many of our fathers in extending religion, marked improvement has come, both as to modes of working and economy of forces, and also as to the ratio of progress made. Persons yet living can remember when there was no regular, liberal, systematic support of missions in our Church; when Liberia and South America were our only foreign missions; when we had no Church Extension Society; when there were no organized, effective, educational movements, no Christian libraries nor Christian literature worth the name; when our Church journalism was weak and scantily patronized; when our Book Concerns were small and feeble; when our Church edifices were plain and unattractive; when our seminaries, colleges, and universities were unendowed and weakly; when the support of our effective ministers was scanty and precarious, and when the support of our superannuates was still more stinted and inadequate; when our statistics were meager and imperfect. It was not until the General Conference of 1856 that our statistics included the number of deaths and of baptisms of infants and adults; the number and value of churches and parsonages; and the contributions for missions from Sunday-schools, and other benevolent collections and doings of our Church. In their insertion into our Discipline I took a leading part.

VII.

In all these, and many other things, wonderful changes have come. I cite a few examples:

Forty-two years ago, I was stationed in Wilkesbarre, Penn., then and now one of the wealthiest of our Methodist charges. I was pastor of the only Methodist Church in that borough. Since then four strong Churches have swarmed from the old hive, each of them having better churches and parsonages than mine were when I went to that charge. My allowance was four hundred dollars, the highest salary paid within the Conference. Our church, erected during my incumbency, was a brick structure, costing ten thousand dollars. It was plain and unpretentious. The parsonage was worth perhaps six hundred or eight hundred dollars.

After settling these four daughters in their several Church homes, the mother Church, which I served, has an elegant edifice, of modern appointments, costing, say, one hundred and fifty thousand dollars. The pastor lives in a fine parsonage, costing, say, fifteen thousand dollars, on a salary of three thousand five hundred dollars. Prior to the Wilkesbarre pastorate was that of Binghamton, N. Y. The church in that place was a square, unsightly object, called "The Eel-pot." My allowance was three hundred and fifty dollars. Here is noted a like advance, as in the former case.

These are only samples. In the march of civilization the whole country has advanced with giant strides. Our Church has kept pace with the material and intellectual progress. Other improvements await.

"Not in vain the distance beacons. Forward, forward let us range!
Let the great world spin forever down the ringing grooves of change.
Through the shadow of the globe we sweep into the younger day;
Better fifty years of Europe than a cycle of Cathay."

VIII.

Of the five years of service I put into the reconstruction of our Church in the South I may not speak in detail. It was harder than the Oregon work, and quite as perilous. I was fired upon in Knoxville before I had been there a month. I was threatened by Ku-klux and conspired against by ex-rebels. Under the severe pressure, my health completely gave way, compelling a suspension of my work there, and my temporary retirement into the less arduous duties of United States consul in Kingston, Jamaica.

In company with Bishop D. W. Clark and Dr. Adam Poe, I was present at the organization of the Holston Conference of the Methodist Episcopal Church, in June, 1865. I also accompanied them to Atlanta, Ga., assisting in reorganizing and arranging our work there. I have never placed as high an estimate upon my service in the South as upon that in Oregon. I hope God will make all he can out of it. Fruitless my labors there were not, yet I should like to have scored a larger, mightier success.

IX.

The best work of my life was in Oregon. From 1851 to 1865—fourteen years—I served the Church as presiding elder and editor, helping to lay, in that then most distant of our Territories, the foundations of civil, social, and religious liberty.

Before and after Oregon was organized into an Annual Conference, I wrought to extend our work in that field. It was a foreign mission when I went. Before its organization as a regular Annual Conference, I was organizing circuits and placing missionaries upon them, and I was doing evangelistic work. One summer I attended seven camp-meetings in as many successive weeks. In these seven weeks myself and wife slept in a house but one night, and in them all we had no rain. In each of them we had precious revivals. At the camp-meeting in the forks of the Santiam, one of the seven, I preached a doctrinal sermon on baptism, of three and a half hours in length. Remarkable as it may seem, the hearers all staid until the close. After Oregon was organized as a part of our regular domestic work, I was appointed the first presiding elder. I was also the first editor and publisher of the *Pacific Christian Advocate*, the first and only Methodist journal ever issued in Oregon. In 1854 I was elected to the presidency of the Oregon Conference, a position I held from Wednesday until Sunday afternoon, when Bishop Simpson reached the seat of the Conference. I found Oregon a sparsely-settled wilderness. I left it a blooming, beautiful garden. It has since become far more attractive and productive than any other equal area of Methodism in any part of the world within my knowledge. Allow a comparison. When, forty years ago, I went to Oregon, we had one district. There were three churches, worth, say, $15,000; and two parsonages, worth, say, $5,000. There were fifteen traveling and seventeen local preachers, and there were four hundred members.

The figures which show the marvelous result seem incredible. Within the limits of the field I literally traversed, twoscore years ago, there are 4 Annual Conferences, 195 traveling and 179 local preachers, 19,000 members, 223 churches, worth $885,000, and 109 parsonages, worth $176,000, equaling $1,061,000 as the value of our church property.

There are to-day fifteen times as many traveling preachers, ten times as many local preachers, forty-seven and one-half times as many members, seventy-four times as many churches, and fifty-four times as many parsonages. The value of the church and parsonage property has increased forty-fold. Consider another aspect of this amazing growth.

It is furnished by later statistics, and these include the following facts as to Oregon alone, and in relation, also, to the statistics of four other leading denominations of Oregon:

Societies,			Members,	
Methodist,	211		10,050	
" Baptist,	107	"	5,043	
" Presbyterian,	70	"	3,575	
" Episcopalian,	32	"	1,600	
" Congregational,	29	"	1,609	
	237			11,827

Thus it is seen that in Oregon, alone, there are almost as many Methodist societies and members, as in the other four leading Churches, altogether.

I have spoken of the *Pacific Christian Advocate*, now in its thirty-seventh volume. You will be interested to learn of its genesis and early history.

The publishing of a weekly religious paper in connection with our work in Oregon was frequently discussed by the leading ministers and laymen—notably by J. R. Robb and Ex-Governor Abernethy, wholesale merchants and lumber-dealers in Oregon City, and by Alexander Abernethy, of Oak Point. Several meetings for consultation were held at Oregon City, Salem, and Portland. These resulted in the creation of a joint-stock company, with a subscription of $3,500, the supposed cost of the necessary outfit.

The subscribers to the stock, as I now recall them, were James R. Robb, Alexander Abernethy, laymen; and Revs. C. S. Kingsley, Alvin F. Waller, Josiah L. Parrish, Thomas H. Pearne, and perhaps, also, Gustavus and Harvey K. Hines, and others; but of these last names I can not be certain.

I was selected editor of the projected paper, and was instructed to order the necessary office fixtures and material. Subsequently the joint-stock company dissolved, and I became sole proprietor, publisher, and editor of the paper.

The first number of the *Advocate* was issued in Salem, early in the summer of 1855.

There was then no provision of the Discipline by which a member of an Annual Conference could be appointed to the conduct of an unofficial religious paper. I was therefore appointed agent of the Willamette University, a nominal appointment, to enable me also to conduct the paper, and still remain a member of Conference.

Although the necessary stock was subscribed, the payments were tardy. I at last assumed the responsibility of ordering an office and a six months' supply of paper. A relative of mine, Francis Hall, Esq., publisher of the New York *Commercial Advertiser*, selected and forwarded the fixtures and material for the new paper. As these had to be shipped *via* Cape Horn, it was nearly six months from the time of ordering them before we received them.

At the ensuing Annual Conference session of 1855, I was elected a co-delegate to the General Conference, which met in Indianapolis, May, 1856, with the late Rev. William Roberts, formerly a superintendent of Methodist missions in California and Oregon.

The General Conference directed the New York Book Agents to purchase the plant of the *Pacific Christian Advocate*, at a cost not to exceed $3,500, and continue the publication of the *Pacific Christian Advocate* in Oregon. I was elected editor of the paper in 1856, by the General Conference, and re-elected in 1860. I was urged by many laymen to be a candidate in 1864, and my Conference urged it upon me to continue in the editorship; but I declined.

The first size of the paper was a mistake. It was a large blanket sheet of four pages. It was unwieldy, inconvenient, and unattractive in size and form. The first issue was badly printed, and on this account it was more unattractive. Yet it succeeded. The publishers have done well to bring it into more portable and compendious form for reading and for preservation.

There was some diversity of view as to the proper location of the office. Some thought Oregon City the better place, as it was between Salem and Portland. Portland was vigorously urged, and really it should have been located there at the start, as it was after several months' publication in Salem, then the capital of the Territory, and afterward of the State. The Salem office of publication was a small, one-story, unpainted building, where cases, press, imposing-stone, and paper supply, were very inconveniently huddled together.

My sanctum was a small room eight or ten feet square. When letters, editorials, and contributions got promiscuously piled in heaps on my table, the confusion was bewildering. It was often the case that answers to important letters were delayed, and editorials were "lost to sight, and yet to memory dear."

The exact date when the first number was issued in Salem I can not now give. An amusing incident occurred in that Salem office, the recital of which will perhaps be enjoyed.

A man who had crossed the Plains on foot, an enthusiastic reformer as to the Indian policy, came into the office. He inquired of me where he could find Rev. Mr. Pearne, the editor of that paper, as he greatly desired to see him. I said:

"Look at me, and you will see the man who bears that name."

"What!" said he, "you Mr. Pearne? It can not be!"

"Why can not it be?" said I.

"Well," said he, "ever since I was a boy I have been reading articles written in Church papers by you, and I expected to see a man of threescore years at least, wrinkled, bowed, and tottering."

"Well," said I, "Pearne is the name I have always borne. I came honorably by it. I am not ashamed of it. I am glad I favorably disappoint you as to my age; and really, I never expect to get old and wrinkled and bowed."

It was somewhat difficult to fix upon a suitable name for the new paper. The following names were proposed: North Pacific Christian Herald, The Pacific, The Pacific Methodist, Oregon Christian Advocate, Oregon Banner, Oregon Banner and Messenger. The first and last names were entirely too long. The Congregationalists in San Francisco were issuing a paper bearing the name, *The Pacific;* for that reason that name was laid aside. The Pacific Methodist was next considered. It was suggested that an aggressive Methodist, or a zealous Methodist, or a shouting Methodist would be in order; but scarcely a Methodist of pacific characteristics.

The *California Christian Advocate* was already under full movement, with Rev. S. D. Simonds as editor, and to have an Oregon Christian Advocate would make it too local. The Oregon Banner, and the Oregon Banner and Messenger were soon dismissed. The name Oregon Christian Advocate was again considered. Rev. Alvin F. Waller, as I now recollect, suggested the name, *Pacific Christian Advocate*. It at once struck all with favor, and it was unanimously adopted. I am glad to credit this suggestion to that grand and true man, Rev. Mr. Waller. He left the impress of his strong personality upon Oregon as perhaps few others have done. Subsequent events have fully vindicated the wisdom of the selection. It preserves the family patronymic, *Christian Advocate*. The word *Pacific* sufficiently locates the patronizing territory of its circulation. If the name Oregon Christian Advocate had been selected, when Washington and Idaho became contiguous Territories, now States, the name would have been offensively exclusive.

It was no small undertaking to publish such a paper in Salem—a hamlet, then, of perhaps six hundred souls. A semi-monthly steamer brought us all the news from the outside world. We had to depend upon home talent and upon indomitable energy and industry to make a current, readable paper. I had heard of Bishop Morris's first editorship of the *Western Christian Advocate*, when he was compelled to write his own correspondence and communications from imaginary places and with fictitious signatures, and also write his own editorial matter as well. I copied his example, doing a larger share of such work.

There was a remarkable improvement in the facilities Portland afforded for news, and other matter for our columns. There was also in Portland, a larger and better class of advertisers. I found it much easier to make a paper in Portland than I did in Salem.

But even under the more favorable conditions in Portland, it was at the same time, drudgery and severe toil, successfully to conduct the *Pacific Christian Advocate*. Probably few, if any editors of our Church papers ever had a berth so hard, or so poorly compensated as was ours in the earlier years of my editorial life. I had no assistants, because there was nothing from which to pay them; no clerks, no book-keeper, no typewriter; scarcely an errand-boy. I did all the editing of the paper, wrote all the editorial matter, conducted all the business correspondence, kept all the accounts, hired and paid all the hands, mailed all the papers, and, with my own hands, directed all the papers, fifteen hundred in number. When all this is considered, as I look back over it, it seems simply to have been impossible that I could accomplish so many things with anything like passable efficiency or correctness. But still more significant, and well-nigh incredible, is it, that for the first few years the compensation was so small. My salary, in the beginning, was only seven hundred dollars a year. For this very inconsiderable compensation I did work fairly worth two thousand dollars a year. Afterwards, it was increased to one thousand dollars a year, and a mailing clerk was allowed me. It was a very hard struggle to keep the concern afloat, and avoid running it into hopeless insolvency. I borrowed and advanced money until, at one time, the *Advocate* owed me four thousand dollars.

I give two incidents of my editorial life in Portland. In the first, the editor was hoaxed. A young man came over to me from Puget Sound, to be baptized by me, as the minister in his circuit was unordained, and could not baptize him. He was a bright lad, and apparently sincere. He came to me well recommended. I baptized him. He went into the Umpqua Valley, in Southern Oregon, to attend school. A few weeks later I received a letter from a gentleman I knew there, a class-leader, stating that this lad in felling a tree had been suddenly killed by the tree falling upon him. The letter stated the sincere and earnest grief of the people over the young man's untimely and shocking death. The letter requested that the name should not appear. I published the incident, withholding the name, as requested. After the paper containing the alleged incident reached the Umpqua Valley, the class-leader informed me that I was the victim of a cruel hoax, as no such event had occurred there. Sending back the copy of the letter I had published, to this class-leader, I found that my young neophyte had practiced this deception and forged the name of the class-leader to the untrue story. His object was notoriety. He gained it.

In the other incident, I fooled a bucking horse. He jumped stiff-legged and tried to unhorse me. My hat went one way and my spectacles another. I spurred him, and rode bareheaded around the square to the no small diversion of gaping crowds. Then returning to the stable, my hat and spectacles were recovered, and I made the trip undertaken.

Everything occurring in those long-gone days is as fresh and vivid as though but of yesterday. How I recall the forms and characters of the living actors contemporary with me in laying the foundations of many generations in Oregon,—the venerable David Leslie, the patriarch of them all; Waller, the typical itinerant; C. S. Kingsley, the versatile teacher, preacher, business man; Gustavus, Harvey K., and Joseph Hines, who have made their imperishable impress upon that land and its dwellers; the suave, dignified, elegant, and eloquent William Roberts; Nehemiah Doane, L. T. Woodward; the saintly man whom everybody loved, James H. Wilbur; Clinton and Albert Kelly; Francis S. Hoyt, ten years president of Willamette University; J. L. Parrish, C. O. Hosford, William Helm, Isaac Dillon, John F. De Vore, John W. Miller, John Flynn, John Spencer, the Royals of three generations. Glorious men! Most of them have already ascended to their crowning. Erelong their few survivors will rejoin them.

Portland is now a city of seventy thousand. When I first saw it, it was a hamlet of perhaps five or six hundred people, in the midst of a dense fir forest. For years the only streets practicable for drays, on account of stumps of trees, were First and Second Streets, running parallel with the river. Portland Academy stood in the midst of timber. I assisted Rev. James H. Wilbur in felling stately fir-trees by boring into them transversely, and firing the intersecting apertures. The trees were so resinous, that those fires so kindled would burn the trunk through, and fell the tree as surely as the woodman's ax could.

X.

Many changes have come to Methodism in the last fifty years. Some of them were important, and some comparatively unimportant. I note a few:

The preaching of the earlier period was of the law and its demands, rather than of the gospel. The guilt and danger of sinners were earnestly enforced. After this, usually in the same sermon, but not always, the remedy was offered. The sermons and exhortations were "not with enticing words of man's wisdom;' but with plain, convincing, direct speech, and "in the demonstration of the Spirit." They were largely doctrinal and controversial. They were distinctively Arminian. In later years, they are more didactic and ethical. As a rule, the sermons of the earlier times were long. The hearers seemed to expect them to be somewhat long. Their length was rarely criticised, unless they extended considerably beyond the usual regulation hour. The hymns were read, and then lined. The prayers were long.

Before my ministry began, and for a few years thereafter, it was not unusual for some matronly and gifted woman to follow the sermon with a rousing exhortation. This fact occasioned but little surprise, as the practice, if an innovation, would have caused; hence I conclude the usage may have had long and general precedent. Some of these exhortations by females produced a profound and overwhelming impression. One I recall was at a quarterly-meeting. After an effective, forceful sermon by Rev. Charles Giles, the presiding elder, the Widow Blair, his sister, asked leave to offer a few words. Her addition was timely and able. On another occasion, during a revival in Paris, N. Y., a lady arose, on the close of my father's sermon, and made an earnest exhortation to the people to come to Christ. Many came forward and were converted, and the revival received a powerful impetus.

In those earlier days there were some men of marked power; yet the rank and file of the early Methodist preachers were not men of eminent genius nor of brilliant abilities. While some of them were scholarly and learned, the most of them were comparatively unlearned. The Rev. George Gary, of whom I have already spoken, was almost entirely unlearned when, in his boyhood, his ministry began. He learned grammar on horseback as he rode his earlier circuits, yet no skilled grammarian could construct sentences more correctly than he.

The Arminian doctrines of free-will, universal atonement, and free grace, equally for all men, appealed to the average American mind as more equitable and equal than the limited atonement and the sovereign decrees of Calvinism. In these stirring times of higher criticism and dissent and doctrinal revision, it is a gratifying fact, and one full of the most encouraging promise, that there has never been any considerable deviation from sound doctrine among the millions of Methodists in the last hundred and fifty years. Now and then a man like Priestley, or Thomas Paine, or Robert Collyer, or H. W. Thomas has described a theological tangent or turned away from Scriptural teachings about Jesus as the Divine Redeemer; but such sporadic deviations have never touched the heart of the Church, which has been as true to sound doctrine as the needle to the pole and the flower to the sun.

A stronger body of Methodist preachers fills the pulpits of Methodism to-day than those of any former period of which I have had knowledge. I believe them equally as consecrated and spiritual as the fathers were, with less of the frontiersman in garb and speech, and with more of refinement and culture and intelligence. They are systematic, learned, and successful. The change from the circuit system to that of stations has come within the last half-century. It has greatly modified the character and form of our ministerial training. The circuit plan was the school in which the younger preachers were trained under the eye and hand of the senior colleague, and also while trainer and trained were both in the work. The advantage of this plan, in our early stage of evolution, was undoubtedly great. When the circuit system ceased, theological schools became a necessity. Their eminent usefulness can not be questioned. Our itinerant system requires annually, say, eight hundred recruits of ministers, and but for the theological schools, we would be unable to keep the ranks full by accessions of trained men for our work. With the introduction of the railway, travel by buggy and on horseback ceased. Thus the time-honored hospitality of the Methodist home to the travel-worn itinerant was no longer needed nor practicable. In large measure the improving, molding influence of the ministerial guest upon the children was wanting.

From the period of the meeting-house, and the chapel, as then called, humble and rude, and severely plain and cheap, we have passed quite over into that of costly, elegant, beautiful churches, challenging the admiration of all persons of refined taste. In these magnificent churches as devout and earnest Christians worship God as ever their rude forefathers were, and as effective workers and planners, and as liberal givers for Christ as ever bore the honored name of Methodist.

Lay delegation has come within the last twenty years. I always favored it. One of the circular resolutions on that subject, which went the round of the Conferences, and which received many votes, was the Oregon resolution, introduced by me into the Oregon Conference in 1859. Lay delegation works well. Perhaps two houses will give more equality or parity of the orders.

One of the most marked changes has come in the economy of forces, by the systematic, organized, connectional movements of these times. These mark the transition and contrasts from the irregular to the ordered, from the partial to the general, from the occasional to the constant, steady giving and doing; from the solicitation and contribution and administration of the few, for great and good objects, to regular, organized, systematic giving and doing for Christ on a large scale, with the breadth of a continent for its field. Take, for example, the Church Extension Board, which in twenty-five years has received and disbursed $4,000,000, aided in the erection of 7,500 churches, and which has $1,500,000 of active capital as a loan fund to perpetuate its mission of blessing. The value of the churches aided is $99,500,000, a gain of 12,000 churches aided, and of net value of churches, $75,000,000.

This is only a sample of Christian giving and doing in one line. There are many. We raised last year, for missions alone, Home and Foreign, in our three Connectional Missionary Societies, over $1,500,000; Board of Church Extension, $300,000; Freedmen's Aid and Southern Education Society, $322,632—increase of receipts over the former year, $55,000; Conference Claimants, $217,000,—in all, $2,339,632, in one year, for Christ's kingdom, where, twenty years ago, the offerings were less than one-quarter as much, and fifty years ago they were, all told, for one year, $140,000, or just one-seventeenth as much. The sum given by Methodists fifty years ago, for all purposes, made an average per member, for that year, of fifteen cents. The amounts raised for benevolences last year, per member, are more than $1.25, an increase of 1,100 per cent.

Since its organization, seventy-two years ago, the Missionary Society has laid upon the altar of Christian missions an average of $347,222 a year, and an aggregate of twenty-five millions.

Let us contrast this connectional form of beneficence, as to Church Extension, with the usage which preceded it. In a village in Chenango County, New York, a Methodist church was much needed; but the society there was unable to build it, and so was the circuit. A wealthy layman, after liberally contributing to the enterprise, entered his buggy, and rode over a radius of one hundred miles, privately soliciting funds to complete the erection of the church. He was out two months in this service, and so gathered some $250 or $300.

One church, of which I had personal knowledge, actually carried a debt of $250 for years, to be able to turn away all private solicitors for aid to build churches. I do not doubt they saved themselves the giving of thousands by this device. Reference has been made to the smallness of our Book Concerns. In 1836 the New York house burned down. The Church contributed $90,000 to restore it. In that contribution every member of my father's family participated. The capital has grown to $2,500,000. For purposes outside of its regular business, the Concern has paid out more than its working capital. For the quadrennium closing in 1848, the sales were $612,625.19, slightly less than $1 a member. For the quadrennium closing in 1888, the sales were $6,920,743.17, or over $3 a member.

According to Dr. Dorchester, the entire value of the religious literature published in the United States by the different denominations was estimated at $140,000,000, of which the Methodist Episcopal Church has issued $50,000,000, or over one-third of the whole, and more than half of this amount in the last sixteen years.

In the modes of conducting Annual Conference business there has been marked improvement. The scope and accuracy of all Conference statistics have been subserved by the changes. Much time has been saved in one particular line of Conference Proceedings. I refer to the passage of character. When the name of a member of Conference was called, and the question was asked, "Is there anything against him?"

he retired from the Conference-room, while, in his absence, the presiding elder represented him and his year's work, sometimes with words of criticism, sometimes with words of eulogy, or both, taking for this considerable time. All this has given place to the present more suitable, and equally thorough and effective mode.

Equal improvement is noted as to the mode of conducting General Conference business. In the first of which I was a member, in 1856, the appeal cases were heard and decided by the whole body of the delegates, taking for the decision of three or four appeals several days. In the General Conference of 1820 two cases of appeal for the location of preachers took parts of nine days, and two cases of appeal for maladministration occupied parts of nine days.

In 1864 a Court of Appeals was held during the General Conference, over which one of the bishops presided. This was followed by the present arrangement of triers of appeals in General Conference Districts.

There has been a growing tendency in the wealthier charges, for the laymen to make choice of their pastors, instead of, as in the earlier stage of our history, leaving the matter in the hands of the bishop.

Unless all charges should alike be practically allowed to designate their pastors, and all ministers to select their charges, the usage is a usurpation of dangerous possibilities.

Love-feast tickets have been used and disused in my time. Band-meetings, within my recollection, have passed into innocuous desuetude.

As a rule, the Sunday-noon class was always held by the officiating preacher when present. I usually led the class after preaching, sometimes, when really

I should have been resting and recovering from the exhaustion induced by the preaching-service. This custom was retained only on circuits and very small stations.

XI.

From this review of changes we turn to the present, with its improved adjustments and methods, and with its more systematic and easy working, and its multiplied facilities for doing for Christ.

Our progress in Christian achievements should keep pace with our increased facilities.

In the earlier times we rode to our circuits and around them on horseback. In the same way we rode to the Annual and General Conferences, four miles an hour. We do these things now by train, thirty miles an hour. By electric power we shall yet travel to Conference, and over presiding elder districts, one hundred miles an hour. We sail the seas twenty miles an hour. In the near future we may fly through space one hundred and fifty miles an hour.

Pessimistic views of the present are wrong. The past was not better. It was not so good. Badness kills itself. It is short-lived. Goodness has inherent and persistent vitality. The stability of a bad cause is only apparent. Slavery thirty years ago seemed a solid institution. It was imbedded in the Constitution, intrenched in commerce and in the social habits, industries, and conditions of the people. It even flourished; and it boasted defenders from the Bible. But how quickly God withered it in the hot flames of the war which its injustice and greed had kindled! It would be as impossible to revivify it as to reanimate the mummy of old Pharaoh.

Within my memory, dueling existed in this country, almost unchallenged. The breath of an enlightened public opinion smote dueling as unmanly and unchristian; and although hoary with age, it died, and there are none so poor to do it reverence.

Never since Jesus hung in bitter agony on Calvary have the forces of truth been so potent, active, and aggressive as at this moment. Of these forces none are wider in their sweep nor grander in their triumph than this Church of our fathers and of us, their sons, planted in this land by our founder, John Wesley, one hundred and seven years ago.

During 1890, eight million copies of the Holy Scriptures have been issued and circulated by the British and Foreign Bible Society and the American Bible Society—from each in equal numbers. A greater number, this, than had been issued in the first eighteen centuries of the Christian era.

Five thousand heathen converts in one of our India Conferences in one year, and in all our foreign missions eleven thousand, are reported in the year 1890. Our total annual increase of members the last year, including deaths, is 108,696; and not including the deaths, the net increase is 80,352. That means an average of nearly three hundred accessions every day in the year.

XII.

Let us cast the horoscope for a hundred years, and see what it reveals. At the rate of increase in the Methodist Episcopal Church since Mr. Wesley died—a hundred years ago—we shall have, in 1991, of traveling ministers, 3,187,000; of members, 1,102,-867,000; of churches, 25,216,849, a seating capacity of fifteen billions. Imagination staggers before these stupendous figures. We must use hyperbole to approximate the expression of the glory God will put upon us.

Isaiah's metaphors, in his sixtieth chapter, assist our words faintly to foretell the sweep of the gigantic extension of God's kingdom in the earth. Gentiles and kings shall come to her light and to the grandeur of her ascension. Her sons shall come from far. The abundance of the sea shall be given her. Even the abundance of the desert shall be hers, brought to her altars by the camels and dromedaries, the ships of the desert. The forces of the Gentiles shall come as clouds and as doves. The queens of Sheba and Seba shall bring gifts. Yea, all nations shall serve her. The gates shall not be shut night nor day. "For brass God will bring gold, for iron silver, and for wood stones, and for stones iron." "A little one shall become a thousand, and a small one a strong city." It is coming, brethren. God shall bring it to pass in his own time. Hallelujah! Let the Lord be magnified!

1. I am glad and thankful that my life has been spent from childhood in God's service in the Methodist Episcopal Church. In my early boyhood I enlisted under the banners of Christ. As the lengthening shadows creep on, there, to the last, my feet shall stand.

2. I wish to say to the young men of the Conference, your possibilities for earth and heaven in the Methodist Episcopal Church are better and grander than in any other.

3. The system of Methodism does not need mending, but working. It is impossible to modify it essentially without destroying it. It should be loyally worked for all there is in it. "Whereunto we have already attained, let us walk by the same rule. Let us mind the same thing."

In 1893 I was appointed presiding elder of the Hillsboro District, which I have served continuously ever since, and am now closing my fifth year of that work.

In October, 1896, our church in Blanchester was burned. The fire in which it perished was a very sweeping and destructive one. Comparatively, as to populations and the wealth of the two places, it was more destructive than the famous Chicago fire of a few years since, which attracted the sympathy of the whole world, and elicited contributions from very many cities of our own and foreign countries. This Church, with a few hundred dollars' assistance from other charges, was rebuilt by a finer and more commodious edifice.

HILLSBORO COLLEGE.

It is worth while to consider a brief sketch of the history of this noble institution, Hillsboro College. The following address was delivered by me at the reopening of the college, January 19, 1896:

This is a memorable occasion. It is a day of retrospect, reaching backward almost seventy years. It is also a day of prospect. Bright with the resplendent achievements of its past, the future beckons us onward by its large promise of intellectual and moral development: the waving harvest of sixty years of sowing. Hillsboro has long been honored as the seat of higher educational institutions.

Threescore and eight years ago, Rev. Joseph McDowell Mathews, D. D., began his illustrious career in this city as an educator of females. For early historical facts on this subject, I am indebted to Hon. James H. Thompson, as I find them in his history of Highland County. In 1829 the Hillsboro Academy was organized. Governor Allen Trimble was the first president of its Board of Trustees, in which relation he continued for twenty-five years. His successors were General Joseph J. McDowell and Samuel E. Hibben, Esq. In this academy Dr. Mathews taught from 1827 to 1836. In 1839, Oakland Female Seminary was established by Dr. Mathews, at the east end of Main Street, between the Chillicothe and Marshall Pikes. Here for eighteen years he taught. During this time one hundred graduates were catalogued, "who," as Judge Thompson attests in his history, "are the mothers and grandmothers of a posterity, which, in every part of our grand country, from the front line of human progress, have justly distinguished themselves." Many of them were then in middle life and in old age, as they had been, with established characters from girlhood the zealous advocates and brave guardians of a very high, pure, and undefiled type of womanhood, which fixes, defines, and gilds the true outline of all chaste society. Judge Thompson pays a high tribute to two historic teachers: "From 1845 to 1851, Professor Isaac Lewis taught a school in every grade of mathematical, classical, and English learning."

Of Dr. Mathews, Judge Thompson adds, that "he has for forty-five years been engaged in founding Oakland Female Seminary, and in teaching females. Dr. Mathews established the first female school in Ohio, in which a thorough collegiate education was given to girls." Some of Dr. Mathews's graduates were among the leading matrons of the past generation. I cite a notable example: the widow of the late Major W. D. Bickham, of Dayton, Ohio. She was one of the leading projectors and managers of the Woman's Christian Association of Dayton. She still holds an important place in its management. Her vigorous and able administration has contributed to make it a model institution of its kind,—a name and a praise in all the land.

To the wise and faithful work of Dr. Mathews is due the elevated and noble character of the women of Highland County for the last half-century—the mothers and grandmothers of the former and present generations of the people of this section. These worthy matrons of his training have impressed their strong personality upon this community, and have made it, for brains, vigor, and enterprise, second to none.

In 1857 the Hillsboro Female College took the place of the Oakland Female Seminary. For three years he was its first president. He was succeeded by Rev. W. G. W. Lewis, Rev. Henry Turner, Rev. Allen T. Thompson, Rev. D. Copeland, then Dr. Mathews, a second term of five years; Rev. John F. Loyd, D. D., Rev. W. C. Helt, and Mr. Gall.

In 1877, as pastor of the Methodist Episcopal Church in Hillsboro, I visited Dr. Mathews, who was then aged and in precarious health. Two years later he died in your midst, full of years and honors. I recall two beautiful incidents. On my first visit, in reply to my inquiry as to his condition, he recited to me, with feeble voice, Charles Wesley's well-known hymn, dictated on his death-bed when he was over fourscore years of age:

> "In age and feebleness extreme,
> Who shall a helpless worm redeem?
> Jesus, my only hope thou art,
> Strength of my failing flesh and heart;
> O could I catch a smile from thee,
> Then drop into eternity!"

On my last visit, some six or eight months before his death, in answer to my inquiries, he whispered: "I am waiting on this side Jordan until my Joshua shall come and divide the waters, and lead me through, dry-shod." A beautiful ending of a lovely life.

Forty-one years ago, out of the Oakland Female Seminary grew the Hillsboro Female College, which a few years ago was made a mixed institution for persons of both sexes. Later still, came Miss Emily Grand-Girard's Female Seminary. Hillsboro College cost fifty thousand dollars. The fathers of the former generation deserve great credit for their self-sacrificing and tireless efforts to create and sustain this edifice, which we are met this day formally to reopen with fitting services, thus dedicating it to its great work of higher education among the young men and women of this community. The graduates from this college alone number one hundred and fifty. May 18, 1894, it was consumed by fire. May we not hope that, like the fabled phœnix, this large and elegant structure, improved in style and finish beyond its predecessor, shall yet be successful in a more extended sphere than its predecessor, and in grander and better work? When the flames on that May-day sent up in smoke and cinders the combustible parts of this dear old college, they left standing the strong, non-combustible walls; and, what was incomparably better still, its friends and patrons have rebuilt it in better form. In doing this they have displayed an energy of purpose and of spirit, which are an assuring prophecy of its success and continuous benefactions.

Rev. Dr. Bashford (President of Ohio Wesleyan University): On behalf of the trustees of the Hillsboro College, I present you this building for appropriate dedicatory services.

Dr. Bashford delivered an eloquent address, and then formally dedicated the building in an appropriate prayer.

Hillsboro Charge is now a very strong Church. Rev. Marion LeSourd is pastor. I have resided here for the last five years. I recently held a quarterly-meeting in Hillsboro. It has over seven hundred members. The sacramental service was very largely attended. I have never seen so many communicants participate at one service in this church, as at this meeting. Probably not less than four hundred received the holy sacrament. The love-feast in the afternoon was almost as largely attended. It was a most spiritual and powerful service. The following article appeared in the *News-Herald* the next day:

During the sacramental service in the Methodist Episcopal Church last Sunday, Dr. Pearne announced some historic facts, as follows:

"This Church was organized in 1805, ninety-three years ago. For ninety-three years our fathers and mothers have sent up prayers to the Lord, and have received showers of blessings in response. Here souls for more than ninety years have come to the mercy-seat, and have found healing and adoption and life. During the last twenty-five years this Church has raised $10,764 for missions, and for general Church purposes $91,761, including the money given for building and improving the church and parsonage. During the same time, in the last twenty-five years, the Sunday-school has given $3,216 for missions, and $2,970 for current Sunday-school expenses; in all, $6,186.

"Eighty-eight ministers and twenty-nine presiding elders have served this Church. Brother M. LeSourd is the eighty-eighth pastor who has officiated in this Church, and I am the twenty-ninth of the presiding elders who have served this people. This Church has sent out two missionaries, Miss Loyd and Miss Ayres, to Mexico. It has sent out an Official Board Blank Record Book, which one of your earnest, working men, L. Detwiler, has prepared, and it is now in nearly two thousand Methodist charges, and it will doubtless be so used as long as Methodism shall continue as a Church. The first preacher in charge in this station, nearly sixty years ago, was Randolph S. Foster, for the last twenty-seven years one of her honored bishops, and one of the grandest and noblest of veterans."

A REMARKABLE BIRTHDAY ANNIVERSARY.

In September, 1894, Rev. R. S. Rust, D. D., LL. D., celebrated the eightieth anniversary of his birthday, at his residence on West Fourth Street, Cincinnati. His friends, in large numbers, crowded his home on the evening of that day. A friend, in Delaware, Ohio, Mrs. Professor L. D. McCabe, sent eighty beautiful white roses, a most fitting and elegant offering. Speeches and music and prayer enlivened and graced the occasion. The writer of this volume, who had been for nearly thirty years a devoted friend and admirer of the noble hero whose life had been full of great and blessed service for the Master, was present, and, being called on, he offered the following remarks:

I am both honored and delighted to be present on this joyous occasion, and to share with you in these most appropriate festivities. As representing the Freedmen's Aid and Southern Education Society, with which our venerable friend has been so long and effectively associated, I am to contribute some brief and befitting statements.

In traveling in different countries, certain marked

features of the landscape have greatly impressed me with their beauty. Repeated observation of these rare but fascinating objects has only augmented their weird spell over my imagination. Two examples are cited for illustration: Thirty years ago I traversed the defile in the mountains of Jamaica, called the bog-walk, through which flows the Rio Cobra. For eighteen or twenty miles the Cobra meanders through a cañon—mountain cleft from summit to base three thousand feet. Between these towering walls, which seem almost to touch each other, in tortuous windings the bold stream pursues its serpentine way, disclosing with every bend of the cañon new forms of beauty. Through this remarkable defile I have often traveled, and always with deepened interest. Fifty-three years ago I first saw Niagara. The majestic crescent, a mile in circuit, over the brink of whose awful depth the waters are foaming and rolling and thundering in a ceaseless downpour, produced an overwhelming effect. I wanted to be silent. I found myself quoting the poet's invocation:

> "Come, then, expressive silence, muse his praise."

Eternity seemed very near. God was revealed in his stupendous works. Many times since I have revisited the mighty waterfall. That gorgeous display of Divine power has always deeply impressed me.

When I recently visited Niagara, a singular marvel had been wrought. The great cataract was still there: its sublime features all unchanged. The human engineer had chiseled in the rocks which shore the floods an unseen chamber, through which a small part of the unused water is diverted and made to fall upon turbine wheels, so generating electricity. This electricity is transmitted over an area of three hundred square miles to flood the populous State of New York with millions of incandescent lights, and to make that vast area vibrant with the whirr and buzz of countless spindles and shuttles, and with hundreds of forges. And all this without at all diminishing the magnificent glory of Niagara. Human genius had utilized God's hidden power.

In this social gathering these material illustrations are suggestive. They furnish most fitting analogies. The earthquakes might have cleaved the mountain to its base, so making a way for the stream and a road for the wayfarer along the picturesque river. For two centuries and a half the mountain of slavery had been growing in this country. God smote it with the terrible thunders of war. In the words of Liberty and Union, the battle-cry of freedom was sung:

"I have read a fiery gospel, writ in burnished rows of steel,
  As ye deal with my contemners, so with you my grace shall deal;
  Let the hero born of woman, crush the serpent with his heel;
        Our God is marching on.

I have seen him in the watchfires of a hundred circling camps;
  They have builded him an altar in the evening dews and damps;
  I have read his righteous sentence by the dim and flaring lamps;
        His day is marching on.

In the beauty of the lilies, Christ was born across the sea,
With a glory in his bosom, which transfigures you and me,
As he died to make men holy, let us die to make men free,
        While God is marching on.

In this case the mountain has become a plain. Slavery has gone down forever. God's own hand buried it in the red gulf of battle.

While the immeasurable power of Niagara has

been tapped by man's device, so transmitting force to be wielded for human uses and needs, so when the mountain of slavery disappeared, God opened in the desert streams of healing and relief for his long-oppressed children. There flowed forth from millions of loyal Christian men and women, first through the channels of the Freedmen's Bureau, and later by the Freedmen's Aid Society, tides of blessing for God's poor; refreshing streams of beneficence in rich abundance. Never has Christian devotion yielded larger nor more prolific results for human uplifting and enrichment.

Eighty years ago to-day God sent into this world, in Massachusetts, one of the chief New England States, a man-child, who contained within himself possibilities as actual as, and relatively far more significant than, the giant oak in the tiny acorn, the Rio Cobra in the Jamaica mountains, and the grand Niagara in the scanty streamlets of Canadian forests. The name given to this newcomer was Richard Sutton Rust. His early years were spent in conditions admirably befitting him for the important place he was so soon and so nobly to fill. He was made of martyr stuff. In his early manhood he championed the then unpopular cause of the slave. He "fought with beasts at Ephesus," where he was mobbed for his Abolitionism; and when he was pleading and working for the freedom of his Brother in Black—"God's image carved in ebony"—he was still further prepared for his great life-work by his direction, for three years, of the educational forces of New Hampshire, as Commissioner of the Public Schools of that State.

Then he came West for a broader theater of action. For some years he was president of the Cincinnati Wesleyan Female College. His first grand achievement in his new field and in his chosen line was in planting and directing Wilberforce University for people of color. It still stands, a growing monument of his wise philanthropic zeal. Later he became corresponding secretary of the Freedmen's Aid Society, which, with steadily increasing efficiency, he administered for twenty-two years. The conditions were peculiar. The mountain of slavery had become the wide plain of freedom for five millions of freedmen then—seven and a half millions now—who for two centuries and a half had been held and accounted as goods and chattels personal. Just as Niagara's hidden forces were developed by human skill and genius into myriad forms of activity and light, so this Freedmen's Aid and Southern Education Society, so ably wielded by our venerable brother, Rev. Dr. Rust, has filled eleven States in the Black Belt with its incalculable benefactions, alike to whites and blacks. He will never be dissociated from the colossal beneficence which he assisted to create and so beneficently administered. That service, in the thought and sympathies of millions of the Freedmen and their descendants, has forever linked him inseparably with our martyr President, Abraham Lincoln. Fourteen years ago the direction of the Society, whose infancy he had nursed and developed to stalwart maturity, passing into other hands, Dr. Rust was elected by the General Conference honorary corresponding secretary of this God-honoring and God-honored philanthropy.

As the child of destiny and man of mark, he is still living at the ripe age of fourscore years, far beyond the ordinary term of human life, to behold in his advancing years the ever-widening circles of beneficence which he set in motion, filling earth and heaven with abundant ripe and golden fruit. For thirty years I have been in touch with him. For a score and a half of years I have known and loved and honored him, and my own life has been the nobler and better for the association.

The cradle is the prophecy of the bridal altar, and that foretypes the cerements of the casket and the grave. But the monuments he has reared in his long life will endure throughout the history of time and the endless cycles of eternity. A higher crowning awaits him, which I expect to witness, amid the splendors of eternity, when God shall place upon his immortal brow the unfading coronal of righteousness, so recognizing and rewarding the triumphs of Christian philanthropy, in augmenting which our distinguished friend bore so eminent and illustrious a part.

Methodism was first organized in Ohio by John Kobler in 1798. The Methodists of the State having determined, by a concerted action of the several Annual Conferences, to celebrate the centennial of its introduction, a committee of one from each Conference was appointed to make the necessary arrangements. They were authorized to appoint the place, devise the program, invite the speakers, attend to transportation and entertainment, and look after the comfort of their guests. The committee fixed upon Delaware as the place, and Commencement-week of the Ohio Wesleyan University as the most suitable time. The exercises began on Tuesday, June 21st, and continued till Friday, June 24, 1898.

Having been requested by the committee to prepare for that occasion a paper on "The Gospel on Horseback," I delivered the following address to a large audience assembled in Gray Chapel:

THE GOSPEL ON HORSEBACK.

The theme assigned me for a brief essay is entitled, "The Gospel on Horseback." With permission, I would like to change it thus: "The Methodist Itinerant on Horseback." Except as the early Methodist preachers carried in their saddlebags the Bible, the hymn-book, the Discipline, and Christian literature for distribution, the gospel can scarcely be said to be on horseback. In Methodist terminology the word itinerant describes neither the fact nor the mode of traveling. In our usage the word itinerant means a pastor who often changes his pastorate, in contradistinction from one who holds a settled or permanent pastorate, and who therefore does not change at all. A Methodist itinerant who rides on horseback is differentiated from a stationed minister, who does not travel, because his position does not admit of his traveling. And yet, in Methodist parlance, the one is as really an itinerant as the other.

The intent of my assigned theme, as I construe it, is to describe the early Methodist preachers who reached their appointments by horse, or who thus rode their circuits. I was probably programmed for this subject, because from my long ministerial life I was supposed to be personally, and from observation, familiar with this subject; and such is, indeed, the fact. Sixty-one years ago I rode on horseback, each Saturday, from Cazenovia Seminary, twenty miles away, to Onondaga Circuit, as a supply. I continued to travel that circuit by horse nearly two years. My circuit lay from four to ten miles south from Syracuse, N. Y. For eight or ten years this was my mode of travel. Fourteen years later, when sent as a missionary to Oregon, both myself and all my Conference associates traveled by horse. For this mode of travel there is ample precedent. Pharaoh's military, who pursued Israel to the Red Sea to recapture and reenslave them, and who met their awful fate by drowning, included horsemen. Miriam's song of victory celebrated this event. "The Lord hath triumphed gloriously. The horse and his rider hath he thrown into the sea." Sennacherib's army, which came hundreds of leagues to besiege Jerusalem, included horsemen. How awful their doom!

> "There lay the rider, distorted and pale,
> With the dew on his brow, and the rust on his mail;
> The tents were all silent, the banners alone,
> The lances unlifted, the trumpet unblown.
>
> And there lay the steed, with his nostril all wide;
> But through it there rolled not the breath of his pride;
> And the foam of their gasping lay white on the turf,
> As the spray of the sea on the wave-beaten surf.

Mounting his fiery Bucephalus, Alexander went forth from Macedon to the conquest of the world. Cortez conquered Mexico by four hundred infantry and fifteen horsemen. Napoleon's marshals and battalions subjugated Europe to his insatiate sway.

It would be strange, indeed, that horses could be used only for purposes of ambition, blood, and death. Nor is it true. The bishops and curates in the days of the Bloody Mary, probably including Latimer and Ridley and others of the Smithfield martyrs, traveled their bishoprics and curacies in this manner. John Wesley and his ministerial and lay helpers rode up and down in Great Britain in the eighteenth century upon horses. It is equally true that to this day some of the large Wesleyan circuits keep a circuit horse for the use of the circuit preachers. For a hundred and fifty years these mounted knights of the cross have been setting the United Kingdom "on a blaze."

In the Colonial times, the Colonists almost exclusively traveled by horse. In the Revolutionary War all the officers, and the cavalry of course, were mounted. Washington traversed Virginia, Ohio, and Pennsylvania on horseback. Circuit judges, barristers, litigants, and doctors rode their routes on horseback. Tradition affirms that the Great Commoner, Henry Clay, and President Andrew Jackson, rode back and forth, to and from Washington, on horseback. In Oregon, at my quarterly-meetings, nearly all the women, as well as the men, who attended the meeting from a distance, came on horseback, some of them with a child in arms and one or two children behind. They were expert riders. I have seen mothers come riding in a lope or canter, with a babe in arms and one or two children behind. All the early Methodist preachers traveled on horseback. This habit prevailed, as late as 1830, all through the Connection. Asbury, Whatcoat, McKendree, George, and Roberts, the first five American Methodist bishops, made their extended continental tours by horse. Nathan Bangs and John Dempster traversed the forests and swamps of Lower Canada in like manner. For the pioneer preachers and people in her extended prairies and forests this was almost their only mode of travel.

When, some sixty or seventy years ago, horse-riding in New York State gave place to buggy-riding, an amusing incident occurred. The Conference met in Wilkesbarre, which was at the southern extreme of the Conference. For the last twenty miles of the distance all the roads converged into one. The buggies were placed upon elliptic springs. They had as great popularity as our modern bikes. As the Conference day approached, the ministers came along this common highway in their buggies. There seemed no end of the long procession. A German and his son were working in a field along the pike. The father threw down his hoe, and cried out, "Vel, den, Hance, py sure, hell is proke loose." But this mode of travel had for the itinerants its special advantages and compensations. While thus riding, they read their Bibles and studied their sermons. They had much time for thought and prayer. They were men of much prayer and deep thought. In this way they mingled freely with the common people. They were, therefore, all the more esteemed, and accounted as of the common people. This gave them large influence and following. None of the people escaped their visits. They found all the settlers. A man and his family emigrated from Northern Georgia into Western Alabama. Before he left Georgia the Methodist itinerant had secured the conversion of the man's wife and children. So he emigrated to get beyond their reach. He had selected his new home and gone upon it; but on the very day of his arrival, and before his household goods were unloaded, the itinerant rode up and sought their acquaintance. The pioneer gave it up. It was no use, he said, to try to get away from these ubiquitous circuit-riders.

Then, moreover, travel on horseback had still other adaptations and compensations. Life in God's open air and sunshine and exercise gave the itinerants stalwart physiques and robust, vigorous, bounding health; large capacity for enduring the exposures, perils, and fatigues of their laborious callings. They had large lung capacity, and loud, strong voices for preaching. In their long rides they sometimes encountered men of keen intellect and of marked skill in debate. I recall and rehearse two notable examples: one of them of intellectual grapple, the other of physical contention. Jacob Gruber entered the traveling connection in 1800, in the Philadelphia Conference. He was eccentric in manner and style, fearless in speech, and a man of unusual capacity for irony, sarcasm, and ridicule. In these lines he very rarely met his superior. Two mounted lawyers overtook him, and conversed with him for several miles. One of them rode on his right hand, and the other on his left. To test his scholarship, they addressed him in Latin. He answered them in German. They probably knew as little of his German, as he did of their Latin. They asked him whether he did not sometimes make mistakes in reading and speaking. He admitted that that was quite probable. They said, "When you make mistakes, do you always stop to correct them?" He replied: "Not always. When the mistake is trivial, I would hardly deem it necessary to stop and correct it. For example, if I were reading the passage, 'Woe unto you, scribes, Pharisees, lawyers,' and if, by mistake, I should read it, 'Woe unto you, scribes, Pharisees, liars,' I would hardly deem it necessary to stop and correct that." They said, "Mr. Gruber, we scarcely know where to place you; *i. e.*, as to whether you are a fool or a knave." "Just now," said he, "I am probably between the two."

They were as badly "left" as Mr. Wesley is reported as having left a bishop of the Church of England in London. Wesley and two of his ministers happened to meet on the pavement the bishop and two of his curates. The bishop held the sidewalk, remarking audibly, "I do n't give up my place on the pavement for a fool." "But I do," said Mr. Wesley, who bowed to the bishop, and stepped off the curb. If that event really occurred, Mr. Wesley answered a fool according to his folly.

The next example was of physical prowess. Rev. Joseph S. Collins, a local preacher, father of the celebrated John A. Collins, of the Baltimore Conference, was a man of gigantic strength. Collins's encounter was quite equal, in its way, to that of Gruber. If Collins had not, like Paul, "fought with beasts at Ephesus," he had had serious grapple with contentious toughs, who required severe handling. A well-mounted stranger overtook Mr. Collins as he was on his way to a certain camp-meeting, which he was to conduct. After exchanging pleasant greetings, the stranger asked him if he could direct him to a certain camp-meeting in that vicinity, and also whether he could inform him whether Mr. Joseph Collins would probably be present. Mr. Collins promised to show him the way, and inquired why he had asked whether Mr. Collins would attend. He said Mr. Collins had put the toughs living in that vicinity under cover. Mr. Collins asked the stranger whether Mr. Collins had ever done him any harm. He answered, "No;" but that he had come forty miles to give Mr. Collins a licking, and put the toughs in heart. Mr. Collins said, "If I were you, and Collins had never done you any harm, I would let him alone." They rode on together several miles. As they drew near the camp-ground, Mr. Collins inquired of him whether he was still of the same mind as when they had first met. The stranger said he was. Mr. Collins dismounted and hitched his horse, and invited the stranger to alight, remarking: "My name is Collins. I am the man you want to lick. We are near the camp-ground, and we may as well have the trial of strength here, and now." When the man had alighted and hitched his horse, Mr. Collins seized him by the collar and the slack of his trousers, and flung him over the fence. The stranger, picking himself up and rubbing the part on which he had fallen, is reported to have said, "Mr. Collins, if you will kindly hand my horse over, we will call it quits."

Mr. Gilruth, the Hercules of the Ohio Conference, is said to have seized an antagonist around the waist, and lifted him off the ground; then raising the bottom rail of the fence with one of his hands, he pushed the man's head under and dropped the rails over his neck, and left him thus in limbo, while Gilruth began to ride off with the honors. The man cried after him for mercy, and was released. He was afterwards converted under Mr. Gilruth's preaching. Many of the old-time veterans could tell of encounters with camp-meeting disturbers.

We are celebrating their entrance into Ohio a hundred years ago, led by the intrepid John Kobler and Henry Smith. Ninety-one years ago the first Methodist Annual Conference was held in Chillicothe, on the Scioto. At that historic session sixty-six Methodist itinerants were present. Bishop Asbury presided. All the preachers who attended that Conference came on horseback. Some of them had ridden by horse a thousand miles to attend. Five presiding elders were present. They were the seniors of the body. William McKendree had entered the traveling connection nineteen years before; William Burke, fifteen; Thomas Wilkerson, fourteen; John Sale, thirteen; and Learner Blackman, seven. Their districts covered four States, Ohio, Kentucky, Tennessee, and Mississippi. Nearly all the others were recent recruits. Thirteen of them were received in 1805. These included the eccentric and renowned Peter Cartwright, one of the great men of the century; James Axley, the intrepid opposer and denouncer of slavery and the liquor-traffic; Jacob and David Young, long the honored pillars of the old Ohio Conference; Jesse Walker, who later was the chivalrous missionary of St. Louis; John Collins, of precious memory; Ralph Lotspeich, the weeping Jeremiah of those early prophets of the Western Conference; and the saintly Samuel Parker. Eleven had joined the Conference in 1806, and eleven men in 1807.

Not alone in the West, but all over the country, some of the greatest men in American Methodism were trained and developed among these early circuit-riders. What a mighty, illustrious array! Freeborn Garrettson, who itinerated on horseback from Halifax to Virginia; Jesse Lee, the first historian of his Church and his times; William Beauchamp, the unequaled theologian; John Dickins, the father of our publishing-houses; Ezekiel Cooper, his eminent successor; George Pickering; John P. Durbin, one of the most distinguished of our educators, an eloquent orator, and for many years the great organizer of the Missionary Society of our Church; John Emory, one of our early bishops; Henry B. Bascom, long a chaplain of the United States Senate, and later a bishop of the Methodist Episcopal Church, South; William Nast, a nonagenarian, one of the earliest of our German annex; L. L. Hamline, John Strange, Joshua Soule, Elijah Hedding, W. B. Christie, Edward R. Ames, Matthew Simpson, Arthur and Charles Elliott; George W. Walker, physically, mentally, and morally one of the grandest of men; Russel Bigelow, Jason and Daniel Lee, and their early associates, who planted our banners in far-off Oregon; and so many more whom time would fail me to mention. They were God's noblemen. Men of brain and brawn, stalwart, sturdy, God-honoring, and God-honored.

This potential equestrian brigade achieved at least three mighty results. They impressed their strong, unique personality upon their age, their century, and their country. They formed the effectual breakwater against the reaction of the American mind from the horrible Augustine theology, which threatened to land the masses of our people, first in the half-way house of Unitarianism, and then into the utter and blank infidelity of Volney, Voltaire, and Rousseau. They arrested this trend by turning the rank and file of the people into the more thinkable and evangelical doctrines of Arminianism. They led the van of our advancing civilization from the Atlantic to the Mississippi. They planted and promoted our cause in the most distant and inaccessible parts of our great Republic. They induced the inclusion of Oregon and Washington and Idaho and Montana into the National domain. The pulsations of American Methodism throb with the impulses of their tremendous and concentrated genius and energy. They climbed the eastern foothills of the Rockies, scaled the Sierras, and planted our system and our agencies amid the golden placers of the Sacramento and along the shores of our mighty Northwest.

In closing this narrative of sixty-one years of itinerant life, I take occasion to make a few inferential statements. The life I have lived has been a very happy one. I had my choice in the beginning to be what my father intended and hoped I would become, a doctor of medicine or a minister. The "necessity" which God put upon me when he called me to the work of the ministry hardly left me to an option, or left an option to me. I felt the inevitable "woe is me, if I preach not the gospel." I yielded to that, and God has given me abundant seals to my ministry. I trust I may have many stars in my crown; but whether or not, I have most certainly had a very successful life. "The hundred-fold in this world" has been my guerdon. I am firmly presuaded that the life everlasting awaits me. Reviewing all that I now know, if I had my life before me at the present to begin, I would most certainly choose the kind of a life I have had.

It is my firm conviction that many young men whom God calls into his ministry, who refuse to yield to God's call, make an awful mistake, and, in very many instances, the mistake has cost them, O so dearly! Their religious experience has been blighted, and not unfrequently their temporal prosperity has either failed to come, or, if it came, it has been delusive and disappointing. "Seek first the kingdom of God and his righteousness, and all these things shall be added unto you," is just as true now as it was when the Divine One announced it.

The success of Methodism—and it has been great, indeed—has been in very large degree, because the Methodist ministers have firmly known, and held by conviction and experience, the blessed reality of the gospel they have preached. Instead of going about to see if they can not find some higher criticism, they have found with delight how abundantly the Word of God has found corroboration in their experience. And what has been true of the ministers who have preached a salvation which they have consciously found true in their own hearts, has been equally true of the laity, rank and file. The testimony of the lay members, men and women, has been re-enforcing to the ministry of Methodism. It would be a sad mistake for the ministers to put forth neat and artistic moral essays for pungent, earnest gospel preaching; and, if possible, a greater mistake for the laymen and laywomen of Methodism to switch off and turn aside from the experience and the practice of the fathers, both in the pulpit and the pew. "Forsake not the old landmarks. Rather inquire for the old paths, and walk therein."

In noting the changes which have come during my long service in the itinerancy, I must name two things. Lay delegation is one of them. It has already done much in promoting our efficiency as a Church, and it will yield yet more fruit in the time to come, and as the system shall be more fully completed to make the lay and ministerial numerically equal. The other noticeable change is the wonderful fact that the Christian women of the world have come to the front as a result of the crusade of the women against the saloon. They are making themselves a great power for God in humanitarian and Christian lines, and in pushing forward the great missionary work in home and foreign fields.

While I have a large measure of catholicity, and can say and mean every word of it, "Grace be to all them that love our Lord Jesus Christ in sincerity and truth," I also have the most clear conviction that Methodism is a chosen plan of God to uplift and to save men; and I advise all young Methodist preachers to "abide in the calling wherein they have been called," and not seek to mend Methodism and improve upon it; but to work it for all there is in it. It needs only an earnest ministry full of faith and the Holy Spirit, and a consecrated, devoted laity full of pentecostal fire and power, to make it even more grandly successful and soul-saving than it has ever been. To your tents, O Israel!

A final remark is this: I address it to the young men and women of Methodism—Have a cheerful religion. Don't allow yourselves to become gloomy, discouraged, depressed. "Be strong in the Lord." Have for your strength "the joy of the Lord," and you will be invincible; nay, more, you will be victorious, triumphantly, immeasurably conquerors, and more than conquerors, over all enemies, obstacles, and difficulties.

www.ingramcontent.com/pod-product-compliance
Lightning Source LLC
Chambersburg PA
CBHW021416300426
44114CB00010B/510